Six Theories of Ch
Revised Formulatio

Six Theories of Child Development

Revised Formulations and Current Issues

Edited by Ross Vasta
Department of Psychology
State University of New York
Brockport

Jessica Kingsley Publishers
London and Philadelphia

First published in the United States of America
as *Annals of Child Development Vol 6* in 1989

First published in paperback in the United Kingdom in 1992 by
Jessica Kingsley Publishers Ltd
116 Pentonville Road
London N1 9JB

Copyright © 1992 Jessica Kingsley Publishers Ltd

British Library Cataloguing in Publication Data
Six Theories of Child Development: Revised
Formulations and Current Issues. – New ed
I. Vasta, Ross
305.23

ISBN 1-85302-137-7

Printed and Bound in Great Britain by
Biddles Ltd, Guildford and King's Lynn

CONTENTS

LIST OF CONTRIBUTORS

Albert Bandura

Department of Psychology
Stanford University

Harry Beilin

Developmental Psychology Program
City University of New York
   Graduate Center

Sidney W. Bijou

Divison of Special Education and
   Rehabilitation
University of Arizona

Urie Bronfenbrenner

Department of Human Development
   and Family Studies
Cornell University

Robert A. Hinde

MRC Unit on the Development and
   Integration of Behaviour
Cambridge University
England

David Klahr

Department of Psychology
Carnegie Mellon University

Paul H. Mussen

Institute of Human Development
University of California
Berkeley

PREFACE

The re-issue of *Six Theories of Child Development: Revised Formulations and Current Issues* in this paperback edition reflects our continued belief that the volume represents a unique and timely collection of chapters by some of the leading developmental scholars of our time. I am confident that it will eventually take its place among the more important works in child psychology emerging from this era.

As I indicated at the time of the original publication three years ago, a particular significance attaches to the diversity of the theoretical viewpoints presented in these models. When compared with physics or biology, child psychology is a relatively young science. Although we have learned an enormous amount in the hundred or so years since the discipline was founded, there continue to be at least as many important and fundamental questions as there are answers. And one of the clearest manifestations of a science in its infancy is the presence of a number of competing theoretical models existing side-by-side—all legitimate, all respected, and all more-or-less successfully accounting for a significant portion of the available data.

In this special volume of the *Annals,* I have selected six contemporary theories of child development that I feel currently are having the greatest impact on scientific progress in the field and also that represent the largest number of developmental researchers. I have correspondingly brought together six distinguished scholars, arguably the pre-eminent spokespersons for these theoretical traditions, and asked them to update the status of each of these models with an eye toward both the current issues of greatest importance, as well as the challenges that lie ahead. In so doing, each of these theories has been at least somewhat revised and reformulated, so that what is contained between the covers of this volume becomes truly a state-of-the-art account of contemporary theories of child development. Paul Mussen, a seventh scholar with a history of bringing together diverse points of view, provides an additional perspective on these theories in his foreword to the volume.

In all likelihood, the passing of the next hundred years will have reduced the number of these competing theories to two or three—with several perhaps failing to adequately account for new findings and thus falling by the wayside, and others (perhaps with further revision of incorporation of now-competing concepts) maintaining their organizing and guiding functions. But which will go and which will survive? Or is yet a seventh approach needed and waiting to emerge? In the pages that follow there may exist some clues to the answer.

Ross Vasta
Series Editor

FOREWORD

The present volume is a uniquely valuable contribution to scholars of human development, for no other source provides such lucid, up-to-date versions of an array of major theories of—or approaches to—child development. Earlier versions of the theories represented are well known, and the chapters in the present volume, although self-contained units, are probably most fully appreciated if they are considered in the context of earlier theoretical writings. This is particularly true of Bandura's stimulating account of a comprehensive social cognitive theory, Beilin's invaluable survey of Piaget's conceptualizations (especially his later—post-1975—works which are not generally available in English), and Bronfenbrenner's extensions of his own ecological approach to human development, now with an emphasis on personality, rather than environmental, dimensions.

The chapters also attest to the intense and pervasive interest in theory construction in developmental psychology and the diversity of conceptualizations that guide empirical investigations. The theories and approaches vary greatly with respect to domains of central interest, comprehensiveness, underlying assumptions, fundamental concepts and propositions. As Klahr amply demonstrates, explanations of different aspects of human development—or, for that matter, different cognitive achievements—may call for different theoretical models.

Yet some striking commonalities in present-day theorizing are apparent in these chapters. Recognizing the inherent complexity of developmental phenomena, contemporary theorists reject simplistic explanatory notions; they are less concerned than earlier theorists with parsimony and the formal aspects of theory building. Contemporary theory construction and revision are guided by meticulous analyses of possible influences on thought and behavior, by new insights, and by findings of empirical studies. Modifications of extant theories involve primarily refinement of fundamental concepts and expansions resulting from the incorporation of significant new dimensions (as in Bandura's, Bijou's, Bronfenbrenner's, and Beilin's chapters). Reciprocal or transactional effects, biological variables, and the interrelationships among biological and environmental influences in human development are more explicit and more strongly emphasized in these latest versions of prominent theories than they were in earlier presentations (most explicitly in Hinde's chapter, but also apparent in Bandura's, Bronfenbrenner's, and Bijou's chapters). In several of the approaches represented, theory and method are closely linked.

Theory construction and theory modification in the field of human development are continuously ongoing, progressive processes. Compared with the theoretical writings published a few decades ago, new theories and modified versions of older ones are more sophisticated, more comprehensive, more clearly relevant to the development of real people in the real world. Given the vigorous search for more adequate theoretical explanations of observed phenomena, we will undoubtedly need another volume comparable to this one a few years from now, presenting even newer, further improved theories. And, to paraphrase Lewin, the better the theories, the more useful they will be.

Paul H. Mussen
Institute of Human Development
University of California, Berkeley
Berkeley, California 94720

SOCIAL COGNITIVE THEORY

Albert Bandura

Many theories have been proposed over the years to explain the developmental changes that people undergo over the course of their lives. These theories differ in the conceptions of human nature they adopt and in what they regard to be the basic causes and mechanisms of human motivation and behavior. The present chapter analyzes human development from the perspective of social cognitive theory (Bandura, 1986). Since development is a life-long process (Baltes & Reese, 1984), the analysis is concerned with changes in the psychosocial functioning of adults as well as with those occurring in childhood. Development is not a monolithic process. Human capabilities vary in their psychobiologic origins and in the experiential conditions needed to enhance and sustain them. Human development, therefore, encompasses many different types and patterns of changes. Diversity in social practices produces substantial individual differences in the capabilities that are cultivated and those that remain underdeveloped.

Annals of Child Development, Volume 6, pages 1-60.
Copyright © 1989 by JAI Press Inc.
All rights of reproduction in any form reserved.
ISBN: 0-89232-979-3

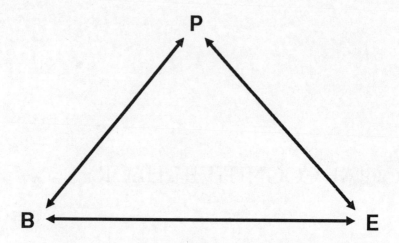

Figure 1. Schematization of triadic reciprocal determinism. *B* signifies behavior; *P* the cognitive, biological and other internal events that can affect perceptions and actions; and *E* the external environment.

MODEL OF CAUSATION

Triadic Reciprocal Determinism

Before analyzing the development of different human capabilities, the model of causation on which social cognitive theory is founded is reviewed briefly. Human behavior has often been explained in terms of one-sided determinism. In such modes of unidirectional causation, behavior is depicted as being shaped and controlled either by environmental influences or by internal dispositions. Social cognitive theory favors a model of causation involving triadic reciprocal determinism. In this model of reciprocal causation, behavior, cognition and other personal factors, and environmental influences all operate as interacting determinants that influence each other bidirectionally (Figure 1). Reciprocal causation does not mean that the different sources of influence are of equal strength. Some may be stronger than others. Nor do the reciprocal influences all occur simultaneously. It takes time for a causal factor to exert its influence and activate reciprocal influences.

Let us consider briefly the major interactional links between the different subsystems of influence. The $P\longleftrightarrow B$ segment of reciprocal causation reflects the interaction between thought, affect and action. Expectations, beliefs, self-perceptions, goals and intentions give shape and direction to behavior. What people think, believe, and feel, affects how they behave (Bandura, 1986; Bower, 1975; Neisser, 1976). The natural and extrinsic effects of their actions, in turn, partly determine their thought patterns and emotional reactions. The personal factor also encompasses the biological properties of the organism. Physical structure and sensory and neural systems affect behavior and impose constraints on capabilities. Sensory systems and brain structures are, in turn, modifiable by behavioral experiences (Greenough, Black, & Wallace, 1987).

The $E\longleftrightarrow P$ segment of reciprocal causation is concerned with the interactive relation between personal characteristics and environmental influences. Human expectations, beliefs, emotional bents and cognitive competencies are developed and modified by social influences that convey information and activate emotional reactions through modeling, instruction and social persuasion (Bandura, 1986). People also evoke different reactions from their social environment by their physical characteristics, such as their age, size, race, sex, and physical attractiveness, quite apart from what they say and do (Lerner, 1982). People similarly activate different social reactions depending on their socially conferred roles and status. For example, children who have a reputation as tough aggressors will elicit different reactions from their peers than those reputed to be unassertive. Thus, by their social status and observable characteristics people can affect their social environment before they say or do anything. The social reactions so elicited affect the recipients' conceptions of themselves and others in ways that either strengthen or alter the environmental bias (Snyder, 1981).

The $B\longleftrightarrow E$ segment of reciprocal causation in the triadic system represents the two-way influence between behavior and the environment. In the transactions of everyday life, behavior alters environmental conditions and is, in turn, altered by the very conditions it creates. The environment is not a fixed entity that inevitably impinges upon individuals. When mobility is constrained, some aspects of the physical and social environment may encroach on individuals whether they like it or not. But most aspects of the environment do not operate as an influence until they are activated by appropriate behavior. Lecturers do not influence students unless they attend their classes, hot stove tops do not burn unless they are touched, parents usually do not praise their children unless they do something praiseworthy. The aspect of the potential environment that becomes the actual environment for given individuals thus depends on how they behave.

Because of the bidirectionality of influence between behavior and environmental circumstances, people are both products and producers of their environment. They affect the nature of their experienced environment through selection and creation of situations. People tend to select activities and associates from the vast range of possibilities in terms of their acquired preferences and competencies (Bandura & Walters, 1959; Bullock & Merrill, 1980; Emmons & Diener, 1986). Through their actions, people create as well as select environments. Aggressive persons produce hostile environments wherever they go, whereas those who act in a more friendly manner generate an amiable social milieu (Raush, 1965). Thus, behavior determines which of the many potential environmental influences will come into play and what forms they will take. Environmental influences, in turn, partly determine which forms of behavior are developed and activated. The growing recognition of reciprocal causation has altered the way in which socialization is viewed. One-sided developmental analyses of how parents influence their children have given way to transactional analyses of how parents and children influence each other (Bell & Harper, 1977; Cairns, 1979; Lewis & Rosenblum, 1974).

Determinants of Life Paths

Psychological theories of human development focus heavily on the growth of capabilities, especially during the earlier formative years when changes occur rapidly. However, the fundamental issues of what determines human life paths has received little attention. Knowledge of the level to which various capabilities have developed does not, in itself, tell us much about the course personal lives will take.

When human development is viewed from a lifespan perspective, the influential determinants include a varied succession of life events that vary in their power to affect the direction lives take (Brim & Ryff, 1980; Hultsch & Plemons, 1979). Many of these determinants include age-graded social influences that are provided by custom within familial, educational, and other institutional systems. Some involve biological conditions that exercise influence over person's futures. Others are unpredictable occurrences in the physical environment. Still others involve irregular life events such as career changes, divorce, migration, accidents, and illness.

Social and technological changes alter, often considerably, the kinds of life events that become customary in the society. Indeed, many of the major changes in social and economic life are ushered in by innovations of technology. Life experiences under the same sociocultural conditions at a given period will differ for people who encounter them at different points in their lifespan (Elder, 1981). Thus, for example, economic depression will have different effects on those entering adulthood than on those who pass through such adverse conditions at a young age. Major sociocultural changes that make life markedly different such as economic adversities that alter livelihoods and opportunity structures, military conflicts, cultural upheavals, new technologies and political changes that modify the character of the society can have strong impact on life courses.

Whatever the social conditions might be, there is still the task of explaining the varied directions that personal lives take at any given time and place. This requires a personal, as well as a social, analysis of life paths. Analysis of behavioral patterns across the lifespan reveals that, in addition to the prevailing sociocultural influences, fortuitous events often exert an important influence on the course of human lives (Bandura, 1982b). There are many fortuitous elements in the events people encounter in their daily lives. They are often brought together through a fortuitous constellation of events, when their paths would otherwise never be crossed. In such chance encounters, the separate paths in which people are moving have their own chain of causal determinants, but their intersection occurs fortuitously rather than through deliberate plan. The profusion of separate chains of events provides innumerable opportunities for fortuitous intersections. It is such chance encounters that often play a prominent role in shaping the course of career pursuits, forming marital partnerships, and altering the future direction of other aspects of human lives (Bandura, 1982b). To cite but a single example, an editor arrives for a talk on the psychology of chance encounters and grabs a seat that happens to be next to a woman psychologist as the lecture hall rapidly fills up. This chance meeting eventually led to their marriage. With only a slight change of time of entry, seating constellations would have altered and this particular social intersect would probably not have occurred. A marital partnership was thus fortuitously formed at a talk devoted to fortuitous determinants of life paths! As this incident illustrates, some of the most important determinants of life paths often arise through the most trivial of circumstances.

Many chance encounters touch people only lightly, others leave more lasting effects, and still others thrust people into new trajectories of life. Psychology cannot foretell the occurrences of fortuitous encounters, however sophisticated its knowledge of human behavior. The unforeseeability and branching power of fortuitous influences make the specific course of lives neither easily predictable nor easily controllable. Fortuity of influence does not mean that behavior is undetermined. Fortuitous influences may be unforeseeable, but having occurred they enter as evident factors in causal chains in the same way as prearranged influences do.

A science of psychology does not have much to say about the occurrence of fortuitous intersections, except that personal attributes and particular social affiliations and milieus make some types of encounters more probable than others. The everyday activities of delinquent gangs and college enrollees will bring them into fortuitous contact with different types of persons. However, psychology can provide the basis for predicting the nature, scope, and strength of the impact such encounters will have on human lives. The power of fortuitous influences to inaugurate enduring change is determined by the reciprocal influence of personal proclivities and social factors. These interactive determinants have been extensively analyzed elsewhere (Bandura, 1982b).

Knowledge of the factors, whether planned or fortuitous, that can alter the course of life paths provides guides for how to foster valued futures. At the personal level, it requires cultivating the capabilities for exercising self-directedness.

These include the development of competencies, self-beliefs of efficacy to exercise control, and self-regulatory capabilities for influencing one's own motivation and actions. Such personal resources expand freedom of action, and enable people to serve as causal contributors to their own life course by selecting, influencing, and constructing their own circumstances. With such skills, people are better able to provide supports and direction for their actions, to capitalize on planned or fortuitous opportunities, to resist social traps that lead down detrimental paths, and to disengage themselves from such predicaments should they become enmeshed in them.

To exercise some measure of control over one's developmental course requires, in addition to effective tools of personal agency, a great deal of social support. Social resources are especially important during formative years when preferences and personal standards are in a state of flux, and there are many conflicting sources of influence with which to contend. To surmount the obstacles and stresses encountered in the life paths people take, they need social supports to give incentive, meaning, and worth to what they do. When social ties are weak or lacking, vulnerability to deleterious fortuitous influences is increased (Bandura, 1982b). The life paths that realistically become open to individuals are also partly determined by the nature of societal opportunity structures. To the extent that societal systems provide aidful means and resources, they increase people's opportunities to influence the course of their lives.

In social cognitive theory, people are neither driven by inner forces nor automatically shaped and controlled by the environment. As we have already seen, they function as contributors to their own motivation, behavior, and development within a network of reciprocally interacting influences. Persons are characterized within this theoretical perspective in terms of a number of basic capabilities, to which we turn next.

SYMBOLIZING CAPABILITY

The remarkable capacity to use symbols provides humans with a powerful tool for understanding and managing their environment. Most external influences affect behavior through cognitive processes. Cognitive factors partly determine which environmental events will be observed, what meaning will be conferred on them, whether they leave any lasting effects, what emotional impact and motivating power they will have, and how the information they convey will be organized for future use. People process and transform passing experiences by means of verbal, imaginal and other symbols into cognitive models of reality that serve as guides for judgment and action. It is through symbols that people give meaning, form, and continuity to the experiences they have had. Symbols serve as the vehicle of thought. Cognitive representations of experiences in knowledge structures provide the substance for thinking. And rules and strategies provide the cognitive operations for manipulating knowledge for different purposes. By symbolically manipulating the information derived from personal and vicarious experiences, people gain understanding of causal relationships and expand their knowledge.

Knowledge and thinking skills provide the substance and tools for cognitive problem solving. Rather than solve problems solely by performing actions and suffering the consequences of missteps, people usually test possible solutions in thought and discard or retain them on the basis of estimated consequences before plunging into action. The remarkable flexibility of symbolization also enables people to create novel and fanciful ideas that transcend their sensory experiences. One can easily think of cows jumping over the moon and elephants riding on flies, even though these feats are physically impossible. Through the medium of symbols they can communicate with others at any distance in time and space. Other distinctive human characteristics to be discussed shortly depend on symbolic capability.

To say that people base many of their actions on thought does not necessarily mean they are always objectively rational. Rationality depends on reasoning skills which are not always well developed or used effectively. Even if people know how to reason they make faulty judgments when they base their reasoning on incomplete or erroneous information, or they fail to consider the full consequences of different choices. They often misread events through cognitive biases in ways that give rise to faulty beliefs about themselves and the world around them. When they act on their misconceptions, which appear subjectively rational to them, they are viewed by others as behaving in an unreasonable or foolish manner. Moreover, people often know what they ought to do but are swayed by compelling circumstances or emotional factors to behave otherwise.

Although the capacity to think vastly expands human capabilities, if put to faulty use, it can also serve as a major source of personal distress. Many human dysfunctions and torments stem from problems of thought. This is because, in their thoughts, people often dwell on painful pasts and on perturbing futures of their own invention. They burden themselves with stressful arousal through anxiety-provoking rumination. They debilitate their own efforts by self-doubting and other self-defeating ideation. They constrain and impoverish their lives through phobic thinking. They drive themselves to despondency by harsh self-evaluation and dejecting modes of thinking. And they often act on misconceptions that get them into trouble. Thought can thus be a source of human failings and distress as well as human accomplishment.

Analysis of how thought enters into the determination of behavior touches on fundamental issues concerning the mind-body relationship. In social cognitive theory, thoughts are brain processes rather than separate psychic entities. The view that cognitive events are brain processes does not mean that psychological laws regarding cognitive functioning must be reduced to neurophysiological ones. Quite the contrary. One must distinguish between cerebral systems and the personal and social means by which they can be orchestrated for different purposes. Mapping the neural circuitry subserving particular skills does not explain the environmental influences that structure those skills or the functional uses to which they will be put. For example, knowing how cortical neurons function in learning does not tell one much about how best to present and organize instructional material, how to code the material to remember it, and how to motivate learners to attend to, process, and rehearse what they are learning. Nor does understanding of how the brain works provide rules on how to construct conditions to produce successful parents, teachers, students or politicians. The influences needed to produce the neural occurrences underlying complex behavior are either external to the organism or act together with cognitively generated ones. The laws of psychology tell us how to structure environmental influences and to enlist cognitive activities to achieve given purposes.

To view cognitions as brain processes raises the intriguing question of how people come to be producers of thoughts that may be novel, inventive, visionary, or that take complete leave of reality, as in flights of fancy. One can get oneself to imagine several novel acts, and then choose to perform one of them. Cognitive production involves intention, creation and exercise of personal agency. The question of interest is not how mind and body act on each other as though they were separate entities, but how people can, through exercise of personal agency, bring into being cognitive or cerebral productions and translate them into actions.

Discrete Global Structures of Specialized Cognitive Competencies

Virtually all theories of cognitive development assume that children become more skilled at abstract reasoning as they grow older. The issue in dispute concerns the nature of cognitive development. According to Piagetian theory, thinking changes in an invariant stage sequence from one uniform way of thinking to another (Piaget, 1970). Cognitive conflict, arising from discrepancies between internal schemata and perceived events, serves as the motivating force for changing from concrete modes of thinking to more abstract forms.

Progression from concrete to abstract reasoning certainly characterizes some aspects of cognitive development. However, cognitive changes are much more diversified and depend on more than intrapsychic conflict. Flavell (1978b) summed up this diversity well when he said, "However much we may wish it to believe otherwise, human cognitive growth may simply be too contingent, multiform, and heterogenous—too variegated in developmental mechanisms, routes, and rates—to be accurately categorized by any stage theory of the Piagetian kind

(p. 187).'' Cognitive development is better analyzed in terms of specialized cognitive competencies rather than discrete uniform ways of thinking.

Cognitive functioning involves knowledge, much of it specialized, and cognitive skills for operating on it. Hence, cognitive attainments require the acquisition of domain-relevant knowledge along with the judgmental rules that apply to that area of activity (Feldman, 1980). For example, the knowledge and rules for reasoning about biological processes will differ from those about mechanical systems or the workings of social relationships. The sequences in which complex cognitive competencies are acquired vary because different domains of activity have different structures.

Within the social cognitive perspective, social factors play an influential role in cognitive development and there are many motivators of the pursuit of competence. Maturational factors and the information gained from exploratory experiences contribute to cognitive growth. However, most valuable knowledge is imparted socially. Those who figure prominently in children's lives serve as indispensable sources of knowledge that contribute to what and how children think about different matters. Indeed, children's intellectual self-development would be stunted if they could not draw on this heritage of knowledge in each realm of functioning and, instead, had to rediscover it, bit by bit, through their own trial-and-error activity. Guided instruction and modeling that effectively conveys abstract rules of reasoning promote cognitive development in children (Bandura, 1986; Brainerd, 1978; Rosenthal & Zimmerman, 1978). Socially-guided learning also encourages self-directed learning by providing children with the conceptual tools needed to gain new knowledge and to deal intelligently with the varied situations they encounter in their everyday life.

With increasing age, human judgment and problem solving depends more heavily on specialized knowledge domains. In efforts to develop their cognitive competencies, people draw on their own experiences and turn to others who are well informed on the matters of concern. Because of the complexity and rapid growth of knowledge, human acquisition of specialized cognitive competencies relies increasingly on modeled expertise. In this process, the knowledge and reasoning strategies for sound judgment are gleaned from those who are highly knowledgeable and skilled in the relevant domain of activity. Development of cognitive competencies can be accelerated by symbolically modeling the reasoning strategies for particular domains in systematic and highly informative ways (Coombs, 1984).

Language Development

A great deal of human thought is linguistically based. Hence, the processes by which language develops are of major interest. Initially, children acquire knowledge about objects and about the relationships between them through non-

linguistic processing of direct and vicarious experience. Such understanding
helps to impart meaning to linguistic symbols. By relating the utterances they
hear to what they understand to be going on at the time, children begin to grasp
what the different linguistic forms signify (Bowerman, 1973; Macnamara, 1972).
The establishment of the linguistic system creates an intricate bidirectional influence between cognitive development and language acquisition (Schlesinger,
1982). After children learn the names for things and how to represent conceptual
relationships in words, language can influence how children perceive, organize,
and interpret events. Language thus becomes not only a means of communication but also a way of shaping the form of thought. The rules for encoding
semantic relations in words are originally learned from discourses regarding concrete events of high interest and meaning to children. As they master linguistic
competencies, language becomes more abstract and is no longer dependent on
the co-occurrence of actual events. This greatly extends the power of language as
a tool of thought.

Generative language is unique to humans. Chimpanzees can be taught signs
representing objects and be prompted to string a few of them together in a loose
order, but this rudimentary communication bears little resemblance to the
generative characteristics of human speech. People are endowed with information-processing capacities for extracting linguistic rules and using them to encode and convey information. The inherent capability to categorize, to abstract
general characteristics from particular instances, to generalize across features of
similarity, and to discriminate by features of dissimilarity provides the basic ap-
paratus for discerning the regularities in language. These basic perceptual
facilities aid recognition of similarities and differences in speech sounds and in
segmenting the flow of speech into recognizable units (Jusczyk, 1981).

Language is the product of multiple determinants operating through a number
of mediating processes. One set of determinants concerns the cognitive skills that
children need to process linguistic information. This requires capabilities to perceive the essential elements of speech, to recognize and remember sequential
structures, to abstract rules from diverse utterances, and to select the appropriate
words and production rules to generate intelligible utterances. These all involve
intricate cognitive subskills. In trying to decipher speech, children have to figure
out how the arrangement of spoken words relates to what they know about what
is going on at the time. Thus, the second set of determinants of language acquisition pertains to children's fund of nonlinguistic knowledge in different areas of
discourse. Such knowledge provides the notions about what the words mean and
how they have to be arranged to convey the child's understood conceptual relations.

Linguistic knowledge is hard to come by, unless notions about words and their
structures are considered and then put to the social test. As in other areas of
functioning, the rate of language acquisition is better predicted from a person's

knowledge that is most pertinent to the area of discourse than from global cognitive structures. The complexity of linguistic input and concrete accompaniments to what is being talked about constitutes the third set of factors governing language acquisition. Interpersonal factors, which govern the communicative functions of speech, serve as a further source of influence on language development. These various determinants will be examined in the sections that follow. When viewed from the broader perspective of communication, the process of language acquisition involves much more than syntactic analysis. Cognitive and social factors are an integral part of the process. However, in the concern over the form of speech, its social function was long neglected.

The contribution of social factors to language development has been downplayed for a long time on the basis of widely shared erroneous assumptions about social learning processes. These misconceptions have been addressed elsewhere and will not be reviewed here (Bandura, 1986). It is mainly through observational learning that children extract syntactic rules from the speech they hear around them. Once they acquire syntactic rules they can generate new sentences they have never heard. In learning to communicate symbolically, children must acquire appropriate verbal symbols for objects and events and syntactic rules for representing relationships among them. The process of acquiring language involves not only learning grammatical relations between words, but also correlating the linguistic forms with the events to which they apply. This requires integrating two relational systems—linguistic and perceptual—both relying on a common base of understanding. Language learning, therefore, depends extensively on nonlinguistic understanding of the events to which the utterances refer. For this reason, it is difficult to transmit linguistic forms that children do not already know by verbal modeling alone.

Adults, of course, do not converse abstractly with young children, who have a poor grasp of speech. Verbal expressions that convey grammatical relations are usually matched to meaningful ongoing activities about which children already have some knowledge. Grammatical features of speech are more informative and distinguishable when the semantic referents to the utterances are present than when they are absent. Young children, for example, are helped to comprehend plural forms if they hear singular and plural labels applied to single and multiple objects, respectively. Acquisition of language rules is greatly facilitated by linking linguistic modeling to ongoing activities to which the speech refers (Brown, 1976; Stewart & Hamilton, 1976; Whitehurst, 1977). Seeing things happen provides informative cues to the meaning of accompanying utterances.

The rate of language acquisition is affected by the complexity of the model's language relative to the children's cognitive capabilities. Children can gain little from modeled speech that exceeds their ability to process what they hear. Linguistic rules must be initially modeled in simplified, as well as in semantically enriched forms to make them more easily learnable. Indeed, parents usually adjust their speech to their children's linguistic competence in an effort to facilitate language acquisition. When addressing young children, parents use utterances that are shorter, more repetitive, and grammatically simpler, than when they speak to older children (Baldwin & Baldwin, 1973; Moerk, 1986; Snow, 1972). Parents also speak slower, which eases the processing of linguistic input, and they use exaggerated intonation as an attention-focusing device. The linguistic environment, of course, is not populated solely with adults. Young children frequently model the language of their peers (Hamilton & Stewart, 1977). Even young children simplify their speech when they are talking to younger children (Shatz & Gelman, 1973). Children master words and linguistic forms at a very early age if provided with enriched language stimulation that matches their cognitive level (Swenson, 1983).

Parents use other modeling devices to promote language development. One method is to expand their children's previous utterances by replacing deletions or adding more complex linguistic elements. Through this process, young children pick up new linguistic forms from the modeled expansions and use them in their own speech (Bloom, Hood, & Lightbown, 1974; Kemp & Dale, 1973; Nicolich & Raph, 1978). The more parents engage in reciprocal modeling, which enhances its social function, the more readily children adopt their parents' modeled expansions (Folger & Chapman, 1978). Children's utterances represent efforts to communicate about meaningful activities that command their attention. Perhaps because of the greater attentional involvement of the children, parental linguistic modeling, which expands children's utterances, increases their spontaneous use of the selected linguistic forms more effectively than does similar parental modeling that is not linked to children's prior speech (Hovell, Schumaker, & Sherman, 1978). Another form of linguistic modeling that accelerates language acquisition involves replying to children's speech by recasting it into a new syntactic form without altering the meaning of what is said. By using modeled recastings, Nelson (1977a, b) selectively promoted children's mastery of advanced syntactic forms they had lacked. Like modeled expansions, recastings address children's immediate communicative concerns and are thus well suited to catch attention and enlist motivation to improve one's linguistic competence.

In summary, modeling, supplemented with semantic aids and devices to focus attention on key linguistic features, is a highly effective way of promoting language acquisition. Sequential analyses of verbal interchanges between parents and their young children show that parents are active language teachers (Moerk, 1986). Their instructive and corrective strategies include repetitive modeling of more advanced linguistic forms, restructuring and elaborating the child's constructions in modeled feedback, simplifying linguistic structures, varying the content around the same structure, rephrasing utterances, prompting, questioning, informing, answering, labeling, pictorial structuring of what is being talked about, and accenting grammatically significant speech elements. Parents tailor their language to the children's level of cognitive and linguistic capabilities. It is not as though children are inundated with speech, but are left otherwise to their own devices to ferret out the rules of grammar from the verbal morass. Rather, parents do much of the abstraction for them by structuring linguistic information in ways that make grammatical rules more easily learnable (Moerk, 1986). As children increase their linguistic competence, parents diminish their instructive activities. Variations in the instructive aspects of parental speech correlate with the rate of children's language development.

Much of the preceding discussion has been concerned with how modeled speech is structured and semantically enriched to enhance language acquisition. Children adopt language because they can do useful and wondrous things with it. Intelligible speech provides many benefits which function as incentives for acquiring communicative competence. In the initial prelinguistic phase, vocal expressions mainly serve interpersonal purposes—it is an effective way for infants to maintain positive interactions. When adults repeat the infants' vocal expressions, the infants' rate of spontaneous vocalizations increases substantially (Haugan & McIntire, 1972). Experience with this type of verbal interplay can enhance the infants' responsiveness to parental linguistic modeling for later language acquisition.

As children begin to recognize the communicative function of speech, their expressive language is influenced by different modes of feedback. We have already seen how language skills can be improved by elaborative and corrective modeling in adult response to incomplete or ungrammatical utterances by children. If children possess sufficient linguistic knowledge, even signs of noncomprehension by adults lead children to correct their own speech in the direction of more accurate forms of language (Kasermann & Foppa, 1981).

Children's language is affected more strongly by its natural consequences than by arbitrary, extrinsic ones. The most effective natural consequences are the benefits derived from influencing the social environment. Success in getting others to do things that bring one different benefits is better achieved by grammatical speech than by unintelligible utterances. The demands for communicative accuracy, although minimal initially, increase as children grow older.

Changes in children's expressive language have been studied when elaborated forms of speech are made highly useful in securing valued outcomes (Hart & Risley, 1978). In these naturalistic studies, young children with limited language skills can get attractive things they want, or assistance with tasks, provided they ask for things in informative ways using appropriate sentence structures. If they do not know the speech forms, they are initially modeled for them in the context of the requests for assistance, whereupon the children are encouraged to use the elaborated speech forms. Children readily adopt advanced speech forms when they can get what they want that way. Moreover, they generalize these elaborated styles of speech across settings, occasions, activities, and people, and they continue to use them after conditions have changed so that simpler speech would do (Hart & Risley, 1975; 1980). Hart and Risley attribute the effectiveness of this motivational system to the fact that language is developed through natural interactions initiated by the children relating to activities that arouse their interest and provide strong incentives to improve their communicative skills. They receive modeled guidance if needed. These are the optimal conditions for learning.

Children use language to gain needed information about things, as well as to gain access to them. Their interest in information grows as they begin to perceive relationships between environmental events and between their actions and outcomes. It is not long before they learn that knowledge which enables them to predict and control events can be very useful. Transmission of information about the workings of the environment requires elaborated language to represent the events of interest. This provides additional incentive for children to enlarge their communicative skills, so they can ask about things and understand what people tell them. They also find language useful in guiding their actions, and in explaining their own behavior to themselves and to others. This can make a big difference in how others treat them. The consequences of verbally-guided action further underscore the many benefits of linguistic competencies. Acting on misunderstandings of what other people say can have adverse effects, as can miscommunications that lead others astray. The outcomes of actions create informative feedback for improving one's understanding and use of speech.

VICARIOUS CAPABILITY

The advanced capability for vicarious learning is another distinctive human quality that receives considerable emphasis in social cognitive theory. Psychological theories have traditionally emphasized learning through the effects of one's actions. If knowledge and skills could be acquired only by direct experience, the process of cognitive and social development would be greatly retarded, not to mention exceedingly tedious and hazardous. A culture could never transmit its language, mores, social practices, and requisite competencies if they had to be shaped tediously in each new member by response consequences without the benefit of models to exemplify the cultural patterns. The abbreviation of the acquisition process is vital for survival as well as for human development because natural endowment provides few inborn skills. Because mistakes can produce costly, or even fatal consequences, the prospects of survival would be slim indeed if one had to rely solely on trial and error experiences. Moreover, the constraints of time, resources, and mobility impose severe limits on the situations and activities that can be directly explored for the acquisition of new knowledge.

Humans have evolved an advanced capacity for observational learning that enables them to expand their knowledge and skills on the basis of information conveyed by modeling influences. Indeed, virtually all learning phenomena resulting from direct experience can occur vicariously by observing people's behavior and its consequences for them (Bandura, 1986; Rosenthal & Zimmerman, 1978). Much social learning occurs either deliberately or inadvertently by observing the actual behavior of others and the consequences for them. However, a great deal of information about behavior patterns and the effects they have on the environment is gained from models portrayed symbolically through verbal or pictorial means.

A major significance of symbolic modeling lies in its tremendous multiplicative power. Unlike learning by doing, which requires altering the actions of each individual through repeated trial-and-error experiences, in observational learning a single model can transmit new ways of thinking and behaving simultaneously to many people in widely dispersed locales. There is another aspect of symbolic modeling that magnifies its psychological and social effects. During the course of their daily lives, people have direct contact with only a small sector of the environment. Consequently, their conceptions of social reality are greatly influenced by vicarious experiences—by what they see and hear—without direct experiential correctives. The more people's images of reality depend upon the media's symbolic environment, the greater is its social impact.

Most psychological theories were cast long before the advent of enormous advances in the technology of communication. As a result, they give insufficient attention to the increasingly powerful role that the symbolic environment plays in present-day human lives. The video system has become the dominant vehicle for disseminating symbolic environments both within and across societies. Whereas previously, modeling influences were largely confined to the behavior patterns exhibited in one's immediate environment, television has vastly expanded the range of models to which members of society are exposed day in and day out. By drawing on these modeled patterns of thought and behavior, observers can transcend the bounds of their immediate environment. New ideas and social practices are now being rapidly diffused by symbolic modeling within a society and from one society to another. Whether it be thought patterns, values, attitudes, or styles of behavior, life increasingly models the media (Bandura, 1986; Pearl, Bouthilet, & Lazar, 1982). Because television occupies a large part of people's lives, the study of acculturation in the present electronic era must be broadened to include electronic acculturation.

Modeling influences can have diverse psychological effects. First, they foster acquisition of new competencies, cognitive skills, and behavior patterns. Second, they affect level of motivation and restraints over behavior that has been previously learned. Modeling influences also serve as social prompts that actuate

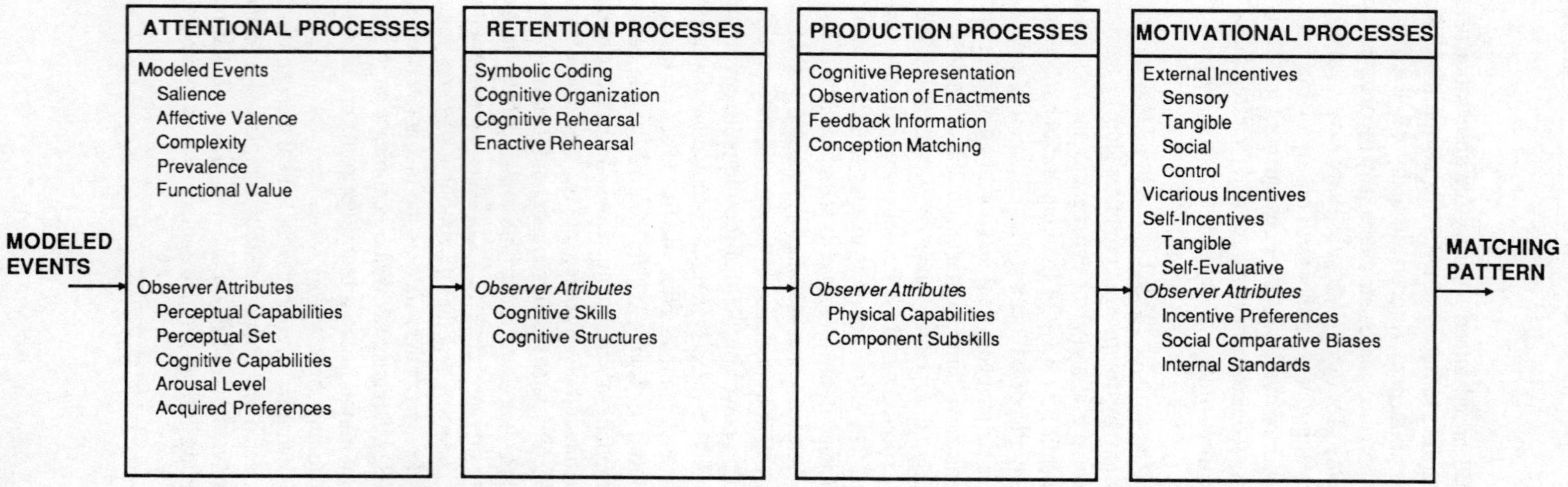

ATTENTIONAL PROCESSES	RETENTION PROCESSES	PRODUCTION PROCESSES	MOTIVATIONAL PROCESSES
Modeled Events	Symbolic Coding	Cognitive Representation	External Incentives
Salience	Cognitive Organization	Observation of Enactments	Sensory
Affective Valence	Cognitive Rehearsal	Feedback Information	Tangible
Complexity	Enactive Rehearsal	Conception Matching	Social
Prevalence			Control
Functional Value			Vicarious Incentives
			Self-Incentives
			Tangible
			Self-Evaluative
Observer Attributes	*Observer Attributes*	*Observer Attributes*	*Observer Attributes*
Perceptual Capabilities	Cognitive Skills	Physical Capabilities	Incentive Preferences
Perceptual Set	Cognitive Structures	Component Subskills	Social Comparative Biases
Cognitive Capabilities			Internal Standards
Arousal Level			
Acquired Preferences			

MODELED EVENTS → → → → MATCHING PATTERN

Figure 2. Subprocesses governing observational learning.

and channel behavior in social transactions. In addition, models often express emotional reactions that tend to elicit emotional arousal in observers. Through such vicarious arousal, people acquire attitudes, values, and emotional dispositions toward persons, places, and things. In sum, modeling influences can serve as instructors, motivators, inhibitors, disinhibitors, social facilitators, and emotion arousers. The determinants and mechanisms governing these diverse modeling effects are addressed in considerable detail elsewhere (Bandura, 1986), and will be reviewed only briefly here.

Observational Learning

Learning from models may take varied forms, including new behavior patterns, judgmental standards, cognitive competencies, and generative rules for creating new forms of behavior. Observational learning is governed by four component subfunctions which are depicted in Figure 2. *Attentional processes* determine what people observe in the profusion of modeling influences and what information they extract from what they notice.

People cannot be much influenced by observed events if they do not remember them. A second major subfunction governing observational learning concerns *retention processes*. Retention involves an active process of transforming and restructuring the information conveyed by modeled events into rules and conceptions for memory representation. In the third subfunction in modeling—the *behavioral production process*—symbolic conceptions are translated into appropriate courses of action. This is achieved through a conception-matching process in which behavioral enactments are adjusted until they match the internal conception of the activity.

The fourth subfunction in modeling concerns *motivational processes*. Social cognitive theory distinguishes between acquisition and performance because people do not perform everything they learn. Performance of observationally learned behavior is influenced by three major types of incentive motivators—direct, vicarious, and self-produced. People are more likely to exhibit modeled behavior if it results in valued outcomes than if it has unrewarding or punishing effects. The observed cost and benefits accruing to others influence the performance of modeled patterns in much the same way as do directly experienced consequences. People are motivated by the successes of others who are similar to themselves, but are discouraged from pursuing courses of behavior that they have seen often result in adverse consequences. Personal standards of conduct provide a further source of incentive motivation. The evaluative reactions people generate to their own behavior regulate which observationally learned activities they are most likely to pursue. They express what they find self-satisfying and reject what they personally disapprove.

Abstract Modeling

Modeling is not merely a process of behavioral mimicry. Highly functional patterns of behavior, which constitute the proven skills and established customs of a culture, may be adopted in essentially the same form as they are exemplified. There is little leeway for improvisation on how to drive automobiles or to perform arithmetic operations. However, in many activities, subskills must be improvised to suit varying circumstances. Modeling influences can convey rules for generative and innovative behavior as well. This higher-level learning is achieved through abstract modeling. Rule-governed behavior differs in specific content and other details but it contains the same underlying rule. For example, the modeled statements, "The dog is *being* petted," and "the window *was* opened" refer to different things but the linguistic rule—the passive form—is the same. In abstract modeling, observers extract the rule embodied in the specific behavior exhibited by others. Once they learn the rule, they can use it to generate new instances of behavior that go beyond what they have seen or heard. Much human learning is aimed at developing cognitive skills on how to gain and use knowledge for future use. Observational learning of thinking skills is greatly facilitated by modeling thought processes in conjunction with action strategies (Meichenbaum, 1984). Models verbalize their thought strategies as they engage in problem-solving activities. The ordinarily covert thoughts guiding the actions of the models are thus made observable and learnable by others.

Modeling has been shown to be a highly effective means of establishing abstract or rule-governed behavior. On the basis of modeled information, people acquire, among other things, judgmental standards, linguistic rules, styles of inquiry, information-processing skills, and standards of self-evaluation (Bandura, 1986; Rosenthal & Zimmerman, 1978). Evidence that generative rules of thought and conduct can be created through abstract modeling attests to the broad scope of observational learning.

Development of Modeling Capabilities

Because observational learning involves several subfunctions that evolve with maturation and experiences, it depends upon prior development. When analyzed in terms of its constituent subfunctions, facility in observational learning is not primarily a matter of learning to imitate. Nor is it a discrete skill. Rather, developing adeptness in observational learning involves acquiring multiple subskills in selective attention, cognitive representation, symbolic transformation, and anticipatory motivation.

Neonates possess greater modeling capabilities than is commonly believed. By several months of age, infants can and do model behavior with some consistency (Kaye, 1982; Meltzoff & Moore, 1983; Valentine, 1930). The development of proficiency in observational learning is grounded in social reciprocation. Infants possess sufficient rudimentary representational capacities and sensorimotor coordination to enable them to imitate elementary sounds and acts within their physical capabilities. Parents readily imitate a newborn's gestures and vocalizations from the very beginning, often in expressive ways that have been shown to facilitate modeling (Papousek & Papousek, 1977; Pawlby, 1977).

The newborn, whose means of communication and social influence are severely limited, learns that reciprocal imitation is an effective way of eliciting and sustaining parental responsiveness. Uzgiris (1984) has given considerable attention to the social function of imitation in infancy. Mutual imitation serves as a means of conveying interest and sharing experiences. Initially, parents tend to model acts that infants spontaneously perform. After the reciprocal imitation is established, parents are quick to initiate new response patterns for imitative sequences that help to expand their infant's competencies (Pawlby, 1977). Successful modeling of these more complicated patterns of behavior requires development of the major subfunctions that govern observational learning. It is to the developmental course of these subfunctions that we turn next.

Attentional Processes

Young children present certain attentional deficiencies that limit their proficiency in observational learning. They have difficulty attending to different sorts of information at the same time, distinguishing pertinent aspects from irrelevancies, and maintaining attention to ongoing events long enough to acquire sufficient information about them (Cohen & Salapatek, 1975; Hagen & Hale, 1973). They are easily distracted. With increasing experience, children's attentional skills improve in all of these respects.

In promoting observational learning, adults alter the behavior they model to compensate for the attentional limitations of children. With infants, parents gain their attention and give salience to the behavior they want to encourage by selectively imitating them. Parents tend to perform the reciprocated imitations in an exaggerated animated fashion that is well designed to sustain the child's attentiveness at a high level during the mutual modeling sequences (Papousek & Papousek, 1977). The animated social interplay provides a vehicle for channeling and expanding infants' attention in activities that go beyond those they have already mastered.

The attention-arousing value of the modeled acts, themselves, also influences what infants are likely to adopt. Infants are more attentive to, and imitate more often, modeled acts when they involve objects and sound accompaniments than when they are modeled silently and without objects to draw attention (Abravanel et al., 1976; Uzgiris, 1979). The more attention infants pay to the modeled activities, the more likely they are to adopt them. As infants' attentional capabilities increase, parents exhibit developmentally progressive activities for them to model.

Representational Processes

In developing representational memory skills, children have to learn how to transform modeled information into symbolic forms and to organize it into easily remembered structures. They also have to learn how to use timely rehearsal to facilitate the retention of activities that are vulnerable to memory loss. It takes time for children to learn that they can improve their future performances by symbolizing and rehearsing their immediate experiences.

In the earliest period of development, experiences are probably retained mainly in imaginal modes of representation. Infants will model single acts, but they have difficulty reproducing coordinated sequences that require them to remember how several actions are strung together (McCall, Parke, & Kavanaugh, 1977). They often start the sequence right and simply forget what comes next. With experience, they become more skilled at delayed modeling. Indeed, infants even as young as 18 months will enact behavior learned from televised models after some time has elapsed. Delayed performances of this type require symbolic memory.

As children begin to acquire language they can symbolize the essential aspects of events in words for memory representation. It is not until children acquire some cognitive and linguistic skills that they can extract rules from modeled performances and make effective use of the more complex linguistic transformations (Rosenthal & Zimmerman, 1978). Children can improve their memory by instruction to anticipate, verbally code, and rehearse what they observe (Brown & Barclay, 1976). The vicarious memorial subskills can also be acquired through modeling. By observing the memory feats of others, children learn what information is worth coding, how events should be categorized, and more general strategies for processing information (Lamal, 1971; Rosenthal & Zimmerman, 1978).

Production Processes

Converting conceptions to appropriate actions requires development of transformational skills in intermodal guidance of behavior. Information in the symbolic mode must be translated into corresponding action modes. This involves learning how to organize action sequences, to monitor and compare behavioral enactments against the symbolic model, and to correct evident mismatches (Carroll & Bandura, 1985; 1989). When children must depend on what others tell them, because they cannot observe fully all of their own actions, detecting and correcting mismatches requires linguistic competencies. Deficiencies in any of these production subskills can create a developmental lag between comprehending and performing.

Motivational Processes

Motivational factors that influence the use to which modeled knowledge is put undergo significant developmental changes. During infancy, imitation functions mainly to secure interpersonal responsiveness. Through mutual modeling with adults, infants enjoy playful intimacy and gain experience in social reciprocation. Before long parents cease mimicking their infant's actions, but they remain responsive to instances of infants adopting modeled patterns that expand their competencies. What continues to serve a social function for young infants changes into an instructional vehicle for parents. This transition requires infants to cognize, on the basis of observed regularities, the social effects their different imitations are likely to produce. To help infants to learn the functional value of modeling the parents make the outcomes salient, recurrent, consistent, and closely tied to the infant's actions (Papousek & Papousek, 1977). With increasing cognitive development, children become more skilled at judging probable outcomes of their actions. Such outcome expectations serve as incentives for observational learning.

What has incentive value for children also changes with experience. At the earliest level, infants and young children are motivated primarily by the immediate sensory and social effects of their actions. In the course of development, symbolic incentives signifying achievements, the exercise of mastery and self-evaluative reactions assume increasing motivational functions. Children soon learn that models are not only sources of social reward but also valuable sources of competencies for dealing effectively with the environment. The benefits of efficacious action and the personal satisfaction it brings become powerful incentives for modeling. Development thus increases the range and complexity of incentives that motivate children to gain knowledge through modeling and to use what they have learned.

When viewed from the developmental perspective of social cognitive theory, observational learning is part of a more general process of cognitive and social development. But observational learning is also one of the basic means by which cognitive competencies are developed and expanded. A comprehensive theory must, therefore, examine not only the cognitive mechanisms of observational learning, but also the social learning determinants of cognition.

Vicarious Affective Learning

Both children and adults are easily aroused by the emotional expressions of others. Although people are endowed with the receptive and expressive capacity for vicarious arousal, social experience largely determines the level and pattern of emotional activation. Expressive displays acquire arousing capacity mainly through correlated social experiences (Bandura, 1986). That is, when individuals are in good spirits they treat others amiably, which produces positive affect. As a result of such occurrences, smiles and other expressions of happiness come to signify a positive state of affairs. Conversely, when individuals are dejected, ailing, distressed, or angry, the people around them are likely to suffer as well in one way or another. Expressive signs of anger or despondency come to forebode aversive experiences.

Research varying the degree to which emotions are experienced jointly confirms the importance of correlated experience in the development of vicarious affective responsivity (Miller, Caul, & Mirsky, 1967; Church, 1959; Englis, Vaughan, & Lanzetta, 1982). To have functional use of the capacity for vicarious arousal determined by experience provides substantial benefits. If people's affective reactions were automatically triggered by innate signals, they would be emotionally burdened much of the time by the expressions of pain, joy, grief, fear, anger, sadness, frustration, and disgust emitted by anyone and everyone in sight.

Vicarious arousal operates mainly through an intervening self-arousal process. That is, seeing others react emotionally to instigating conditions activates emotion-arousing thoughts and imagery in observers. As children develop their capacity for cognitive self-arousal, they can generate emotional reactions to cues that are only suggestive of a model's emotional experiences (Wilson & Cantor, 1985). Conversely, they can neutralize or attenuate the emotional impact of modeled distress by thoughts that transform threatening situations into non-threatening ones (Cantor & Wilson, 1987; Dysinger & Ruckmick, 1933).

Cognitive self-arousal can take two forms—by personalizing the experience of another, or by taking the perspective of another. In the personalizing form, observers get themselves emotionally aroused by imagining things happening to themselves that are either similar to the model's experiences or have been generalized from previous positive and aversive experiences. In the perspective-taking form, observers come to experience the emotional states of others by putting themselves in their place and imagining how they might feel. What little evidence exists suggests that observers gain better understanding of other's emotions and react more emotionally to another's affective experiences if the observers imagine how they themselves would feel in that situation than if they try to imagine how the other person might feel (Hughes, Tingle, & Swain, 1981; Stotland, 1969).

If the affective reactions of models only aroused observers fleetingly, it would be of some interest as far as momentary communication is concerned, but of limited psychological import. Thus, if modeled affectivity got children to avoid a threat, but they learned nothing from that experience, they would require the presence of an emoting model to tell them how to behave in every future encounter with the same threat. What gives significance to vicarious influence is that observers can acquire lasting attitudes, emotional reactions, and behavioral proclivities toward persons, places, or things that have been associated with the model's emotional experiences. Thus, observers learn to fear the things that frightened models, to dislike what repulsed them, and to like what gratified them (Bandura, 1988b; Duncker, 1938; Mineka, 1987). Fears and intractable phobias are ameliorated by modeling influences that convey information about coping strategies for exercising control over the things that are feared. The stronger the instilled sense of coping self-efficacy, the bolder the behavior (Bandura, 1982). Values can similarly be developed and altered vicariously by repeated exposure to modeled preferences.

Gender-Role Development

Many aspects of human functioning, such as the interests and competencies people cultivate, the occupational paths they pursue, and the conceptions they hold of themselves and others are prescribed by cultural sex typing. The stereotypic gender conceptions that people adopt have lasting effects on how they perceive and process experiences and how they use their capabilities (Bem, 1981; Betz & Hackett, 1986; Spence & Helmreich, 1978). Because so much of human experience is affected by gender differentiation, the processes of sex typing have been the subject of much developmental theorizing and research. The kinds of attributes and social roles that are culturally linked to masculine and feminine gender should be distinguished from biological sex differences. Although biological characteristics form a basis for gender differentiation, many of the social roles that get tied to gender are not ordained by biological differences. Gender-role development is largely a psychosocial phenomenon.

Sex typing is promoted through a vast system of socialization practices beginning at birth with infants clothed in pink or blue apparel depending on their sex. Before long boys are attired in rugged trousers, girls in pastel skirts, and each is given a different hair style as well. Children come to use differential physical attributes, hair styles, and clothing as indicants of gender (Thompson & Bentler, 1971). As soon as young children begin to comprehend speech, they notice that verbal labeling in masculine and feminine terms is used extensively by those around them. It does not take them long to learn that children are categorized into girls and boys, and adults into mothers and fathers, women and men. Gender labeling gives salience not only to sorting people on the basis of gender, but also to the features and activities that characterize each gender. Children begin to develop a sense of their own gender identity from such experiences.

Gender-role learning requires broadening gender conceptions to include behavioral, social, and vocational aspects. Knowledge about gender roles is more difficult to grasp than is gender identity for several reasons. First, children must achieve gender differentiation before they can organize knowledge about what roles are appropriate for males and females. Second, the stylistic and role behaviors that traditionally typify male and female orientations are not uniformly sex-linked. Not all males are aggressive, nor are all females unassertive. As a result, children have to rely on the relative prevalence of the social examples they observe. If children routinely see women performing homemaking activities, while males only occasionally try their hand at it, homemaking readily gets sex-typed as a woman's role. But if they often observe both men and women gardening, it is not as easily sex-typeable.

Much early role learning occurs in play. The forms play takes is not untouched by social influences. Parents stereotypically stock their sons' rooms with educational materials, machines, vehicles, and sports equipment, and their daughters' rooms with baby dolls, doll houses, domestic items, and floral furnishings (Rheingold & Cook, 1975). The sex-typed play materials with which children are provided channel their spontaneous play into traditionally feminine or masculine roles. Even during the first year of a child's life, fathers promote stereotypically sex-appropriate play, although they are stricter in sex-role differentiation for sons than daughters (Snow, Jacklin, & Maccoby, 1983). Not surprisingly, even very young children believe their parents expect them to conform to stereotypic gender roles (Albert & Porter, 1982).

Socializing agencies outside the home add their influence to the gender-role stereotyping. Peers are sources of much social learning. In the social structuring of activities, children selectively associate with same-sex playmates pursuing gender-typed interests and activities (Huston, 1983). In these interactions children reward each other for gender-appropriate activities and punish gender-inappropriate behavior (Lamb, Easterbrooks, & Holden, 1980). The sanctions work their effects. Children also get criticized by their teachers for engaging in play activities considered inappropriate for their sex, and this is especially true for boys (Fagot, 1977).

The differentiation of the sexes extends beyond the realms of attire, make-believe play, and free activities. Whenever appropriate occasions arise, parents and others instruct children in the kinds of behavior expected of girls and boys. While obviously not all parents are inflexible sex stereotypers in all activities, most accept, model, and teach the sex roles traditionally favored by the culture. In the development of career interests and pursuits, cultural practices encourage a wider range of career options for males than for females (Betz & Hackett, 1986). Such differential practices constrict the career pursuits for which women judge themselves to be efficacious.

Superimposed on this differential tuition that leaves few aspects of children's lives untouched is a pervasive cultural modeling of stereotypic sex roles. Modeling serves as a major conveyer of sex-role information. Children are continually exposed to models of sex-typed behavior in the home, in schools, on playgrounds, in readers and storybooks, and in representations of society on the television screens of every household (Courtney & Whipple, 1974; Jacklin & Mischel, 1973; Miller & Reeves, 1976). Males are generally portrayed as directive, venturesome, enterprising, and pursuing engaging occupations and recreational activities. In contrast, women are usually cast in subordinate roles, either tending the household or performing lower status jobs, and otherwise acting in dependent, unambitious, and emotional ways. Heavy viewers of the media display more stereotypic sex-role conceptions than do light viewers (McGhee & Frueh, 1980). Nonstereotypic modeling expands children's aspirations and the range of role options they consider appropriate for their sex (Ashby & Wittmaier, 1978; O'Bryant & CorderBolz, 1978). Repeated symbolic modeling of egalitarian role pursuits by males and females enduringly reduces sex role stereotyping in young children (Flerx, Fidler, & Rogers, 1976).

In everyday life, children have ample opportunities to observe how many members of each sex behave. Perry and Bussey (1979) show that several models displaying the same behavior within each sex is a stronger conveyer of gender-linked rules of conduct than is divergent modeling. The propensity for children to pattern their preferences after models of the same sex increases as the percentage of same-sex models displaying the same preferences increases. That multiple modeling serves as a basic mechanism in the sex-typing process is further corroborated by other studies encompassing varied activities, preferences, and stylistic behaviors (Bussey & Bandura, 1984).

Based on these multiple sources of gender-role information, young children form a conception of the attributes that typify masculinity and femininity and the behaviors appropriate for their own sex. In identifying the determinants of gender-role learning, it is essential to distinguish between the acquisition of gender-typed behaviors and their spontaneous performance. Children do not suspend observational learning of sex-typed activities until the time they discover whether they are girls or boys. Rather, they learn many of the things that typify gender roles from the male and female models around them before they have formed a clear gender identity and have fully comprehended the social significance attached to sexual status. Nor do children watch and gain knowledge only from same-sex models, even after they have developed a clear conception of their own sex.

Children observe and learn extensively from models of both sexes, but they are selective in what they express behaviorally. In tests for acquisition, which encourage children to reveal all they have learned observationally, they display many modeled activities they have acquired but ordinarily do not express, because they judge them inappropriate for their sex (Bandura, 1965; Bussey & Bandura, 1984; Dubanoski & Parton, 1971). Developmental research may confuse, rather than inform, when theories about sex-typed learning are tested with measures of sex-typed performance, rather than of learning.

Numerous factors govern the performance of sex-typed behavior. Prevailing social sanctions make outcomes partly dependent on the sex-appropriateness of actions. Hence, children soon learn to use sex-typing information as a predictive guide for action. The negative sanctions for cross-sex behavior are generally more severe for males than for females. Boys are therefore more likely than girls to use the sex stereotyping of the activity as a guide for action (Serbin, Connor, & Citron, 1981).

Knowledge about the sex appropriateness of behavior patterns does not depend entirely on directly experienced sanctions. Observing what consequences befall others also conveys knowledge of gender-roles for regulating conduct. As children begin to adopt standards of behavior through precept and example, much sex-typed behavior is further regulated through internal standards and self-evaluative reactions to their own conduct. They perform gender-role behaviors that bring them self-pride and eschew those that violate their own standards.

In the cognitive-developmental theory articulated by Kohlberg (1966), children infer stereotypic conceptions of gender from what they see and hear around them. Once they achieve gender constancy—a conception of their own gender as fixed and irreversible—they positively value, and seek to adopt, only those behaviors congruent with the gender concept they have acquired. A major problem for a theory that makes the understanding of gender constancy a prerequisite for gender-linked modeling is that children clearly differentiate and prefer sex-typed objects and play patterns, long before they view themselves as unchangeably boys or girls (Huston, 1983; Maccoby & Jacklin, 1974). Moreover, growing awareness of gender constancy does not increase children's preferences for same-sex roles, activities, and peers (Marcus & Overton, 1978; Smetana & Letourneau, 1984). Nor is attainment of gender constancy a precondition for same-sex modeling (Bussey & Bandura, 1984). Same-sex modeling seems to rely on classifying males and females into distinct groups, recognizing personal similarity to one group of models, and tagging that group's behavior patterns in memory as the ones to be used to guide behavior (Bussey & Bandura, 1984). Gender labeling and differential structuring of social experiences teach children to use the sex of the model as a guide for action (Huston, 1983).

Young children thus learn to use gender as an important characteristic for classifying persons and activities, and to use gender features as a guide for selective modeling, without having to wait until they realize that their gender is permanent and irreversible. Simple awareness of gender identity—that one is a boy or girl—is sufficient to foster the acquisition of information and competencies traditionally linked to one's own sex.

The view that same-sex modeling can proceed on the basis of gender identity alone, and that social factors also exert selective influence on what characteristics are adopted accord with Spence's (1984) formulation. She posits that gender identity facilitates the adoption of prototypic gender-congruent attributes, but interacting social and personal factors determine what particular constellations of gender-related characteristics are developed. When long hair and culinary skill are in vogue, men with long flowing locks who perfect cooking skills perceive themselves as masculine, just as do men with closely cropped hair who eschew the skillet. Thus, people within each sex can develop heterogeneous patterns of gender-related attributes while retaining a confirmed personal sense of masculinity and femininity.

It is not as though the environment provides the grist for ascertaining one's gender, but after the self-categorization as a boy or girl occurs the development of educational, occupational, avocational, and social competencies is motivated intrapsychically by a drive to match one's gender conception. Social realities bear hard throughout the lifespan on the kinds of lives men and women pursue in a given society. Over the years, women have had to emancipate themselves from inequitable and constraining social systems rather than from their concept of gender. In centering their theory on gender conceptual learning, cognitive theorists neglect the social realities of gender-role functioning, which are of considerable import. Gender conception is a contributing factor but it does not dictate the course of self-development oblivious to social reality. A comprehensive theory of how roles get linked to gender must extend well beyond gender conception to a social analysis of how institutional systems and sanctions shape gender roles. The social determinants of gender roles, which are largely ignored in cognitivistic approaches, receive considerable attention in social cognitive theory (Bandura, 1986).

FORETHOUGHT CAPABILITY

A third distinctive human characteristic is the capability for forethought. People do not simply react to their immediate environment, nor are they steered by implants from their past. Most human behavior, being purposive, is regulated by forethought. The future time perspective manifests itself in many different ways. People anticipate the likely consequences of their prospective actions, they set goals for themselves, and they otherwise plan courses of action that are likely to produce desired outcomes. Through exercise of forethought, people motivate themselves and guide their actions anticipatorily.

The capability for intentional and purposive action is rooted in symbolic activity. Future events cannot be causes of current motivation and action. However, by being represented cognitively in the present, foreseeable future events are converted into current motivators and regulators of behavior. Thoughts of desirable future events tend to foster the behavior most likely to bring about their realization. Forethought is translated into incentives and action through the aid of self-regulatory mechanisms, which will be reviewed later.

Anticipatory Outcomes as Motivators and Guides

Human behavior is extensively regulated by its effects. Behavior patterns that produce positive outcomes are readily adopted and used, whereas those that bring unrewarding or punishing outcomes are generally discarded. But external consequences, as influential as they often are in guiding selection of behavior, are not the only kind of outcomes that influence human behavior. People partly guide their actions by observed consequences. This enables them to profit from the successes and mistakes of others as well as from their own experiences. As a general rule, they are inclined to do things they have seen succeed and avoid those they have seen fail. However, observed outcomes exert their influence through judgments that one is likely to experience similar outcomes for similar courses of action. Such judgments are affected by perceived similarity to those undergoing the experiences and belief about one's capabilities to achieve similar levels of performance (Bandura, 1986). People also influence their own motivation and behavior by the positive and negative consequences they produce for themselves. This mode of self-regulation will be considered later in some detail.

Outcomes affect motivation and action largely by creating beliefs about the effects actions are likely to have under different circumstances. Because outcomes exert their influence through forethought, they have little or no impact until people discover how and when actions affect the occurrence of outcomes (Brewer, 1974). In everyday life, actions usually produce mixed effects, they may occur immediately or far removed in time, and many factors influence how actions affect the environment. Such bewildering patterns of determinants provide a fertile ground for misjudgment. When belief about the effects of actions differs from actuality, behavior is weakly controlled by its actual consequences until repeated experience instills realistic beliefs. But it is not always one's beliefs that change in the direction of social reality. Acting on erroneous beliefs can alter how others behave, thus shaping the social reality in the direction of the misbeliefs (Snyder, 1981).

Ambiguity and Variability of Outcome Information

Constructing conceptions of how the environment operates on the basis of response outcomes alone can be a slow and difficult process. This is because the information conveyed by response outcomes is often variable and ambiguous, especially when the outcomes are socially mediated. Usually, many factors enter into determining what effects, if any, given actions will have. The same behavior may, therefore, produce diverse effects depending on when and where it is performed and the persons toward whom it is directed. Multiple determinants create ambiguity about how given actions will affect the environment.

In addition to multiple causation, some of the important outcomes occur long after the behavior has been performed. Intervening happenings create confusion about what caused what. Gaining knowledge about the environment from the diverse effects of one's actions, therefore, requires careful sorting out of personal and vicarious experiences. In constructing a cognitive model of how to affect their environment, people must vary in their actions and observe the differences in the immediate and later results it produces in different situations, at different times, and toward different persons. Much of this information is gained vicariously.

Developmental Changes in Forethought

The ability to envision the likely outcomes of actions undergoes developmental changes. Infants have difficulty recognizing that what they do has effects and representing such predictive knowledge symbolically. During the first few months of life, infants do not possess the attentional and memorial capabilities to profit much from contingent experiences, even when the effects of their actions are delayed only briefly (Millar, 1972; Watson, 1979). There is some evidence to suggest that, during the initial months of life, infants' ability to foresee response outcome is developed better by providing them with opportunities to effect changes in the physical environment than to influence the social environment (Gunnar, 1980). This is because manipulation of physical objects usually produces immediate, conspicuous, predictable effects. After shaking a rattle repeatedly and hearing the resultant sound, infants cannot help but notice that their actions produce environmental effects. However, younger infants have difficulty learning, even from the physical effects of their actions, if the effects are displaced in time and space (Millar & Schaeffer, 1972). Their problem stems more from inadequate attention to events than from cognitive incapacities to link actions to outcomes.

The social effects of infants' behavior, depending as they do on the availability of vagaries of others, are not only more delayed and variable, but they often occur independently of the infants' behavior. That is, others frequently attend to, and initiate activities with infants, regardless of what the infants may be doing at the time. A cry may bring others instantly, some time later, or not at all. Others often appear in the absence of crying. It is difficult to learn from such mixed social experiences, in which actions do not always produce social reaction, and social reactions often occur on their own through the initiative of others (Watson, 1979).

Parents often structure contingent experiences in ways that help infants discover how their actions affect the environment and the behavior of others (Papousek & Papousek, 1979). Parents establish close eye contact with the infant to ensure adequate attentiveness. They react quickly in animated ways to their infants' actions to create highly noticeable immediate effects. To aid the perception that actions produce outcomes, the social transactions are enacted repeatedly. These types of social interactions create a cognitive set to look for causal relationships in instances where behavior is more complexly related to its effects. When infants are provided with many salient opportunities to observe that they can produce environmental effects, they become more skilled in foreseeing the likely outcomes of actions (Finkelstein & Ramey, 1977).

Discerning rules for predicting the effects of actions requires several cognitive subskills that develop with experience. To begin with, rule induction partly depends on preexisting level of knowledge, which can be used to discover the factors governing response outcomes. The discovery process is further aided by the use of focusing strategies for narrowing down different possibilities to the appropriate rules. This is achieved by a verification process in which notions are tested by acting on them and seeing whether they produce the expected effects. The outcomes of action under different circumstances must, therefore, be closely monitored and the information synthesized and retained over a series of experiences. Moreover, learners have to remember what ideas they tried and how well they worked. Deficits in any of these component skills—formulating notions from a knowledge base, applying efficient rule induction strategies, monitoring situational factors and response outcomes, remembering outcome information, and matching ideas to action effects—can retard rule learning.

Improvement of cognitive subskills can enhance adeptness at foreseeing the effects of actions. When deficiencies in rule learning stem from inadequate perception of ongoing events, attentional skills must be developed that expand children's use of the situational and outcome information available to them. If they quickly forget what they have observed, they do not have much relevant information to process. The development of memory skills helps children to remember what actions in what situations produced what outcomes, so they have available the information needed to formulate rules of behavior. Additional problems may arise from what they make of the outcome information they have perceived and retained. Development of reasoning skills can teach children how to apply decision rules to the information they gain to come up with appropriate solutions. These component skills are best developed initially on simpler activities involving minimal delay of effects and then extended to more complex ones requiring greater attentional, organizational, and memorial demands.

Learning from consequences is improved if young children are taught the required cognitive skills for processing outcome information (Brainerd, 1978; Eimas, 1970). Such findings indicate that it is more fruitful to explore the cognitive skills that underlie learning than to ascribe learning difficulties to global cognitive deficiencies. Adults also vary in the extent to which they have mastered the constituent skills for extracting rules of behavior from outcome information. Those who are inept in ferreting out what is relevant in their experiences or who use faulty inferential reasoning do not profit much from experience. When they are taught how to process outcome information more effectively, they learn rules of behavior more effectively from the outcomes of their actions (Eimas, 1970).

Role of Forethought in Social and Technical Change

Analysis of the role of forethought in human development and well-being musty be extended beyond the processes governing acquisition of outcome rules for individual behavior. Forethought takes more complex forms in judging probable distal outcomes of social practices and technologies. Many technical innovations that provide current benefits also entail hazards that can take a heavy future toll on human beings and the environment.

The capacity to extrapolate future consequences from known facts enables people to take corrective actions that avert disastrous futures. It is the expanded time perspective and symbolization of futures afforded by cognition that increases the prospects of human survival. Had humans been ruled solely by immediate consequences, they would have long destroyed most of the environmental supports of life. Threats to human welfare arise repeatedly because the ability to create new technologies outstrips the knowledge of their likely full effects. In such instances, people know not what they are unleashing by their creations.

Development of risk-analysis methods for estimating the likelihood and severity of harmful effects of modern technologies has become a matter of considerable interest (Rasmussen, 1981). They are used to bring estimated future consequences to bear on protective current behavior. In the health field, for example, toxicological methods, which speed up the cumulative effects in animals with concentrated dosages, are used to identify potentially injurious substances before the public has suffered the consequences of extensive exposure to them. The carcinogenicity of the things people consume and the environmental conditions to which they are exposed are assessed in this way. Biochemical methods have been devised for assessing the capacity of different substances to cause injury to microorganisms and cell cultures (Ramel & Rannug, 1980). Computers provide a ready means for estimating the effects of technical and social changes through computational enactments without having to carry out actual trials. After a sound model of the system has been developed, it permits the user to vary factors and to observe the effects of the simulated changes. Computers can serve as a tool to greatly extend human ability to manipulate, test, redesign, and refine physical and social systems for desired purposes and to gauge their long-term effects.

Structuring Behavior by Response Outcomes

The discussion so far has been concerned with learning rules for predicting the likely outcomes of actions. New patterns of behavior can also be formed by response outcomes. In learning by doing, outcomes serve as an unarticulated way of informing performers about the characteristics of appropriate behavior. By observing which actions work and which do not, people eventually construct conceptions of new behavior patterns and when it is appropriate to perform them.

In social cognitive theory, learning from the effects of actions is a special case of observational learning. In learning by direct experience, people construct conceptions of behavior from observing the effects of their actions; in learning by modeling, they derive the conceptions from observing the structure of the behavior being modeled. Conceptions of complex behavior can be learned faster from observing the behavior patterns displayed in an already integrated form than from attempting to construct them bit by bit by trying different actions and examining how well they work. Another limitation to learning from the effects of action is that it does not ensure that the best solutions will be developed. This is because, in most domains of activity, different solutions are possible which vary in adequateness. Once people hit upon a solution that is sufficient, they keep using it without considering other alternatives, even though better ones exist (Schwartz, 1982). Sufficing outcomes can thus operate as barriers to discovery.

SELF-REGULATORY CAPABILITIES

Parental guidance and sanctions greatly influence the socialization process. However, neither parents nor other significant adults can be continuously present to guide children's behavior. Successful socialization, therefore, requires the gradual substitution of internal controls and direction for external sanctions and mandates. Once the capability for self-direction is achieved, self-demands and self-sanctions serve as major guides, motivators and deterrents. In the absence of internal standards and self-sanctions, individuals would behave like weathervanes, constantly shifting direction to conform to whatever momentary influence happened to impinge upon them. Theories that seek to explain human behavior as solely the product of external rewards and punishments present a truncated image of human nature because people possess self-directive capabilities that enable them to exercise some control over their thoughts, feelings, and actions by the consequences they produce for themselves. Psychosocial functioning is, therefore, regulated by an interplay of self-produced and external sources of influence.

Motivational Standards

Self-regulation of motivation and behavior through internal standards distinguishes between aspirational standards and social and moral standards. The capacity to exercise self-influence by personal challenge and evaluative reaction to one's own attainments provides a major cognitive mechanism of motivation and self-directedness. Motivation based on aspirational standards involves a cognitive comparison process between internal standards and personal attainments. The motivational effects do not stem from the standards themselves, but rather from several self-reactive influences. These include affective self-evaluation of one's attainments, perceived self-efficacy to fulfill one's standards, and adjustment of personal standards to keep them within attainable bounds (Bandura, 1988a; Bandura & Cervone, 1983).

Standards motivate by enlisting self-evaluative involvement in the activity. People seek self-satisfactions from fulfilling valued goals, and are prompted to intensify their efforts by discontent with substandard performances. Perceived self-efficacy is another cognitive factor that plays an influential role in the exercise of personal control over motivation. Whether negative discrepancies between internal standards and attainments are motivating or discouraging is partly determined by people's beliefs that they can attain the goals they set for themselves. Those who harbor self-doubts about their capabilities are easily dissuaded by failure. Those who are assured of their capabilities intensify their efforts when they fail to achieve what they seek and they persist until they succeed. The standards people set for themselves at the outset of an endeavor are likely to change, depending on the progress they are making. They may maintain their original standard, lower their sights, or adopt an even more challenging standard. Thus, the third constituent, self-influence, in the ongoing regulation of motivation, concerns the readjustment of personal standards in light of one's attainments. Csikszentmihalyi (1979) examined what it is about activities that fosters continuing deep engrossment in life pursuits. The common factors found to be conducive to enduring self-motivation include adopting personal challenges in accordance with one's perceived capabilities and seeing oneself make progress toward the hoped for goal.

The effectiveness of aspirational standards in regulating motivation and action depends partly on how far into the future they are projected. A proximate standard serves to mobilize self-influences and direct what one does in the here and now. Distal standards alone are too far removed in time to provide effective incentives and guides for present action. There are usually too many competing influences at hand for distant cognized events to exert much control over current behavior. Subgoals not only enlist self-reactive motivators, they also help to develop self-efficacy and intrinsic interest (Bandura & Schunk, 1981). Without standards against which to measure their performance, people have little basis for gauging their capabilities. Subgoal attainments provide rising indicants of mastery for enhancing one's sense of efficacy. People display enduring interest in activities at which they feel self-efficacious and from which they derive self-satisfaction. Challenging standards enlist sustained involvement in tasks needed to build competencies that foster interest. When people aim for and master valued levels of performance, they experience a sense of satisfaction. The satisfactions derived from goal attainments build intrinsic interest.

Many theories of self-regulation are founded on a negative feedback control system. The system functions as a motivator and regulator of action through a discrepancy reduction mechanism. Perceived discrepancy between performance and the reference standard triggers action to reduce the incongruity. Discrepancy reduction clearly plays a central role in any system of self-regulation. However, in the negative feedback control system, if performance matches the standard the person does nothing. A regulatory process in which matching a standard begets inertness does not characterize human self-motivation. Such a feedback control system would produce circular action that leads nowhere. Nor could people be stirred to action until they receive feedback that their performance is discrepant from the standard.

Human self-motivation relies on *discrepancy production* as well as on *discrepancy reduction*. It requires *proactive control* as well as *feedback control*. People initially motivate themselves through proactive control by adopting performance standards that create a state of disequilibrium and then exert themselves on the basis of anticipatory estimation of how much effort would be required to succeed. Feedback control comes into play in subsequent adjustments of effort expenditure to achieve desired results. After people attain the standard they have been pursing, they generally set a higher standard for themselves. The adoption of further challenges creates new motivating discrepancies to be mastered. Similarly, surpassing a standard is more likely to raise aspiration than to lower subsequent performance to conform to the surpassed standard. Self-motivation thus involves a dual cyclic process of disequilibrating discrepancy production followed by equilibrating discrepancy reduction.

Cognitive motivation has been explained by some theorists in terms of an inborn automotivator. According to Piaget (1960), discrepancies between the cognitive schemata children already possess and perceived events create internal conflict that motivates exploration of the source of discrepancy until the internal schemata are altered to accommodate to the contradictory experiences. Empirical tests of this type of automotivator reveal that discrepancy of experience alone does not guarantee cognitive learning. Indeed, if disparities between perceived events and mental structure were, in fact, automatically motivating, everyone should be highly knowledgeable about the world around them and continually progressing toward ever higher levels of reasoning. The evidence does not seem to bear this out.

In the social cognitive view, people function as active agents in their own motivation. Self-motivation through cognitive comparison requires distinguishing between standards of what one knows and standards of what one desires to know. It is the latter standards, together with perceived self-efficacy, that exert selective influence over which of many activities will be actively pursued. Aspirational standards determine which discrepancies are motivating and which activities people will strive to master. Strength of self-motivation varies curvilinearly with the level of discrepancy between standards and attainments: Relatively easy standards are insufficiently challenging to arouse much interest or effort; moderately difficult ones maintain high effort and produce satisfactions through subgoal achievements; standards set well beyond a person's reach can be demotivating by fostering discouragement and a sense of inefficacy.

Social and Moral Standards

In areas of functioning involving achievement strivings and cultivation of competencies, the internal standards that are selected as a mark of adequacy are progressively altered as knowledge and skills are acquired and challenges are met. In many areas of social and moral behavior the internal standards that serve as the basis for regulating one's conduct have greater stability. That is, people do not change from week to week what they regard as right or wrong or good or bad. In the course of socialization, people develop moral standards from a variety of influences (Bandura, 1986). These include direct instruction in the precepts of moral conduct, the approving and disapproving reactions to their conduct by significant persons in their lives, and the moral standards modeled by others. People do not passively absorb moral standards from whatever influences happen to impinge upon them. Rather, they construct for themselves generic standards from the evaluative rules that are prescribed, modeled, and taught. This process is complicated because those who serve as socialization influencers, whether designedly or unintentionally, often display inconsistencies between what they practice and what they preach. Moreover, people usually differ in the standards they model, and even the same person may model different standards in different social settings and domains of conduct.

Evaluative self-reactions provide the mechanism by which standards regulate conduct. The anticipatory self-pride and self-criticism for actions that match or violate personal standards serve as the regulatory influencers. Individuals do things that give them self-satisfaction and a sense of self-worth. They refrain from behaving in ways that violate their moral standards because it will bring self-disapproval. Self-sanctions thus keep conduct in line with internal standards.

Self-directed influences are not governed solely by moral standards. Actions give rise to self-reactions through a process of moral reasoning in which conduct is evaluated in relation to environmental circumstances as well as personal standards. Situations with moral implications contain many decisional ingredients that not only vary in importance, but may be given lesser or greater weight depending upon the particular constellation of events in a given moral predicament. Thus, for example, judgments of the reprehensibility of conduct will vary depending upon the nature of the transgression; the degree of norm violation; the contexts in which it is performed; the perceived situational and personal motivators for it; the immediate and long-range consequences of the action; whether it produces personal injury or property damage; and the characteristics of those toward whom the action is directed and their perceived blameworthiness. In dealing with moral dilemmas people must, therefore, extract, weight, and integrate morally relevant information in the situations confronting them. Factors that are weighed heavily under some combinations of circumstances may be disregarded or considered of less importance under a different set of conditions. This process of moral reasoning is guided by multifaceted rules on how to combine different sorts of information to judge the morality of conduct (Bandura, 1988d; Lane & Anderson, 1976; Surber, 1985).

Development of Moral Standards

There are some universal features to the development of standards of conduct. These commonalities arise from basic uniformities in the types of biopsychosocial changes that occur with increasing age in all cultures. People vary in what they teach, model, and sanction with children of differing ages. At first, guidance of behavior in children who have a poor command of language is necessarily external and highly dependent on physical sanctions. As children mature, social and verbal sanctions increasingly replace physical ones as influential guides for how to behave in different situations. Parents and other adults explain standards of conduct and the reasons for them. Social sanctions that disapprove transgressive acts and commend valued conduct add substance to the standards. It is not long before children learn to discriminate between approved and disapproved forms of conduct and to regulate their actions on the basis of anticipated social consequences (Bandura & Walters, 1959; Sears, Maccoby, & Levin, 1957).

As moral standards are gradually internalized, they begin to serve as guides and deterrents to conduct by the self-approving and self-reprimanding consequences children produce for themselves. Not only do the sanctions change from a social to a personal locus, but with advancing age the range of moral considera-

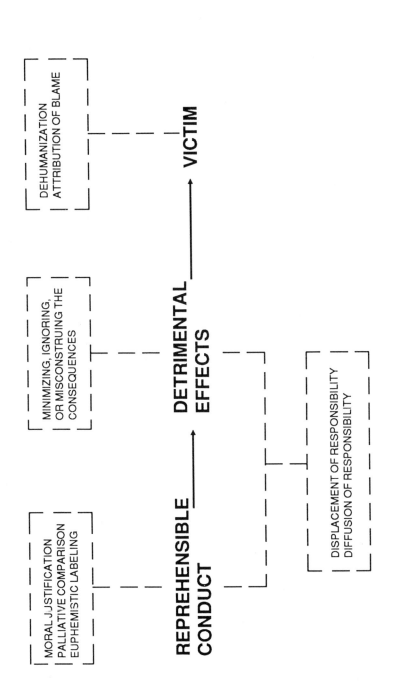

Figure 3. Mechanisms through which internal control is selectively activated and disengaged from detrimental conduct at different points in the regulatory process.

tions expands. As the nature and seriousness of possible transgressions change with age, parents and other significant adults in the child's life add new aspects to the moral persuasion. For example, they do not appeal to legal arguments when handling preschoolers' misconduct, but they do explain legal codes and penalties to preadolescents to influence future behavior that can have serious legal consequences. An expanding social reality requires more generalized and complex moral standards.

Children model the rules their parents use to integrate information in judging the morality of transgressive conduct (Leon, 1984). Parents react differently to their children's misconduct at different ages (Denny & Duffy, 1974). They increase the complexity of their moral reasoning as their children get older. The more complex the parent's moral reasons in dealing with misconduct, the more elaborate is their children's moral reasoning. Variation in social influences contributes to developmental changes in what factors are considered to be morally relevant and the relative weight they are given. Parents, of course, are not the exclusive source of childrens' standards of moral judgments and conduct. Other adults, peers, and symbolic models play influential roles as well. Children exposed to adult and peer models who exemplify conflicting standards adopt different standards of conduct than if adults alone set the standard, or if adults and peer models subscribe to the same standards (Bandura, Grusec, & Menlove, 1967; Brody & Henderson, 1977). To the developing child, televised modeling influences the development of moral judgments by what it portrays as acceptable or reprehensible conduct, and by the sanctions and justifications applied to it. As the preceding comments indicate, a varied array of interacting societal influences contribute to the development of moral perspectives.

Adoption of internal standards does not necessarily encompass every domain of activity or completely supplant other forms of control. Even the most principled individuals may, in some domains of activity and under some circumstances, regulate their behavior mainly by anticipated social or legal consequences. Moreover, during the course of development, children learn how to get around moral consequences of culpable behavior that can gain them personal benefits. They discover that they can reduce the likelihood of reprimands by invoking extenuating circumstances for their misdeeds (Bandura & Walters, 1959). As a result, different types of vindications become salient factors in moral judgments. Even very young children are quite skilled in using mitigating factors to excuse wrongdoing (Darley, Klosson, & Zanna, 1978). Later they learn to weaken, if not completely avoid, self-censure for reprehensible conduct by invoking self-exonerating justifications. A theory of moral reasoning must, therefore, be concerned as well with how cognitive processes can make the immoral inconsequential or even moral.

The self-regulation of conduct in not entirely an intrapsychic affair. Rather, it involves a reciprocity of influence between thought, conduct, and a network of social influences. Under social conditions in which transgressive behavior is not easily self-excusable, conduct is likely to be congruent with more standards. But self-regulation of moral conduct can be weakened or nullified by exonerative moral reasoning and social circumstances. The forms that these mechanisms of moral disengagement take are analyzed in the following section.

Selective Activation and Disengagement of Internal Control

Moral standards do not function as fixed internal regulators of conduct. Self-regulatory mechanisms do not operate unless they are activated, and there are many processes by which moral reactions can be disengaged from inhumane conduct (Bandura, 1986; 1988c). Selective activation and disengagement of internal control permits different types of conduct with the same moral standards. Figure 3 shows the points in the self-regulatory process at which internal moral control can be disengaged from censurable conduct.

One set of disengagement practices operates on the construal of the behavior itself by *moral justification*. People do not ordinarily engage in reprehensible conduct until they have justified to themselves the morality of their actions. What is culpable is made personally and socially acceptable by portraying it in the service of moral purposes. Moral justification is widely used to support self-serving and otherwise culpable conduct. Moral judgments of conduct are also partly influenced by what it is compared against. Self-deplored acts can be made righteous by contrasting them with more flagrant transgressions. The more outrageous the comparison activities, the more likely are one's reprehensible acts to appear trifling. Since examples of human culpability abound, they lend themselves readily to cognitive restructuring of transgressive conduct by *advantageous comparison*. Activities can take on a very different appearance depending on what they are called. *Euphemistic labeling* provides another convenient device for masking reprehensible activities or even conferring a respectable status upon them. Through convoluted verbiage, reprehensible conduct is made benign and those who engage in it are relieved of a sense of personal agency.

Cognitive restructuring of behavior through moral justifications and palliative characterizations is the most effective psychological mechanism for promoting transgressive conduct. This is because moral restructuring not only eliminates self-deterrents but engages self-approval in the service of transgressive exploits. What was once morally condemnable becomes a source of self-valuation.

Another set of dissociative practices operates by obscuring or distorting the relationship between actions and the effects they cause. People will behave in ways they normally repudiate if a legitimate authority sanctions their conduct and accepts responsibility for its consequences (Diener et al., 1975; Milgram, 1974). Under conditions of *displacement of responsibility*, people view their actions as springing from the dictates of others rather than their being personally responsible for them. Since they are not the actual agent of their actions, they are spared self-prohibiting reactions. The deterrent power of self-sanctions is also weakened when the link between conduct and its consequences is obscured by *diffusion of responsibility* for culpable behavior. Through division of labor, diffusion of decision making, and group action, people can behave detrimentally without any one person feeling personally responsible (Kelman, 1973). People behave more injuriously under diffused responsibility than when they hold themselves personally accountable for what they do (Bandura, Underwood, & Fromson, 1975).

Additional ways of weakening self-deterring reactions operate through *disregard* or *distortion of the consequences of action*. When people pursue detrimental activities for personal gain or because of social inducements, they avoid facing the harm they cause or they minimize it. They readily recall the possible benefits of the behavior but are less able to remember its harmful effects (Brock & Buss, 1962, 1964). In addition to selective inattention and cognitive distortion of effects, the misrepresentation may involve active efforts to discredit evidence of the harm they cause. As long as the detrimental results of one's conduct are ignored, minimized, distorted, or disbelieved there is little reason for self-censure to be activated.

The final set of disengagement practices operates at the point of recipients of detrimental acts. The strength of self-evaluative reactions to injurious conduct partly depends on how the perpetrators view the people toward whom the behavior is directed. To perceive another as human enhances empathetic or vicarious reactions through perceived similarity (Bandura, 1988c). As a result, it is difficult to mistreat humanized persons without risking self-condemnation. Self-sanctions against cruel conduct can be disengaged or blunted by *dehumanization*, which divests people of human qualities or attributes bestial qualities to them. While dehumanization weakens self-restraints against cruel conduct (Diener, 1977; Zimbardo, 1969), humanization fosters considerate, compassionate behavior (Bandura, Underwood, & Fromson, 1975).

Attribution of blame to one's antagonists is still another expedient that can serve self-exonerative purposes. Deleterious interactions usually involve a series of reciprocally escalative actions, in which the antagonists are rarely faultless. One can always select from the chain of events an instance of the adversary's defensive behavior and view it as the original instigation. Injurious conduct thus becomes a justifiable defensive reaction to belligerent provocations. Others can, therefore, be blamed for bringing suffering on themselves. Self-exoneration is similarly achievable by viewing one's detrimental conduct as forced by circumstances rather than as a personal decision. By blaming others or circumstances, not only are one's own actions excusable but one can even feel self-righteous in the process.

Because internalized controls can be selectively activated and disengaged, marked changes in moral conduct can be achieved without changing people's personality structures, moral principles, or self-evaluative systems. It is self-exonerative processes rather than character flaws that account for most inhumanities. The massive threats to human welfare stem mainly from deliberate acts of principle rather than from unrestrained acts of impulse.

SELF-REFLECTIVE CAPABILITY

If there is any characteristic that is distinctively human, it is the capability for reflective self-consciousness. This enables people to analyze their experiences and to think about their own thought processes. By reflecting on their varied experiences and on what they know, they can derive generic knowledge about themselves and the world around them. People not only gain understanding through reflection, they evaluate and alter their own thinking by this means. In verifying thought through self-reflective means, they monitor their ideas, act on them or predict occurrences from them, judge from the results the adequacy of their thoughts, and change them accordingly.

Modes of Thought Verification

Judgments concerning the validity and functional value of one's thoughts are formed by comparing how well thoughts match some indicant of reality. Four different modes of thought verification can be distinguished. They include *enactive, vicarious, persuasory,* and *logical* forms. Enactive verification relies on the adequacy of the fit between thought and the results of one's actions. Good matches corroborate thoughts; mismatches tend to refute them. In the vicarious mode of thought verification, observing the effects produced by somebody else's actions serves as a way of checking the correctness of one's own thinking. Vicarious thought verification is not simply a supplement to enactive experience. Symbolic modeling greatly expands the range of verification experiences that cannot otherwise be attained by personal action. A related mode of thought verification relies on comparing one's thoughts to the judgments of others. When experiential verification is either difficult or impossible, people evaluate the soundness of their beliefs by comparing them to the judgments of others. In the course of development, people acquire rules of inference. By reasoning from what is already known, they can derive knowledge about things that extend beyond their experience and check the validity of their reasoning.

Such metacognitive activities usually foster veridical thought (Flavell, 1978a), but they can produce faulty thought patterns as well. Forceful actions arising from erroneous beliefs often create social effects that confirm the misbeliefs (Snyder, 1980). Verification of thought by comparison with distorted televised versions of social reality can foster shared misconceptions (Hawkins & Pingree, 1982). Social verification can foster bizarre views of reality if the shared beliefs of the reference group with which one affiliates are peculiar (Winfrey, 1979). Deductive reasoning will be flawed if the propositional knowledge on which it is based is faulty or biases intrude on reasoning processes (Falmagne, 1975).

Self-Efficacy Appraisal

Among the types of thoughts that affect action, none is more central or pervasive than people's judgments of their capabilities to exercise control over events that affect their lives. The self-efficacy mechanism plays a central role in human agency (Bandura, 1982a; 1986). Self-judgments of operative capabilities function as one set of proximal determinants of how people behave, their thought patterns, and the emotional reactions they experience in taxing situations. In their daily lives, people continuously have to make decisions about what courses of action to pursue and how long to continue those they have undertaken. Because acting on misjudgments of personal efficacy can produce adverse consequences, accurate appraisal of one's own capabilities has considerable functional value.

It is partly on the basis of judgments of personal efficacy that people choose what to do, how much effort to invest in activities and how long to persevere in the face of obstacles and failure experiences. People's judgments of their capabilities additionally influence whether their thought patterns are self-hindering or self-enhancing, and how much stress and despondency they experience during anticipatory and actual transaction with the environment.

Judgments of self-efficacy, whether accurate or faulty, are based on four principal sources of information. These include performance mastery experiences; vicarious experiences for judging capabilities in comparison with performances of others; verbal persuasion and allied types of social influences that one possesses certain capabilities; and physiological states from which people partly judge their capableness, strength, and vulnerability. In the self-appraisal of efficacy these different sources of efficacy information must be processed and weighed through self-referent thought. Acting on one's self-efficacy judgment brings successes or missteps requiring further self-reappraisals of operative competencies. The self-knowledge which underlies the exercise of many facets of personal agency is largely the product of such reflective self-appraisal.

Self-reflectivity entails shifting the perspective of the same agent rather than reifying different internal agents or selves regulating each other. Thus, in their daily transactions people act on their thoughts and later analyze how well their thoughts have served them in managing events. But it is one and the same person who is doing the thinking and later evaluating the adequacy of one's knowledge, thinking skills, and action strategies. The shift in perspective does not transform one from an agent to an object. One is just as much an agent reflecting on one's experiences as in executing the original courses of action.

Developmental Analysis of Self-Efficacy

As previously noted, accurate appraisal of one's own capabilities is highly advantageous and often essential for effective functioning. Very young children lack knowledge of their own capabilities and the demands and potential hazards of different situations. They would repeatedly get themselves into dangerous predicaments were it not for the guidance of others. Adult watchfulness and guidance sees young children through this early formative period until they gain sufficient knowledge of what they can do and what different situations require in the way of skills. With development of cognitive self-reflective capabilities, self-efficacy judgment increasingly supplants external guidance.

Beginnings of Perceived Causal Efficacy

Children's exploratory experiences and observation of the performances of others provide the initial basis for developing a sense of causal efficacy. However, newborns' immobility and limited means of action upon the physical and social environment restrict their domain of influence. The initial experiences that contribute to development of a sense of personal agency are tied to infants' ability to control the sensory stimulation from manipulable objects and the attentive behavior of those around them. Infants behave in certain ways, and certain things happen. Shaking a rattle produces predictable sounds, energetic kicks shake their cribs, and screams bring adults.

Realization of causal efficacy requires both self-observation and recognition that one's actions are part of oneself. By repeatedly observing that certain environmental events occur with action, but not in its absence, infants learn that actions produce effects. Infants who experience success in controlling environmental events become more attentive to their own behavior and more competent in learning new efficacious responses, than do infants for whom the same environmental events occur regardless of how they behave (Finkelstein & Ramey, 1977; Ramey & Finkelstein, 1978).

Development of perceived self-efficacy requires more than simply producing effects by actions. Those actions must be perceived as part of oneself. The self becomes differentiated from others through dissimilar experience. Thus, if self action causes pain, whereas seeing similar actions by others does not produce experienced pain, one's own activity becomes distinct from that of all others. Infants acquire a sense of personal agency when they begin to perceive environmental events as being personally controlled—a growing realization that they can make events occur.

During the initial months of life, the exercise of influence over the physical environment may contribute more to the development of a child's sense of causal efficacy than does influence over the social environment (Gunnar, 1980). This is because manipulating physical objects produces quick, predictable, and easily observable effects. Highly noticeable correlation between actions and effects facilitates perception of personal agency in infants whose attentional and representational capabilities are limited. In contrast, causal agency is more difficult to discern in noisier social contingencies, where actions have variable social effects, and some of them occur independently of what the infants are doing. However, with the development of representational capabilities infants can begin to learn from probabilistic and more distal outcomes of personal actions. Before long the exercise of control over the social environment begins to play an important role in the early development of self-efficacy.

Familial Sources of Self-Efficacy

Children must gain self-knowledge of their capabilities in broadening areas of functioning. They have to develop, appraise and test their physical capabilities, their social competencies, their linguistic skills, and their cognitive skills for comprehending and managing the many situations they encounter daily. Development of sensorimotor capabilities greatly expands the infants' available environment and the means for acting upon it. These early exploratory and play activities, which occupy much of their waking hours, provide opportunities for enlarging their repertoire of basic skills.

While developing their capabilities during this initial period of immaturity, most of the infants' gratifications and well-being must be mediated by adults. Because of this physical dependency, infants quickly learn how to influence the actions of those around them by their social and verbal behavior. Many of these transactions involve the exercise of proxy control in which young children get adults to effect changes that the children themselves cannot bring about. Efficacy experiences in the exercise of personal control are central to the early development of social and cognitive competence. Parents who are responsive to their infants' communicative behavior, and who create opportunities for efficacious actions by providing an enriched physical environment and permitting freedom of movement for exploration, have infants who are relatively accelerated in their social and cognitive development (Ainsworth & Bell, 1974; Yarrow, Rubenstein, & Pedersen, 1975). Parental responsiveness increases cognitive competence, and infant capabilities elicit greater parental responsiveness in a process of reciprocal causation (Bradley, Caldwell, & Elardo, 1979). Acquisition of language provides children with the symbolic means to reflect on their experiences and what others tell them about their capabilities and, thus, to begin to gain self-knowledge of what they can and cannot do.

The initial efficacy experiences are centered in the family, but as the growing child's social world rapidly expands, peers assume an increasingly important role in children's developing self-knowledge of their capabilities. It is in the context of peer interactions that social comparison processes come most strongly into play. At first, the closest comparative age-mates are siblings. Families differ in number of siblings, how far apart in age they are, and in their sex distribution. Different family structures, as reflected in family size, birth order, and sibling constellation patterns, create different social references for comparative self-efficacy appraisal.

Comparative appraisals of efficacy require not only evaluation of one's own performances, but also knowledge of how well others do, cognizance of non-ability determinants of their performances, and some understanding that it is those who are slightly better than oneself, who provide the most informative social criterion for comparison. With development, children become increasingly discriminative in their use of comparative efficacy information. Developmental analyses conducted by Morris and Nemcek (1982) show that effective use of social comparative information for self-efficacy appraisal lags behind perception of ability rankings.

Peers and the Broadening and Validation of Self-Efficacy

Children's efficacy-testing experiences change substantially as they move increasingly into the larger community. It is in peer relationships that they broaden and particularize self-knowledge of their capabilities. Peers serve several important efficacy functions. Those who are most experienced and competent provide models of efficacious styles of thinking and behavior. A vast amount of social learning occurs among peers. In addition, age-mates provide the most informative points of reference for comparative efficacy appraisal and verification. Children are, therefore, especially sensitive to their relative standing among the peers with whom they affiliate in activities that determine prestige and popularity.

Peers are neither homogeneous nor selected indiscriminately. Children tend to choose close associates who share similar interests and values. Selective peer association will promote self-efficacy in directions of mutual interest, leaving other potentialities underdeveloped (Bandura & Walters, 1959; Ellis & Lane, 1963; Krauss, 1964). The influences are undoubtedly bidirectional—affiliation preferences affect the direction of efficacy development, and self-efficacy, in turn, partly determines choice of peer associates and activities. Because peers serve as a major agency for the development and validation of self-efficacy, disrupted or impoverished peer relationships can adversely affect the growth of personal efficacy. Perceived social inefficacy can, in turn, create internal obstacles to favorable peer relationships (Wheeler & Ladd, 1982). Development of personal efficacy in coercive styles of behavior may likewise be socially alienating. Thus, children who readily resort to aggression perceive themselves as highly efficacious in getting things they want by aggressive means (Perry, Perry, & Rasmussen, 1986).

School as an Agency for Cultivating Cognitive Self-Efficacy

During the crucial formative period of children's lives, the school functions as the primary setting for the cultivation and social validation of cognitive competencies. School is the place where children develop the cognitive competencies and acquire the knowledge and problem-solving skills essential for participating effectively in society. Here their knowledge and thinking skills are continually tested, evaluated, and socially compared.

As children master cognitive skills, they develop a growing sense of their intellectual efficacy. Many social factors, apart from the formal instruction, such as peer modeling of cognitive skills, social comparison with the performances of other students, motivational enhancement through proximal goals and positive incentives, and instructors' interpretations of children's successes and failures in ways that reflect favorably or unfavorably on their ability also affect children's judgments of their intellectual efficacy (Schunk, 1984; 1987). Enhanced perceived self-efficacy fosters persistence in seeking solutions, cognitive skill development and intrinsic interest in academic subject matters (Bandura & Schunk, 1981; Schunk, 1984; Relich, Debus, & Walter, 1986).

The task of creating learning environments conducive to development of cognitive skills rests heavily on the talents and self-efficacy of teachers. Those who are well-versed in their subject matter and have a high sense of efficacy about their teaching capabilities can motivate low achievers and enhance their cognitive development (Ashton & Webb, 1986; Gibson & Dembo, 1984). The staffs of successful schools, whether they serve predominantly advantaged or disadvantaged students, have a strong group sense of efficacy to fulfill their academic purpose and resiliency of perceived efficacy in the face of social realities strewn with frustrations (Lightfoot, 1983).

There are a number of school practices that, for the less talented or ill prepared, tend to convert instructional experiences into education in inefficacy. These include lock-step sequences of instruction, which lose many children along the way; ability groupings which further diminish the perceived self-efficacy of those in the lower ranks; and competitive practices where many are doomed to failure for the success of a relative few.

Classroom structures affect perceptions of cognitive capabilities, in large part, by the relative emphasis they place on social-comparative versus self-comparative appraisal. Self-appraisals of less able students suffer most when the whole group studies the same material and teachers make frequent comparative evaluations (Rosenholtz & Rosenholtz, 1981). Under such a monolithic structure, which highlights social comparative standards, students rank themselves according to capability with high consensus. Once established, reputations are not easily changed. In a personalized classroom structure, individualized instruction tailored to students' knowledge and skills enables all of them to expand their competencies and provides less basis for demoralizing social comparison. As a result, students are more likely to compare their rate of progress to their personal standards than to the performance of others. Self-comparison of improvement in a personalized classroom structure raises perceived capability. Educational practices should be gauged not only by the skills and knowledge they impart for present use, but also by what they do to children's beliefs about their capabilities, which affects how they approach the future. Students who develop a sense of self-efficacy are well equipped to educate themselves when they have to rely on their own initiative.

Growth of Self-Efficacy Through Transitional Experiences of Adolescence

Each period of development brings with it new challenges for coping efficacy. As adolescents approach the demands of adulthood, they must learn to assume full responsibility for themselves in almost every dimension of life. This requires mastering many new skills and the ways of adult society. Learning how to deal with sexual relationships and partnerships becomes a matter of considerable importance. The task of choosing what lifework to pursue also looms large during this period. Self-judged capabilities influence the range of career options seriously considered, the degree of interest shown in them, and the vocational paths that are pursued (Betz & Hackett, 1986; Lent & Hackett, 1987). These are but a few of the areas in which new competencies have to be acquired.

With growing independence during adolescence some experimentation with risky behavior is not all that uncommon (Jessor, 1984). Adolescents expand and strengthen their sense of efficacy by learning how to deal successfully with potentially troublesome matters in which they are unpracticed as well as with advantageous life events. Development of resilient self-efficacy requires some experience in mastering difficulties through perseverant effort. Triumphs over difficulties instill a strong belief in one's capabilities that provides the staying power in the face of difficulties. Insulation from problematic situations leaves one ill-prepared to cope with adversities. Impoverished high-risk environments present harsh realities with minimal resources and social supports for culturally-valued pursuits, but extensive modeling, incentives and social supports for transgressive styles of behavior. Such environments severely tax the coping efficacy of youth enmeshed in them to make it through adolescence in ways that do not irreversibly foreclose many beneficial life paths.

Adolescence has often been characterized as a period of psychosocial turmoil. While no period of life is ever free of problems, contrary to the stereotype of "storm and stress," most adolescents negotiate the important transitions of this period without undue disturbance of discord (Bandura, 1964; Petersen, 1988; Rutter, Graham, Chadwick, & Yule, 1976). Indeed, transitional school experiences generally sustain or even increase a sense of personal competence (Nottelmann, 1987). However, youngsters who enter adolescence beset by a disabling sense of inefficacy transport their vulnerability to distress and debility to the new environmental demands. The ease with which the transition from childhood to the demands of adulthood is made similarly depends, in no small measure, on the strength of personal efficacy built up through prior mastery experiences.

Self-Efficacy Concerns of Adulthood

Young adulthood is a period when people have to learn to cope with many new demands arising from lasting partnerships, marital relationships, parenthood, and careers. As in earlier mastery tasks, a firm sense of self-efficacy is an important contributor to the attainment of further competencies and success. Those who enter adulthood poorly equipped with skills and plagued by self-doubts find many aspects of their adult life stressful and depressing. The lower their sense of parenting efficacy, the more vulnerable they are to despondency (Cutrona & Troutman, 1986).

By the middle years, people settle into established routines that stabilize their self-appraised efficacy in the major areas of functioning. However, the stability is a shaky one because life does not remain static. Rapid technological and social changes constantly require adaptations calling for self-reappraisals of capabilities. In their occupations, the middle-aged find themselves pressured by younger challengers. Situations in which people must compete for promotions, status, and even work itself, force constant self-appraisals of capabilities by means of social comparison with younger competitors (Suls & Mullen, 1982).

Reappraisals of Self-Efficacy With Advancing Age

The self-efficacy problems of the elderly center on reappraisals and misappraisals of their capabilities. Discussions of aging focus extensively on declining abilities. Many physical capacities do decrease as people grow older, thus, requiring reappraisals of self-efficacy for activities in which the mediating biological functions have been significantly affected. However, gains in knowledge, skills, and expertise compensate some loss in physical capacity. When the elderly are taught to use their intellectual capabilities, their improvement in cognitive functioning more than offsets the average decrement in performance over two decades (Baltes & Willis, 1982). Because people rarely exploit their full potential, elderly persons who invest the necessary effort can function at the higher levels of younger adults. By affecting level of involvement in activities, perceived self-efficacy can contribute to the maintenance of cognitive functioning over the adult life span.

Major life changes in later years are brought about by retirement, relocation, and loss of friends or spouses. Such changes place demands on interpersonal skills to cultivate new social relationships that can contribute to positive functioning and personal well-being. Perceived social inefficacy increases older person's vulnerability to stress and depression both directly and indirectly by impeding development of social supports which serve as a buffer against life stressors (Holahan & Holahan, 1987a; 1987b).

Much variability exists across behavioral domains and educational and socioeconomic levels, and there is no uniform decline in beliefs in personal efficacy in old age (Baltes & Baltes, 1986). Whom the elderly compare themselves against contributes much to the variability in perceived self-efficacy. Those who measure their capabilities against people their age are less likely to view themselves as declining in capabilities than if younger cohorts are used extensively in comparative self-appraisal. There is evidence that perceived cognitive inefficacy is accompanied by lowered intellectual performances (Lachman, Steinberg, & Trotter, 1987). A declining sense of self-efficacy, which often may stem more from disuse and negative cultural expectations than from biological aging, can thus set in motion self-perpetuating processes that result in declining cognitive and behavioral functioning. People who are beset with uncertainties about their personal efficacy not only curtail the range of their activities but undermine their efforts in those they undertake. The result is a progressive loss of interest and skill. In societies that emphasize the potential for self-development throughout the lifespan, rather than psychophysical decline with aging, the elderly lead productive, self-fulfilling lives.

FAMILIAL AND SOCIAL TRANSMISSION MODELS

Psychological theories have traditionally assumed that values, standards and behavioral patterns are transmitted via parent-child relationships. In a provocative paper, Reiss (1965) contrasts theories based on the familial transmission model with those emphasizing transmission by broader social systems. He offers several reasons why the familial transmission model cannot adequately explain socialization processes and outcomes. Assuming, at least, a 20-year procreation difference between generations, a long time intervenes between parents' imparting values and standards to their children and when they can, in turn, pass on those values to their own offspring. The long time lag between succeeding descendants would produce a very slow rate of social change, whereas, in fact, extensive society-wide shifts in standards and normative behavior often occur within a single generation. The marked change in sexual standards and practices and cohabitation patterns within a relatively short time span is but one example. Reiss, therefore, argues that the parent-child relationship cannot be the major agency of cultural transmission. Rather, standards of behavior are primarily disseminated by institutionally organized systems (e.g., educational, mass media, religious, political, and legal agencies) and regulated by collectively enforced sanctions. In Reiss' view, psychosocial changes originate primarily at the social systems level, whereas changes emerging within the family are of lesser social impact. Thus, for example, racial segregation in public accommodations and infringement of voting rights were changed more rapidly by collective protest and Supreme Court decisions than by waiting for prejudiced parents to inculcate in their children more acceptant attitudes which they would display toward minority groups when they became restauranteurs and motel operators thirty or forty years later.

In accord with Reiss' main thesis, social cognitive theory assumes that values and behavior patterns arise from diverse sources of influence and are promoted by institutional backing. Because social agencies possess considerable rewarding and punishing power, collectively enforced sanctions can produce rapid and widespread societal changes. However, a social systems theory alone is insufficient to explain why there is often substantial variation in values and behavior patterns, even within the same subcultures. Differences arise partly because institutional prescriptions for the youth of a society must be implemented by parents, teachers and community members. Those who, for whatever reason, do not subscribe to the institutional codes will undermine the broader social transmission effort. Barring strong sanctions, parents often find new values as discordant and resist adopting them for some time. Families who are estranged from the mainstream social systems also pay little or no heed to institutional values.

A comprehensive theory of social transmission must also explain what produces and sustains the values, standards and behavior patterns promulgated by the cultural institutions. They are products of influences wielded by members of the society. Changes in social systems are often initiated by determined dissenters acting on values modeled largely from individuals who have opposed prevailing social practices (Bandura, 1973; Keniston, 1968; Rosenhan, 1970). Dissenters create their own subsystems to support their efforts to reform social systems (King, 1958).

In discussing the limitations of personality theories of socialization, Reiss states that, in such approaches, social change can arise only when there is a breakdown in transmission between generations. This type of criticism is applicable to theories assuming that parental values are introjected by children *in toto* and then are later passed on unmodified to their progeny. In social cognitive theory, the adoption of values, standards and attributes is governed by a much broader and more dynamic social reality. Social learning is a continuous process in which acquired standards are elaborated and modified, and new ones are adopted. Children repeatedly observe and learn the standards and behavior patterns not only of parents, but also of siblings, peers, and other adults (Bandura, Grusec, & Manlove, 1967; Davidson & Smith, 1982). Moreover, the extensive symbolic modeling provided in the mass media serves as another prominent extra-familial source of influence (Liebert, Sprafkin, & Davidson, 1982). Hence, children's values and attributes are likely to reflect amalgams of these diverse sources, rather than simply the unaltered familial heritage. Even if psychosocial patterns arose solely from familial sources, significant changes could emerge across generations through familial transmission. This is because the attributes and standards of the two parents are rarely identical and siblings add further variety to what is modeled in the familial environment. The attributes children develop are composites of different features of parental and sibling values at each generation. Thus, children within the same family can develop somewhat different composite systems of attributes and values that are neither solely those of the parents nor of the siblings (Bandura, Ross, & Ross, 1963).

Some of the criticisms levied by Reiss against the familial transmission model are debatable, but his contention that social institutions often play a heavier role in perpetuating and changing psychosocial patterns than do familial influences is well taken. However, an interactional theory that treats human development as a product of both familial and social system influences holds greater promise of furthering our understanding of the process than does a dichotomized view that pits one system against the other. This broader transmission model provides the vehicle for cultural evolution and the transmission of cultural patterns both within generations and from one generation to the next. Boyd and Richerson (1985) analyze the mechanisms of cultural evolution from a population view of social learning. In their analysis, environmental conditions, multiple modeling influences, and personal experiences operate interactively to change the frequency of behavioral variants in the population. Social learning influences shape the form of cultural evolution by favoring behavioral variants that are efficacious in particular milieus.

THE NATURE OF HUMAN NATURE

Seen from the social cognitive perspective, human nature is characterized by a vast potentiality that can be fashioned by direct and vicarious experience into a variety of forms within biological limits. To say that a major distinguishing mark of humans is their endowed plasticity is not to say that they have no nature or that they come structureless (Midgley, 1978). The plasticity, which is intrinsic to the nature of humans, depends upon specialized neurophysiological mechanisms and structures that have evolved over time. These advanced neural systems, which are specialized for processing, retaining, and using coded information, provide the capacity for the very characteristics that are distinctly human— generative symbolization, forethought, evaluative self-regulation, reflective self-consciousness, and symbolic communication.

Plasticity does not mean that behavior is entirely the product of post-natal experience. Some innately organized patterns of behavior are present at birth; others appear after a period of maturation. One does not have to teach infants to cry or suck, toddlers to walk, or adolescents how to copulate. Nor does one have to create physiological motivators arising from hunger, thirst, and pain or somatically-based rewards. Infants come equipped with some attentional selectivity and interpretive predilections as well (von Cranach, Foppa, LePenies, & Ploog, 1979). The inborn programming for basic physiological functions is the product of accumulated ancestral experiences that are stored in the genetic code.

Most patterns of human behavior are organized by individual experience and retained in neural codes, rather than being provided ready-made by inborn programming. While human thought and conduct may be fashioned largely through experience, innately determined factors enter into every form of behavior to some degree. Genetic factors and neural systems affect behavioral potentialities and place constraints on capabilities. Both experiential and physiological factors interact, often in intricate ways, to determine behavior. Even in behavioral patterns that are formed almost entirely through experience, rudimentary elements are present as part of the natural endowment. For example, humans are endowed with basic phonetic elements which may appear trivial compared to complex acquired patterns of speech, but the elements are, nevertheless, essential. Similarly, action patterns regarded as instinctual, because they draw heavily on inborn elements, require appropriate experience to be developed. Sensory systems and brain structures are alterable by environmental influences. The level of psychological and physiological development, of course, limits what can be acquired at any given time. Because behavior contains mixtures of inborn elements and learned patterns, dichotomous thinking, which separates activities neatly into innate and acquired categories, is seriously inaccurate.

Humans have an unparalleled capability to become many things. The qualities that are cultivated and the life paths that realistically become open to them are partly determined by the nature of the cultural agencies to which their development is entrusted. Social systems that cultivate generalizable competencies, create opportunity structures, provide aidful resources, and allow room for self-directedness increase the chances that people will realize what they wish to become.

ACKNOWLEDGEMENT

Preparation of this chapter was facilitated by Public Health Research Grant MH-5162-25 from the National Institute of Mental Health. Some sections of this chapter include revised and expanded material from the book, *Social Foundations of Thought and Action: A Social Cognitive Theory*, 1986, Prentice-Hall.

REFERENCES

Abravanel, E., Levan-Goldschmidt, E., & Stevenson, M. B. (1976). Action imitation: The early phase of infancy. *Child Development, 47*, 1032–1044.

Ainsworth, M. D. S., & Bell, S. M. (1974). Mother-infant interaction and the development of competence. In K. Connolly & J. Bruner (Eds.), *The growth of competence* (pp. 97–118). London: Academic Press.

Albert, A. A., & Porter, J. R. (1982). Children's perception of parental sex-role expectations. *The Journal of Genetic Psychology, 140*, 145–146.

Ashby, M. S., & Wittmaier, B. C. (1978). Attitude changes in children after exposure to stories about women in traditional or nontraditional occupations. *Journal of Educational Psychology, 70*, 945–949.

Ashton, P. T., & Webb, R. B. (1986). *Making a difference: Teachers' sense of efficacy and student achievement*. White Plains, NY: Longman, Inc.

Baldwin, A. L., & Baldwin, C. P. (1973). The study of mother-child interaction. *American Scientist, 61*, 714–721.

Baltes, M. M., & Baltes, P. B. (Eds.). (1986). *The psychology of control and aging*. Hillsdale, NJ: Erlbaum.

Baltes, P. B., & Reese, H. W. (1984). The life-span perspective in developmental psychology. In M. H. Bornstein & M. E. Lamb (Eds.), *Developmental psychology: An advanced textbook* (pp. 493–531). Hillsdale, NJ: Erlbaum.

Baltes, P. B., & Willis, S. L. (1982). Plasticity and enhancement of intellectual functioning in old age: Penn State's adult development and enrichment project (ADEPT). In F. I. M. Craik & S. Trehub (Eds.), *Advances in the study of communication and affect* (Vol. 8): *Aging and cognitive processes* (pp. 353–389). New York: Plenum.

Bandura, A. (1964). The stormy decade: Fact or fiction? *Psychology in the Schools, 1*, 224–231.

Bandura, A. (1965). Influence of models' reinforcement contingencies on the acquisition of imitative responses. *Journal of Personality and Social Psychology, 1*, 589–595.

Bandura, A. (1973). *Aggression: A social learning analysis*. Englewood Cliffs, NJ: Prentice-Hall.

Bandura, A. (1982a). Self-efficacy mechanism in human agency. *American Psychologist, 37*, 122–147.

Bandura, A. (1982b). The psychology of chance encounters and life paths. *American Psychologist, 37*, 747–755.

Bandura, A. (1986). *Social foundations of thought and action: A social cognitive theory*. Englewood Cliffs, NJ: Prentice-Hall, Inc.

Bandura, A. (1988). Self-regulation of motivation and action through goal systems. In V. Hamilton, G. H. Bower, & N. H. Frijda (Eds.), *Cognitive perspectives on emotion and motivation* (pp. 37–61). Dordrecht: Kluwer Academic Publishers, 1988.

Bandura, A. (1988b, in press). Social cognitive theory and social referencing. In S. Feinman (Ed.), *Social referencing and social construction of reality*. New York: Plenum.

Bandura, A. (1988c, in press). Mechanisms of moral disengagement in terrorism. In W. Reich (Ed.), *The psychology of terrorism: Behaviors, world-views, states of mind*. New York: Cambridge University Press.

Bandura, A. (1988d, in press). Social cognitive theory of moral judgment and action. In W. M. Kurtines & J. L. Gewirtz (Eds.), *Moral behavior and development: Advances in theory, research, and applications* (Vol.1). Hillsdale, NJ: Erlbaum.

Bandura, A., & Cervone, D. (1983). Self-evaluative and self-efficacy mechanisms governing the motivational effects of goal systems. *Journal of Personality and Social Psychology, 45*, 1017–1028.

Bandura, A., Grusec, J. E., & Menlove, F. L. (1967). Some social determinants of self-monitoring reinforcement systems. *Journal of Personality and Social Psychology, 5*, 449–455.

Bandura, A., Ross, D., & Ross, S. A. (1963). A comparative test of the status envy, social power, and secondary reinforcement theories of identificatory learning. *Journal of Abnormal and Social Psychology, 67*, 527–534.

Bandura, A., & Schunk, D. H. (1981). Cultivating competence, self-efficacy and intrinsic interest through proximal self-motivation. *Journal of Personality and Social Psychology, 41*, 586–598.

Bandura, A., Underwood, B., & Fromson, M. E. (1975). Disinhibition of aggression through diffusion of responsibility and dehumanization of victims. *Journal of Research in Personality, 9*, 253–269.

Bandura, A., & Walters, R. H. (1959). *Adolescent aggression.* New York: Ronald Press.

Bell, R. Q., & Harper, L. V. (1977). *Child effects on adults.* Hillsdale, NJ: Erlbaum.

Bem, S. L. (1981). Gender schema theory: A cognitive account of sex typing. *Psychological Review, 88*, 354–364.

Betz, N. E., & Hackett, G. (1986). Applications of self-efficacy theory to understanding career choice behavior. *Journal of Social and Clinical Psychology, 4*, 279–289.

Bloom, L., Hood, L., & Lightbrown, P. (1974). Imitation in language development: If, when, and why. *Cognitive Psychology, 6*, 380–420.

Bower, G. H. (1975). Cognitive psychology: An introduction. In W. K. Estes (Ed.), Handbook of learning and cognition (pp. 25–80). Hillsdale, NJ: Erlbaum.

Bowerman, M. (1973). Structural relationships in children's utterances: Syntactic or semantic? In T. E. Moore (Ed.), *Cognitive development and the acquisition of language* (pp. 197–213). New York: Academic Press.

Boyd, R., & Richerson, P. J. (1985). *Mechanisms of cultural evolution.* Chicago: University of Chicago Press.

Bradley, R. H., Caldwell, B. M., & Elardo, R. (1979). Home environment and cognitive development in the first two years: A cross-lagged panel analysis. *Developmental Psychology, 15*, 246–250.

Brainerd, C. J. (1978). The stage question in cognitive-development theory. *The Behavioral and Brain Sciences, 2*, 173–213.

Brewer, W. F. (1974). There is no convincing evidence for operant of classical conditioning in adult humans. In W. B. Weimer & D. S. Palermo (Eds.), *Cognition and the symbolic processes* (pp. 1–42). Hillsdale, NJ: Erlbaum.

Brim, O. G., Jr., & Ryff, C. D. (1980). On the properties of life events. In P. B. Baltes & O. G. Brim, Jr. (Eds.), Life-span development and behavior (Vol.3, pp. 367–388). New York: Academic Press.

Brock, T. C., & Buss, A. H. (1962). Dissonance, aggression, and evaluation of pain. *Journal of Abnormal and Social Psychology, 65*, 197–202.

Brock, T. C., & Buss, A. H. (1964). Effects of justification for aggression and communication with the victim on postaggression dissonance. *Journal of Abnormal and Social Psychology, 68*, 403–412.

Brody, G. H., & Henderson, R. W. (1977). Effects of multiple model variations and rationale provision on the moral judgments and explanations of young children. *Child Development, 48*, 1117–1120.

Brown, A. L., & Barclay, C. R. (1976). The effects of training specific mnemonics on the metamnemonic efficiency of retarded children. *Child Development, 47*, 71–80.

Brown, I., Jr. (1976). Role of referent concreteness in the acquisition of passive sentence comprehension through abstract modeling. *Journal of Experimental Child Psychology, 22*, 185–199.

Bullock, D., & Merrill, L. (1980). The impact of personal preference on consistency through time:

The case of childhood aggression. *Child Development, 51*, 808–814.

Bussey, K., & Bandura, A. (1984). Gender constancy, social power, and sex-linked modeling. *Journal of Personality and Social Psychology, 47*, 1242–1302.

Cairns, R. B. (Ed.). (1979). *The analysis of social interactions: Methods, issues, and illustrations.* Hillsdale, NJ: Erlbaum.

Cantor, J., & Wilson, B. J. (1988). Helping children cope with frightening media presentations. *Current Psychological Research and Reviews, 7*, 58–75.

Carroll, W. R., & Bandura, A. (1985). Role of timing of visual monitoring and motor rehearsal in observational learning of action patterns. *Journal of Motor Behavior, 17*, 269–281.

Carroll, W. R., & Bandura, A. (1989, in press). Representational guidance of action production in observational learning: A causal analysis. *Journal of Motor Behavior.*

Church, R. M. (1959). Emotional reactions of rats to the pain of others. *Journal of Comparative and Physiological Psychology, 52*, 132–134.

Cohen, L. B., & Salapatek, P. (1975). *Infant perception: From sensation to cognition: Vol.1. Basic visual processes.* New York: Academic Press.

Coombs, M. J. (Ed.). (1984). *Developments in expert systems.* London: Academic Press.

Courtney, A. E., & Whipple, T. W. (1974). Women in TV commercials. *The Journal of Communication, 24*, 110–118.

Csikszentmihalyi, M. (1979). Intrinsic rewards and emergent motivation. In M. R. Lepper & D. Greene (Eds.), *The hidden costs of reward* (pp. 205–216). Morristown, NJ: Erlbaum.

Cutrona, C. E., & Troutman, B. R. (1986). Social support, infant temperament, and parenting self-efficacy: A mediational model of postpartum depression. *Child Development, 57*, 1507–1518.

Darley, J. M., Klosson, E. C., & Zanna, M. P. (1978). Intentions and their contexts in the moral judgments of children and adults. *Child Development, 49*, 66–74.

Davidson, E. S., & Smith, W. P. (1982). Imitation, social comparison and self-reward. *Child Development, 53*, 928–932.

Denny, N. W., Duffy, D. M. (1974). Possible environmental causes of stages in moral reasoning. *The Journal of Genetic Psychology, 125*, 277–284.

Diener, E. (1977). Deindividuation: Causes and consequences. *Social Behavior and Personality, 5*, 143–156.

Diener, E., Dineen, J., Endresen, K., Beaman, A. L., & Fraser, S. C. (1975). Effects of altered responsibility, cognitive set, and modeling on physical aggression and deindividuation. *Journal of Personality and Social Psychology, 31*, 328–337.

Dubanoski, R. A., & Parton, D. A. (1971). Imitative aggression in children as a function of observing a human model. *Developmental Psychology, 4*, 489.

Duncker, K. (1938). Experimental modification of children's food preferences through social suggestion. *Journal of Abnormal Social Psychology, 33*, 489–507.

Dysinger, W. S., & Ruckmick, C. A. (1933). *The emotional responses of children to the motion-picture situation.* New York: Macmillan.

Elder, G. H. (1981). History and the life course. In D. Bertaux (Ed.), *Biography and society: The life history approach in the social sciences* (pp. 77–115). Beverly Hills: Sage.

Eimas, P. D. (1970). Effects of memory aids on hypothesis behavior and focusing in young children and adults. *Journal of Experimental Child Psychology, 10*, 319–336.

Ellis, R. A , & Lane, W. C. (1963). Structural supports for upward mobility. *American Sociological Review, 28*, 743–756.

Emmons, R. A., & Diener, E. (1986). Situation selection as a moderator of response consistency and stability. *Journal of Personality and Social Psychology, 51*, 1013–1019.

Englis, B. G., Vaughan, K. B., & Lanzetta, J. T. (1982). Conditioning of counter-empathetic emotional responses. *Journal of Experimental Social Psychology, 18*, 375–391.

Fagot, B. I. (1977). Consequences of moderate cross-gender behavior in preschool children. *Child Development, 48*, 902–907.

Falmagne, R. J. (1975). *Reasoning: Representation and process in children and adults.* Hillsdale, NJ: Erlbaum.

Feldman, D. H. (1980). *Beyond universals in cognitive development.* Norwood, NJ: Ablex.

Finkelstein, N. W., & Ramey, C. T. (1977). Learning to control the environment in infancy. *Child Development, 48,* 806–819.

Flavell, J. H. (1978a). Metacognitive development. In J. M. Scandura & C. J. Brainerd (Eds.), *Structural-process theories of complex human behavior* (pp. 213–245). Alphen a. d. Rijn, The Netherlands: Sijithoff and Noordhoff.

Flavell, J. H. (1978b). Developmental stage: Explanans or explanadum? *The Behavioral and Brain Sciences, 2,* 187–188.

Flerx, V. C., Fidler, D. S., & Rogers, R. W. (1976). Sex role stereotypes: Developmental aspects and early intervention. *Child Development, 47,* 998–1007.

Folger, J. P., & Chapman, R. S. (1978). A pragmatic analysis of spontaneous imitations. *Journal of Child Language, 5,* 25–38.

Gibson, S., & Dembo, M. H. (1984). Teacher efficacy: A construct validation. *Journal of Educational Psychology, 76,* 569–582.

Greenough, W. T., Black, J. E., & Wallace, C. S. (1987). Experience and brain development. *Child Development, 58,* 539–559.

Gunnar, M. R. (1980). Contingent stimulation: A review of its role in early development. In S. Levine & H. Ursin (Eds.), *Coping and health* (pp. 101–119). New York: Plenum Press.

Hagen, J. W., & Hale, G. A. (1973). The development of attention in children. In A. D. Pick (Ed.), *Minnesota Symposium on Child Psychology* (Vol. 7, pp. 117–140). Minneapolis: University of Minnesota Press.

Hamilton, M. L., & Stewart, D. M. (1977). Peer models and language acquisition. *Merrill-Palmer Quarterly of Behavior and Development, 23,* 45–56.

Hart, B., & Risley, T. R. (1975). Incidental teaching of language in the preschool. *Journal of Applied Behavior Analysis, 8,* 411–420.

Hart, B., & Risley, T. R. (1978). Promoting productive language through incidental teaching. *Education and Urban Society, 10,* 407–430.

Hart, B., & Risley, T. R. (1980). In vivo language intervention: Unanticipated general effects. *Journal of Applied Behavior Analysis, 13,* 407–432.

Haugan, G. M., & McIntire, R. W. (1972). Comparisons of vocal imitation, tactile stimulation, and food as reinforcers for infant vocalizations. *Developmental Psychology, 6,* 201–209.

Hawkins, R. P., & Pingree, S. (1982). Television's influence on social reality. In D. Pearl, L. Bouthilet, & J. Lazar (Eds.), *Television and behavior: Ten years of scientific progress and implications for the eighties* (Vol. II, pp. 224–247). Rockville, MD: National Institute of Mental Health.

Holahan, C. K., & Holahan, C. J. (1987a). Self-efficacy, social support, and depression in aging: A longitudinal analysis. *Journal of Gerontology, 42,* 65–68.

Holahan, C. K., & Holahan, C. J. (1987b). Life stress, hassles, and self-efficacy in aging: A replication and extension. *Journal of Applied Social Psychology, 17,* 574–592.

Hovell, M. F., Schumaker, J. B., & Sherman, J. A. (1978). A comparison of parents' models and expansions in promoting children's acquisition of adjectives. *Journal of Experimental Child Psychology, 25,* 41–57.

Hughes, R., Jr., Tingle, B. A., & Swain, D. B. (1981). Development of empathic understanding in children. *Child Development, 52,* 122–128.

Hultsch, D. F., & Plemons, J. K. (1979). Life events and life-span development. In P. B. Baltes & O. G. Brim, Jr. (Eds.), *Life-span development and behavior* (Vol. 2, pp. 1–36). New York: Academic Press.

Huston, A. C. (1983). Sex typing. In P. H. Mussen (Ed.), *Handbook of child psychology* (Vol. 4., pp. 387–467). New York: Wiley.

Jacklin, C. N., & Mischel, H. N. (1973). As the twig is bent—sex role stereotyping in early readers. *The School Psychology Digest, 2,* 30–38.

Jessor, R. (1984). Adolescent development and behavioral health. In J. D. Matarazzo, N. E. Miller, J. A. Herd, & S. M. Weiss (Eds.), *Behavioral health: A handbook of health enhancement and dis-*

ease prevention (pp. 69–90). Silver Spring, MD: Wesley.

Jusczyk, P. W. (1981). Infant speech perception: A critical appraisal. In P. D. Eimas & J. L. Miller (Eds.), *Perspectives on the study of speech* (pp. 113–164). Hillsdale, NJ: Erlbaum.

Kasermann, M. L., & Foppa, K. (1981). Some determinants of self correction: An interactional study of Swiss-German. In W. Deutsch (Ed.), *The child's construction of language* (pp. 97–104). London: Academic Press.

Kaye, K. (1982). *The mental and social life of babies: How parents create persons.* Chicago: University of Chicago Press.

Kelman, H. C. (1973). Violence without moral restraint: Reflections on the dehumanization of victims and victimizers. *Journal of Social Issues, 29*, 25–61.

Kemp, J. C., & Dale, P. S. (1973). *Spontaneous imitations and free speech: A developmental comparison.* Paper presented at the meeting of the Society for Research in Child Development, Philadelphia.

Keniston, K. (1968). *Young radicals.* New York: Harcourt, Brace and World.

King, M. L. (1958). *Stride toward freedom.* New York: Ballantine Books.

Krauss, I. (1964). Sources of educational aspirations among working-class youth. *American Sociological Review, 29*, 867–879.

Lackman, M. E., Steinberg, E. S., & Trotter, S. D. (1987). The effects of control beliefs and attributions on memory self-assessments and performance. *Psychology and Aging, 2*, 266–271.

Lamal, P. A. (1971). Imitation learning of information-processing. *Journal of Experimental Child Psychology, 12*, 223–227.

Lamb, M. E., Easterbrooks, M. A., & Holden, G. W. (1980). Reinforcement and punishment among preschoolers: Characteristics, effects and correlates. *Child development, 51*, 1230–1236.

Lane, J., & Anderson, N. H. (1976). Integration of intention and outcome in moral judgment. *Memory and Cognition, 4*, 1–5.

Leon, M. (1984). Rules mothers and sons use to integrate intent and damage information in their moral judgments. *Child Development, 55*, 2106–2113.

Lent, R. W., & Hackett, G. (1987). Career self-efficacy: Empirical status and future directions. *Journal of Vocational Behavior, 30*, 347–382.

Lerner, R. M. (1982). Children and adolescents as producers of their own development. *Developmental Review, 2*, 342–370.

Lewis, M., & Rosenblum, L. A. (Eds.). (1974). *The effect of the infant on its caregiver.* New York: Wiley.

Liebert, R. M., Sprafkin, J. N., & Davidson, E. S. (1982). *The early window: Effects of television on children and youth* (2nd ed.). Elmsford, NY: Pergamon.

Lightfoot, S. L. (1983). *The good high school.* New York: Basic Books.

Maccoby, E. E., & Jacklin, C. N. (1974). *The psychology of sex differences.* Stanford, CA: Stanford University Press.

Macnamara, J. (1972). Cognitive basis of language learning in infants. *Psychological Review, 79*, 1–13.

Marcus, D. E., & Overton, W. F. (1978). The development of cognitive gender constancy and sex role preferences. *Child Development, 49*, 434–444.

McCall, R. B., Parke, R. D., & Kavanaugh, R. D. (1977). Imitation of live and televised models by children one to three years of age. *Monograph of the Society for Research in Child Development, 42*(5, Serial No. 173).

McGhee, P. E., & Frueh, T. (1980). Television viewing and the learning of sex-role stereotypes. *Sex Roles, 6*, 179–188.

Meichenbaum, D. (1984). Teaching thinking: A cognitive-behavioral perspective. In R. Glaser, S. Chipman, & J. Segal (Eds.), *Thinking and learning skills* (Vol. 2): *Research and Open Questions* (pp. 407–426). Hillsdale, NJ: Erlbaum.

Meltzoff, A. N., & Moore, M. K. (1983). The origins of imitation in infancy: Paradigm, phenomena, and theories. In L. P. Lipsitt & C. K. Rovee-Collier (Eds.), *Advances in infancy research* (Vol. 2., pp. 266–301). Norwood, NJ: Ablex Publishing.

Midgley, M. (1978). *Beast and man: The roots of human nature.* Ithaca, NY: Cornell University Press.

Milgram, S. (1974). *Obedience to authority: An experimental view.* New York: Harper & Row.

Millar, W. S. (1972). A study of operant conditioning under delayed reinforcement in early infancy. *Monographs of the Society for Research in Child Development, 37*(2, Serial No. 147).

Millar, W. S., & Schaffer, H. R. (1972). The influence of spatially displaced feedback on infant operant conditioning. *Journal of Experimental Child Psychology, 14,* 442–453.

Miller, R. E., Caul, W. F., & Mirsky, I. A. (1967). Communication of affect between feral and socially isolated monkeys. *Journal of Personality and Social Psychology, 7,* 231–239.

Miller, M. M., & Reeves, B. (1976). Dramatic TV content and children's sex role stereotypes. *Journal of Broadcasting, 20,* 35–50.

Mineka, S. (1987). A primate model of phobic fears. In H. Eysenck & I. Martin (Eds.), *Theoretical foundations of behavior therapy* (pp. 81–111). New York: Plenum Press.

Moerk, E. L. (1986). Environmental factors in early language acquisition. In G. J. Whitehurst (Ed.), *Annals of child development* (Vol. 3, pp. 191–236). Greenwich, CT: JAI Press.

Morris, W. N., & Nemcek, D., Jr. (1982). The development of social comparison motivation among preschoolers: Evidence of a stepwise progression. *Merrill-Palmer Quarterly of Behavior and Development, 28,* 413–425.

Neisser, U. (1976). *Cognition and reality: Principles and implications of cognitive psychology.* San Francisco: Freeman.

Nelson, K. E. (1977a). Aspects of language acquisition and use from age 2 to age 20. *Journal of American Academy of Child Psychiatry, 16,* 584–607.

Nelson, K. E. (1977b). Facilitating children's syntax acquisition. *Developmental Psychology, 13,* 111–117.

Nicolich, L. M., & Raph, J. B. (1978). Imitative language and symbolic maturity in the single-word period. *Journal of Psycholinguistic Research, 7,* 401–417.

Nottelmann, E. D. (1987). Competence and self-esteem during transition from childhood to adolescence. *Developmental Psychology, 23,* 441–450.

O'Bryant, S. L., & Corder-Bolz, C. R. (1978). The effects of television on children's stereotyping of women's work roles. *Journal of Vocational Behavior, 12,* 233–244.

Papousek, H., & Papousek, M. (1977). Mothering and the cognitive head-start: Psychobiological considerations. In H. R. Schaffer (Ed.), *Studies in mother-infant interaction.* London: Academic Press.

Papousek, H., & Papousek, M. (1979). Early ontogeny of human social interaction: Its biological roots and social dimensions. In M. von Cranach, K. Foppa, W. LePenies, & D. Ploog (Eds.), *Human ethology: Claims and limits of a new discipline* (pp. 456–478). Cambridge, England: Cambridge University Press.

Pawlby, S. J. (1977). Imitative interaction. In H. R. Schaffer (Ed.), *Studies in mother-infant interaction.* London: Academic Press.

Pearl, D., Bouthilet, L., & Lazar, J. (Eds.). (1982). *Television and behavior: Ten years of scientific progress and implications for the eighties.* Rockville, MD: National Institute of Mental Health.

Perry, D. G., & Bussey, K. (1979). The social learning theory of sex differences: Imitation is alive and well. *Journal of Personality and Social Psychology, 37,* 1699–1712.

Perry, D. G., Perry, L. C., & Rasmussen, P. (1986). Cognitive social learning mediators of aggression. *Child Development, 57,* 700–711.

Petersen, A. C. (1988). Adolescent Development. In M. R. Rosenzweig & L. W. Porter (Eds.), *Annual Review of Psychology* (pp. 583–607). Palo Alto, CA: Annual Reviews, Inc.

Piaget, J. (1960). Equilibration and development of logical structures. In J. M. Tanner & B. Inhelder (Eds.), *Discussions on child development* (Vol. 4, pp. 98–115). New York: International Universities Press.

Piaget, J. (1970). Piaget's theory. In P. H. Mussen (General Ed.), W. Kessen (Vol. Ed.), *Handbook of child psychology* (4th ed., Vol. 1, pp. 103–128). New York: John Wiley & Sons.

Ramel, C., & Rannug, U. (1980). Short-term mutagenicity tests. *Journal of Toxicology and Environmental Health, 6*, 1065–1076.

Ramey, C. T., & Finkelstein, N. W. (1978). Contingent stimulation and infant competence. *Journal of Pediatric Psychology, 3*, 89–96.

Rasmussen, N. C. (1981). The application of probabilistic risk assessment techniques to energy technologies. *Annual Review of Energy, 6*, 123–138.

Raush, H. L. (1965). Interaction sequences. *Journal of Personality and Social Psychology, 2*, 487–499.

Reiss, A. J., Jr. (1965). *Social organization and socialization: Variations on a theme about generations.* Working paper 1, Center for Research on Social Organization, University of Michigan, Ann Arbor, MI.

Relich, J. D., Debus, R. L., & Walker, R. (1986). The mediating role of attribution and self-efficacy variables for treatment effects on achievement outcomes. *Comtemporary Educational Psychology, 11*, 195–216.

Rheingold, H. L., & Cook, K. V. (1975). The context of boys' and girls' rooms as an index of parents' behavior. *Child Development, 46*, 459–463.

Rosenhan, D. L. (1970). The natural socialization of altruistic autonomy. In J. Macaulay & L. Berkowitz (Eds.), *Altruism and helping behavior: Social psychological studies of some antecedents and consequences* (pp. 251–268). New York: Academic Press.

Rosenholtz, S. J., & Rosenholtz, S. H. (1981). Classroom organization and the perception of ability. *Sociology of Education, 54*, 132–140.

Rosenthal, T. L., & Zimmerman, B. J. (1978). *Social learning and cognition.* New York: Academic Press.

Rutter, M., Graham, P., Chadwick, O. F. D., & Yule, W. (1976). Adolescent turmoil: Fact or fiction? *Journal of Child Psychology and Psychiatry, 17*, 35–56.

Schlesinger, I. M. (1982). *Steps to language: Toward a theory of native language acquisition.* Hillsdale, NJ: Erlbaum.

Schunk, D. H. (1984). Self-efficacy perspective on achievement behavior. *Educational Psychologist, 19*, 48–58.

Schunk, D. H. (1987). Peer models and children's behavioral change. *Review of Educational Research, 57*, 149–174.

Schwartz, B. (1982). Reinforcement-induced behavioral stereotype: How not to teach people to discover rules. *Journal of Experimental Psychology, 111*, 23–59.

Sears, R. R., Maccoby, E. E., & Levin, H. (1957). *Patterns of child rearing.* Evanston, IL: Row, Peterson.

Shatz, M., & Gelman, R. (1973). The development of communication skills: Modifications in the speech of young children as a function of listener. *Monographs of the Society for Research in Child Development, 38*(5, Serial No. 152).

Smetana, J. G., & Letourneau, K. J. (1984). Development of gender constancy and children's sex-typed free play behavior. *Developmental Psychology, 20*, 691–696.

Snow, C. E. (1972). Mothers' speech to children learning language. *Child Development, 43*, 549–565.

Snow, M. E., Jacklin, C. N., & Maccoby, E. E. (1983). Sex-of-child difference in father-child interaction at one year of age. *Child Development, 54*, 227–232.

Snyder, M. (1980). Seek, and ye shall find: Testing hypotheses about other people. In E. T. Higgins, C. P. Herman, & M. P. Zanna (Eds.), *Social cognition: The Ontario symposium on personality and social psychology* (Vol. 1, pp. 105–130). Hillsdale, NJ: Erlbaum.

Snyder, M. (1981). On the self-perpetuating nature of social stereotypes. In D. L. Hamilton (Ed.), *Cognitive processes in stereotyping and intergroup behavior* (pp. 182–212). Hillsdale, NJ: Erlbaum.

Spence, J. T. (1984). Gender identity and its implication for concepts of masculinity and femininity. In T. B. Sonderegger (Ed.), *Nebraska Symposium on Motivation* (Vol. 32). Lincoln: University of Nebraska Press.

Spence, J. T., & Helmreich, R. L. (1978). *Masculinity and femininity: Their psychological dimensions, correlates, and antecedents.* Austin: University of Texas Press.

Stewart, D. M., & Hamilton, M. L. (1976). Imitation as a learning strategy in the acquisition of vocabulary. *Journal of Experimental Child Psychology, 21,* 380–392.

Stotland, E. (1969). Exploratory investigations of empathy. In L. Berkowitz (Ed.), *Advances in experimental social psychology* (Vol. 4, pp. 271–314). New York: Academic Press.

Suls, J., & Mullen, B. (1982). From the cradle to the grave: Comparison and self-evaluation across the life-span. In J. Suls (Ed.), *Psychological perspectives on the self* (Vol. 1, pp. 97–125). Hillsdale, NJ: Erlbaum.

Surber, C. F. (1985). Applications of information integration to children's social cognitions. In J. B. Pryor & J. D. Day (Eds.), *The development of social cognition* (pp. 59–94). New York: Springer-Verlag.

Swenson, A. (1983). Toward an ecological approach to theory and research in child language acquisition. In W. Fowler (Ed.), *Potentials of childhood* (Vol. 2). *Studies in early developmental learning* (pp. 121–176). Lexington, MA: Lexington Books.

Thompson, S. K., & Bentler, P. M. (1971). The priority of cues in sex discrimination by children and adults. *Developmental Psychology, 5,* 181–185.

Uzgiris, I. C. (1979). The many faces of imitation in infancy. In L. Montada (Ed.), *Fortschritte der entwicklungpsychologie* (pp. 173–193). Stuttgart: Verlag W. Kohlhammer.

Uzgiris, I. C. (1984). Imitation in infancy: Its interpersonal aspects. In M. Perlmutter (Ed.), *The Minnesota symposia on child psychology* (Vol. 17, pp. 1–31). Hillsdale, NJ: Erlbaum.

Valentine, C. W. (1930). The psychology of imitation with special reference to early childhood. *British Journal of Psychology, 21,* 105–132.

von Cranach, M., Foppa, K., LePenies, W., & Ploog, D. (Eds.)(1979). *Human ethology: Claims and limits of a new discipline.* Cambridge, England: Cambridge University Press.

Watson, J. S. (1979). Perception of contingency as a determinant of social responsiveness. In E. B. Thoman (Ed.), *Origins of the infant's social responsiveness* (Vol. 1, pp. 33–64). New York: Halsted.

Wheeler, V. A., & Ladd, G. W. (1982). Assessment of children's self-efficacy for social interactions with peers. *Developmental Psychology, 18,* 795–805.

Whitehurst, G. J. (1977). Comprehension, selective imitation, and the CIP hypothesis. *Journal of Experimental Child Psychology, 23,* 23–38.

Wilson, B. J., & Cantor, J. (1985). Developmental differences in empathy with a television protagonist's fear. *Journal of Experimental Child Psychology, 39,* 284–299.

Winfrey, C. (1979, February 25). Why 900 died in Guyana. *The New York Times Magazine,* p. 39.

Yarrow, L. J., Rubenstein, J. L., & Pedersen, F. A. (1975). *Infant and environment: Early cognitive and motivational development.* New York: Halsted.

Zimbardo, P. G. (1969). The human choice: Individuation, reason, and order versus deindividuation, impulse, and chaos. In W. J. Arnold & D. Levine (Eds.), *Nebraska symposium on motivation, 1969* (pp. 237–309). Lincoln: University of Nebraska Press.

BEHAVIOR ANALYSIS

Sidney W. Bijou

This chapter is an update of the behavior analysis theory of child development introduced by Bijou and Baer (1961, 1978). It contains a sketch of the history of the theory, an elaboration on its philosophy of science, details that complete the unit of analysis, an expansion on the processes of development, and a refinement and extension of the stages of development to include the entire life span. It also includes a brief review of the contributory effects of this theory on applied developmental research and practice, a discussion of some current issues, and an expression of my hopes for its further advancement.

I. HISTORY

The history of this perspective begins with the initial presentation of the theory in 1961 and ends with a discussion of a revision of some aspects of the theory and a clarification of some persistently misunderstood features.

Annals of Child Development, Volume 6, pages 61-83.
Copyright © 1989 by JAI Press Inc.
All rights of reproduction in any form reserved.
ISBN: 0-89232-979-3

Initial Statement of the Theory

The initial statement of the theory was presented in *Child Development I: A Systematic and Empirical Theory* (Bijou & Baer, 1961). There we described the formulation as a natural science approach based on the philosophies of science of radical behaviorism (Skinner, 1953) and interbehaviorism (Kantor, 1959). Merging these views, we hypothesized first, that general psychology, the parent science, is the study of the behavior of individual organisms in interaction with the environment, and second, that the task of psychology is to analyze behavior as a function of the current situation, past events bearing on the current situation, and genetic inheritance. The relationship between behavior and environmental stimulation was considered to be *linear* (i.e., either stimuli-preceded responses as in classical conditioning, and stimuli-preceded responses followed by stimuli as in operant conditioning) and *functional*, with functional and causal relationships being regarded as synonymous. We also took the position that, although psychology is an independent natural science, it is, nevertheless, closely related to organismic biology and cultural anthropology in that the former is pertinent to an adequate analysis of both response and stimulus variables and the latter to the stimulating conditions to which an individual is exposed.

We defined developmental psychology as that branch of general psychology that specializes in studying *progressions (and regressions) in interactions* between an individual's behavior and environmental events. The developing individual was conceptualized as a pattern of psychological responses in interaction with the functional environment. The functional environment—meaning the constellation of stimuli to which the individual actually responds, or is attending to—consists of specific stimuli and setting events. Specific stimuli, which may be physical, chemical, organismic (those originating in the physiology of the individual), and social, are analyzed in terms of their physical and functional dimensions. Functional dimensions refer to the effects that stimuli may have on a person. Thus, a stimulus may have a discriminative function, which means that if a person behaves in a certain way in a given situation, certain consequences are likely to occur. For example, greeting a friend with "Hello, how are you today?" is likely to result in a response such as, "I'm fine. How are you?" The setting component of the environment is a stimulus-response interaction which, simply because it has occurred, will affect other stimulus-response relationships that follow. A mother who routinely puts her 18-month-old daughter in a playpen after her afternoon nap observes that during the next hour or so the child plays contentedly with toys and engages in vigorous vocal play. One day the child is kept awake during her nap time by the loud, persistent noise of a power lawn mower being run close to her bedroom window. On this day, during playpen time, she throws her toys around, whimpers, cries, and is generally fussy.

Although the flow of interactions between an individual and the environment is continuous from fertilization to death, it may be "stopped down" at any point to study the details of a specific event. Thus, the flow of development may be studied in terms of three stages: universal, basic, and societal (Kantor, 1959).

Progressions in development were considered to depend on opportunities and circumstances provided by the individual's physical make-up (developmental level, health status, and handicapping condition) and the physical and social environments, present and past. And increments in development were brought about by *respondent* of Pavlovian processes that involve responses controlled by antecedent stimulation and by *operant* processes wherein responses are controlled by consequences (Skinner, 1938, 1953).

Respondent processes, which play a central role in unconditioned and conditioned feelings and emotional interactions, develop new eliciting stimulus functions through pairings with unconditional stimuli, such as a child's fear reaction to the sight of a dog that had nipped him the day before. The resulting eliciting functions of a conditioned stimulus (e.g., the child's fear reaction) may be weakened by the elimination of such pairing (extinction). Conditioned respondent behavior may also be elicited by stimuli that physically resemble conditioned stimuli (generalization). The acquisition of a stimulus function by generalization may be "corrected" by differential reinforcement, or discrimination training, that is, by reinforcing responses to the training stimulus and not reinforcing responses to all other stimuli.

Operant interactions are acquired and maintained by contingent stimuli having primary (e.g., food when deprived of food) or acquired (e.g., money) positive reinforcing functions and by the removal of stimuli having primary or acquired negative reinforcing functions. They are weakened by contingent neutral reinforcing functions (extinction) and by contingent primary or acquired aversive stimulus functions.

The strength of operant interactions, measured in terms of their frequency of occurrence, is affected by such conditions as time that elapses between the response and the contingency, the number of reinforcements previously received, and the schedule of reinforcement (the proportion of reinforced to nonreinforced responses).

Discriminative stimuli, or antecedent controlling stimuli, acquire their functions from pairings with operant reinforcement. Like stimuli in respondent interactions, they can also acquire their functions through generalization, which in turn can be virtually eliminated by differential reinforcement.

Respondent and operant interactions are influenced by the context in which they occur (setting events) and are modified when stimuli with opposing functions are simultaneously involved (conflict). In everyday life, respondent and operant processes occur in various combinations with each other. Take, for example, a child waking early on Christmas morning, running to the Christmas tree, and discovering the bicycle he has long yearned for. The running and the discovery of the bike are operant interactions. The sight of the bike itself may cause him to break out in "goose pimples," flush, or breathe faster, in short, to be "thrilled." These are respondent reactions, elicited by the sudden availability of a powerful positive reinforcer.

Application to the Universal Stage of Infancy

The concepts and principles of the theory were first applied to an analysis of development during the universal stage of infancy (Bijou & Baer, 1965). This period is characterized by extreme physiological immaturity, reflex (respondent) behavior, and the transition from random movements to biologically coordinated responses that are followed by ecological interactions (i.e., exploration).

As a preface to the analysis of development during infancy, we sketched growth from conception to birth to show the continuity of prenatal and postnatal development. We also surveyed the psychological equipment of the neonate and concluded that the neonate is a biological organism having individual anatomical and physiological characteristics that are shaped from the moment of fertilization by the interaction of heredity (genotype) and the organic-physical conditions and events. The neonate possesses only individual biological characteristics; he or she cannot be said to have a personality, fixed innate intelligence, innate psychic drives, consciousness, or an innate morality, that is, he or she is neither morally good nor bad.

The evolution of manual dexterity, body management, locomotor skills, socialization, perception, and language behavior was analyzed primarily as operant processes in specific settings; the early development of feeling and emotional repertoires were analyzed as combinations of operant and respondent processes.

We concluded our analysis with the statement that although each infant is unique in his or her anatomical structure and physiological functioning, there is considerable similarity in the psychological changes that take place during the universal stage. Throughout most of this period, the infant functions as a biological organism and much of the behavior observed is common to his or her species characteristics. Contacts with the social and physical world are for the most part related to optimizing biological functioning. For most infants, the social and physical settings are fairly homogeneous, not only because of the similarity in limitations imposed by the extreme biological immaturity, but also because of the relatively extensive uniformity in infant-caring practices in a culture.

Application to the Basic Stage of Early Childhood

The concepts and principles of the theory subsequently were applied to an analysis of development during the *basic stage* of early childhood (Bijou, 1976). In this period, extending roughly from two to five years of age, the basic personality structure is laid down. Exploratory behavior, curiosity, and play; cognitive abilities, problem solving, intelligence, and competence; and the roots of moral behavior were selected for analysis because of their prevalence during this period and the potentiality for development in the succeeding period.

Exploratory behavior, or curiosity, was analyzed as interactions between the physical environment, which includes (a) the physical aspects of the social environment, and the organism's own physiology, (b) ecological reinforcers (those generated by exploratory activities), and (c) setting factors. Exploratory interactions result in repertoires that are essential for entering behaviors ("readiness") for subsequent behaviors, such as concept formation, and as a source for developing new reinforcers, such as likes and interests.

Play was considered to be a child's activities when someone, including the child, says he is playing. Such interactions often serve to foster the acquisition of new activities, knowledge, motivation, imaginative activities, and problem-solving skills, or to maintain those already in the repertoire.

The analysis of cognitive, or knowing, behavior included knowing how to do things (abilities), knowing about things (knowledge), and problem-solving skills. In all three classes of interactions, the responses involve sequences of attending, perceiving, and consummatory, or terminal behaviors, which may or may not have a direct effect on the environment. Intelligence in the normative, psychometric sense was analyzed as performance on a sample of cognitive tasks selected on the basis of their correlation with school achievement. A child's score on an intelligence test is an indication of aptitude for school work, compared with similar children, and is a function of his or her interactional history. Measures on such norm referenced tests provide information for the selection and classification of school children. Competence was also viewed as performance on samples of cognitive tasks although the factors were selected on the basis of their relevancy to practical activities in the culture at large. Scores on such tests, known as criterion referenced tests, are the basis for established starting points for teaching and training programs.

Finally, initial moral behavior was analyzed as the behavior the child must learn so as to comply with the family's moral code. Such behavior is gradually acquired through both incidental learning and deliberate instruction.

Discussed as well were two areas of the application of behavior analysis: the clinical treatment of child behavior problems and preschool education. The treatment approach stressed two basic facts: Every problem has its own unique history, and the treatment program should be individually tailored to the specific problem behavior. The application of behavioral principles to preschool education was oriented to helping parents, teachers, and school administrators determine the overall preschool goals, and to assisting teachers not only to translate these goals into specific objectives but to employ empirically based learning procedures for carrying out the objectives.

Revision of the Theory

In 1978, we made four revisions of the theory (Bijou & Baer, 1978). The first pertained to the unit of analysis. Originally, we stated that the unit was behavior in a linear relationship to past and present stimuli. It was changed to: a unit is an interactional situation, or behavior segment, consisting of a stimulus and response function in a symbiotic relationship with each other, and a setting factor. To elaborate: a stimulus function is the meaning of a stimulus to an individual as a consequence of previous contacts with the object or event, that is, his or her interactional history. As a child interacts more and more with objects and events in different settings, he or she acquires an increasing number of stimulus and response functions. For a crawling child, a chair is an object to avoid; for a child learning to stand upright, it is an object with which to pull oneself up; for a child with locomotor skills, it is an object to sit at a table; for an agile child, it is an object to stand on to reach the proverbial cookie jar; etc. The particular stimulus and response function in effect in a given future situation depends on the degree of similarity between its setting and the setting in which the stimulus and response functions were acquired. Thus, the concept of stimulus and response functions brings the effects of a person's interactional history into the analysis of the current situation without resorting to hypothetical mental processes.

The second revision was a change in the definition of a setting event from "... a stimulus-response interaction, which, simply because it has recurred, will affect other stimulus-response relationships that follow it" (Bijou & Baer, 1961, p. 2) to "a condition that influences an interactional sequence by altering the strengths and characteristics of a particular stimulus and response function involved in an interaction" (Bijou & Baer, 1978, p. 26). As indicated in the discussion of stimulus and response functions above, the setting factor may be said to "select" the stimulus and response function that is appropriate for a set of circumstances.

The third was a redefinition of emotional and affective interactions. Although both had been defined as patterns of respondent and operant responses, they were separated in the revision. An emotional interaction was redefined as "... a momentary cessation of behavior on the occasion of a sudden change in the environment" (ibid., p. 108), as when one is driving a car along a city street when suddenly a child on skates darts in front of the right side of the car. The previous smooth car driving behavior becomes momentarily but completely disorganized. This is the emotional interaction. It is followed by two phases. The first consists of a rapid recovery from the totally disrupted condition and is marked by a new stimulus function which calls forth a response function involving applying the brakes and turning the steering wheel sharply to the left thereby avoiding the child. The second phase involves the onset of violent organic and visceral activities, such as a rapid increase in heart rate, breaking out in a sweat, dryness of the mouth, trembling of the arms and legs, etc. The more violent the physiological reflex actions, the longer they persist. During the period of their persistence, they function collectively as a setting condition for this phase. The driver may be distracted for a while and think or say repeatedly, "I was sure lucky to have missed that kid!"

An affective interaction was redefined as one with a feeling component (bodily response) to a variety of circumstances, such as nonreinforcement (frustration, anger, etc.); removal of strong, generalized, social discriminative stimuli (loneliness, grief, etc.); strong, natural or acquired aversive stimulation (anxiety, fear, etc.); natural or acquired powerful positive reinforcing stimuli (joy, happiness, etc.); and certain strong setting events (extreme deprivation of life-sustaining substances, drugs, etc.).

A more thorough analysis of complex interactions including conflict, decision making, biofeedback, problem-solving, thinking, and creative behavior comprised the fourth change. For example, creative behavior was viewed as a class of problem-solving interactions with unusual or original solutions. It is a reaction to a problematic situation that the individual cannot resolve because he or she lacks the repertoires necessary to cope with the prevailing conditions. Designating a solution as unusual depends on its rare occurrence in a group, as in normative and actuarial accounts; or with reference to its initial occurrence in the history of a particular person in a single problem-solving setting; or with reference to all previous problem-solving settings. This analysis has been the basis for research on creativity in the painting and block-building activities of preschool children (see Goetz, 1982; Goetz & Baer, 1971; Goetz & Salmonson, 1972).

Added to the newer version was a brief discussion of basic and applied research which conclude that the main difference between the two was merely the objective of the study. In basic research, the aim is to see what happens when certain conditions are arranged or rearranged; in applied research, it is to see whether the results of arranging or rearranging conditions provide an answer to a socially significant problem.

Further Clarifications

Unfortunately, both the initial theory and its revision have been persistently misunderstood or misrepresented on several counts (Bijou, 1979; 1984a). Among the most frequently encountered is the criticism that the theory is a learning theory and as such it is too simplistic to account for complex behavior, particularly language (e.g., Lerner, 1976; White, 1970). While it is true that this perspective evolved from a learning theory, it has matured into a self-sufficient *system of psychology* having an articulate philosophy of science, a characteristic research methodology, a set of empirical concepts and principles, and an explicit procedure for interrelating basic and applied research (Keller, 1973; Michael, 1985; Reese, 1982). Furthermore, it has in fact been applied to an analysis of complex behavior, including language. For reference one has only to look at Skinner's treatment of complex social behavior (1953), his extension of operant principles to verbal behavior (1957), educational processes (1968), and rule-governed behavior (1969), and to Kantor and Smith's treatment of every conceivable form of behavior in psychology (1975).

That the approach does not deal with the causes of behavior is another erroneous impression. This criticism is based on the assumption that explanations in psychology must either be couched in hypothetical terms, such as cognitive structures and processes, which occur in an unspecified realm such as the mental life, or that they must involve presumed physiological (primary brain and neurological) processes. The latter, which attempt to explain the phenomena of one science in terms of the principles of a "lower" science, are referred to in philosophy as *reductionistic*. The behavior analysis position is that statements of *general functional relationships* among all the variables in a situation are derived from observation of actual interactions (i.e., empirical laws) provide adequate explanation, a view consistent with life-span developmental psychology (Reese, 1982).

Still another misunderstanding is that in this formulation an individual is passive, responding only when stimulated. Whereas this criticism is pertinent to J. B. Watson's early view of the individual (Watson, 1913), it is in no way applicable to contemporary behaviorism, which regards the individual as *always* being in an interactive relationship with the environment. In other words, the individual is described in behavioral psychology as *adjustive*, not reactive, as in biology. But to conceptualize an individual as being active does not imply that internal events such as thoughts, feelings, and ideas are among the determiners of behavior (see Morris, 1988). It presumes that they are implicit interactions that are a function of past interaction and the current situation. Some implicit interactions mediate overt behavior, such as carrying out a well-thought-through plan; some combine with explicit behavior, as in problem solving; and some have no effect on the immediate external situation, as in the acquisition of a new orientation to a situation (knowledge). Furthermore, according to this model, the environment is not the sole cause of behavior. An adequate explanation of a psychological event requires a description of all the factors in an interactional unit in terms of general functional relationships (Kantor, 1959).

Yet another misconception is that the application of behavior concepts and principles to child rearing practices, early education, and child therapy may have harmful effects on a child's mental development, and even may mislead practitioners into believing that their procedures, as they view them, are based on scientific findings (e.g., Farnham-Diggory, 1981; Katz, 1972). That this is true can hardly be disputed, but critics making this claim overlook the fact that the practical application of *any* scientific finding may have a detrimental rather than a beneficial effect when the practitioner is ill-informed, misunderstands, or misinterprets the concepts and principles being applied (Reese, 1982). Applied behavior analysis has no monopoly on such problems. Fortunately, criticisms of this sort do serve to remind us that there are few if any standards for evaluating the various approaches to child rearing practices, early education, and child therapy; that practitioners should be trained more adequately; that more rigorous procedures for screening potential practitioners should be initiated; and that so-cial, legal, and ethical safeguards against inferior and unethical practices should be legislated (see Kazdin, 1981b; Reese, 1982).

II. CURRENT STATUS

In this section, we shall comment further on the philosophy of science of the ap-proach, provide further details about the unit of analysis, extend the list of developmental processes, refine and characterize the stages of development, comment on advances in applied research, and outline the advantages of a be-havior analysis of human development.

Philosophy of Science

Earlier we stated that the philosophy of science of this approach is a combina-tion of radical behaviorism and interbehaviorism (see Morris, Higgins, & Bickel, 1982). If we were to list all the assumptions that constitute this philosophy, we would find that taken together they by no means fit neatly into any one of the world hypotheses described by Pepper (1942), namely, formalism, mechanism, contextualism, and organicism. If, however, we were forced to characterize the theory according to Pepper's categories, we would probably say that it is a com-bination of mechanism and contextualism. This conclusion is based on the fact that behavior analysis involves the analysis and synthesis of interactions, and represents historical events in current activities under specific setting conditions.

Analysis of events takes the form of segmenting (a) the stream of a person's life-history interactions into episodes, (b) the functional environment into specific stimuli and setting conditions, and (c) psychological behavior into response systems with the related physiological components and the subinterac-tions. Synthesis of events takes the form of conceptualizing (a) all the variables existing in a unified field of conditions free of local determiners (i.e., all condi-tions contribute to change in a situation), (b) stimuli as organizations of elements, and (c) psychological behavior as the action of the whole individual. Finally, past interactions are represented as interrelated stimulus and response functions in the current situation.

Pepper's categories of world hypotheses aside, the philosophy of science of this approach is best described as one which assumes that "all psychological events consist of interactions of organisms and stimulus objects which evolve during the lifetime of individuals as they proceed on the biological curve from a point near birth and which ends at death. The behavior performed and observed constitutes adjustments or interactions to ambient things and conditions" (Kantor, 1977, p. xiv).

Unit of Analysis

In the 1978 version of our theory, we described the unit of analysis as consisting of the behavior of a child as a response function in reciprocal interaction with a stimulus function in a particular setting (Bijou & Baer, 1978). To refine this formulation we now add two other components: media of contact, and reaction systems (Kantor, 1959).

The *media of contact* is not a specific stimulus or setting event but a condition that enables an individual to interact with stimulus objects. Included here are light, air waves, and gaseous particles when stimulating objects are at a distance; chemicals for taste interactions; and physical contact for pain, pressure, pinching, etc. Like a setting condition, variations in the medium of contact affect the relationship between stimulus and response functions, and consequently, the final outcome of an interaction.

The *reaction systems* of an interaction refer to the detailed composition of a psychological response function. Although the individual responds as a unified entity, his or her reactions can be abstracted into the physiological components involved, such as the motoric aspect, neural aspect, glandular factors, and action of the receptors and effectors, as well as the psychological subinteractions, such as attending, perceiving, meaning, cognizing, and consummating responses. Not all units of analysis include all of the above psychological sub-interactions, as will be shown in the descriptions of categories below.

Categories of Units of Analysis

Units of analysis are classified as effective, affective, cognitive, or linguistic, depending on the consummatory, or final reaction system (Bijou, 1984b). An *effective* unit terminates in a response that has a direct effect on the object or event interacted with (e.g., removing a cloth to see the covered object). For the most part, it involves operant conditioning processes (Bijou & Baer, 1978; Catania, 1979; Michael, 1985; Skinner, 1953). As our analyses of development during infancy and early childhood show, effective interactions are dominant in the initial development of a child's psychological equipment.

An *affective*, or feeling, unit is one that terminates in some bodily functioning (mostly glandular) and is sometimes accompanied by a general response pattern (e.g., a sulking reaction to a low grade on an examination) (Kantor, 1966). It functions in the mode of respondent conditioning (Bijou & Baer, 1978; Catania, 1979; Skinner, 1953) and carries a wide range of positive and negative feeling labels (e.g., anger, grief, fear, pleasure, and joy). Ordinarily an affective interaction *does not* directly modify the object or event with which it interacts.

Excluded from the category of affective interactions are emotional, turbulent, and chaotic behaviors resulting from a sudden and threatening change in the environment. "For a brief time period the individual does not act as a psychological organism but reverts to a stage of uncoordinated biological action including the performance of numerous visceral and skeletal muscle reflexes as well as vocal action of no adjustmental significance" (Kantor, 1966, p. 403). Thus, there is a clear separation between feeling and emotional reactions.

A *cognitive*, or knowing, unit terminates for the most part in an orienting *implicit* response. Like an affective interaction, it does not generally modify the object or event interacted with (Skinner, 1974). In complexity these units range from simple cognizing interactions (reactions to the elementary properties of things) to understanding (describing the development, operation, and future changes in some event or phenomenon) (Kantor & Smith, 1975). In our approach, terms frequently included in the cognitive category, viz., thinking and learning (see Lipsitt & Reese, 1979), are treated as processes and are analyzed separately.

A *linguistic* unit consists of two types of interaction—referential and symbolizing (Kantor, 1977). In a *referential* unit, a person's linguistic response ("This is a handy gadget") interacts with two stimulus functions, one inherent in the listener (e.g., a peer), the other in the thing or event referred to (e.g., a pen knife). A referential interaction can be either narrative or mediative. It is narrative if the listener's response is referential, as when the listener in a conversation says to the friend who is admiring the pen knife, "I always carry a pen knife." It is a mediative if the listener performs a nonlinguistic act, such as handing the speaker the knife he has asked for. On those occasions when someone talks to himself or herself that person at that time is both the speaker and the listener.

A *symbolizing* unit, on the other hand, involves a response to a *substitute stimulus function*, or a symbol, such as a mark on a calendar, a road directional sign, or an object of nature. In a simple symbolizing interaction, the terminal response is usually an implicit orienting reaction; (e.g., noticing a sign indicating that the speed limit is 35 miles an hour). In a complex symbolizing interaction, it is an implicit orienting response to a symbol, followed by an interaction with the object or situation symbolized (e.g., understanding the meaning of a stop sign, then stepping on the brake to stop at the designated intersection).

Although all four classes of interactions intermingle in all possible combinations in everyday behaviors, we can nonetheless as a rule identify the dominant interaction and observe in what way or ways the others are interrelated.

Developmental Processes

The initial formation of behavior and its subsequent integration and elaboration comes about through a variety of processes. In our treatment of infancy and early childhood (Bijou & Baer, 1965; Bijou, 1976), we emphasized the role of operant and respondent processes. Here, other processes will also be reviewed, albeit briefly, namely, unlearned behavior or capacities, habituation and facilitation (sensitization), and intellectual fatigue.

Among unlearned processes we include simple reflex behavior, capacity for certain reflexes to be conditioned to neutral stimuli and for certain types of stimulation to increase the frequency of the behavior they follow, and complex released behavior. Of those named, the only one that requires some discussion is complex released behavior, a phenomenon observed in nonhuman species. "It is an empirical matter in each case whether these kinds of behavior are built-in response patterns triggered by specific though complex stimuli or the effect of special kinds of reinforcement that develop and maintain the specific form of behavior" (Michael, 1985, p. 102).

There are serious doubts about the existence of released behavior in the human species. Perhaps what resembles this behavior most is "primitive" imitation in the young infant (Meltzoff & Moore, 1983). Here the stimulation is a limited number of facial expressions presented to the child under appropriate conditions and the response is a rough approximation of the stimulus pattern.

The processes of habituation and facilitation, apparent throughout the life span, receive most attention when learning is studied in contrived settings. Habituation connotes a decrement in responding with repeated stimulation, particularly with the startle and orienting reactions in respondent behavior. So that if we, for example, repeatedly elicit a startle response in a newborn by clapping our hands every ten seconds, eventually that response will dissipate. Facilitation, or sensitization, refers to the opposite effect, that is "to an increase in the eliciting effect of one stimulus as the result of presentation of some other stimulus; one stimulus amplifies the eliciting effect of another stimulus (for example, a flash of light may make it more likely that a later sound noise will produce a startle reaction)" (Catania, 1979, p. 53).

Intellectual fatigue refers to loss in efficiency after prolonged concentration on reading, thinking, and problem solving tasks, most of which can usually be restored to the previous level of performance by a change of activity.

Noteworthy is the fact that modeling, observational learning, and imitation (but not "primitive" imitation, mentioned under unlearned processes) are not considered to be separate processes. They are a class of operant interactions in which there is a similarity in the topography of the stimulus and response functions.

Research Methodology and Empirical Laws

One critical feature of a behavior analysis of human development is that it is a *psychology of the individual*, like Lewin's (1954) and others, rather than a psychology of groups. Yet we must hasten to add that it differs from other individual psychologies in that its focus is entirely on the behavior of an *individual in symbiotic relationships* with the environment. Being a psychology of the individual, its research methods use single subject designs, or within-subject comparisons in order to derive concepts and principles pertaining to individuals as they interact with objects and events (see Sidman, 1960).

In research with humans in laboratory, semi-laboratory, and natural settings, diverse measures have been employed. The most frequently used parameter in early studies was rate of responding, an influence stemming from laboratory research with nonhumans. Later investigators, particularly those dealing with linguistic, social, cognitive, and intellectual problems, utilized additional measures, namely, duration (e.g., length of utterance), latency (e.g., time between the utterance of a speaker and the response of the listener), and magnitude (e.g., loudness of a request).

Typically, single subject designs, which have proliferated during the past decade (Kratochwill, 1978; Tawney & Gast, 1984), yield data that are analyzed and presented in terms of simple descriptive statistics or visual inspection. Inferential statistics have been found wanting for at least two reasons (Michael, 1985; Poling & Fugua, 1986). First, few inferential statistical techniques exist that are appropriate for single subject designs. Second, and even more important, is the fact that this type of behavioral research is designed to demonstrate functional relationships, not to test theories. The generalized functional relationships derived from single subject research constitute the empirical laws of the behavioral approach.

Stages of Development

While the foundational, basic, and societal stages of personality development have been a serviceable scheme for analyzing changes in behavior during a child's early years, they need to be revised to deal with development throughout the life span.

The reader should be reminded that these stages are *empirical*, that is, the beginning and end points are based on mixed criteria, some from an individual's biological status and some from human circumstances (Bijou, 1984b; Lipsitt,

1967). They are simply analytical tools meant to help investigators to deal with
long and intricate interactions. Thus they differ with the concept of stages in
other developmental theories such as those by Erikson (1950), Freud (1949), and
Piaget (1970) which have attributed to them explanatory or causal properties. In
these approaches, behavior is often "explained" on the basis of the child's stage
of development. For example, a child's aggression toward his father may be attributed to his or her oedipal psychosexual stage of development.

Foundational Stage

Analysis of interactions in the foundational stage, previously referred to as the
universal stage (Bijou & Baer, 1965), requires changes in four respects. First is
the treatment of ecological behavior (Bijou, 1980). Heretofore, it has been discussed as part of the basic stage (Bijou, 1976), but because it closely follows the
development of basic biological coordination skills such as manual dexterity,
body balance, and locomotion, it should rightly be included in the analysis of the
foundational stage. Second, the development of language behavior should be
edited so that it begins initially with nonlanguage interchanges (communication)
between the infant and the mother (Clark, 1978). In addition, the development of
referential language and symbolizing behavior should be treated separately because they involve different processes, as noted in the description of the linguistic unit of analysis above (also see Bijou, in press). Third, initial socialization
should be updated to take into account more of the details as to how affectionate
attachments are acquired and maintained (see Schaffer, 1984). And finally, discussion of the foundational stage should include a summary of the literature on
child-rearing practices that point out the influence of early stimulation on affec-
tional and linguistic behaviors.

Basic Stage

Instead of treating the basic stage as a single period of development, it should
be divided into three stages—early childhood, middle childhood, and adolescence—in order to describe in more detail the steadily declining influences of
biological immaturity and the equally steadily increasing influences of peer and
community socialization.

Development taking place during these three sub-stages should be described in
terms of longitudinal changes in play and recreational behavior, linguistic skills,
basic preacademic and academic skills, repertoires of knowledge, and moral behavior. A summary of the literature dealing with the treatment of child and
adolescent behavior problems, and programs for parent training and remedial
education are likewise essential.

Societal Stage

The societal stage is also too gross for adequate analysis. It should be sub-divided into three periods: adulthood, middle age, and old age. Adulthood and middle age, both essentially free of biological immaturity and almost completely dominated by community influences, need differential treatment only in terms of the differences in developmental tasks in the two stages of life. For example, the preparation for vocational adjustment and the "settling in" of vocational oc-cupation. Analyses of the progressions during these epochs, which are continua-tions of the developments in adolescence, include recreational behavior, family socialization, vocational adjustment, with emphasis on increases in repertoires of knowledge, and the development of specialized vocabularies associated with vocational occupation and recreational activities.

In addition to such a longitudinal analysis, there should be a cross-sectional analysis of young-adult and middle-aged persons on the basis of "life-style," that is, according to their departure or adherence to cultural norms, for example, the idiosyncratic or eccentric personality, or the culturally bound personality with thoughts, manners, and beliefs that adhere closely to those of the community.

Old age, which is characterized by biological and psychological deterioration, should be analyzed in terms of the variations in progression from middle age and the conditions that promote new dependencies on one hand, and compensatory behaviors on the other.

Applied Human Development

Its clear impact on applied research and practical application is a distinctive hallmark of behavior analysis (see Kazdin, 1979; 1981a). During the late 50s and early 60s, its concepts and principles were applied to the everyday problems of nursery school children, the retarded, the severely disturbed (e.g., autistic), and institutionalized clients. Without waiting for a systematic formulation of a be-havior analysis of human development, workers in those fields proceeded full bore to apply the principles derived from many sources, but mostly from inter-pretations of complex behavior in Skinner's *Science and Human Behavior* (1953).

The rapid expansion of applied behavioral research, which led to the founding of the *Journal of Applied Behavior Analysis* in 1968, has been augmented by a formulation of a behavior analysis theory of child development, particularly by psychologists who have made outstanding contributions to both basic and ap-plied problems. Among the more prominent are Donald M. Baer, Barbara C. Etzel, Emilio Ribes, Todd R. Risley, and Murray Sidman.

Currently, the extensive behavioral research literature ranges widely over many areas of application: child behavior therapy, classroom management, the design of instructional materials, compensatory preschool education, the treatment of retarded and developmentally disabled children, delinquency, parent training, social skills training, behavioral medicine, management of personal problems of adolescence and old age, training in sports, exercise, and recreational activities, and more (see Lutzker & Martin, 1981).

Advantages of the Approach

We conclude our presentation of a behavior analysis of human development by enumerating its distinct advantages:

1. It treats the study of human development as a branch of general psychology viewed as a natural science.
2. It is ontological and compatible with ontogenetic evolution.
3. It is related to human biology without treating physiological processes as causes of psychological behavior, that is, without being reductionistic.
4. It is related to the sciences (physical and cultural anthropology) that are concerned with the origin and nature of things and events that make up the social environment of development.
5. It is systematic. A consistency prevails in the way the subject matter is defined and investigated, and in the way its concepts and laws are derived from data.

III. ISSUES AND PROBLEMS

At the heart of the issues and problems of a behavior analysis of human development are the divergent conceptions of behaviorism. Behavioral psychologists believe that their approach is a movement that has been and continues to be a program that has helped psychology move toward becoming a natural science. Nonbehavioral psychologists, on the other hand, believe behaviorism to be a fad that will be replaced by cognitive psychology (see Baars, 1986). These conflicting views are probably founded on different conceptions of psychology as a science. I have selected for discussion only two issues and problems stemming from these differences: the treatment of unobservable interactions, or mental processes, and the mixture of data sources for the construction of concepts and principles.

Treatment of Unobservable Interactions

Underlying this issue is the question as to whether behavioral psychologists can deal with unobservable interactions. Nonbehavioral psychologists usually deal with unobservables by creating—on the basis of various kinds of data—hypothetical mental structures and processes (e.g., cognitive maps and information processing) or fictitious physiological activities (e.g., explaining perception in terms of neural and brain activities). Behavioral psychologists, in contrast, treat unobservable interactions primarily in two ways: (a) by recognizing the existence of mental processes but conceding that the behavioral approach is unable to deal with them (the position taken by the founder of behaviorism, J. B. Watson (1913), and (b) by treating mental processes as they would any other event in a natural science. The latter is the view held by both radical behaviorists and interbehaviorists. Skinner (1953) refers to mental processes as private events and Kantor (1959; Kantor & Smith, 1975), as implicit interactions.

Inasmuch as these contemporary behavioral treatments of unobservables seem not to be too widely known, some elaboration is in order. In analyzing an unobservable event, we make several assumptions. The first is that an implicit response is always related to a substitute stimulus function. One does not imagine a horrible war scene without stimulation from a surrogate stimulus generated directly or indirectly from an external environment. The second is that an implicit interaction may be independent of or subordinate to overt or effective behavior. Daydreaming and reminiscing activities that do not lead to practical consequences are examples of independent implicit interactions; a civil engineer's planning phase for the construction of a bridge is an example of a subordinate implicit interaction. The third assumption is that all implicit interactions originate in contacts with objects and events. In a novel, characters are created from combinations of living, and sometimes historical, models. And finally, implicit interactions take many forms. One form, for example, is the revived interaction in which a person relives an extraordinary or a traumatic experience. Another form is the anticipatory interaction in which a person responds implicitly to a future imagined event, such as an interview for a job. In general, the analysis of an unobservable interaction involves a thorough review of a person's past and present interactions and his or her behavioral equipment, and drawing inferences about the nature of the interaction and its relationship to other interactions.

Mixture of Bases for Concepts and Principles

It is difficult, if not impossible, to arrive at a unified natural science of psychology with concepts and principles that have been derived from a variety of data sources (Bijou, 1968). The concept and principles applied to development during infancy and early childhood are generally those based on a *functional analysis of individuals* whereas those describing development at the later stages are for the most part derived from *correlational analyses* or the performance of groups. Another example is the mixture of data sources for terms like intelligence and abilities. The meaning of an IQ is based on its relationship to other scores in the distribution of the standardization population. Yet it is often used to describe an individual's intellectual competence and even to predict his or her future employment. Perhaps developmental psychologists should work toward establishing two bodies of knowledge, one based on concepts and principles derived entirely from research on the behavior of individuals, the other on the behavior of groups—a developmental sociology.

IV. FUTURE DIRECTIONS

Future projections of any approach to the study of human development are undoubtedly a combination of extrapolation of current trends and the writer's optimistic hopes for greater productive activities in relatively dormant areas. From the behavioral perspective, three directions are imperative: (1) More studies of the full range of psychological events at all stages of development, (2) greater focus on research on language development and performance, and (3) more descriptive studies conducted in natural settings.

More Studies on the Full Range of Events

To date, research by behavioral psychologists has not generated a substantial number of studies dealing with complex interactions such as thinking, reasoning, and creative behavior. There have nonetheless been some analyses and investigations of complex interactions, including problem solving (e.g., Parsons & Ferraro, 1977; Skinner, 1969) and creative play (Goetz, 1982). Perhaps the assumption held by Skinner (1947) and others during the past 40 years or so, that a general theory of behavior will evolve most expeditiously when research progresses from simple to more and more complex problems has discouraged many behaviorists from working on complex interactions. Still some behavioral psychologists have advocated the study of all kinds of events at all levels of development (see Baer, 1973; Kantor, 1970), contending that behavioral psychologists are not only well equipped to study the full range of psychological events, but that their contributions are sorely needed to advance the field as a whole.

Greater Focus on Language Research

A greater interest in research on language behavior and development has been evidenced during the past decade by the increasing number of presentations at national conventions, the larger number of articles in journals, and the founding of a journal specializing in the behavior analysis of language, *The Analysis of Verbal Behavior*. It is our hope that the trend toward more research activity on language will continue at an accelerated rate. A better understanding of the differences between language products (such as words and sentences) and actual language interactions (speech), and the interrelationships between language interactions and effective, affective, and cognitive interactions is vital to the advancement of developmental psychology.

We hope that future researchers will, of course, continue to focus on the operant analysis of verbal behavior (Skinner, 1957) but will also devote attention to other behavioral formulations, for example, psychological linguistics (Kantor, 1977). For beginnings in the latter direction see Bijou, Chao, and Ghezzi (1988), Bijou, Umbreit, Ghezzi, and Chao (1986), Parrott (1984), and Parrott (1985).

More Descriptive Studies in Natural Settings

From time to time behaviorists plead for more research in natural settings. While this appeal seems to be appreciated, it nevertheless fails to induce much action. Notably sparse are publications describing interactions as they actually occur in the home, school, community, workplace, and institutions. Apparently the experimental laboratory history of behavior analysts is so strong that they find it difficult to engage in research other than that designed to demonstrate functional relationships through systematic manipulation of conditions.

Calls for more descriptive research in natural settings have usually been supported by the argument that many classes of human development, such as language behavior, moral behavior, and affectionate relationships cannot be fully understood without knowledge about the relevant conditions and events as they occur in natural surroundings. The feasibility of this type of research is well demonstrated by Hart's research on initial language development at the University of Kansas (Hart & Risley, 1984). Selecting children from 46 families varying in socioeconomic status, race, and family size, Hart observed and recorded longitudinally the relationship between the family's interactional patterns and the child's language progress. Having begun with 7- to 12-month-olds, the investigation will continue until they have reached the age of three.

V. SUMMARY AND CONCLUSION

Set forth in this chapter is an explication of a behavior analysis of human development, covering the history, current status, persistent issues and problems, and future directions.

The first version of the formulation appeared in 1961 with the title, "A Systematic and Empirical Theory of Child Development." Based on a combination of radical behaviorism (Skinner) and interbehaviorism (Kantor), it presented child development from a natural science perspective. Among the assumptions advanced were: (1) The subject matter of behavioral psychology is the interaction between an individual and environmental events. (2) The unit of analysis is behavior in a functional relationship to stimuli. (3) Psychological development consists of progressions in interactions between a biologically maturing person and changes in the environment, which is primarily social. (4) The behavior of the individual is analyzable in terms of operant and respondent processes. (5) The flow of development can be segmented into three stages: universal, basic, and societal.

In 1965, the theory was applied to development during the universal stage of infancy, focusing on manual and locomotor skills, initial socialization, perception, language, and emotional behavior. Somewhat later, in 1976, it was applied to development during the basic stage of early childhood, which includes children ages two to five years. Exploratory behavior, cognitive abilities, intelligence, moral behavior, nursery school education, and the treatment of behavior problems were the focuses of analysis.

The theory was revised in 1978. Major modifications included changing the unit of analysis to the reciprocal interaction between stimulus and response functions under a setting condition; redefining a setting condition to mean one that influences stimulus and response functions; separating and redefining emotional and affective interactions; and analyzing several complex interactions.

Two papers were published, in 1979 and 1984, that aimed at clarifying recurring misunderstandings of the approach. Explanations dealt with the systematic status of the theory, the concept of causation, the passivity-activity aspect of the individual, the analysis of language and other complex interactions, and the misuse of behavior analysis in practical applications.

Further revisions and extensions since 1978 have brought the theory to its current status. The modifications include: (1) completing the unit of analysis by adding media of contact (e.g., air and sound waves for visual and auditory contacts) and response systems (the physiological participating components and subinteractions, such as attending, perceiving, and cognizing); (2) classifying the units of analysis into effective, affective, cognitive, and linguistic interactions; (3) adding unlearned behavior, capacity for learning, habituation, sensitization, and intellectual fatigue to operant and respondent processes; (4) extending the list of response measures to include latency, magnitude, and duration; and (5) dividing the basic stage into early and middle childhood and adolescence, and the societal stage into adulthood, middle age, and old age.

We also pointed out that the kinship between behavior analysis and applied behavior analysis has, during the past 30 years, led to significant advances in research on an extensive range of practical problems.

Two persistent issues and problems were addressed, one centering on the treatment of unobservable interactions, or mental processes, the other on the confusion created by mixing concepts and principles based on different data sources, that is, from single subject and group design research.

The future progress of the theory depends on more research on the full range of behavior, including language development and performance, and more studies in natural settings.

REFERENCES

Baars, B. J. (1986). The cognitive revolution in psychology. New York: The Guilford Press.

Baer, D. M. (1973). The Control of Developmental process: Why wait? In J. R. Nesselroade & H. W. Reese (Eds.), *Life-span developmental psychology: Methodological issues.* New York: Academic Press.

Bijou, S. W. (1968). Ages, stages, and the naturalization of human development. *American Psychologist, 23,* 419–427.

Bijou, S. W. (1976). *Child development: The basic stage of early childhood.* Englewood Cliffs, NJ: Prentice-Hall.

Bijou, S. W. (1979). Some clarifications on the meaning of a behavior analysis of child development. *The Psychological Record, 29,* 3–13.

Bijou, S. W. (1980). Exploratory behavior in infants and animals: A behavior analysis. *The Psychological Record, 30,* 483–495.

Bijou, S. W. (1984a). Actualization del analisis de conducta del desarrollo infantil. *Revista de Psicologia General Y Applicada, 39,* 21–45.

Bijou, S. W. (1984b). Cross-sectional and longitudinal analysis of development: The interbehavioral perspective. *The Psychological Record, 34,* 525–535.

Bijou, S. W. (in press). Psychological linguistics: Implications for a theory of initial development and research. *Advances in Child Behavior and Development.* New York: Academic Press.

Bijou, S. W. & Baer, D. M. (1961). *Child development: A systematic and empirical theory.* Vol. 1. Englewood Cliffs, NJ: Prentice-Hall.

Bijou, S. W. & Baer, D. M. (1965). *Child development: Universal stage of infancy.* Vol. 2. Englewood Cliffs, NJ: Prentice-Hall.

Bijou, S. W. & Baer, D. M. (1978). *Behavior analysis of child development.* Englewood Cliffs, NJ: Prentice-Hall.

Bijou, S. W., Chao, C. C., & Ghezzi, P. M. (1988). Manual of instructions for analyzing referential language interactions II. *The Psychological Record, 38,* 401–414.

Bijou, S. W., Umbreit, J., Ghezzi, P. M., & Chao, C. C. (1986). Manual of instructions for identifying and analyzing referential interactions. *The Psychological Record, 36,* 491–516.

Catania, A. C. (1979). *Learning.* Englewood Cliffs, NJ: Prentice-Hall.

Clark, R. A. (1978). The transition from action to gesture. In A. Lock (Ed.), *Action, gesture and symbol* (pp. 231–257). New York: Academic Press.

Erickson, E. (1950). *Childhood and society.* (2nd ed.) New York: Norton.

Farnham-Diggory, S. (1981). How do we shape up rigorous behavioral analysts? *Developmental Review, 1,* 58–60.

Freud, S. (1949). *Outline of psychoanalysis.* New York: Norton.

Goetz, E. M. (1982). A review of functional analyses of preschool creative behaviors. *Education and Treatment of Children, 5,* 157–177.

Goetz, E. M. & Baer, D. M. (1971). Descriptive reinforcement of "creative" blockbuilding by young children. In E. A. Ramp & B. L. Hopkins (Eds.), *A new direction for education: Behavior analysis.* Lawrence, KS: University of Kansas Press.

Goetz, E. M. & Salmonson, M. M. (1972). The effect of general and descriptive reinforcement on "creativity" in easel painting. In G. B. Semb (Ed.), *Behavior analysis education*. Lawrence, KS: University of Kansas Press.

Hart, B. & Risley, T. R. (1984, May). The "natural" conditions for learning to talk. Paper presented at the meeting of the Association for Behavior Analysis, Nashville, TN.

Kantor, J. R. (1959). *Interbehavioral psychology*. (2nd rev. ed.) Bloomington, IN: Principia Press.

Kantor, J. R. (1966). Feelings and emotions as scientific events. *The Psychological Record, 16*, 377–404.

Kantor, J. R. (1970). An analysis of the experimental analysis of behavior (TEAB). *Journal of the Experimental Analysis of Behavior, 13*, 101–108.

Kantor, J. R. (1977). *Psychological linguistics*. Chicago: Principia Press.

Kantor, J. R. & Smith, N. W. (1975). *The science of psychology: An interbehavioral survey*. Chicago: Principia Press.

Katz, L. G. (1972). Condition with caution. *Young Children, 27*, 277–280.

Kazdin, A. E. (1979). Advances in child behavior therapy: Applications and implications, *American Psychologist, 34*, 981–987.

Kazdin, A. E. (1981a). Behavior modification in education: Contributions and limitations. *Developmental Review, 1*, 34–37.

Kazdin, A. E. (1981b). Uses and abuses of behavior modification in education: A rejoinder. *Developmental Review, 1*, 61–62.

Keller, F. S. (1973). *The definition of psychology* (2nd ed.). New York: Appleton-Century-Crofts.

Kratochwill, T. R. (1978). *Single subject research: Strategies for evaluating change*. New York: Academic Press.

Lerner, R. M. (1976). *Concepts and theories of human development*. Reading, MA: Addison-Wesley.

Lewin, K. (1954). Behavior and development as a function of the total situation. In L. Carmichael (Ed.), *Manual of child psychology*. (Rev. ed.) (pp. 918–983). New York: Wiley.

Lipsitt, L. P. (1967, April). "Stages" in developmental psychology. Paper presented at the meeting of the Eastern Psychological Association, Boston, MA.

Lipsitt, L. P. & Reese, H. W. (1979). *Child development*. Glenview, IL: Scott, Foresmann and Co.

Lutzker, J. R. & Martin, J. A. (1981). *Behavior change*. Monterey, CA: Brooks/Cole.

Meltzoff, A. N. & Moore, M. K. (1983). Newborn infants imitate adult facial gestures. *Child Development, 20*, 187–192.

Michael, J. L. (1985). Behavior analysis: A radical perspective. In B. L. Hammond (Ed.), *Master lecture series, Volume 4, Psychology of learning* (pp. 99–121). Washington, D.C.: American Psychological Association.

Morris, E. K. (1988). Not so worlds apart: Contextualism, radical behaviorism, and developmental psychology. *The Interbehaviorist, 16*, 8–15.

Morris, E. K., Higgins, S. T., & Bickel, W. K. (1982). The influence of Kantor's interbehavioral psychology on behavior analysis. *The Behavior Analyst, 5*, 159–173.

Parrott, L. J. (1984). Listening and understanding. *The Behavior Analyst, 7*, 29–40.

Parrott, L. J. (1985). Toward a descriptive analysis of verbal interactions. *Experimental Analysis of Human Behavior Bulletin, 3*, 12–15.

Parsons, J. A. & Ferraro, D. P. (1977). Complex interactions: A functional approach. In B. C. Etzel, J. M. Le Blanc & D. M. Baer (Eds.), *New developments in behavioral research: Theory, method and application* (pp. 237–245). Hillsdale, NJ: Erlbaum.

Pepper, S. C. (1942). *World hypothesis*. Berkeley: University of California Press.

Piaget, J. (1970). Piaget's theory. In P. H. Mussen (Ed.), *Carmichael's manual of child psychology*. (3rd ed.), Vol. 2, (pp. 703–732). New York: Wiley.

Poling, A. & Fugua, R. W. (1986). *Research methods in applied behavior analysis*. New York: Plenum.

Reese, H. W. (1982). Behavior analysis and life-span developmental psychology. *Developmental Review, 2*, 150–161.

Schaffer, H. R. (1984). *The child's entry into a social world*. New York: Academic Press.

Sidman, M. (1960). *Tactics of scientific research*. New York: Basic Books.

Skinner, B. F. (1938). *The behavior of organisms.* Englewood Cliffs, NJ: Prentice-Hall.

Skinner, B. F. (1947). Current trends in experimental psychology. In W. Dennis (Ed.), *Current trends in psychology* (pp. 16–49). Pittsburgh: University of Pittsburgh Press.

Skinner, B. F. (1953). *Science and human behavior.* New York: Macmillan.

Skinner, B. F. (1957). *Verbal behavior.* New York: Appleton-Century-Crofts.

Skinner, B. F. (1968). *The technology of teaching.* Englewood Cliffs, NJ: Prentice-Hall.

Skinner, B. F. (1969). *Contingencies of reinforcement: A theoretical analysis.* Englewood Cliffs, NJ: Prentice-Hall.

Skinner, B. F. (1974). *About behaviorism.* New York: Knopf.

Tawney, J. W. & Gast, D. L. (1984). *Single subject research in special education.* Columbus, OH: Charles E. Merrill Publishing.

Watson, J. B. (1913). Psychology as the behaviorist views it. *Psychological Review, 20,* 158–177.

White, S. H. (1970). The learning theory approach. In P. H. Mussen (Ed.), *Carmichael's manual of child psychology* (pp. 657–701). Vol. 1. New York: Wiley.

PIAGETIAN THEORY

Harry Beilin

Jean Piaget died in 1980 at the age of 84 years. Such longevity is not in itself exceptional. What is exceptional is a productive career that began at the age of 14, with his first publication (a note on molluscs), and lasted to the year of his death. His final manuscripts are still in the process of being published. What is equally remarkable is that his theories, which were controversial in the 1920s when they first appeared, remain so in the present and will undoubtedly continue to be for some time. They are controversial first because the theory's assumptions challenge time-honored presuppositions of classical models. The theoretical interpretations Piaget gives to counter-intuitive facts uncovered in his by-now classical experiments, such as the conservation and object permanence studies, have provoked countless attempts at disconfirmation. Last, his methods of inquiry until most recently were the source of much criticism. What has not been controversial are the many clever and seemingly simple experiments devised by the Genevans that have become standard equipment in the developmental psychologist's tool box.

It is an unfortunate feature of the contemporary understanding of Piaget's theory that much of what is written about and commented on in the theory refers

Annals of Child Development, Volume 6, pages 85-131.
Copyright © 1989 by JAI Press Inc.
All rights of reproduction in any form reserved.
ISBN: 0-89232-979-3

to research completed some years back, work typically published prior to 1975. It is unfortunate because the theory developed and elaborated after 1975 in many ways marks a radical departure from the earlier theory.

In this chapter, I propose to do three things. First, to discuss the assumptions that are fundamental to Piaget's theory: those core elements in his research program to which he has been committed from his earliest days, and to those assumptions that have changed from the earlier to the later theory.[1,2] Second, I will briefly detail what might be called Piaget's standard theory, those aspects of the research program developed for the most part before 1975 that delineate and account for the stages in cognitive development. Third, the major part of the chapter, will be devoted to the later or new theory, principally what has appeared since 1975.

PART 1.   CORE ASSUMPTIONS OF PIAGET'S RESEARCH PROGRAM

It is difficult to know where to start in detaining the fundamental tenets of the program, in that they are more than trivially interrelated. It seems appropriate to start with Piaget's biological model, inasmuch as his professional career began as a biologist; his doctoral dissertation was concerned with a biological problem, and it has a central place in the theory.

Mind as a Developmental Process

Piaget's theory rests on two assumptions (he calls them hypotheses). First, cognitive mechanisms are extensions of organic biological regulations from which they are derived. Second, these mechanisms are specialized and differentiated "organs" of such organic regulations, resulting from their interactions with the external world (1971, p. 346).[3] The organic regulations are first manifest in the innately determined reflex and instinctual patterns evident in the processes of perception, conditioning, memory and habit formation. But the acquisition of knowledge goes well beyond inherited capacities shared with other species. Piaget wishes to identify the sources of knowledge and these are said to relate to the nature of knowledge as constructed by the human species. Human cognitive development consequently results in three kinds of knowledge. First, the kind of knowledge linked to hereditary mechanisms, already mentioned; second, physical knowledge derived from experience; and third, logico-mathematical knowledge, the result of the coordination of operations, which for Piaget is the fundamental "regulatory organ" of intelligence (1971, p. 100). Thus, the most sophisticated and rational forms of thought are derived from an innate legacy of organized instinctive and reflex forms of behavior.

It is important for Piaget's theory that the development of cognitive mechanisms proceed from a base of organized or structured forms. He assumes that no form of knowledge, not even knowledge derived from perception, simply registers or is a "copy" of reality; it always entails a process of assimilation into previously existing structure. The significance of assimilation is that it provides the basis of meaning in that all knowledge arrived at by assimilation results in meaning, from the most primitive perceptual signals to conditioned responses, and in the symbolic function basic to the most advanced cognition. Assimilation is also critical in that it entails the assumption that all knowledge is connected with an action. "To know an object or a happening is to make use of it by assimilation into an action schema" (1971, p. 6).[4]

The concept of assimilation is also important in the way it differentiates Piaget's theory from empiricist theories of an associationist or S→R type. Instead of an association assumed between stimulus and response as in conditioning theory, Piaget conceives of associations as a state singled out from a more complex process of assimilation. Thus, the S→R formulation is more appropriately denoted as S→(AS)→R (where AS symbolizes assimilation into a scheme). Piaget's claim that the differentiation of cognitive mechanisms derives from an organic base in the ensuing interactions with the world appears to him to distance his theory as well from nativist accounts of the origins of mind. A further claim of the theory is that the differentiated cognitive mechanisms, particularly those that give rise to logico-mathematical thought, derive from a self-regulating system that provides balance between assimilation and accommodation processes. The latter process is one of modifying (differentiating) internal structures in response to the incorporation of "objects" from the environment, in conditions in which one cannot exist without the other. That is, there is no assimilation to an existing structure without the structure making adjustments (accommodations) to the products of the assimilation. An example from infancy is of the 5- to 6-month-old, who, in seizing objects in both hands shows, first, the existence of an assimilation scheme in the act of seizing the object. By stretching out or bringing in the hands in accord with whether the object is far or near marks the accommodation of the scheme (1971, pp. 8–9).

Distancing his theory from nativism also requires Piaget to reject preformationism. (I will say more about preformationism in the discussion of Piaget's constructivism.) An alternative to preformationism is to conceive of cognitive development as the product of epigenesis. In this Piaget follows Waddington, who describes the development of biological systems as homeorrhetic, to contrast them with (homeostatic) closed systems, such as those in a home thermostat. Homeorrhetic systems, by virtue of self-regulating devices, constantly adjust the ongoing system so as to maintain equilibrium despite tendencies from environmental inputs towards disequilibrium. The regulatory devices thus keep the system on a trajectory within necessary routes or channels (termed "chreodes," by

Waddington). The various channelings and auto-corrections are under the control of a "time-tally" mechanism that acts as a "speed control" for the processes of assimilation and organization. The systems that impel cognitive development are seen by Piaget as analogs to the homeorrhetic character of biological systems and under similar kinds of control as exhibited by the time tally mechanism.

The Stage Assumption

Stages have played a major role in Piaget's model of development, and its source is clearly in its analogy with biological, principally embryological, development. At the same time, he says, "psychologists have relied too much on the notion of stage" (1971, p. 17). In recent years, the stage concept has been played down in the theory and the characterization of stages has undergone some change (Gruber & Voneche, 1977; Vuyk, 1981). In the past, other's stage notions have been criticized, for example, Freud's stages, which he avers has led to "arbitrary" thinking about development. The term is used by Piaget (1971, p. 17) when: (1) a series of developments is constant, independent of speeding up or delays due to experience or the social context; (2) it can be identified by a "whole structure" that defines all the cognitive factors at that stage and not identified solely by a dominant property (as in Freud's and Erikson's stage theories). This feature of Piaget's stage concept, the so-called structure of the whole *(structure d' ensemble)* has been one of the most criticized elements in his theory (see Brainerd, 1978 for a debate on the issues); and (3) where the structures (the *structure d' ensembles)* are constituted by a process of integration in which each structure is prepared for by the preceding one and is integrated into the one that follows. (Piaget's delineation of the stages in cognitive development will be briefly outlined later.)

Controversy over stages well predates Piaget and is not confined to developmental psychology, or to psychology alone for that matter (see Beilin, 1971). Controversy is concerned principally with continuity and discontinuity in development. Piaget was not naive on the issue. According to him development is fundamentally *continuous*. He says, "continuity would depend fundamentally on a question of scale; for a certain scale of measurement, we obtain discontinuity when with a finer scale we should get continuity" (Piaget, 1960, p. 121). The problem for Piaget's theory on this score is in his description of qualitative changes due to successive structurations that appear discontinuous. His claim of qualitative discontinuity appears to contradict his other claim that structures are in fact constituted gradually, i.e., continuously. But the general problem with stages goes even further than the continuity/discontinuity issue. There is the theoretical question as to whether development is domain specific, a widely held current view, or whether it is characterized by unified abstract entities (whole structures) that function across cognitive domains. The related empirical issue is as to whether intercorrelations and convergences of performance across Piagetian tasks in a purported stage are high enough to support the "structured whole" concept. To many, the data, at least in some critical respects, do not. The critical attack on the stage notion which has been widespread and long lasting appears to have affected Piaget's thinking on the matter and Vuyk (1981) reports from her conversations with Piaget that he was "less and less" interested in stages (p. 192). Vuyk, mirroring Piaget's views, says, "thinking in terms of stages, one runs the risk of looking too much for periods of rest or equilibrium, while in fact development is never static. Piaget now considers development a spiral, and though one may call a stage 'a detour of the spiral,' this indicates that periods of equilibrium are relatively unimportant" (1981, p. 192).

For the *structure d' ensembles* (structured whole) concept itself, Inhelder, Piaget's longtime collaborator, is said to hold that it was an "unfortunate expression" that should not be taken literally . . ." (Vuyk, 1981, p. 193). The de-emphasis on stages is accompanied by a shift in Piaget's research program away from the more structured aspects of thought to its more functional and process features. Nonetheless, in recognizing the de-emphasis on stages one should not conclude that the stage description of development disappeared from Piaget's picture of developmental change. Quite the contrary, even among his last works stage and levels analysis forms the framework in which the data of particular developing cognitive systems are described and explained. Thus it would be an error to divorce the stage concept from Piaget's theory. It plays too critical a role in understanding development for it to be displaced. At the least, it points to the need to explain the mechanisms by which stage-like changes occur, and account for the transformation of one stage to the next.

Structure and Function

There is no best way to create a metatheoretical framework for psychological theory, nor for developmental theory. One may distinguish theories as mechanistic or organismic and thereby emphasize particular aspects of their properties, and it is in these terms that developmental theories often have been differentiated. I do not believe this distinction presently serves as well as another. When Titchener introduced the distinction between functionalist and structuralist theories in psychology (Beilin, 1983) it provided a metatheoretical framework for marking the assumptions underlying then current conceptually and empirically driven positions. Developments in theory in the past 30 years have made the functionalist/structuralist distinction even more relevant to an understanding of theoretical debates within the social sciences. The terms of the distinction have changed in meaning since they became popular in Titchener's time, and even now they do not lend themselves to unequivocal definition, but in general they bear on the differences between structural and functional explanation in psychological theory. In the present cognitive era in psychology, structure tends to be identified with mental structure and function with psychological process.

Piaget's theory is a good example of a theory that is both structuralist and functionalist. At various times it has been identified as predominantly one or the other, or as both. Piaget's early theory, up to about the 1940s, was described as functionalist (by no less an authority than Boring). In the era from the 1940s to about 1975 it was structuralist, as Piaget sympathized with the then current wave of structuralist theorizing, in both the social and biological sciences (as evident in Piaget's book *Structuralism* [1970]). From about 1975 to the present there has been a decided shift toward the functionalist elements in the theory. In actuality, Piaget's theory building strategy has combined structural and functional analysis from the start. His method is to begin with a functional analysis of data obtained by his so-called clinical method, either from direct observation of the child's activity or from action elicited by experimenter-designed materials, specific instruction, and open-ended questions. The first (functional) level of analysis typically yields empirical generalizations reported along with details of the experimenter's observations. These functional descriptions that detail how the child functions in specific contexts yield to a structural analysis in which patterns that are observed are mapped onto formal systems, either logical or mathematical that best fit the data. These logico-mathematical, theoretically-generated forms are posited by Piaget to underlie and account for the consistencies in action and thought that cut across domains of activity and constitute the structures of mind of the child. Although Piaget recognizes that these formal models or axiomatic systems are theorist-generated, he believes mental structures have these formal properties so long as they adequately describe, explain, and predict the actions of the child in the course of reasoning and problem solving.

There is thus an intimate relation between mental structures and the manner in which the child functions in either linguistic or action contexts. In essence, the road to the structure of mind is through the way mind functions. Consequently, there is no structure without function, and no function without structure.

Although Piaget's theory is decomposable into functionalist and structuralist elements, they are nevertheless closely associated in a coherent system. The basic functionalist elements are those provided by the biology of the system, which Piaget calls the functional invariants. They are the fundamental processes of assimilation, accommodation and self-regulation and constitute the components of Piaget's theory of equilibration. These processes account for the acquisition of knowledge. They are "invariant" in the sense that they do not change with development and operate in all domains of the organism's experience. They also operate, in accord with cybernetic principles, to maintain equilibrium in the system despite and because of constant change in the organism's mental functioning. Piaget does not list abstraction and reflective abstraction among the functional invariants, but they certainly function as such. These are general functions of mind and are the processes that give rise to the operations and structures of mind.

Constructivism

In almost every work of Piaget's, an effort is made to distance his theory from the two classic sources for the origins of mind, experience in the world and genetically-given predetermined structures, in essence, the empiricist and rationalist accounts. Piaget ignores the fact that there are no purely empiricist or rationalist accounts of the origins of mind. No empiricist holds that the human organism comes into the world without some natively-given equipment that makes the acquisition of knowledge possible, nor are there nativists who hold that experience plays no role in the acquisition of knowledge. In rejecting environmentalism, and copy theories in particular, at one pole and nativist theories at the other, Piaget proposes instead that the child's active engagement with the material and social worlds results in the construction of a conception of reality. This conception is not the consequence of the effects of the environment on the child, even when the child incorporates conventional knowledge from membership in a social community by way, for example, of language. In such cases the child is said to make that knowledge his own by a reconstruction through existing mental structures. Alternatively, Piaget rejects preformationist views in which all possibilities in mental development are predetermined by initial, presumably genetically-given, conditions. Piaget's solution is in his equilibration theory account of how knowledge is constructed. Both natively-given structures and experience have a role but the operations and structures of mind are constructed from the actions of the child on the world. The actions are at first physical, then they become mental by a process of internalization (mental activity is as much "activity" for Piaget as is physical activity). Again, the processes by which these constructions occur are those of abstraction, the source for physical knowledge (for example, some objects become known to be heavier than others) and reflective abstraction, the source of logico-mathematical knowledge (when one object is heavier than a second and the second is heavier than a third, the first is inferred to be [necessarily] heavier than the third).

Empiricist (mostly associationist and behaviorist) theories are also "constructive." They differ from Piaget's constructivism in that they are devoid of holistic assumptions. They tend toward atomism, most are not "active organism" theories (the organism is assumed to be passive), and most tellingly, their acquisition assumptions are devoid of assimilation requirements (no acquisition or learning without appropriate existing structure). Piaget's constructivism is probably the most distinctive and radical feature of his theory, although some aspects of his constructivism are no longer as revolutionary as they once were. Few contemporary developmental or learning theories, for example, conceive of the organism as "passive" in the acquisition of knowledge.

In essence, the development of cognition results from the interaction of a knowing subject and reality i.e., from the action of subject on object. Mental development depends on the subject's activity, on existing and newly composed structures, on a self-regulating mechanism and on the characteristics of the object (the environment, both social and physical).

Activity

Although the constructivist aspect of Piaget's theory is based on the assumption of an active organism, it is important to understand the classic alternatives to the origin of knowledge that Piaget rejects or excludes. He repudiates the traditional empiricist view of the origin of "ideas" in perception and language. Although there are psychologists of perception who hold that visual perception requires activity of the visual system, as in the integration of information from saccadic eye movement (Hochberg, 1972), or unconscious inferencing, the remainder of that community base their views, like those of Gibson (1979) on direct information pick-up from the environment; or, if they reject direct perception, hold to some variant of information-processing theory (Marr, 1982; Ullmann, 1980).

For language, the prevailing view is that thought, at least beyond infancy, is accounted for linguistically rather than the reverse. One problem with the Piagetian view that thought is derived from activity is the difficulty in distinguishing "activity" from any other psychological process. Perception involves activity and so does language (as linguistic or verbal activity). In fact all psychological functioning—by its very definition—entails activity. That does not mean however that all theories of development or change are necessarily constructivist. It does mean however that the construction of knowledge by perception and language cannot be rejected because they are not based on activity, as Piaget holds.

Universals

Piaget has always insisted that what he was interested in was the "nomethetic" aspects of development, the universals or invariants in cognition. He was not interested in individual differences as such, or the nature of conventional knowledge, or the effects of context on the acquisition of knowledge.

The individual for Piaget is a microcosm of the forces and mechanisms operative in the population or species (Piaget, 1971, p. 283), and studying individuals singly or collectively should provide insight into the general laws governing development. Piaget's early descriptions of his own children's cognitive development (Piaget, 1952), that added much to his early reputation, rest on this assumption. They were also the source of much criticism because of the universalist generalizations he was willing to make based on observations of one, two, or three subjects. His later works, carried out on larger samples, nevertheless seek to identify the same universal mechanisms in development.

A critical distinction is made in the theory between the "individual subject" and the "epistemic subject," the latter referring to the "cognitive nucleus which is common to all subjects at the same level" (1970, p. 139). The epistemic subject, who is not a psychological subject in the common understanding of the term, is the object ultimately of Piaget's interest. The universal properties or structures of mind identified with the epistemic subject are the products of the structural analysis in the Piagetian research program.

Development, seen as the differentiation and integration of increasingly abstract structures, is said to exercise a constraining influence over processes of learning. "Learning" for Piaget is not the source of development but under the "control" of developmental processes. Since the child's actions are always only assimilable to existing structure, the form and nature of existing structure acts to constrain the consequences of the child experience. Although it is evident that children approach the world in their actions with different strategies, and the rich protocols that report Piaget's observations attest to this, the early and middle era works tended to ignore or relegate such data to the background. The research of the last period reverses this tactic and new meaning is given to variability and to strategy differences, in essence, to the functional aspects of development. Nonetheless, even with this seeming reversal in research strategy, the goal is the same—to demonstrate how universals emerge from process and function.

In Piaget's view the structures constructed by successive regulations have general application to contexts of diverse content. The *structure d' ensembles* notion embodies this holistic emphasis. When it became clear from both Genevan and non-Genevan research that cognitive acquisitions did not occur across all domains to which a structure should apply (according to the earlier theory, for example, all conservations should have been achieved concurrently by virtue of common underlying structure), the notion of decalage (time lags in acquisition) was introduced. A theoretical account was later added to save the nomethetic character of the theory by suggesting that acquisitions result from the interaction of two types of structure (Inhelder, Sinclair, & Bovet, 1974); general structures (for example, in conservation: the reversibility and identify operations) and domain structures (for example, the knowledge associated with weight, number or length). Although domain characterization would more clearly have to be taken into account as a consequence of this amendment to the theory it hasn't.

The current trend to base developmental theory on domain specificity and away from the structured whole concept, has never been fully embraced by classical Piagetians despite moves to accommodate to notions of functional variation.

Dialectics of Stability and Change

Piaget's theory may be said to be a "dialectic constructivism" (1971, p. 212). The dialectic of the theory reflects the effort to balance the idea of structure with that of "genesis, history and function" (1970, p. 120). It is dialectic in its emphasis on "historical development" (of individual and species), on "the opposition between contraries (assimilation/accommodation, affirmations/negations)," on "synthesis" (the integrative aspects of structure) and on "wholeness" (the totalities that integrate and organize knowledge) (1970, p. 121). Cognitive growth produces forms of increasing complexity, in which the elementary forms are integrated in the more complexly evolved forms. This dialectic in development requires a change from linear or tree models of development to a notion of "spirals" (nonvicious circles) that is more characteristic of the interactions that occur in growth (1970, p. 125). The dialectic within this course of spiral development is inherent in the "uninterrupted process of coordinating and setting in reciprocal relations. It is (this) process which is the true "generator" of structures as constantly under construction and reconstruction. The subject exists because, to put it briefly, the being of structures consists in their coming to be, that is their being, 'under construction' " (1970, pp. 139–140). Thus the structures of mind in Piaget's view are not static entities—*"there is no structure apart from construction, either abstract or genetic"* (italics in original, p. 140). Thus Piaget's genetic epistemology (as he identifies his position) is designed to take into account the forms of knowing and the processes that account for the progressions or transitions from one level or structure to more evolved forms qualitatively different in their properties and functions. Some critics claim that Piaget's theory is "destinational" (Toulmin, 1981) in that it assumes three features of development: (1) it holds to invariant sequences in development; (2) there is a final stage in development; and (3) the final stage is formal operations. On the first assumption, it is true that Piaget claims there is an invariant sequence in the construction of forms and structures. This invariant sequence, however, is not linear but "spiral." To assert "a final stage" is to misunderstand Piaget's dialectic constructivism. There can be no more a final stage in the evolution of mind than there can be in the evolution of the species. The argument seems to be more against Piaget's concept of universal structures of mind, and the characterization of adult thought as having the properties of formal operations. On one sense, it is difficult to see how there cannot be a "final state" in development, as in the adult forms of language to which prior development "leads." This does not exclude development on a horizontal level, so to speak, with increasingly enriched and delineated forms. If development is to be dialectic it would have to be so. But biological and therefore mental development, like evolution, involves constraints on the complexity of evolved structures for a particular species—at a particular time. The notion of a single cause in development leading to adult cognitive structures is also objected to by Toulmin. If alternatively one believes that development proceeds by a succession of local rules or generalizations that derive from each encounter with reality in its various contexts, then development surely never ends and knowledge is more a succession of facts or complexes of facts than the Piagetian idea of generalized structures that cut across domains of knowledge. But the latter is a process that never ends either, except with death. Whether the issue can be resolved solely by empirical evidence is at present unclear. Nevertheless, the issue is being vigorously debated (see for example Levin, 1986).

Holism

In setting out the assumptions of Piaget's theory there is the danger of decomposing the theory in such a way as to miss its integrated quality. Piaget's theory is a synthesis of structuralism and ''geneticism,'' the desire to account for conservation (invariance) as well as transformation in development: the conservation of structures that are able to maintain an identity even as they are transformed. The integrity of the organism as a whole maintains its identity. Inasmuch as any structure is by definition a totality, the totality gives meaning and coherence to each of its constituent parts, even as they may change.

PART 2. THE STANDARD THEORY

The assumptions spelled out in Part One are both inherent in and specified as part of Piaget's theory. They are, however, of a general nature; in part theoretical, in part metatheoretical. The ''meat and potatoes'' of Piaget's developmental theory consists in Piaget's characterization of the Kantian categories of knowledge, space, time, number, causality, etc., their precursors, and how they develop. These are detailed principally within the framework of the stage theory. There is no consistency in the way the stages are demarcated, but their main divisions are set off in three or four main stages, with substages. There are three stages when Piaget chooses to consider concrete operations as a substage of representative intelligence (Piaget, 1983). We will, following more traditional practice, detail four principal stages.

I. *Sensorimotor Intelligence.* This level lasts till about eighteen months to two years, and is divided into two subperiods with six substages. The first subperiod is defined by concentration on the child's own body (till 7 to 9 months); the second subperiod, the objectivization and spatialization of the schemes of practical intelligence.

Sensorimotor development proceeds from substage I (the use of reflexes) (in the first month) to substage VI (at 18 months to 2 years), in which the emergence of the symbolic (or semiotic) function permits of mental representation, and the invention, through mental activity, of functions hitherto only carried out in physical action. It is a period in which objects, play, space, time, and causal relations become known through practical activity, and objects become increasingly differentiated from subjects and from each other. From the point at which the subject/object relation is undifferentiated (substages I and II), the child, in substage III, begins to explore the world, not just perceptually as before this, but in action, largely through the direction and control of arm and hand movements. By virtue of these controls, the child is observed to develop procedures to "make interesting sights last." Events, in which chain rattles and swinging objects, that at first are accidentally activated, are then with intention made to continue in their movements, noises, etc. This substage is particularly important in the development of "intentional cognition" (Flavell, 1963).

Repetition in action plays a major role in sensorimotor development, becoming increasingly refined in the process of exploring objects. Repetition appears in three levels of "circular-reactions" (a term adopted from J. M. Baldwin), which culminate at the third level in varied repetitions that exploit, through exploration, an object's full potentialities. A typical achievement of this level of circular reaction appears in substage V when an object that rests on a support (e.g., a blanket) out of reach is pulled by the child to himself by means of the support. Here is a means-end sequence that is new to the child and results from both exploratory activity (groping) and circular activity that is directed toward a goal. Substage VI marks the advent of representational capacities in the form of symbolic (more generally semiotic representation) that make mental activity possible and the beginning of implicitly carried out actions.

II. *Period of representational thought (1$^1/_2$ – 2 years to 6 years)*. When cognition becomes representational, the expression of the possibilities open to the child to engage the world (of persons, objects and events) increases many fold. The most obvious indicator of the transition is the rapid acquisition of language and concepts (or what Piaget at first preferred to call preconcepts). After his earliest studies of language, Piaget came to consider language as a socially derived conventional system that the child does not construct but merely reconstructs, consequently, language is subsidiary to thought or (nonlinguistic) cognition. It is probably in this light that one must explain the relative neglect at first of this developmental period in Piaget's research, and in which he was inclined to contrast the achievements of the period with the more striking changes that occur at 6 to 7 years with the advent of concrete operations.

The representational period, prior to and paving the way for the period of concrete operations, is typified by the development of one-way mappings, one-way functions or semilogics (each of these terms is used to describe the period).[5] The one-way mappings (or directional functions, as they are referred to in Piaget, 1983), are called "one-way" because they lack mental reversibility, that is, as logical (or semilogical) relations they lack the ability to be reversed, the property of logical operations that appears with concrete operations. Defined mathematically they are represented as $y = f(x)$ (1983, p. 110). As with any developmental period, there are new achievements (the positive) and limitations (the lack of what will appear later) reflected in intellectual distortions of the period. In the functional period, this is manifest in the achievements of the concept of "order," but it also is the source of error. For example, in length comparisons "longer" is understood as "going farther"; in conservation of liquid quantity it is evident in the centration on single dimensions, as in taking only the level of the liquid into account and not the dimensions of the container (the condition known as nonconservation).

Functions represent dependencies, y is a function of (or depends upon) x, and not a simple relation as would be entailed in a comparison, as in "x in relation to y" (e.g., "longer than"). Thus in an experiment with weights attached to a vertically hanging string riding over a fixed pulley and going horizontally to a spring, attached to a wall, the string will be pulled down (and the spring extended) as a function of the weight on the string. Children in the range of 4 to 5 years do not understand that there is a reciprocal relation between the length of the string from below the pulley (vertical) and that of the string beyond the pulley. That is, as one segment of string increases, the other decreases. They do understand, however, that when the weight increases the string will go down.

Piaget refers to the early functions of this period as *constitutive functions*. These prepare the way for *constituted functions*, which play a role in (two-way) operations and in understanding causality. The constitutive functions are said to arise out of and are expression of the dependencies inherent in schemes of action. They are essentially qualitative (and ordinal, that is, only ordered one-way), and devoid of quantification, except for establishing equalities by correspondence.

Another feature of the preoperatory period defined by one-way functions is the child's ability to deal with correspondences (Piaget, 1979). Piaget's treatment of correspondences is theoretically significant because it represents a major change in one of the theory's assumptions. Earlier, Piaget maintained that "to know is to transform," or more precisely to discover or construct the invariances that exist despite transformations in objects, events and properties. A correspondence, however, is not a transformation. Correspondences are arrived at by a process of comparison without modifying the states that are compared. Comparisons, Piaget discovers, are at all levels of development. At the sensorimotor level, assimilations to schemes of actions are correspondences, as in the case of the infant in the crib who accidentally hits a suspended rattle and makes it swing. In repeating the action with other objects the infant indicates that it has made a comparison between the new situation and the original and established a correspondence between them. At the representative level there are correspondences whenever generalization occurs such that new elements are responded to as to those already known. All operations entail correspondences as well. In development, correspondences (as the functions already discussed) pave the way for transformations, in that there are no transformations without the child first having established some correspondence (as in the conservations). A second stage follows in which transformations and correspondences are in interaction. In the third stage, new correspondences, as between direct operations (one-way mappings) and their inverses, result from the construction of operational structures themselves (Piaget, 1979). An example from the preoperational period shows how correspondences can result in precocious conservation. The traditional conception of conservations is that they always require transformations (i.e., conservation is the maintenance of quantitative invariances across transformations) as in the case of a clay sausage that is transformed (i.e., changed in shape to a ball or the reverse) and the nonconserving child claims that the quantity has changed, or else conserves the quantity and says the amount of clay has not changed. In the new experiments instead of a transformation in the shape of the clay, a piece of clay is transferred (cut off) from one end and added to the other end. Young children (5½ years) when asked whether the quantity is the same with the piece cut off say, no. When the detached piece is added to the other end and children are asked whether the amount is the same as before the detachment they reply that the quantity is the same since the piece cut off is the same as the piece put on ("you took it away and then put it back ... " 1979, p. 21). Three-fourths of the subjects respond correctly at this age, whereas conservation (with transformations) proper is not achieved until about six or seven years (in Piaget's samples).

When correspondences are conserved they are inferred to have structure; structure that Piaget refers to as "morphisms." In turn, morphisms constitute categories. Categories are classes of objects with all their possible morphisms (Piaget, 1977). Categories are at present a matter of lively interest among mathematicians, largely based on the category theory of MacLane and Eilenberg (Piaget, 1977a). The application of category theory to psychological processing in both the preoperational and operational periods represents a significant addition to the logico-mathematical formulations that Piaget introduced into his theory, principally to axiomatize the structures of the concrete and formal operational periods. Category theory should play an important role in future extensions of the theory and will be discussed again, later in this chapter.

III. *Concrete operations (6 to 11 years)*. The period best known and most researched by other investigators is concrete operations, which is initiated by the achievement of the first of the logical structures characterized as reversible. The logical form of the period underlies three major logico-mathematical domains; the conservations that signal the onset of the period, the classification and categorization logics, and the ordering relations, or logics. Each domain has a typical structure but underlying them all is a more abstract logico-mathematical system that Piaget calls the "groupings."

The conservations, those of number, length, weight, continuous and discrete quantities, area, mass, and volume (namely, all quantitative concepts), have an underlying logic with two forms of reversibility, reversibility by inversion or negation and reversibility by compensation. An identity rule (if nothing is added or taken away, it remains the same) accompanies both reversibilities.

Satisfying the identity rule alone, however, is not sufficient for attaining the conservation concept, it must be accompanied by reversibility. Whereas the identity rule is related to and derived from the concept of the permanent object (attained at 18 months), the first conservations are not attained till about 6 or 7 years. Acquiring all the conservations may take 4 or 5 years.

Logical operations of the concrete operational period are to be distinguished from infralogical operations. Operations are actions carried out mentally, and logical operations are those operations, either one-way or reversible, onto which logical or mathematical forms may be mapped. Logical operations are involved in one-to-one correspondence, adding, subtracting, multiplying, classification and ordering—all those that involve numerable or discrete quantities. Infralogical operations are involved in measurements, time, space and others that are based on continuous rather than discrete quantities. The logico-mathematical structures, basic to classification, the "groupings," differ according to whether they refer to the addition or subtraction of classes (which participate in setting up classification hierarchies), or involve the multiplication or division of classes (as are involved in the construction of matrices with one property on one axis and another on the intersecting axis). The combination of the addition (subtraction) and multiplication (division) dimensions define four of the grouping structures applied to classes. A parallel set of structures apply to ordering relations (seriations, as in setting up a size order of sticks). The eight groupings that result are hypothetical and are said to define the manner in which children go about classifying and ordering objects. The groupings have been criticized by logicians and mathematicians because of their limitations as logical or mathematical systems. Piaget, in his defense (1978), says that although these structures are acquired piecemeal and are logically inelegant, from the time of Linneus to the present, they nevertheless are in accord with structures that provide the basis for all zoological and botanical classification.

Since categories are based on morphisms, it suggests to Piaget that groupings apply not only to a system of operations (based on transformation) but also to correspondences (and thus comparisons). The morphisms bear not only on classifications but also on seriations and conservations. The new "groupings" and conservations based on morphisms and category theory are said to pave the way for the "groupings" based on transformation.

Although logico-mathematical models are applied to concrete operational thought their full development is in thought of the formal operational period.

IV. *Formal Operations (11 years on)*. This period is distinguished by the advent of propositional operations, the so-called INRC or four-group, as well as by combinatorial structures. Concrete operations may be thought of as operations of the first order, or first power; formal operations consist in applying operations to operations and transformations to transformations, a second order of operations.

The data to which Piaget's logico-mathematical models are applied come principally from such experiments as involve combinations of liquids that yield colors that can be reversed by the addition of other liquids. The purpose of such experiments is to see how older children and adolescents go about solving such problems. What Piaget concludes from these experiments is that it is not till adolescence that hypothetical mental combinations can take the place of physical trial and error to solve the same problems.

When given a pendulum, for example, and permitted to vary the length and amplitude of its oscillations, the weights on the arm, and the initial impulse, subjects in the concrete operational period (7 to 12 years) vary the factors in a haphazard manner. At best, they classify, order serially and set up correspondences between the results they obtain from their manipulations. Subjects 12 to 15 years (at their best) after a few trials, formulate all possible hypotheses and arrange their manipulations as a function of the formulated hypotheses.

Thinking, for the subject at this level, is propositional, that is, it is based on statements whose truth value can be tested. When concrete operations are put in the form of propositions, they can be acted on by means of various logical operations, thus relating them by implication ($p \supset q$), conjunction (p.q), disjunction (pvq), identity, etc. The result is a powerful system of logical analysis for the purpose of logical deduction in problem-solving and reasoning, with wide applicability to all domains of thought, scientific and otherwise.

These logical operations in natural thought are not disconnected, they are related to each other in a structure, the Klein four-group, which Piaget labels the INRC group.

The propositional structure of INRC group combines the two forms of reversibility, inversion(N) and reciprocity (R), previously separated in concrete operational thought, into a single system. Inversion is the form of reversibility entailed in the operations of classes; reciprocity with the operations of relations. Piaget shows that the combinational system, the second feature of formal operations, is a generalization of classification applied to multiplicative products (1953, p. 31). In classifying the products in all possible ways a combinatorial system results. By combining the four basic conjunctions, 16 binary operations of 2-value propositional logic result. The table of 16 propositional operations is isomorphic with a truth-value table for two propositions, in which all the possible products are tested. In turn, relationships between the elements in this table are the set of transformations of the INRC group (Piaget, 1953).

Two things should be noted. First, the hypothetical propositional structures the adolescent of adult starts with in an experiment or problem-solving situation and uses to direct his actions is a truth-testing process. As Piaget puts it, the logic of propositions leads from the possible (i.e., the theoretical) to the actual in the process of truth-testing. Second, the 16 binary propositional system is hypothesized to be used by subjects in actual problem-solving situations. The latter assumption has been seriously questioned by various investigators, some of whom also question the very applicability of this logical system to adolescent and adult thought. In essence, they question the psychological reality of the system, which Piaget holds, constitutes a closed logical structure, and is the "final stage" in the development of thought. Or so he did until the last years of his life.

PART 3. THE NEW THEORY

The new direction in Piaget's research program began to emerge with Inhelder *et al.*'s (1974) work on learning and development. In this work the Genevans began to emphasize strategies and procedures in cognitive functioning in a systematic way. In the sections of the chapter that follow, the essence of the research and theory reported on and published, or in press, since 1974 will be presented and discussed. In general, the order of the works follows the order in which the investigations were carried out. The research in its totality represents a return to the functionalist emphasis of the early phase of Piaget's work. Once having gone through a structuralist phase, however, the new work bears the marks of a synthesis between structural and functional aspects of cognitive development. Nevertheless the later work in many ways revises significantly the structuralist character and emphasis of the theory, as it existed in the early 1970s, and what I refer to as the standard theory.

Procedures and Structures[6]

The approaches children use to solve problems are made up of two com-

ponents, structural knowledge and knowledge of procedures (which include algorithms and heuristics) that are an indissociable pair. They are however subject
to contradictions and characteristically, as in any dialectic relation, are over-
come. They are not the only such dialectic pairs in cognitive functioning, and as
do the others, they reflect the distinction between "knowing how" and "knowing why."[7] The other pairs are (1) action and the meaning of the action, (2)
transformations and comparisons, (3) function and comprehension, (4) finality
and causality, (5) internal and external finality, (6) previously constructed
schemes that are reused and schemes that are newly constructed (retroactive and
proactive processes), and finally, the synthesis of the six pairs in, (7) *knowing
how* and *knowing why*.

The seven contrasting pairs play a distinct but complex role in the relationship
between structures and procedures despite their common base in transformations.
Procedures carry out or utilize transformations in achieving specific goals. Consequently, procedures are temporal processes; structures, on the other hand, link
transformations and extract connections from atemporal systems. Constructing
structures requires a variety of procedures but procedures can play a role even in
nontransformational correspondences and morphisms.

Although procedures are everywhere and psychologists make much of them,
particularly in an era of functionalist thinking, skepticism abounds about structures. Consequently, Inhelder and Piaget feel obliged in response to criticisms to
point out that although children are aware of eating and breathing, their stomachs
and lungs do not exist only in the minds of physiologists (Inhelder & Piaget,
1980, p. 23). By the same token, evidence for the existence of structures in the
child's thought and action, although established by inference, comes from what
the child considers possible, impossible and necessary and are not the psychologist's invention. Procedures, by contrast, are more observable.

A second difference between structures and procedures, aside from tem-
porality, is that structures are integrated entities, whereas procedures are only
connected serially. Structures are closed systems that are progressively elaborated and integrated into larger systems. This is the case, for example, with the
schemes of the sensorimotor period, such as those involved in object permanence, which are integrated into the more general schemes in the mathematical group of displacements. These are followed by the conservation of matter and
integrated into the more general observation structures of weight. The later
developing grouping structures in turn are integrated into the groups of the formal operational period. Procedures are not integrated in the same way, instead
they are chained. First, they proliferate with each new task and each new goal.
The chaining is made up of successive replacements and diversifications.

Taking into account the differences between procedures and structures, *knowing how* and *knowing why* are involved differently in each. Knowing how, is evident in the discovery and deployment of procedures as structures are put to use.

Understanding the reasons why (knowing why) has a different role. Carrying out the operations of a structure is not possible without knowledge of the (structural) constraints of the system, inasmuch as structures are closed systems of operations. For example, classifying means consciously searching for similarities and differences, which involves both procedures and structures. However, knowing the reasons for using a particular procedure are not strictly necessary; comprehension takes a secondary role to success in this case. Nevertheless, it is not possible to structure *contents* without at the same time knowing "why" and "how." Thus children are able to give reasons for their classifying or seriating objects in particular ways, or in more complex problem-solving situations, offer justifications that reflect on the structures relating propositions.

A dialectical process leads to the progressive development of structures. As a structure is expanded into one more advanced forms, the older structure is integrated into the newer one and the newer one replaces the older, totally or partially. Procedures are not subject to this dialectical process. Procedures are identified by diversification, whereas unification is the rule for structures. Procedures are not immune from the generalization of successful practices, however, so the subject clearly profits from developing an enlarged repertoire of procedures. There is no accretion of structures in the same fashion, for unless they are systematically integrated, they are not likely to be effective. Whereas the richness of procedure rests on their variety and number, the richness of structures depends on their coherence and complexity.

Despite these differences, structures and procedures are ultimately interdependent. "Every structure is the result of a procedural construction, and every procedure makes use of some of the aspects of structures" (Inhelder & Piaget, 1980, p. 26).

As is usual with Piaget, there is a larger epistemological lesson to be seen in this dynamic relation. Science could not exist, he says, without the structural instruments inherent in and derived from psychological development, starting from early childhood. Technology in turn derives from its procedures. Technology is thus neither the offshoot of science nor the root of science, although science and technology are clearly interdependent.

On Causality

Causality, by his own admission, has been a troublesome issue for Piaget. One of his earliest studies, published in 1930 (Piaget, 1930) was concerned with it. As he later reconsidered the relationships between causality and operational thought and examined (with R. Garcia, a historian of science) causal notions in the history of science, he felt forced to revise his theory of causal thinking (Piaget & Garcia, 1974).

In his early depiction of causal understanding he felt that "the mind believes itself to be apprehending an external reality that is independent of the thinking subject" (1930, p. 237). The early studies were experiments on the nature of air, the origin of wind and breath, on clouds and heavenly bodies, water currents, the floating of boats, shadows, etc. The later experiments treat with changes in states of matter, the direction of thrusts and pulls, action and reaction, energy and work, as well as some of the earlier notions, such as sound and air. The essential problem remained the same as to the nature of the relation of operational thought to causal explanation. The conclusion he comes to in the newer theory is that causal explanation consists in the use of actions and operations, by virtue of which the subject creates models and "attaches" them to objects, not simply applies them to objects. Objects thus become operators, functioning like operations in our thought, and thereby make actions comprehensible. Inasmuch as the actions on objects create or lead to operations, to that extent are they not simply creations of mind but the result of an interaction between subject and object.

The dilemma faced by Piaget and the motivation for reexamining causal reasoning was that in explaining any phenomenon by means of a set of conditions considered as causal amounted to showing by what transformations it was produced, and how the new result corresponds to transmissions from the initial stages (Piaget & Garcia, 1974, p. 1). These aspects of transformation and conservation, however, are characteristic of both operations and causality, since there is an intimate relation between the two, in that the former entails transformations of the real, and causality expresses what objects do as they act on one another and the subject. The question then is as to which element is primary. Piaget's conclusion is that at every level, development of the understanding of causality interacts with the development of operations. Each of these developments is in a dialectic relation with the other with periods of nondifferentiation, mutual deformation, opposition, and then periods of coordination.

The common roots to both operations and causal explanation are evident in sensorimotor actions. Activity itself is a biologically-based causal mechanism in that the infant in manipulating and moving objects is causally involved with the environment (Inhelder, 1980). These very activities generate schemes that also serve as the origins of logico-mathematical operations.

The level of representational thought ($1\frac{1}{2}$ to 2) years marks the appearance of preoperational structures (semilogical functions) and precausal notions. This is the period in which semilogical (nonreversible) operations dominate thought. Thus, when sugar is dissolved in water, neither its quantity nor its weight nor its volume are conserved. Concomitantly, causal explanations are marked by animistic and finalistic explanations—the water level is said not to change because an ink mark on the jar that coincides with the water level is holding it up. Piaget believes that it is this nondifferentiation between causal and operative aspects of thinking, in particular, the irreversible nature of all forms of causality, that retards the development of operations. It inhibits them from becoming reversible.

At the same time, causality, by virtue of the one-way nature of operations at this level, can become neither objective nor rational.

At this level as well, the child, who does not distinguish the general case from the particular, believes that a shadow made by an object on a table (particular) is caused by the shadow of trees (general). This type of thinking, reported in the earlier (1930) work is said to be an example of analogical or transductive reasoning typical of children at this age. Further, in the realm of (semilogical) operations, the difficulties with class inclusion (the relation of "all" to "some") and the attendant absence of quantification, appear as the most consistent difficulties in causal thinking at this stage.

When concrete operations and reversible operations are achieved (6 to 7 years), the child's logical operations and the attribution of models to reality begin to be differentiated and begin to affect one another. Nonetheless the differentiation is limited by the very nature of concrete operational thought. Concrete operations bear directly on objects in that their properties are most intimately related to physical causality. The "resistance" of physical properties to operational development delays the formation of the latter and results in the step-by-step compositions typical of this period. The final period (formal operations) marks the differentiation of causality from mental operations. Operations are differentiated enough from content to function in a formal fashion, and the "attributions" of the resulting models are responsible for definite progress in causal reasoning. At this level adolescent thought becomes functionally similar to the scientist's in the application of deductive models to reality.

The general result from this body of research is the claim that causality entails the attribution of operational structures to the object. Causality is thus more than a system of transformations reduced to cause and effect. Going even further, Piaget suggests that operations are causal structures applicable to extratemporal forms; physical causality in turn is a system of operations brought about by material objects. This correspondence works because the organism itself is a physical object subject to causality like all other objects.

The Grasp of Consciousness/Success and Understanding (Piaget, 1976, 1978)

These two works represent the first and second steps in a single enterprise. The first reports on the development of the child's awareness of its own action, contrasting awareness with the ability to perform the action. Piaget wishes to do for conscious awareness what Freud did for the unconscious, to see it recognized as "a continually active dynamic system" (1976, p. 332). The passage from the unconscious to the conscious requires reconstructions and does not simply result from a process of illumination, in which light is merely thrown on a hitherto obscure situation that conscious awareness is ordinarily thought of as being. Rather, cognizance (the act of becoming conscious) of an action transforms the

action scheme into a concept—thus, cognizance is in essence an act of conceptualization. This process only provides the "knowing how" aspect to understanding cognizance. The "knowing why" of cognizance requires seeking the
functional reasons for it.

Cognizance starts upon the conscious awareness of success or failure in seeking a goal. The consequence of failure is seeking the reason, and in Piaget's vec-
torial model of the process, this leads to cognizance of "the more central regions
of the *action*" (1976, p. 335). Upon starting from the vantage point of the *object*,
due to failure to reach the goal, the subject tries to discover why his available
schemes could not be applied successfully to accommodate to the object. Attention is thereby drawn to the means used and to how they might be corrected or
replaced. By virtue of this "two-way movement" between object and action,
cognizance comes nearer to the actions internal mechanism—going from "the
periphery to the center" (p. 335). This implies that cognizance results, only
when there is a failure of adaptation (accommodation of scheme to object), but
Piaget holds it also occurs with successful achievement of the goal. In this case
cognizance results from the assimilation process itself, in that the object is assimilated to a practical scheme. If the results of action are susceptible to consciousness while still generalizable, the scheme becomes a concept, and the
assimilation becomes representative. In becoming a representative instrument it
is increasingly capable of future application.

As a consequence of this two-way process, cognizance of the object (goal) extends to the action (means), inasmuch as each is dependent upon the other. The
need for causal explanation that is the inevitable consequence of this sequence is
therefore not limited to objects since the latter are "known" only through actions. Thus the manner in which Piaget explains causal thought is integrated into
the explanation of cognizance. A basic law of movement is defined from periphery to two centers (c and c1). Piaget uses the terms periphery and center, because
the internal factors at the start escape the subject's consciousness, and second because knowledge originates in the interaction between subject and object (i.e.,
from point P), which is peripheral to both subject (S) and object (O). The law of
movement is not limited to cognizance of physical action, because the interiorization of action leads in mental action to consciousness of the problem to be
solved, and then to the external means to solve them. This theoretical account,
which is an application of Piaget's account of reflective abstraction, is documented by the child's recounting of how he discovered the specific means by
which he achieved a goal. The younger child simply recounts his successive actions, often only with gestures, whereas the older child, says, for example, "I
saw that ... so I thought ..." or "so I had the idea ..." (1976, p. 337).

The mechanism basic to this process, again, is the transition from assimilation
of the object into an existing scheme (practical assimilation) to an assimilation
through concepts. A subsidiary claim, following on the claim that cognizance en-

tails conceptualization, is that conscious awareness by virtue of the process of conceptualization (transforming actions into representative concepts), is a significant source of cognitive change in problem-solving and reasoning. To the possible counterclaim that the cognitive processing that occurs in problem-solving takes place unconsciously and cognizance is only awareness after the process occurs, Piaget offers a number of arguments in support of his own position, based as usual on some experimental findings.

One of these experiments employs a wooden ball held in a cord sling. The sling is swung by the child around his head and then released so that the ball hits a designated target on the wall. Even young children learn to succeed at the task. The object of the study though is to determine when and how the child comes to awareness of the ball's position when it is released so as to hit the target (at 3 o'clock or 9 o'clock on a hypothetical clock model of rotation). Piaget says that the young child conceptually distorts what he observes, rather than simply records (describes) how he did it. In the experiment, even though children know very well how to throw the wooden ball tangentially (at 3 o'clock or 9 o'clock) so that it hits the target (at 12 o'clock), they say (i.e., believe) that they released it at 12 o'clock. If consciousness were merely a reflection of something going on unconsciously, the child's response would be in accord with the correct adjustment of the actions to the goal. Instead, the child makes inferences of what he did, which identifies the conceptualization inherent in the conscious awareness of the goal-oriented actions. The process of inferencing requires that the child construct a spatial representation of the actions necessary for understanding the ball's departure at a tangent to the target. His resulting construction is in conflict, however, with the subject's earlier (conscious) scheme. This results in the child's move to release the ball opposite (12 o'clock) to the (12 o'clock) target with the consequence that he ends up sending the ball wide of the target. Before the conscious scheme is corrected, the least advanced children (level IA) simply distort their observations and "seem to drive the source of the conflict into the unconscious" (p. 339). The child in this instance does not have difficulty with his motor coordination, nor is the contradiction in the child's consciousness (i.e., he is not conscious of the tangential release). Therefore, Piaget concludes, it must be in the process of conceptualization inherent in the process of cognizance.

The cognizance studies lead to a reconceptualization of the theory of equilibration, particularly as to how reflective abstraction leads to knowledge, but this will be detailed in the later section on equilibration. The cognizance studies and the theory developed from them have further epistemological significance. The process that leads from the periphery to the "central regions" of the action, "c," is the process of interiorization, and the process leading from the periphery to the object, "c1," is that of externalization. Interiorization results in the construction of logico-mathematical structures, and externalization results in physical knowledge and thus to causality. In the sensorimotor period, the interiorization process leads to reciprocal assimilation of schemes and to the central coordination of schemes. The result is a "logic" of schemes prior to language and thought. (This insight will have an important consequence in the proposed theory of meaning to be discussed later.) The logic of schemes provides the principal elements of later operatory structures and are important in the principal coordinations of the sensorimotor period: the relation of the order, the embedding of schemes, correspondences, and interconnections. But externalization is also evident at this level, in the accommodations of schemes to objects, in instrumental behaviors, and in spatio-temporal physical structures.

At the level of representational thought (in the present context Piaget refers to it as the conceptualization level) there is growth in cognizance of action. This is the consequence of the interiorization of physical actions into meaning-bearing representations, such as language and mental imagery. Cognizance is marked at this level by empirical abstraction and reflective abstraction. By virtue of reflective abstraction, conceptualization leads to operative structures, making reasoning and structural organization (in seriation, classification, and numbers) possible. Reflective abstraction in this is essentially unconscious. Externalization results in two analogous processes. Empirical abstraction (from objects) leads to the representation of observable features, leading to functions and general laws. Reflective abstraction results further in operations that permit the integration of events bearing on objects—that is, in the formation of causal attributions to objects. Again causal attributions and logico-mathematical inferences remain unconscious.

At the third level (formal operations), reflected abstractions are the conscious products of the process of reflective abstraction. Cognizance is now extended to the reflection of thought upon itself. Interiorization is evident in the ability to theorize with many new logico-mathematical instruments of thought; by virtue of externalization the subject is able to vary the dimensions or parameters of experiments. The consequence is a much closer relation between the concrete facts of experimentation and the abstract processes of conceptualization and thus of cognizance.

The study of cognizance consequently fits into the general model Piaget has elaborated of the circular relationship between subject and object. "The subject only learns to know himself when acting on the object, and the latter can become known only as a result of progress of the actions carried out on it . . . this explains the harmony between thought and reality, since action springs from the laws of an organism that is simultaneously one physical object among many and the source of the acting, then thinking, subject" (1976, p. 353).

Success and Understanding (1978)

The studies reported in the companion volume, *The Grasp of Consciousness,* were concerned with walking on all fours, launching an object by a sling, putting back-spin on a ping-pong ball so it returns after being projected forward, etc., and are described by Piaget as achieved precociously, that is, without many developmental steps (or stages).

The studies reported in *Success and Understanding*, however, involved the "resistance" of objects, so that the subject comes to acquire the means to deal with them only in stages. These studies are designed to confirm the view developed earlier of the "initial autonomy of action, and of the process of conscious conceptualization as it progresses from periphery to central mechanism" (1978, p. 213). Additionally, the new data cast light on the reverse effect of conceptualization on actions and on the roles of practical success and understanding. What result from an examination of these data, as well, are new views of implicative and explicative processes in comprehension, and of the relationship between affirmations and negations in the development of the child's thought.

The experiments, again, are most simple. For example, building "roofs" with two cards, houses of four cards, the "domino effect" with a row of dominoes, transmission of movement in closely placed suspended balls, etc. Results of the earlier study, showing the lag of consciousness behind action, were confirmed in these experiments. In all successes at the first stage, conceptualization was seen to lag behind action, and cognizance started from the external results of the action, followed by the analysis of the means employed, and appeared last in the general coordinations (reciprocity, transitivity, etc.) of the at-first unconscious mechanisms of action.

At level two, the picture changes as conceptualization and action have reciprocal effects on each other. This is evident in an experiment of the transmission of movement in a row of almost touching suspended balls. The subject almost immediately appeals to mediate transmission, that is, the subject says each ball is touching the next ball and budging it. What conceptualization at this level appears to do is engender greater use of anticipation and of the greater possibilities of immediate implementation of their conceptions. Nevertheless, there is a relatively long phase in which action and its conceptualization are practically at the same level, with constant interaction between trial and error and conceptual inference.

At level three, there is a reversal between conceptualization and action in which, by virtue of reflected abstraction, the subject can plan the entire action starting from the conceptualization. In contrast to level two, there is no longer the instability in the interactions between conceptualization and action, even when they begin to be effective. At level three, practice appears to be guided by theory.

The studies reported on in this volume led Piaget to an important new step in theoretical extension, although as in most changes of this order, there are anticipations in earlier works. He states that the most general characteristic of conscious states, from the most elementary grasp of consciousness evident in goal-oriented actions to higher-level conceptualization, is that they express sig-nifications and are connected by what he calls "signifying implications" (1978, p. 221). All action and its contents can be considered as significative repre-sentations when translated into language and mental images (i.e., by semiotic in-struments). The center of the coordinations, which remains causal in actions, have their equivalent in thought in the system of operational coordinations. These transform the objects of thought in the same way that action transforms physical objects. It is important in this new conception to see that an operation is not a *representation* of an act, although strictly speaking it is still an action in that it produces new constructions. It is a "signifying" action, not a physical ac-tion, in that its connections are implicative and not causal. There is hence an isomorphism of causality and implication, which is why Piaget usually refers to an operation as an internalized action (1978, p. 221). This account does much to answer criticism of one aspect of Piaget's theory, which seemed to give action in the mind properties of physical actions. In making the relations implicative, the "actions" are logical and not physical (nor for that matter linguistic, see foot-note, 1978, p. 221).

The consequence of the system of signifying implications is that it supplies something not included in either goals or means. What it provides is under-standing that extracts the reasons of things, whereas process reflects effective ap-plication or use. Understanding goes beyond success in that it yields knowledge that can make action unnecessary.

Affirmations and Negations

Every action, says Piaget, tends, despite being directed to an aim and being es-sentially positive, to change or negate an initial state for a new one. Operations are similar in that every operation entails an inverse operation. Hence, every cog-nitive activity whether a physical action or a mental operation, has positive ele-ments that are fully compensated by negative elements. Nonetheless, it is characteristic of young children at the more elementary levels of thought to neglect the negative elements and focus on positive, more salient properties. Ex-perimentally, this is seen in the construction of equivalent paths (in order to travel equal distances), in which young subjects typically focus on the end points of the paths and neglect the starting points. In a dominoes task employing the domino effect, younger subjects again neglect the starting point, holding that the first domino will topple the second irrespective of the distance between them—similarly with rotations. Subjects fail to realize that to raise one end of a pivoting bar the other end must be pulled down. In fact, in study after study, subjects show that they are concentrating on positive elements and neglecting negative ones. Thus, in these experiments subjects were taking one dimension or feature of the problem into account, usually a positive one contributing to the effect, and neglecting other elements, resulting in a lack of success.

On the basis of the consistency of the effect in these experiments, Piaget, arrives at a general rule of the initial primacy of the positive over negative elements in development. The rule applies particularly to the mechanisms of cognizance. Affirmations, devoid of the negative features logically attached to them, lie at the periphery of the subject's activities in that objects and events are perceived in their positive elements before their logically negated elements can be considered. For example, an object is seen as red, square and on top of another before it can be registered as not blue, not round and not on the same table as another. Hence, negative elements are usually not considered, except in comparisons, in failed predictions, or when needs are not satisfied. Negations consequently, lie closer, in Piaget's model, to the central regions in that they involve correlations, coordinations and inferences on the part of the subject. Second, negative elements often impede early success and give rise to failures when the negative elements are connected to the conditions preceding an action. Third, in the case of gradual success, neglect of negative elements produces all sorts of conflicts and contradictions that become more evident in the studies on contradiction.

On Contradiction

In the theory of equilibration, disequilibria are the principal "motor" of developmental change. In the earlier theory "conflict" was the principal element is creating disequilibrium. In the present work, *Experiments in Contradiction* (1980), conflict is only one form of disequilibrium, along with adaptive failure and oppositions, all of which appear in the subject's consciousness as contradictions. In these studies Piaget states his aim as determining the relations between contradiction and the disequilibria of action and thought. Is cognitive disequilibrium, he asks, the result of contradiction, or is disequilibrium simply experienced as contradiction.

The method basic to the studies reported is to look for the source of contradiction in situations in which the same action appears not to give the same results, in which two contrary actions do not completely compensate each other, and in which inferential coordinations lack necessity.

The contradictions Piaget is concerned with are those that occur in natural thought, in distinction to those that occur in logical thought. These natural contradictions are more akin to the contradictions in dialectics where contradictions are capable of being "transcended"; logical or formal contradiction on the other hand is only corrected or eliminated. Whereas logical contradiction entails the simultaneous assertion of the truth of a proposition and its negation, in natural thought contradictions arise when questions asked cannot be resolved in advance of testing them. Such questions consist in asking whether an action is compatible with another action favorable to its being carried out, incompatible, or an impediment to it. At more developed stages of thought, anticipating the answer to these questions results in conceptualizing such outcomes in varying degrees.

In setting out and classifying different forms of contradiction in natural thought, prior to their formalization later in development, Piaget is concerned most with the transcendencies that occur in resolving contradictions. The transcendencies appear to be marked by two interdependent processes, one extensional, the other intensional (i.e., in comprehension). The first involves widening the field of reference and the second involves a relativization of notions. An example of this is seen in a balance beam experiment, in which the subject only takes weight into account and, in doing so, sees it lead to contradictory results. The subject is thus forced to supplement the judgment by taking into account distance from the fulcrum. In this action there is simultaneously an extension of the field of reference and a relativization of the action of the weights in respect to their position. Both processes require new compensations between affirmations and negations, and result in the puzzling fact that despite sometimes glaring contradictions children will lack consciousness of these contradictions till later in development, and often with great difficulty. This is evident in the classic conservation of number experiment in which there is a contradiction between two schemes, one involving one-to-one correspondence of objects in two rows, the other involving the ordinality of the newly staggered or rearranged rows. In this case, children do not become conscious of the contradiction till about 6 years of age. What Piaget concludes is that transcendence is the result of compensations derived from negations constructed for that purpose.

The easiest condition for achieving consciousness is the one in which a prediction is contradicted by evidence against that prediction. In this instance, negation is not constructed, it is imposed from the outside. In the more difficult case, consciousness of a contradiction between schemes is not produced until the subject becomes capable of transcending it. The very contradiction between schemes makes the need for negation evident; without the negation the subject produces a series of local and isolated affirmations (e.g., equality for correspondences, inequality for rows of different length).

In data from a variety of experiments, contradictions experienced with springs, with scales, with mirror images, with conservations, etc., affirmations overwhelm negations in systematic ways, until the operatory level of thought. At the earliest perceptual level, there are only affirmations, that is, only positive characteristics are perceived. In sensorimotor actions, there is no endogenous negative behavior, only movements directed at removing obstacles. With the beginning of conceptualization (1½ – 2 years) come elementary negative judgments ("it is little, not big," or "grandpa gone"). In early verbal expression, language never expresses comparative relations except in positive terms ("more or less heavy"). Only at operatory levels with reverse operations, and thus negation, is it possible to place negation into correspondence with each direct operation or affirmation. These facts, says Piaget, account for why affirmations are dominant over negations and why there is such a lack of negation in the early years.

Contradictions may be considered as incomplete compensations between affirmations and negations. Dialective contradictions, and natural thought is essentially dialectical in its succession of disequilibria and reequilibrations, fall within the scope of the same mechanisms. Whether dialectical or natural, contradictions are merely the expression and *not* the cause of the disequilibria. When formalization begins, formal contradictions and those with contents are nevertheless distinguishable.

What Piaget has done in this work is to redirect attention from logical and formal aspects of contradiction, and their structural properties, to their functions alone. Inasmuch as functioning precedes and prepares structures, it justifies his conception of the relation of disequilibria to contradictions, as also prior to structures. Second, the oppositions that result from disequilibria are dependent on the *content* of thought and action alone, and this requires a functional understanding of the processes involved in the developments related to contradiction.

Possibility and Necessity (1987)

Again, a series of studies, undertaken prior to 1979, play a critical role in further developments in Piaget's theory. Piaget's new proposal is to view the development of knowledge as the consequence of previously created possibilities. Possibilities, once transformed and realized, lead to yet newer possibilities. Thus with development there is a gradual building up of the set of possibilities, as seen from the vantage point of the subject. To study the phenomenon, a broad series of experiments was undertaken designed to determine how subjects conceive of possibilities for creation and invention with given sets of materials presented them. These included opportunities for arranging objects in various ways, imagining various possible shapes of partially concealed objects, seeing the possibilities in free as well as constrained combinations, and the possibilities in the construction of geometric shapes.

For the present purpose, Piaget introduces a new (or revised) classification of schemes: *Presentative schemes* (both sensorimotor and representational) that "involve simultaneous characteristics of objects" (pp. 4–5), and are conserved in combination with others in a hierarchy of schemes. *Procedural schemes* refer to the means created or used to reach a goal. These may be ordered in a sequence and are not necessarily conserved. They are context dependent and unlike presentative schemes of action are not easily generalizable. *Operational schemes* are a synthesis of the previous two. They are procedural in that they are performed in "real time," and yet they have an atemporal structure, from the combinatorial laws that regulate them and mark them as higher order presentative schemes.

What Piaget proposes, and it is a new notion, is that development of operational structures is the outcome of a more general evolution, and is not to be explained by operational development in and of itself. Operations require the synthesis of possibility and necessity. Possibility is provided by procedural freedom (flexibility); necessity is provided by self-regulation and system-bound compositions.

It would appear from Piaget's description that possibility and necessity are the consequence of subjects' autonomous activity. In this view, reality would appear "dominated" and "absorbed" into the subjects' schemes by capacities not derived from reality. This is not quite so, however. To avoid the accusation of idealism, Piaget insists that since the epistemic subject (the structures) and the psychological subject (the problems and procedures) are themselves part of reality, that reality is made richer by virtue of the fact that every event appears as an outcome among a variety that are possible, within a system of logico-mathematical transformations (p. 150). Thus, as possibility, reality, and necessity are differentiated, each of the three is modified. What results is a new integration, with objects incorporated in the subject, with the aid of mathematics, and the subject becoming a part of the object, through biology.

Consequently each person is constituted of two complementary cognitive systems, the presentative, made up of stable schemes and structures, whose function is that of understanding the world; and the procedural system, whose functioning ensures successful performance, and works toward the satisfaction of needs. The presentative system forms the basis of the epistemic subject; the procedural, the psychological subject. Once a possibility is actualized by means of a procedural scheme, a new presentative scheme results, accounting for the complementarity of the systems.

Limitations play an important role in this scenario, from which subjects have to be liberated, and also to account for the creation of possibilities. The initial limitations come from the early lack of differentiation between reality, possibility and necessity. This lack prevents subjects from seeing things as they are, and also leads them to believe that what they believe is necessarily so, excluding the possibility of things changing or being changed. These Piaget calls *pseudonecessities* and *pseudo-impossibilities*, which he observes are not only characteristic of children but also of thought in the history of science and mathematics. Whereas in earlier discussions of equilibration, stress was placed on the self-regulating aspects of the system, in the present work stress is on the possibilities generated by equilibration processes. The need for the newer version derives from the fact that self-regulation, that is, the process of improving and evaluating a structure, is constituted of procedures only, not presentative schemes (or structures themselves). These self-regulations are determined by the possible, and the mechanisms that lead to the possible.

Accompanying the reexamined theory of equilibration is a development model of the possible. At the preoperational level (I) possibilities are generated locally by successive analogies. At the level of initial concrete operations (IIA), *concrete* co-possibilities are formed, wherein several possibilities are anticipated at the same time, before being tested. At the next level (IIB—the level of equilibration of concrete operations), is the *abstract* co-possible, in which each possibility realized is treated as one among many others that are conceivable. At level III (hypothetico-deductive operations), are the indeterminate co-possibilities: the possible in its most general form, possibilities seen as unlimited in number.

The consequence of this newer developmental framework is to see operations as the product of possibilities and not as their source. Once possibility, necessity, and reality are differentiated and coordinated, possibilities and operational structures are subordinated to a third type of equilibration between differentiation and integration.

Revising the theory of equilibration, which these studies led to, resulted from considering that each new possibility is simultaneously a construction and an "opening," in that possibility generates an innovation and at the same time a new gap to be filled—"a limitation and a disturbance to be compensated for" (p. 151). Hence disturbances drive transitions that turn into compensations and possibilities. Possibilities thus constitute a continuous source of reequilibrations that are constructive as well as compensatory. In the end, this process is one in which possibility is both an instrument and a motive force in development. In the course of development, any possibility and procedural scheme may lead to presentative schemes, and thus to structures. Structures, then, have their start as procedures. The consequence of these relations and developments, together with the observation that psychological subjects have many traits in common, led Piaget to replace the dichotomy of epistemic subject and psychological subject with a trichotomy: the individual subject, the common or general (temporal and causal) subject, and the epistemic (nontemporal and exclusively implicative) subject.

Necessity. Up to this point we have considered Piaget's treatment of possibility, primarily. We now consider the other side of the coin, necessity.

Necessity develops in a way similar to the development of possibility. Sensorimotor development provides the initial form in simple local necessities resulting from the elementary compositions (coordinations), and culminates at the end of the period in preoperational representation. At the level of concrete operations some systematic types of necessity appear, such as conservation, recursiveness and transitivity. At the formal operational stage, necessity takes on a general form.

Piaget proposes another general law of development that encompasses reality, possibility, and necessity, with three periods in their relations. Nondifferentiation is the mark of the first period: reality includes many pseudonecessities, and possibility consists in simple, direct extensions of actual realities. Necessity is thus bound up in local coordinations.

The second period (coincident with concrete operations and the grouping structures) is one in which differentiation among the three occurs: possibilities become families of co-possibilities, and necessity goes beyond local coordination, with operational compositions defining the necessary forms. Reality consists in concrete contents.

In the third period, the three modalities are integrated in a total system. Reality, however, is subordinated to systems of necessary connections.

The experiments on which the developmental sequence is based were conducted on subjects' responses to rotations, constructions of slopes, length measures, multiplications, and the construction of proofs. The experiments led to the conclusion that: (1) necessity is the result of compositions carried out by the subject and is not inherent in objects; (2) it is the result of a process (necessitation) and not the indication of a state; and (3) although it is related to the constitution of possibilities that yield differentiations, necessity itself is related to integration. The two together are complementary and in equilibrium.

There are three dimensions of necessity that enter into the process of necessitation. First, the general logical principle, the principle of non-contradiction: p and not-p cannot exist at the same time; second is the principle of sufficient reason, which does not specify what this reason is. Piaget offers a reason himself for the necessitation process. "Is it necessary that necessities exist," without specifying what they are. If this were not so, he says, thought would constantly contradict itself. He observes further that the integration of the past, and all its assertions, with the present state is the source of necessity.

Necessity, consequently, is defined in this context, as "those processes the composition C of which cannot be negated without leading to a contradiction" (p. 130). Only the subject's own actions (or operations) permit the verification of the contradictory nature of non-C, since reality can only indicate that not-C never occurs, and is insufficient to demonstrate its impossibility. Hence the subjective nature of necessity, and the integration of past and present, which is a condition for logico-mathematical necessity that can only be inferential, in contrast to other subject actions.

Necessitation starts in development with the formation of concepts capable of mutual composition when subjects first use incompatible criteria that lead to contradictions (e.g., in the judgment of lengths). They finally adopt homogeneous criteria that make associative compositions possible (by virtue of which, for example, they are able to judge lengths as similar or dissimilar). The process continues as operative processes such as reflective abstraction and completive generalizations are brought to bear on problems. Finally, they arrive at those fundamental operations Piaget now calls *significant implications*, which he claims are at the base of all inferential logic, in which p ⊃ q (p implies q) is necessary to the extent that the meaning of q is included in that of p. This is an application of the entailment (or relevance) logic of Anderson and Belnap, who take necessity as inherent in the operation itself, which in the case of Piaget's significant implications, is the relation of p ⊃ q, wherein q can be deduced from p by natural inference (p. 138).

Necessitating processes extend to the construction of logico-mathematical structures upon the acquisition of these operations. In this circumstance, closures (equilibrium in structures) are complemented by new openings (possibilities), and extend further to explanatory physical models. The processes of structuring and modeling result in the need for justification and explanation. This in turn leads to new necessities. That is, the newly acquired capacities, just as in the case of possibilities, and complementary to them, lead to new extensions, and to further development.

There are two forms of necessity, one is structural *force*, and the other relates to functional stages, of which there are three, but they are not developmental. They refer to phases in the solution of a problem or to the construction of a model of a structure, or protostructure.

The first is *preparatory determination* with the search, first, for necessary conditions, then, for necessary and sufficient conditions.

The second is *elaboration* or *analysis*. This is the search for an explanation, A, of the necessity of a particular construction, which is succeeded by explanation B for A, C for B, etc. in a continuing process. This is seen as the "principal driving force" in the search for necessity. It is distinguished from mere extensional generalization, and it occurs at about 7 years of age with the transition from generalizing from one case to another (extensional generality) to deductive justification. The third phase is *amplification*. It consists in deriving necessary consequences from previously *necessitated* constructions.

In regard to procedural knowledge, discussed previously in relation to presentative schemes and possibility, there seems to be no reason to distinguish a procedural from a structural kind of necessity. A procedure is oriented to success, not understanding. Thus it can provide sufficient but not necessary conditions. When necessity plays a role in procedural action, as it usually does, it is in understanding the reasons for success and failure, not at the level of the results as such.

On Equilibration

The studies reported in the *Grasp of Consciousness* (1976) and *Possibility and Necessity* (1987) led Piaget to refine and extend the theory of equilibration, as already indicated. His book on equilibration (Piaget, 1977, 1985)[8] appears to embody views also developed in the *Grasp of Consciousness*.

He starts first with a distinction, between observable and nonobservable coordinations between objects and actions. An observable feature is one that can be recorded through factual (empirical) observation. This encompasses events, repeatable relationships, temporary and regular covariations to the extent that a functional dependence or law can be said to apply to them. Regular relationships or functions between two observable features are also observable features. This contrasts with "inferential coordinations," those coordinations or connections that are not observed but are deduced through what Piaget calls operatory composition: in essence, constructions of mind that go beyond extension and generalization. Whereas, observable features are created by objects and by actions, inferential coordinations, even those attributed to objects (as in causal attributions), originate in the subject's logic—the logic inherent in the general coordinations of the subject's own actions.

This led to a distinction between empirical abstraction, applied to observable features, and reflective abstraction, applied to the coordination of internalized actions. Abstractions from the features of objects is essentially empirical. Action, however, gives rise to both empirical and reflective abstraction. (Note: the term "reflexive" is used by some translators, "reflective" by others; I abide by the latter convention.) There are in Piaget two levels of reflective abstraction, when it refers to inferences drawn from coordinations. One is unconscious, and is the source of inferential coordinations, the second conscious, and entails reasoning. Reflective abstraction can become conscious when the subject compares two actions taken in problem-solving attempts to discern the common element in the steps he has taken, for example in solving a tower of Hanoi problem. This conscious level Piaget refers to as "reflected abstraction"—the past tense indicating the consequence of the "reflective" process. (It is sometimes denoted by some translators as "reflexive" to indicate the reflexivity of the thought process: thought turned upon itself.)

The basic elements to consider in the process of equilibration are, first, those that result in constructions, and second, those that form the compensations that are required because constructions invariably entail contradictions. Consequently, the process of equilibration involves regulations of various kinds: regulation of object-observables, regulation related to action and awareness, regulation of relations between observables, and regulation of coordinations (causality; logico-mathematical). The regulations are required inasmuch as the subject in seeking knowledge acts to avoid incoherence and tends instead toward various forms of equilibrium, which are always temporary. Even logico-mathematical structures offer only local and temporary stability, for, as indicated earlier, once completed the new structures reopen or create new problems. Thus for Piaget even the most developed science "remains a continual becoming" (1978, p. 178), with disequilibria functioning so as to require regulations. The central problem now seen by Piaget is to account for successive improvement in the forms of equilibration.

The forms of equilibrium that play a role in this, and parallel the regulations, are: (1) the equilibrium of relations between subject and object that forms the basis of physical knowledge, (2) the equilibrium of coordinations between schemes or subschemes that are associated with logico-mathematical knowledge, and (3) the general equilibrium between whole and parts, that is, between differentiation of schemes and their integration into a total system. The last of these dominates the other two and is implicated in the termination of actions. In other words, where a "gap" exists by virtue of a re-equilibration it is filled by differentiations that, together with the subject's relations with objects, and the coordinations between schemes, provide the means and goals that proceed only in relation to the equilibrium of the system as a whole.

Two questions are posed by Piaget. What is the mechanism (the "why") that leads to improvement in regulations and increased coherence? The "how" of improvement is accounted for by the fact that new forms include earlier forms or contents and act upon them—in an endogenous process, inasmuch as objects play little if any role in this process. Endogenous construction is essentially the process of reflective abstraction that extracts from earlier forms the elements that are constituted in the new, later forms. Improvement in equilibration is the consequence of new regulations that act on a more complex set of assimilations and accommodations. The new forms are richer by consequence of having a greater number of compositions. They offer the possibility of greater and greater control as a hierarchy of regulations is built with development, leading to self-regulation and self-organization.

The reason why new constructions occur lies in the balance between constructions and compensations that always go together. The essential fact is that as each new structure is constituted it opens up new possibilities. These may be disturbing to the present state of the system but they are compensated by coherent integrations into the system. Thus an extension of an earlier system produces an improved equilibrium only to the degree that a disturbance in the system is attenuated by being incorporated into the system. Many instances of such constructions and compensations can be given at each level of cognitive development, culminating in the composition of inversions and reciprocities that lead to the INRC group in formal operations.

Psychologically, the perturbations or disequilibria, the gaps in a structure, are experienced as the feeling that there is something left to be done; that not all possibilities have been exhausted. These obstacles represent a threat to an existing structure and motivate the subject to seek new solutions. It is only when the new solutions are integrated together with the older structures into a new construction that the higher level totality resolves the distress, at least temporarily. Since the new structure opens up new possibilities that did not exist previously, the process goes on continually.

Finally, all three varieties of equilibration, which reflect different relations between subjects and objects or between subjects' schemes, require compensations between affirmations and corresponding negations—and play a determining role in all equilibrations. In the initial stages there is primacy of affirmations that result in many disequilibria, because inverse operations and regulations by negations are lacking (as for example, provided by the logical reversibilities). Thus, when there is compensation, it requires constructing negations that are at first missing. Although Piaget had earlier maintained that equilibration was closely tied to developing reversibilities, in a new theory of equilibration, perturbations (disequilibria) and compensations, as general phenomena, are concretized and made verifiable by the detailed study of later developing negations and the difficulties subjects have in constructing them.

Psychogenesis and the History of Science.

It has been a long-standing claim of Piaget's that the history of concepts in science has a developmental course that parallels the development of the individual, or more appropriately, the epistemic subject. Another way of putting it is to say that genetic epistemology, the science of the genesis of knowledge, applies to both the history of scientific ideas as well as to the development of knowledge across individuals. In accord with this view, Piaget has over the years drawn parallels between the history of mathematics, as well as the physical and biological sciences, and the course of cognitive development. It was evident, however, that the "fit" was far from even approximately parallel. This was the case with geometry. In his earlier description of the development of geometric cognition, Piaget (1960) described a development that proceeded from an ability to deal with topological relations and concepts to those of Euclidean and projective concepts. The history of geometry, however, was more or less in reverse, starting with Euclid's geometry and proceeding eventually to topology and beyond. With the more recent collaboration of R. Garcia, a historian and philosopher of science, Piaget (Piaget & Garcia, in press) has revised his description of relations among geometric concepts and expanded the analysis to include detailed studies of exemplars in algebra, and mechanics. They detail a general developmental account that is said to apply equally well to specific instances. In each example there is a development, on the part of scientists and mathematicians from interrelating internal properties of the field of application (the intraoperational phase) to understanding these properties as invariants within transformations. This is followed by the discovery of transformations (the interoperational phase). The interoperational is followed by the interpretation of such transformations as aspects of total structures, from which the transformations are derivable as intrinsic variations (the transoperational phase). A relativisation of concepts and a reinterpretation of the meaning of variables (or concepts) accompanies the progression through these stages.

In respect to geometry, the new version details the progression in geometric concepts from the intrafigural to the inter-figural and finally to the transfigural. An extended historical-epistemological analysis shows the parallels between the history of both geometry and algebra and their interrelations, and a parallel development in the child's reasoning about geometry and space. The "why" and "how" of this development is explained in similar terms to those expounded in the general theory of equilibration. Subjectively, in each science or mathematics there is a search for explanation (filling the gaps), and objectively, the achievement of "necessity" (that is, logically necessary relations), which always remains relative. In characterizing the equilibration process, the emphasis is on endogenous processing and the role of reflective abstraction, although in the work on the history of science there is greater attention given to the social evolution of knowledge. For cognitive development there is also greater account taken of the fact that to the child objects are not "pure," they are defined by their social roles as well. When language develops, objects are even more complexly interpolated into a system of social interpretation that cannot but affect the process of assimilation. The problem for genetic epistemology is to explain how assimilation is conditioned by such social meaning and how particular experience depends on such meanings. Whereas the history of science shows the clearest examples of the influence of the framework of meanings into which objects and events are interpreted by society, the same, Piaget says, is not true for intellectual development, where speculation holds the ground, in the absence of experimental data.

For the history of science, Piaget and Garcia appear to accept insights from Kuhn (and Feyerabend) as to the manner in which social paradigms become dominant epistemic frameworks and act in the manner of ideologies blocking development outside the accepted conceptual frame. From that point on, however, Piaget and Garcia part company not only with Kuhn and Feyerabend but also with Popper and Lakatos.

They emphasize that the only factors that are truly universal in both cognitive development and in the history of science are functional and not structural. These involve the assimilation of novelties to existing structures and the accommodation to new discoveries. The functional aspect in cognitive development (the process of equilibration) explains the relative stability of structures once formed, as well as the disequilibria of structures, and the reequilibrations that lead to higher order structures. The change from one structure to the next is clearly discontinuous, a "leap," but the change is neither predictable nor subject to norms.

Nevertheless, structures elaborated in the course of genesis have no internal stability that resist perturbations (in accord with Kuhn and against Popper, who holds that change in science comes from refutation). At the same time, structures undergo change that follow an internal logic. Piaget and Garcia fault Popper and Lakatos for neglecting the epistemological aspects of change, that is, in establishing what precisely is involved in the change from a "lower level" theory to a higher level theory.

The neglect of this way of investigating the issues results from other's disregard, particularly by Kuhn, of what is known (presumably from a Piagetian account) of how knowledge develops in the child. Instead, Kuhn is accused of falling back on a neo-positivist interpretation of that development. (Kuhn in talking of a "gestalt switch" would appear, however, to be using a modified gestalt characterization of change.)

Using a (newer) Piagetian formulation as a guide leads to a different view of scientific development. It emphasizes functional continuity from the "natural" and prescientific to the scientific, which can include "breaks, leaps, disequilibria and re-equilibrations," and in which there is a relative absence of conscious knowledge of its own mechanisms of construction and change. This account, however is not to the neglect of the social context. In a dialectical account, the object is always located within a network of social relations.

Here Piaget confronts a seeming paradox. If society is to have the influence claimed, how can one then claim to find the same cognitive processes operating in different periods of human history, and in all children irrespective of social group and ethnicity? Knowing the nature of the mechanisms by which knowledge is acquired in the interaction between subject and object, and of how objects, capable of being assimilated, appear to the subject, suggests an answer. Society modifies the objects but not the mechanisms of knowledge acquisition. The meanings attributed to objects are affected by the social context, but the way the meanings, however defined, are acquired depends on the subject's cognitive mechanisms and not on the contributions of the social group. The social group, through the environment it creates and through social models, affects how the subject's attention is directed toward certain objects and situations, and how objects are located in particular contexts, but these do not modify how the biological mechanisms of acquisition function in all manner of social and cultural contexts.

Meaning and Truth.

Piaget often amended and transformed his theory, yet rarely accounted or indicated that a change was taking place or that he rejected an earlier view. He did just that in regard to egocentrism, stages, and equilibration, but these were rare exceptions. It was therefore a revelation to see, in a note published in 1980, the last year of his life (Piaget, 1980), a statement that his logic of operations "was too closely linked to the traditional model of extensional logic and truth tables. A better way, I now believe, of capturing the natural growth of logical thinking in the child is to pursue a kind of logic of meanings ... which ... would be a decanted version of our former logic of operations and I hope it will provide a better way of accounting for the contribution of new knowledge" (1980, pp. 5–7).

One might think that a statement of such seeming importance would have caused considerable stir in Geneva, and in Piagetian scholarship elsewhere. To date, it has not. The forthcoming publication of Piaget's last book, devoted to the logic of meaning, may change that (Piaget & Garcia, in press). The significance of this change in the theory, as important as any made by Piaget, will be discussed with a description of what Piaget proposes.

It is well known that Piaget's logico-mathematical models, particularly the groupings, the combinatorial and propositional logics, and the INRC groups that he maps onto the child's natural thought have been under considerable attack from logicians, mathematicians and psychologists. The reasons are many, but they can be reduced to two main issues. First, they violate in a number of instances the logical and mathematical assumptions as well as details of the theories from which they are drawn. Second, those models, as psychological models, are of questionable psychological reality in that their implications do not accord well with relevant empirical data. Nonetheless, up to the present, Piaget appears to have been quite loyal to his own theory. The changes he made previously were principally additions to the logic of operations. The most important of these was the addition of category theory (from mathematics) to account for correspondences, principally in preoperational thought. This addition also led to a change in the theory of groupings that play an important role in concrete operations. So the natural question to ask is whether the new theory of meanings represents a signal change in direction, or whether it is an extension of his logical theory. It appears to be both. On the one hand, Piaget appears not to be rejecting combinatorial or propositional logics or the INRC groups, but rather to reinterpret their place within a larger logical framework. The theory is very different in its emphasis on meaning, or to be more precise, on intensional rather than the extensional logics he favored in the past. Extensional logic is concerned principally with validity or the truth value of statements (i.e., propositions) and the utility of those logics for Piaget was that they mapped onto the data that were forthcoming from his group's studies of problem solving and scientific and mathematical reasoning. He neglected for the most part the well-known distinction made by Frege between *(Sinn)* "sense" and *(Bedeutung)* "truth value," or more broadly between meaning and truth. Although he did identify meaning with the assimilation process, even in his early work, it was not a central focus of the theory, except in adopting the classical distinction between intension and extension and insisting that "true" knowledge of a concept requires understanding both of the extension and intension of the concept or term. What distanced Piaget from many other students of cognitive development was his insistence that having a true concept required integrating its extensional properties with its intensional. Thus a true quantitative concept was not acquired till concrete operations at about 7 years of age, since it is not till then that the child could deal with part/whole and inclusion relations, and thus with extension of a term. The new theory of meaning puts a different face on those relations.

The goal of the new theory is to reconstruct and expand operational logic in two ways. First, to construct a logic of meaning from which operational logic could be derived, and second to reformulate propositional logic in part by loosening its tie to extensional (truth table) logic. True to Piaget's usual method he attempts to show that the origins of logical thought are to be found in sensorimotor actions, more precisely in the implications that exist between sensorimotor actions. Consequently, the logic of meaning rests on implications that go beyond that of statements, a view long consistent with Piaget's claim that language is not the origin of thought. Thus all action entails meaning to the subject by way of implications; consequently systems of implication reside in the meanings of action, which only later are to be seen in the meanings of operations. The subject's expectations and anticipations in the course of action imply the existence of early inferences, although it is necessary to distinguish between the meaning of actions and the causality of actions (the verifiability of outcomes), probably the earliest instances of the distinction between meaning and truth. That is, an action in itself is neither true nor false, it is evaluated in terms of its outcome in respect to a goal. An action implication, however, involved in expectations or anticipations of actions, may be true or false and thus constitutes a logic at the most elementary levels of development. The source of meaning is the assimilation of an object in a scheme. Inasmuch as any assimilation by its nature generates meaning, a causal succession of agents can lead to implications between meanings.

Piaget proposes a series of levels of meaning implication in early development, the most elementary of which are included in the construction of action, object, and relation schemes. These are said to derive from the earlier "global perspective pictures" of the child's undifferentiated universe. Hence, the first cognitive achievements appear in the first action schemes. Concepts of objects and relations are composed (in the intensional sense) and the first inferences and implications between meanings and actions rest on these. Possibly the more significant developments are those that develop around the construction of "relation schemes." The example given is of inserting smaller cubes into larger ones at about 10 months of age. The container-content scheme, a relational scheme, is said to arise by reflective abstraction from the often-used daily scheme of "putting something in one's mouth." These relational schemes may be coordinated further when a positive action (inserting) is followed by a reverse action (taking out), which suggests the first implications among actions, "action x implies the possibility of the reverse action."

This initial level is defined by Piaget as "protological" to suggest a preparatory phase for a later period in which deduction proper appears.[9] This phase is marked by the appearance of the first assimilation schemes and consequently the first meaning implications (e.g., relations are established between grasping and seeing with progressively improved computation of distances).

The second of the sensorimotor levels is marked by systematic action implications that yield stable structures, such as those of object permanence. These structures imply that positions and displacements are sufficiently coordinated to form a "group of displacements." As with the first level, positive implications are blended with negations.

With the appearance of the semiotic function (18 months to 2 years) action implications are expressible in statements and hence the formation of meaning implications among statements. This level is also determined by meanings (intensions) and is not reducible to extensions. These meanings are dependent on what Piaget calls "nestings" and "inherences" and are still not referable to truth tables. The early operations, appear at this level, in regard to which Piaget makes some striking claims. He says that these early formed operations cannot be organized into structural wholes (such as groupings). Taken separately, however, each is isomorphic with one of the 16 binary operations of propositional logic. It "astonished" Piaget to "find" the 16 operations at the level of the coordinations among actions, long before the appearance at 11 or 12 of formal operations.

Adding the logical connectives, "and" as well as "or," and negations to the combinations, results in many more than 16 operations (as a function of the various forms of conjunctions, disjunctions, etc.). These combinations are elaborated by subjects on each occasion in a particular context and on the basis of meaning implications. Theoretically, the result is that the foundation of logic, based on implications and negations, is inferential in nature, and the logic of meanings so elaborated prepares for the operatory logic. The operatory logic, which in the past was closely tied to extension, is now tied to intension and the logic of meaning.

Piaget proposes that the formation of meanings, and "meaning implications" (implications between actions and operations) are distinct entities that nevertheless are indissociable. Their unity lies in some shared features, but more importantly they grow in a dialectical relation as two poles in a cycle, within the spiral of development.

In development, from elementary forms to later logical operations, the genetic "roots" are meanings and meaning implications. The beginnings are in implicit action implications that become explicit in consciously formulated statements. Meanings and meaning implications take various forms. The simplest meaning form is the predicate (defined by similarities and differences between object properties and other predicates). Predicates are bound by preoperations of

"conjunctions" that are either "constrained" (necessary, with a mutual implication, as in shape and size) or "free" (contingent, as with shape and color). In-be-
tween are "coupled predicates," based on "pseudo-constrained" conjunctions
(a form of "incorrect" reasoning seen in young subjects).

Piaget goes on to detail the various forms of meaning implication. First, he
"replaces" classical extensional implication, $p \supset q = (p.q \ v \ \overline{p}.q \ v \ \overline{p}.\overline{q})$ by *meaning implication*: A ---> B, A implies B if at least one meaning of B is included in
(= inheres) in the meaning of A and is transitive (i.e., the meaning of C is included in that of B, that of D in that of C, B, A, etc.). By virtue of this definition,
any action, in addition to being carried out (its causal aspect), has a meaning,
consequently, by necessity, there are implications between actions that go
beyond the traditional view of only implications between statements. From the
very beginning, then, there is a logic of actions which is the basis of the logic of
operations.

Meaning implications are the first structures to result from interacting meanings. Combinations of these initial fragments of structure prepare for the groupings of the concrete operational period (7–8 years on). They also prepare for the
more complex 16 cases in the truth table, which now must be interpreted in terms
of meanings (intensions). Thus intersections, incompatibilities, etc. are formed
early at the level of actions.

Piaget's project for a new theory of meaning appears to have been carried out
only partially. The part of the project only programmatically detailed is the
"decanted" version of the former operatory logic. Inasmuch as Anderson and
Belnap's logic of entailment, which Piaget clearly intended as a model for his
theory of meanings, is inclusive of truth functional logic, it does not require a
total rejection of the operatory logic Piaget previously developed. From the
description of Piaget's new theory it appears that he did not intend that it be
eliminated but amended as well as pruned, leaving a "decanted" residue.[10]

According to one view (discussed in Ricco, in press), Anderson and Belnap's
logic of entailment is a formal, mathematical logic, with the role of content or
meaning limited and indirect and given an abstract treatment. As a consequence,
post-Piagetians such as Le Bonniec (Ricco, in press), reject entailment logic as a
basis for developing an adequate logic of natural thought. Her approach instead
is through modal logic, which Piaget in turn dismissed as a possible alternative.

Where to From Here?

The final question is, whither Piagetian theory and research in the future? The
attitudes of Genevans themselves take two forms (Inhelder et al., 1987), both
conservative. The more conservative view is that Piaget's theory has left a rich
legacy, the value of which has not been fully extracted. The task should be to

develop from the theory all it implies; testing further its implications, and extending these to as many domains as possible. The other stand views the theory as in need of some modification and even elaboration, in areas that later research has shown to be inadequately conceptualized. In my view, each of these positions is reasonable but should be augmented by a third, following Piaget's own model for change. That is, to delete from the theory that which does not adequately account for the research evidence, substitute other models for those that are nonfunctional and augment and modify them as psychological reality dictates (Beilin, 1985).

The evidence from Geneva itself shows considerable reluctance to tamper with the received legacy, particularly the logical models, with minor exceptions.[11] Those who have had prior affiliations with Geneva, appear to be much more outspoken in this regard. Apostle (1982), for example, offers a detailed attack on many features of Piaget's logic, including some assumptions that appear in the new theory of meanings (such as the equating of relations and intension). His view of the direction that Piaget's logic should take is to expand the theory with both functional logic and modal logic.

If one looks at the research agenda of various Genevans (the original Piaget research group is now located in a series of interest-based units within different departments), they appear to divide into the traditional Piagetians who carry on in somewhat the same vein as the original Piagetian program (logic, functional aspects of development, pragmatics, constructivism, etc.) and a self-styled group of neo-Piagetians who are concerned with those aspects of research neglected by Piaget: social relations, cultural influences, affectivity and the biological infrastructure of development; relations between normal and pathological cognitive development, and the application of the Piagetian approach to education (Shulman et al., 1985, pp. 12–13; Mogdil & Mogdil, 1982).

CONCLUSION

What we see in the new Piagetian theory is what we have seen in Piaget's theory historically, a commitment to basic indispensable elements in the core of the research program that nevertheless have changed in various ways. This occurred, sometimes by deletion, but more often through theory additions, and by the incorporation of models from outside of psychology. The consequent reorganizations and integrations, however, have always tended toward coherence. The theory remains structural in many respects, but the principal thrust of research and theory development in the years after 1975 are essentially in the direction of building up the functional aspects of the theory, and in this Piaget was very much in touch with his times. How the theory will fare in the future is difficult to foretell, despite Piaget's outward confidence that it would survive, whereas other equally strong theories might not. As he might have put it himself, the later theory opens up many new possibilities. It remains to be seen what they lead to.[12]

NOTES

1. Laudan (1979), dissenting from Lakatos's characterization of the hard core of research programs as unchanging, holds instead that hard core assumptions may in fact be altered with developments in a research tradition. If Piaget's theory can be taken as a prototype of a psychological research program, then the evidence appears to favor Laudan's view. Piaget's hard core consists of some assumptions that have remained unaltered and others that changed as significant elements were added to it. A striking example is the addition of correspondences and morphisms to the theory. This addition altered the assumption that all cognition entails transformation.

2. The fundamentals of the theory stirred considerable debate among scholars. I will consider only a small number of these; just those that have resulted in later changes in the theory.

3. References in the bibliography give the dates for the English/French editions, only the English edition dates are given in the text.

4. Piaget distinguishes between scheme (pl. schemes) and schema (pl. schemata). Scheme refers to operational activities, to that which is repeatable and generalizable in an action (for example, that which is common in "sucking," "pushing," or "hitting"). A schema, in the figurative aspects of thought (imagery, memory, perception) provides a representation of reality with no attempt to transform it, as occurs in a scheme. In his early reports, Piaget used the term schema that in later work is referred as scheme.

5. Although this material is part of the newer Piagetian theory, it is introduced here to place it in an appropriate context.

6. The Genevan position on strategies and procedures is developed in a number of works published between 1974 and 1980 (see Inhelder & Piaget 1980). A history of research on strategies may be found in Gholson, 1980. The Genevans in their approach to strategies and procedures were undoubtedly influenced by information-processing theories, which become important in American and English psychology in the 1960s and 1970s.

7. Piaget makes a subtle change from the philosopher's "knowing that" to "knowing why."

8. There are two English language translations of the 1975 work (Piaget, 1978, 1985).

9. For some years now, Langer (1980, 1986) has pursued a research program devoted to a study of the development of protological forms in the sensorimotor and preoperational periods. There is overlap and non-overlap in Langer's and Piaget's approaches. The latter of course is grounded in the new theory of meaning.

10. The description of Piaget's new theory of meanings is based, at the time of this writing, on the availability of only the first half of the volume by Piaget and Garcia (in press) that Piaget had prepared. In the second half, Garcia details the relations between Anderson and Belnap's logic of implication, based on relevance and necessity, and Piaget's operatory logic and shows how the latter is subsumed by the former.

11. In the Seventh Advanced Course of the "Fondation (FR.) Archives Jean Piaget" held in Geneva in 1985 on the theme "Piaget Today," even with two presentations on Piaget's logic, the new theory of meanings was not mentioned (except by myself). It is referred to, however, in the introduction to the volume, which consists of papers and subsequent discussion presented in the "course" (Inhelder, DeCaprona, & Cornu-Wells [1987]).

12. Two late works, one posthumous, await publication:
Piaget, J. et al. (1980b) *Les formes elementaires de la dialectique.*
Paris: Gallimard.
Piaget, J., & Henriques, G. (in press) *To compare and transform.*
Hillsdale, NJ: Erlbaum.

REFERENCES

Apostel, L. (1982). The future of Piagetian logic. *Revue Internationale de Philosophie, 36*, 567–611.

Beilin, H. (1971). Developmental stages and developmental processes. In D. Green, M. Ford & G. Flamer (Eds.), *Measurement and Piaget*. New York: McGraw-Hill.

Beilin, H. (1983). The new functionalism and Piaget's program. In E. K. Scholnick (Ed.), *New trends in conceptual representation: Challenges to Piaget's theory?* Hillsdale, NJ: Lawrence Erlbaum Associates.

Beilin, H. (1985). Dispensable and core elements in Piaget's research program. *The Genetic Epistemologist, 13*, 1–16.

Boden, M. A. (1979). *Piaget*. London: Fontana.

Brainerd, C. (1978). The stage question in cognitive-developmental theory. *The Behavioral and Brain Sciences, 1*, 173–182.

Cohen, L. (1979). On developing knowledge of infant perception and cognition. *American Psychologist, 34*, 894–899.

Flavell, J. H. (1963). *The developmental psychology of Jean Piaget*. Princeton, NJ: D. Van Nostand.

Gelman, R. & Gallistel, C. R. (1978). *The child's understanding of number*. Cambridge, MA: Harvard University Press.

Gholson, B. (1980). *The cognitive-developmental basis of human learning: Studies in hypothesis testing*. New York: Academic Press.

Gholson, B. (1985). Kuhn, Lakatos and Laudan: Applications in the history of physics and psychology. *American Psychologist, 40*, 755–769.

Gibson, J. J. (1979). *The ecological approach to visual perception*. Boston: Houghton-Mifflin.

Gruber, H. E., & Voneche, J. J. (Eds.), (1977). *The essential Piaget*. New York: Basic Books.

Harris, P. L. (1983). Infant cognition. In P. H. Mussen (Ed.), *Handbook of child psychology*. (4th Edition). Vol. 2. *Infancy and developmental psychobiology*. H. H. Haith & J. J. Campos (Eds.). New York: Wiley and Sons.

Hochberg, J. (1982). The representation of things and people. In E. Gombrich, J. Hochberg & M. Black, *Art, perception and reality*. Baltimore, MD: Johns Hopkins Press.

Inhelder, B. (1980). Genetic epistemology and psychology of physical causality. *Cahiers de la Fondation Archives Jean Piaget No. 1*.

Inhelder, B. (1982). Outlook. In S. Modgil & C. Modgil (Eds.), *Jean Piaget: Consensus and controversy*. New York: Praeger.

Inhelder, B., de Caprona, D., & Cornu-Wells, A. (Eds.). (1987). *Piaget today*. London & Hillsdale, NJ: Lawrence Erlbaum Associates.

Inhelder, B., & Piaget, P. (1980). Procedures and structures. In D. R. Olson (Ed.), *The social foundations of language and thought: Essays in honor of Jerome S. Bruner*. New York: Norton.

Inhelder, B., Sinclair, H., & Bovet, M. (1974). *Learning and the development of cognition*. Cambridge, MA: Harvard University Press.

Langer, J. (1980). *The origins of logic: Six to twelve months*. New York: Academic Press.

Langer, J. (1986). *The origins of logic: One to two years*. New York: Academic Press.

Laudan, L. (1977). *Progress and its problems*. Berkeley: University of California Press.

Levin, I. (Ed.). (1986). *Stage and structure: Reopening the debate*. Norwood, NJ: Ablex Publishing.

Marr, D. (1982). *Vision: A computational investigation into human representation and processing of visual information*. San Francisco: W. H. Freeman.

Modgil, S., & Modgil, C. (Eds.), (1982). *Jean Piaget: Consensus and controversy*. New York: Praeger.

Montangero, J. (1985). *Genetic epistemology: Yesterday and today*. New York: CUNY/Graduate School and University Center.

Piaget, J. (1930/1927). *The child's conception of physical causality*. London: Routledge and Kegan Paul.

Paiget, J. (1952/1936). *The origins of intelligence in children*. New York: International Universities Press.

Piaget, J. (1953). *Logic and psychology*. Manchester: Manchester University.

Piaget, J. (1960). The general problems of the psychobiological development of the child. In J. M. Tanner & B. Inhelder (Eds.), *Discussions on child development*. Vol. 4. New York: International Universities Press.

Piaget, J. (1962/1945). *Play, dreams and imitation in childhood*. New York: Norton.

Piaget, J. (1970/1968). *Structuralism*. New York: Basic Books.

Piaget, J. (1971/1967). *Biology and knowledge: An essay on the relations between organic regulations and cognitive processes*. Chicago: University of Chicago Press.

Piaget, J. (1977). Some recent research and its link with new theory of groupings and conservations based on commutability. In R. Rieber & K. Salzinger (Eds.), The roots of American psychology: Historical influences and implications for the future. *Annals of the N.Y. Academy of Sciences, 291*, 350–357.

Piaget, J. (1978b/1975). *The development of thought: Equilibrations of cognitive structures*. Oxford: Blackwell.

Piaget, J. (1985/1975). *The equilibration of cognitive structures. The central problem of intellectual development*. Chicago: University of Chicago Press.

Piaget, J. (1976/1974). *The grasp of consciousness: Action and concept in the young child*. Cambridge, MA: Harvard University Press.

Piaget, J. (1978/1974). *Success and understanding*. Cambridge, MA: Harvard University Press.

Piaget, J. (1979). Correspondences and transformations. In F. B. Murray (Ed.), *The impact of Piagetian theory: On education, philosophy, psychiatry and psychology*. Baltimore, MD: University Park Press.

Piaget, J. (1980/1974). *Experiments in contradiction*. Chicago: University of Chicago Press.

Piaget, J. (1983). Piaget's theory. In P. H. Mussen (Ed.), *Handbook of child psychology*. (4th Edition). Vol. 1. W. Kessen (Ed.), *History theory and methods* (pp. 103–128). New York: Wiley & Sons.

Piaget, J. (1987/1981). *Possibility and necessity*. Vol. 1. *The role of possibility in cognitive development*. Vol. 2. *The role of necessity in cognitive development*. Minneapolis: University of Minnesota Press.

Piaget, J., & Garcia, R. (1974/1971). *Understanding causality*. New York: W.W. Norton.

Piaget, J., & Garcia, R. (in press). *Psychogenesis and the history of science*. New York: Columbia University Press.

Piaget, J., & Garcia, R. (in press). *Towards a logic of meanings*. Hillsdale, NJ: Lawrence Erlbaum Associates.

Piaget, J., Grize, J. B., Szeminska, A., & Bang, V. (1977). *Epistemology and the psychology of functions*. Dordrecht, Holland: D. Reidel Publishing.

Piaget, J., Inhelder, B., & Szeminska, A. (1960/1948). *The child's conception of geometry*. New York: Basic Books.

Piaget, J., & Voyat, G. (1979). The possible, the impossible and the necessary. In F. B. Murray (Ed.), *The impact of Piagetian theory*. Baltimore, MD: University Park Press.

Ricco, R. B. (in press). Necessity and the logic of entailment. In W. F. Overton (Ed.), *Reasoning, necessity, and logic: Developmental perspectives*. Hillsdale, NJ: Lawrence Erlbaum Associates.

Rotman, B. (1977). *Jean Piaget: Psychologist of the real*. Ithaca: Cornell University Press.

Scholnick, E. K. (1983). *Current trends in conceptual representation: Challenges to Piaget's theory?* Hillsdale, NJ: Lawrence Erlbaum Associates.

Shulman, V. L., Restaino-Baumann, L. C., & Butler, L. (Eds.), (1985). *The future of Piagetian theory: The neo-Piagetians*. New York: Plenum.

Spelke, E. S. (1985). Object perception and the object concept in infancy. In M. Perlmutter (Ed.), *Minnesota Symposium on Child Development*, Vol. 18. Minneapolis: University of Minnesota Press.

Toulmin, S. (1981). Epistemology and developmental psychology. In E. Gollin (Ed.), *Developmental plasticity*. New York: Academic Press.

Ullmann, S. (1980). Against direct perception. *The Behavioral and Brain Sciences, 3*, 373–416.

Vuyk, R. (1981). *Overview and critique of Piaget's genetic epistemology 1965–1980*. Vol. 1 & 2. New York: Academic Press.

INFORMATION-PROCESSING APPROACHES

David Klahr

1. CHARACTERIZING INFORMATION-PROCESSING APPROACHES

Reflections on the intellectual history of a field often reveal a long period between the occurrence of fundamental insights and the first concrete steps based on those insights. Over 25 years ago, Herbert Simon (1962) suggested the general form of an information-processing approach to cognitive development:

> If we can construct an information processing system with rules of behavior that lead it to behave like the dynamic system we are trying to describe, then this system is a theory of the child at one stage of the development. Having described a particular stage by a program, we would then face the task of discovering what additional information processing mechanisms are needed to simulate developmental change—the transition from one stage to the next. That is, we would need to discover how the system could modify its own structure. Thus, the theory would have two parts—a program to describe performance at a particular stage and a learning program governing the transitions from stage to stage (Simon, 1962, pp. 154–155).

Annals of Child Development, Volume 6, pages 133-185.
Copyright © 1989 by JAI Press Inc.
All rights of reproduction in any form reserved.
ISBN: 0-89232-979-3

This provocative idea[1] motivated my own early research with Iain Wallace (cf. Klahr & Wallace, 1970a, 1970b, 1972), but not until 10 years after Simon's suggestion did an entire volume explicitly focused on "Information Processing in Children" (Farnham-Diggory, 1972) appear. The chapters in that book represent an interesting contrast between traditional approaches to perception and memory (e.g., Pollack, 1972; Hagen 1972), Genevan views on information-processing issues (Inhelder, 1972; Cellerier, 1972), and important considerations surrounding information-processing approaches to development (Newell, 1972).

A few years later, when Iain Wallace and I were writing a monograph entitled "Cognitive Development: An Information Processing View" (Klahr & Wallace, 1976), we chose the indefinite article in our title carefully. The field of adult information-processing psychology was expanding rapidly and diffusely, and we were well aware that our view of important issues and proposed solutions was neither comprehensive nor representative. Indeed, we believed that, with respect to adult cognition, there was no single perspective that could characterize the entire field of information processing, and therefore no single vantage point from which to present *the* information-processing view of cognitive development.

With the passage of another dozen years, the definitional task has become no easier. The very pervasiveness of information-processing psychology contributes to the difficulty, and the imperialism implicit in some definitions exacerbates it. Another problem in deciding what is and is not an example of the information-processing approach is that, "many developmental psychologists ... are not aware that they have accepted certain assumptions and methods of the information-processing approach" (Miller, 1983, p. 249). Further complicating the problem is the fact that others have already reviewed this discipline and have offered their own definitions of information-processing psychology in general (e.g., Lachman, Lachman, & Butterfield, 1979; Palmer & Kimchi, 1986) and information-processing within the field of cognitive development (e.g., Bisanz et al., 1987; Siegler, 1983; Neches, 1982; Rabinowitz et al., 1987; Klahr & Wallace, 1976). Nevertheless, in this chapter I accept the challenge presented by the Editor of this volume, and I attempt to say something about "information processing" that may be useful to readers of *Annals of Child Development*.

Few people would disagree with the recent claim that, with respect to alternative approaches for understanding *adult* cognition:

the one that has dominated psychological investigation for the last decade or two is information processing. For better or worse, the information-processing approach has had an enormous impact on modern cognitive research, leaving its distinctive imprint on both the kinds of theories that have been proposed and the kinds of experiments that have been performed to test them. Its influence has been so pervasive, in fact, that some writers have argued that information processing has achieved the exalted status of a "Kuhnian paradigm" for cognitive psychology (Lachman, Lachman, & Butterfield, 1979). It is unclear whether or not this claim is really justified, but the fact that it has even been suggested documents the preeminence of information processing in modern cognitive psychology (Palmer & Kimchi, 1987, p. 37).

Deciding whether information processing is equally preeminent in cognitive development depends in large part on how far one chooses to cast one's definitional net. The broadest definitions of information-processing approaches to cognitive development usually invoke the family resemblance concept: An approach qualifies for inclusion to the extent that it manifests a certain set of features. Although no single approach uses all of them, the more features that are present in a piece of work, and the more highly articulated those features, the more typical it is of the approach.

It will be convenient in this paper to propose a dichotomy between "hard core" and "soft core" information-processing approaches, based on the set of features that they exhibit. To preview the set of features that will be used, I have listed them all in Table 1, and they will be elaborated in subsequent sections. The hard/soft distinction serves to organize this paper, but the terms should not be viewed as mutually exclusive. In fact, all of the soft core features can be mapped into their stronger versions in the hard core set. The mapping will become evident as the features are described. It will also become evident that the univer-

Table 1. Features of Information-processing Approaches
to Cognitive Development

Features of Soft-core information processing approaches:

THEORETICAL FEATURES

- S1: The assumption that the child's mental activity can be described in terms of processes that manipulate symbols and symbol structures.
- S2: The assumption that these symbolic processes operate within an information processing system with identifiable properties, constraints, and consequences.
- S3: The characterization of cognitive development as self-modification of the information processing system.

METHODOLOGICAL FEATURES

- S4: Use of formal notational schemes for expressing complex, dynamic systems.
- S5: Modeling the time-course of cognitive processing over relatively short durations: chronometric analysis.
- S6: Use of high-density data from error-patterns and protocols to induce and test complex models.
- S7: Use of highly detailed analyses of the environment facing the child on specific tasks.

Features of Hard-core Information Processing Approaches:

- H1: Use of computer simulation.
- H2: Commitment to elements of the simulation as theoretical assertions, rather than just a metaphor or computational convenience.
- H3: Goal of creating a complete self-modifying simulation that accounts for both task performance and development.

sality of information-processing to which Palmer and Kimchi refer applies only to the soft-core approaches, while the hard core, as it will be defined here, applies to a relatively small, but influential, part of the field.

The chapter is organized as follows. In the remainder of this section, I characterize the defining features of information-processing approaches to cognitive development. This will include a sample of illustrative instances. In Section 2, I describe a particular information-processing approach—one based on production-system models—that is becoming very influential. Finally, in Section 3, I summarize what the major accomplishments have been so far, and I speculate about future directions.

1.1 Soft-core Information-processing Approaches to Cognitive Development

The features that characterize soft-core approaches can be grouped into two categories: theoretical assumptions and methodological practices.[2]

1.1.1 Theoretical Assumptions

S1: The child's mental activity can be described in terms of processes that manipulate symbols and symbol structures. My use of the terms "symbol" and "symbol-structure" here is quite distinct from the notion of symbolic thought associated with Vygotsky's "symbolic play" or Piagetian questions about when a child makes a transition from pre-symbolic to symbolic functioning. Symbolization in that diffuse sense concerns the general issue of the power of the child's representational capacity, not whether or not symbols are involved. Instead, I am using symbols at a more microscopic level, in the sense intended by Newell (1980), where symbols provide access to other symbols. Such symbols comprise the elementary units in *any* representation of knowledge including sensory-motor knowledge or linguistic structures. Thus, distinctions between dense and articulated symbols (Goodman, 1968) or personal and consensual symbols (Kolers & Smythe, 1984) are not relevant at the level of underlying symbols necessary to support all symbolic capacity. Given this microscopic interpretation of what a symbol is, it seems to me that the symbolic assumption is so deeply embedded in the field that often it is only implicit, and its use ranges from interpretations of relatively focused studies to all-encompassing theoretical positions.

For example, DeLoache (1987) discovered an abrupt improvement between 30 and 36 months in children's ability to understand the symbolic relationship between a model of a room and the real room. She summarizes this as a milestone in "the realization that an object can be understood both as a thing itself and as a symbol of something else" (DeLoache, 1987, p. 1556), and she notes that the younger children fail "to think about a symbolic object both as an object and as a symbol'' (p. 1557). Thus, at the global (or conventional) level, DeLoache's results suggest that the 2.5-year-old children are "pre-symbolic" (at least on this task). But it is clear that if one were to formulate detailed models of children's knowledge about this task at both levels of performance, then one would, in both cases, postulate systems that had the ability to process symbols at the microscopic level defined above. Thus, even in an ingenious research program—such as DeLoache's—directed at determining when children "become symbolic," the assumption of underlying symbol-processing capacity remains.

The second example of implicit assumptions about symbol processing comes from Case's (1985, 1986) theory. He postulates *figurative schemes, state representations, problem representations, goals, executive control structures,* and *strategies* in order to account for performance at specific levels of development, and *search, evaluation, retagging,* and *consolidation* to account for development from one performance level to the next. Case makes no explicit reference to *symbol structures,* but his central theoretical construct—what he calls *Short Term Storage Space* (STSS)—clearly implies that the kinds of things that get processed are comprised of symbols and symbol structures. Thus, although Case commonly contrasts his own approach (cf. Case, 1985, pp. 43–50) with hard-core information-processing approaches that rely on computer simulation, I view his work as being well within the domain of soft-core information processing.

Explicit assumptions about the centrality of symbol structures are exemplified by the "knowledge is power" approach to cognitive development. The general goal of this line of work is to demonstrate that much of the advantage that adults have over children derives from their more extensive knowledge base in specific domains, rather than from more powerful general processes. The most convincing evidence supporting this position comes from Chi's studies (Chi, 1976, 1977, 1978) in which children who have more domain-specific knowledge than adults (e.g., children who have more knowledge about chess or dinosaurs or classmates' faces) outperform their adult counterparts on a range of tasks in which access to the specific knowledge is a determining factor in performance. In all of these, and related, studies, the major explanatory variable is access to symbolic structures (chunks, semantic nets, etc.) that supports the superior performance of the children.

S2: These symbolic processes operate within an information processing system with identifiable properties, constraints, and consequences. Typically, developmentalists interested in a variety of cognitive processes have assumed an architecture having cannonical form of the STM/LTM model of the late 1960s and early 1970s (cf. Atkinson & Shiffrin, 1968; Craik & Lockhart, 1972; Norman, Rumelhart, & LNR, 1975). This architecture is comprised of several sensory buffers (e.g., "iconic" memory, an "acoustic buffer," a limited capacity short-term memory, and an unlimited, content-addressable long-term memory. Newell

(1972, 1973, 1980) developed the concept of *cognitive architecture* of the mind, and both he and Anderson (1983) have made very specific proposals about how it is structured. Cognitive architectures can be cast at several levels, just as one can discuss the architecture of a computer chip, or the entire central processing unit, or the micro-code, and so on, up to the architecture of a high-level user application. The cognitive architectures proposed by Newell and by Anderson span several of these levels, starting with the structure of the program interpreter and continuing down to the level of basic processes, such as the rates and capacities of short-term memory, and the relation between short- and long-term memory.

Developmental researchers interested in higher-level problem-solving processes such as seriation, arithmetic, and problem-solving (e.g., Baylor & Gascon, 1974; Neches, 1987; Klahr & Wallace, 1972; Young, 1976) have adopted a very specific form of the higher level cognitive architecture: the production system architecture proposed by Newell and Anderson. But the topic of specific architectures, such as production systems, takes us from soft-core to hard-core information processing, so I will defer that discussion until later.

Note that proposals for cognitive architectures are not the same as theories that attempt to characterize the "structure of thought." Such approaches, best exemplified by Piaget, have been recently refined and extended by such theorists as Halford (1975) and Fischer. For example, Fischer's skill theory (Fischer, 1980; Fischer & Pipp, 1984) is cast entirely in terms of abstract structures with scant attention to processes. The transition processes that he does discuss—substitution, focusing, compounding, differentiation and intercoordination—are presented only in terms of their global characteristics, and are not constrained by an underlying architecture that processes information.

S3: Cognitive development occurs via self-modification of the information-processing system. This assumption shows up in several guises, ranging from Piaget's original assertions about assimilation, accommodation, and the active construction of the environment, to proposals for various kinds of structural reorganizations (e.g., Case, 1986; Halford, 1970; Fischer, 1980), to interaction between performance and learning (Siegler, 1988), to explicit mechanisms for self-modifying computer models (Klahr, Langley, & Neches, 1987). This emphasis on self-modification does not deny the importance of external influences such as direct instruction, modelling, and the social context of learning and development. However, it underscores the fact that whatever the form of external environment, the information-processing system itself must ultimately encode, store, index, and process that environment. Here too, the soft-core approaches tend to leave this somewhat vague and implicit, whereas the hard-core approaches make specific proposals about each of these processes. However, all information-processing approaches to development acknowledge the fundamental importance of the capacity for self-modification.

1.1.2 Methodological Practice

S4: Use of formal notational schemes for expressing complex, dynamic systems. While using computer simulation languages may be *sine qua non* of hardcore information processing, there are several lesser degrees of formalization that mark the soft-core methods including such devices as scripts, frames, flowcharts, tree diagrams, and pseudo-programming languages. Compared to verbal statements of theoretical concepts and mechanisms, each of these notations offers increased precision and decreased ambiguity. Flow charts are perhaps the most common type of formal notation used by information-processing psychologists. For example, Sternberg and Rifkin (1979) used a single flow chart to represent four distinct models of analogical reasoning. Their depiction clearly indicates how the models are related and what parameters are associated with each component of each model.

Another type of formal notation commonly used in research on children's comprehension of stories is the *story grammar* (Mandler & Johnson, 1977; Stein & Glenn, 1979), and Nelson has analyzed children's event representations in terms of *scripts* (Nelson & Gruendel, 1981). Mandler (1983) provides a comprehensive summary of how these kinds of representations have been used in developmental theory. In both areas the underlying theoretical construct has been the *schema*. As Mackworth (1987) wryly notes, to simply assert that some aspect of the mind can be characterized as a schema is to say almost nothing at all, because the schema concept

> has repeatedly demonstrated an ingenious talent for metamorphosis. A schema has been variously identified with a map, a record, a pattern, a format, a plan, a conservation law (and a conversation law), a program, a data structure, a co-routine, a frame, a script, a unit, and an agent. Each of these concepts has, in turn, considerable variability and ambiguity.

However, if one goes further, and makes specific proposals for how the schema is structured, organized, and processed, then this kind of formalization can be useful. For example, Hill and Arbib (1984) have attempted to clarify some of the different senses in which "schema" has been used, and they go on to describe a schema-based computational model of language acquisition.

The issue of how to evaluate different forms of knowledge representation is discussed at length by Klahr and Siegler (1978). They list the following criteria that a theorist could use in choosing a representation:

1. The representation must be sufficient to account for behavior. Thus, it must have a clear mapping onto the empirical base it is supposed to account for.
2. It should be amenable to multiple-level analyses. That is, it should be easy to aggregate and disaggregate the grain of explanation. For the design of

well-controlled experiments or curriculum design, the representation will have to be stated in terms of averages across many subjects; it must be a modal form. For detailed study of individual strategies and component processes, it must be capable of disaggregation without drastic revision.

3. The representation should not violate well-established processing constraints.

4. The representation should have "developmental tractability" (Klahr & Wallace, 1970b). That is, it should allow us to state both early and later forms of competence and provide an easy interpretation of each model as both a precursor and successor of other models in a developmental sequence (Klahr & Siegler, 1978, p. 65).

The attractive property of any type of formal notation is that it renders explicit what may have only been implicit, and it frequently eliminates buried inconsistencies. Siegler (1983) illustrates this point in his account of the evolution of his ideas about children's number concepts:

> ... I have recently adopted a more detailed representational language to characterize preschoolers' knowledge of numbers. This format involves task-specific flow diagrams operating on a semantic network; the semantic network includes the types of information that the rule models did not explicitly represent. I have had to revise my models of counting, magnitude comparison, and addition several times after I thought they were complete, because when I reformalized the ideas, the models revealed gaps and contradictions. The concreteness of the flow diagrams and semantic networks thus has added to the conceptual rigor of the ideas, forcing me to face vagueness and incompleteness in my thinking that I otherwise might have overlooked (pp. 163–164).

What about mathematical modelling of developmental phenomena? Should it be included in the set of formal notational schemes that signal soft-core information processing? The situation is not straightforward. On the one hand, mathematical modelling meets the criteria of formalization and precision. But on the other hand, most of the mathematical models in developmental psychology typically characterize information at a very abstract level: in terms of states and transition probabilities, rather than in terms of structural organization and processes that operate on that structure (cf. Brainerd's [1987] Markov models of memory processes). As Gregg and Simon (1967) demonstrated very clearly with respect to stochastic models of concept learning, most of the interesting psychological assumptions in such models are buried in the text surrounding the mathematics, and "the accurate predictions of fine-grain statistics that have been achieved with [stochastic theories] must be interpreted as validations of the laws of probability rather than of the psychological assumptions of the theories" (p. 275). For example, Wilkinson and Haines (1987) use Markov learning models to propose some novel answers to the important question of how children assemble simple component skills into reliable strategies. However, they couch their analysis in terms of the probabilities of moving between abstract states, while their discussion in the text is rife with undefined processes whereby the child "discovers," "adopts," "retains," "invokes," "moves," "prefers," "abandons," or "reverts." As is often the case in the use of mathematical models, the formalism of the mathematics obscures the informality of the underlying theory. Perhaps this is the reason why mathematical modelling has not played a central role in information-processing approaches to development.

S5: Modelling the time-course of cognitive processing over relatively short durations: chronometric analysis. Among adult experimentalists, one of the methodological hallmarks of an information-processing approach is the use of chronometric analysis. It is based on several assumptions. First, there is a set of distinct, separable, processes that underlie the behavior under investigation. Second, the particular process of interest can be isolated, via a task analysis, such that experimental manipulations can induce the system to systematically increase or decrease the number of executions of the focal process. Third, that the experimental manipulations affect *only* the number of executions of the focal process, and nothing else about that process or the total set of processes in which it is embedded. (For a thorough discussion of the history and methodology of chronometric studies, primarily with adults, see Chase, 1978.)

One of the first studies to use chronometric analysis with children was Groen and Parkman's (1972) analysis of how first graders did simple addition problems. Groen and Parkman proposed several plausible alternative models and, from each, predicted a pattern of reaction times as a function of different relations among the two addends (sum, difference, min, max). One of these models was called the "min strategy," in which subjects compute the sum by starting with the larger of the two addends and counting up the number of times indicated by the smaller of the two, producing a final result that is the sum of the two. By assuming that the initial determination of the maximum takes a fixed amount of time, this model predicts that reaction times should be a linear function of the smaller of the two arguments. Based on their analysis of mean reaction times across subjects and trials, Groen and Parkman concluded that the "min strategy" was the best fitting model. (There were some exceptions to this general result, and this process has been further elaborated with respect to individual variations across problems and subjects by Siegler [1989], and older children by Ashcraft [1982] but the initial Groen and Parkman work still stands as a pioneering effort in chronometric analysis of children's performance.)

Another use of chronometric methods with children is exemplified by Keating and Bobbitt's (1978) extension of Sternberg's (1966) memory-scanning paradigm. The basic task is to present children with a set of digits, followed by a "probe" digit. The child's task is to decide whether the probe digit was in the original set. Reaction time is measured from the onset of the probe until the child responds. In addition to the general assumptions listed above, the paradigm assumes that the items in the set are stored in some kind of passive buffer, and that there is an active process that sequentially compares the probe with each of the items stored in the buffer. The empirical question is how long each comparison (and move to the next item) takes for children at different levels of development.

Additional examples of chronometric analysis include Chi and Klahr's (1975) work on rates of subitizing and counting in 5-year-olds, and Kail, Pellegrino, and Carter's (1980) study of mental rotation speeds in 9-year-olds. All of these share another common feature of information-processing experiments: their goal is to go beyond testing hypotheses about some component of the cognitive system by *measuring* some of its properties. That is, the purpose of a study such as Keating and Bobbitt's is not just to demonstrate that children's memory scanning process was organized in the same way as adults', but to estimate some of the critical parameters of processes such as the scanning rate.[3] Kail (1988) presents an elegant example of the extent to which chronometric analysis can illuminate important developmental questions. For each of the 15 ages from 8 to 22 years (e.g., 8-year-olds, 9-year-olds, etc.), he estimated the processing rate for five tasks: mental rotation, name retrieval, visual search, memory search and mental addition. Then he plotted the processing rate vs. age function for each task, and showed that the exponential decay functions for all tasks could be fit by a single decay parameter. He interprets these results by positing an increasing amount of common, nonspecific processing resources that become available to children as they develop.

S6: Use of high-density data from error-patterns and protocols to induce and test complex models. It has often been noted that pass/fail data provide only the grossest form of information about underlying processes. Nevertheless, a casual glance through the journals overflowing my in-basket reveals that most of the empirical research in cognitive development is still reported in terms of percentage of correct answers. Another characteristic of information-processing approaches is the belief that much more can be extracted from an appropriate record of children's performance. The basic assumption is that, given the goal of understanding the processing underlying children's performance, we should use all the means at our disposal to get a glimpse of those processes as they are occurring, and not just when they produce their final output. Verbal protocols, eye-movements, and error patterns (as well as chronometric methods, mentioned above) all provide this kind of high-density data.

This position is neither novel nor radical. Once again, Piaget turns up as a charter member of the soft-core information-processing club. He was probably the first to demonstrate that children's errors could reveal as much, or more, about their thought processes as their successes, and a substantial proportion of his writing is devoted to informal inferences about the underlying knowledge structures that generate children's misconceptions in many domains. Siegler (1981) puts the issue this way:

> Many of Piaget's most important insights were derived from examining children's erroneous statements; these frequently revealed the type of changes in reasoning that occur with age. Yet in our efforts to make knowledge-assessment techniques more reliable and more applicable to very young children, we have moved away from this emphasis on erroneous reasoning and also away from detailed analyses of individual children's reasoning. . . . The result may have been a loss of valuable information about the acquisition process. . . . [My] hypothesis is that we might be able to increase considerably our understanding of cognitive growth by devoting more attention to individual children's early, error-prone reasoning (p. 3).

The basic assumption in error-analytic methodologies is that children's knowledge can be represented as a set of stable procedures that, when probed with an appropriate set of problems, will generate a characteristic profile of responses (including specific types of errors). Application of this idea to children's performance reached perhaps its most elegant form in the BUGGY models of children's subtraction errors (Brown & Burton, 1978; Brown & Van-Lehn, 1982). Brown and his colleagues demonstrated that a wide variety of subtraction errors could be accounted for by a set of "bugs" that children had in their subtraction procedure. For example, two of the most frequent bugs discovered by Brown and Burton were:

BORROW FROM ZERO:

When borrowing from a column whose top digit is 0, the student writes 9, but does not continue borrowing from the column to the left of the zero.

$$\begin{array}{r} 103 \\ -\ 45 \\ \hline 158 \end{array}$$

SMALLER FROM LARGER:

The student subtracts the smaller digit in a column from the larger regardless of which one is on top.

$$\begin{array}{r} 254 \\ -118 \\ \hline 144 \end{array}$$

These and dozens of more subtle and complex bugs were inferred from the analysis of thousands of subtraction test items from 1,300 children. The key to the analysis was the creation of a network of subprocedures that comprise the total knowledge required to solve subtraction problems. This procedural network can then be examined for possible points of failure, any one of which would result in a bug.

Another highly productive research program based on the analysis of error patterns is Siegler's well-known "rule assessment" methodology (Siegler, 1976; Siegler, 1981). The basic idea in this and other developmentally-oriented error-analysis work (e.g., Baylor & Gascon, 1974; Fay & Mayer, 1987; Klahr & Robinson, 1981; Young, 1976) is that children's responses at any point in the development of their knowledge about an area are based on what they know at that point, rather than on what they don't know. In order to characterize that (imperfect) knowledge, the theorist attempts to formulate a model of partial knowledge that can generate the full set of responses—both correct and incorrect—in the same pattern as did the child. The model thus becomes a theory of the child's knowledge about the domain at that point in her development.

Fay and Mayer (1987) extended the Brown and Burton (1978) approach from the domain of "simple" arithmetic to the more complex domain of spatial reference in a graphics programming environment. They investigated children's naive conceptions about spatial reference by examining how children (from 9 to 13 years old) interpreted Logo commands to move and turn from various initial orientations. Children were presented with problems that varied in initial orientation of the "turtle," the type of command (move or turn), and the value of the argument (how far to move or turn). Their task was to predict the final orientation of the turtle, given its initial orientation and command. Fay and Mayer first constructed an ideal model, comprised of about a dozen elementary operations. Then, based on the general characteristics of children's errors, they proposed six types of misconceptions (e.g., that a right-turn command actually *slides* the turtle to the right) and formulated models for the micro-structure of each misconception, in terms of degenerate versions of relevant parts of the ideal model. For the subjects to which these degenerate models were applied, Fay and Mayer were able to account for nearly every one of the (mostly) incorrect responses to the 24 items in their test battery.

Error-analyses of this type are not only useful for cognitive developmental theory, but they also have pedagogical implications. The potential for facilitating remedial instruction is what originally motivated the BUGGY work, and it continues to be a valuable by-product of detailed error-analysis research:

> ... novice Logo programmers appear to enter the Logo environment with individual confusions and misconceptions that they apply fairly consistently during instruction. Diagnosis of the specific confusions—such as a misunderstanding of what left and right mean or a misunderstanding of what degrees of rotation means—provides a more detailed and potentially useful evaluation of students' knowledge than the traditional global measurement of percentage correct (Fay & Mayer, 1987, p. 265).

I believe that this kind of work illustrates the basic premise of this aspect of information-processing approaches: Careful and creative analysis of complex error patterns can provide an extremely informative window into the child's mental processes.

Protocol analysis is another form of high-density data that is often associated with information-processing approaches. The basic idea here is that in addition to final responses on tasks, the subject can generate external indications of inter-mediate states, and that this pattern of intermediate indicators (the protocol) can be highly informative about the underlying processes that generated the final response. Included here are not only verbal protocols, but also sequences of eye movements (Just & Carpenter, 1978) and other motor responses (Rumelhart & Norman, 1981). The classic verbal protocol analyses with adults are reported in Newell and Simon (1972), and a rigorous theoretical and methodological treat-ment is offered in Ericsson and Simon (1984). Here too, there is a common mis-conception that protocol analysis requires subjects to give an introspective account of their own behavior, and therefore is unreliable and unacceptably sub-jective (Nisbett & Wilson, 1977). Clearly, this would be a fatal flaw in the methodology, especially if it is to be used with children. But the criticism is un-founded. As Anderson (1987) summarizes the issue:

> Many of these unjustified criticisms of protocols stem from the belief that they are taken as sources of psychological theory rather than as sources of data about states of the mind. For the latter, one need not require that the subject accurately interpret his mental states, but only that the theorist be able to specify some mapping between his reports and states of the theory (p. 472).

In adult information-processing psychology, protocol analysis is a widespread method, but it is only infrequently used in more than a casual fashion by current cognitive developmentalists. This is very surprising, when one considers the fact that Piaget was the most prolific collector and analyzer of verbal protocols in the history of psychology.

Klahr and Robinson (1981) used a combination of motor and verbal protocol analysis and error analysis to explore pre-school children's problem-solving and planning skills. Children were presented with puzzles requiring from 2 to 7 moves to solution, and they were instructed to describe the full sequence of moves that would enable them to reach the goal configuration. Children were video-taped as they described—verbally and by pointing—what sequence of moves they would use to solve the problem, but the pieces were never actually moved. The protocols enabled Klahr and Robinson to infer the children's internal representation of the location of each object, and the processes whereby children made moves. They then constructed several alternative models of children's strategies, and used the error-analysis technique described earlier to identify each child's response pattern with a specific strategy. Note that nowhere were the children asked to reflect on their own mental processes, or to give a report on what strategies they were using while solving the problems.

The information extracted from the protocols in the Klahr and Robinson study consisted of a planned sequence of well-defined moves of discrete objects, and this level of mapping from the protocol to hypothesized representations and processes is characteristic of the kind of protocol analyses presented in Newell and Simon's (1972) seminal work. A "richer" use of protocols, similar to some of the later examples in Ericsson and Simon (1984), provides the basis of Dunbar and Klahr's (1988) analysis of children's strategies for scientific reasoning. Children (ages 8 to 11 years old) and adults were presented with a programmable robot, taught about most of its operating characteristics, and then asked to discover how some additional feature worked. They were asked to talk aloud as they generated hypotheses, ran experiments (i.e., wrote programs for the robot and ran them), and made predictions, observations and evaluations. These verbal protocols were then analyzed in terms of different classes of hypotheses, the conditions under which experiments were run, how observed results were assessed, and so on. Based on this analysis, Dunbar and Klahr were able to suggest some important differences in scientific reasoning skills between children and adults.

S7: Use of highly detailed analyses of the environment facing the child on specific tasks. Both chronometric techniques and error analysis require at least a rudimentary analysis of the task environment. In addition, there are some information-processing approaches in which complex and detailed task analysis plays a central role, even when neither error analysis or chronometrics are used. In a sense, these approaches consist almost *entirely* of task analysis. While such work is typically preliminary to further work in either error analysis or computer simulation (or both), it is often useful for its own sake, as it clarifies the nature of the tasks facing children. As Kellman (1988) notes: "The realization that investigation of psychological processes presupposes a highly developed, abstract analysis of the task and available constraints has perhaps been the major advance in psychology in the last several decades" (p. 268).

Klahr and Wallace's (1970b) task analysis of class inclusion is an example of such a formal characterization of an important developmental task. Their goal was to illustrate how a common "Piagetian experimental task" (i.e., the full set of components involved in the class inclusion task, including finding some objects, finding all objects, comparing subsets of objects, etc.) involved the coordination of several more basic information processes. They proposed a network of interrelated processes (similar to Gagne's learning hierarchies) in which some processes had common subcomponents, while others were relatively independent. Klahr and Wallace's analysis enabled them to explain how surface variations in a task could invoke different processes, that, in turn, would have profound effects on performance, even though the underlying formal logic of the task remained invariant.

In the area of children's counting, Greeno, Riley and Gelman (1984) formulated a model for characterizing children's competence. Their model is much more complex than the early Klahr and Wallace analysis of classification, but it is fundamentally similar with respect to being a formal task analysis whose primary goal is to elucidate the relations among a set of underlying components. Klahr and Carver's (1988) work on debugging Logo programs provides another example of detailed task analysis. Based on their analysis of the components of the debugging process, they formulated a set of "cognitive objectives" for insertion in a programming curriculum. In addition to the instructional elements, their debugging model provided a framework for assessment of debugging skills, for creation of transfer tasks, and for evaluation of transfer.

1.1.3 Topic areas and subject populations

There is, at best, a loose association between the use of information-processing approaches and the choice of topic and/or subject population. The developmental topics studied within this approach range from higher cognitive processes, such as problem solving (Resnick & Glaser, 1976) and scientific reasoning (Kuhn & Phelps, 1982; Dunbar & Klahr, 1988), to more basic processes, such as attention and memory (Chi, 1981; Kail, 1984). Subject populations typically range from toddlers, through preschoolers, to late adolescents, and are typically normal, although gifted (Davidson, 1986), aging (Hoyer & Familant, 1987; Madden, 1987), and retarded and learning-disabled (Geary, et al., 1987; Spitz & Borys, 1984) populations have been studied under the information-processing rubric. In the case of special populations, issues are usually framed by the theoretical or empirical results emerging from studies of normal populations, and the question of interest is the qualitative or quantitative difference in a particular information-processing construct. For example, Spitz and Borys (1984) have studied the differences in search processes between normal and retarded adults on the classic Tower of Hanoi puzzle.

Because the focus of this chapter is *cognitive* development, I have drawn the conventional—and arbitrary—boundary that precludes an extensive discussion of perceptual/motor or language development. I can find no principled basis for excluding either of these areas from mainstream information processing, for in both of them one can find many examples of the approach (cf. MacWhinney, 1987; Yonas, 1988). MacWhinney's (1987) edited volume on mechanisms of language acquisition contains an array of information-processing approaches that run the gamut from soft- to hard-core features. In the area of perceptual development, Marr's (1982) seminal work, which advocates computational models as the proper approach to constructing theories of vision, is increasingly influential. Indeed, Banks (1988), in presenting his own computational model of contrast constancy, argues that perceptual development is a much *more* promising area in which to construct computational models than cognitive or social development, because there are more constraints that can be brought to bear to limit the proliferation of untested (and untestable) assumptions. Nevertheless, for reasons of brevity, neither perceptual/motor nor language development will be treated extensively in this chapter.

1.1.4 Soft-core information processing: What's not included?

Even with these caveats and exclusions, the soft-core version of the term *information processing* has become so pervasive in cognitive development that it appears to have achieved the same dubious status as *structuralism*, of which Flavell (1982) says, with characteristic insight and frankness:

> I think . . . that we should give up using 'structuralism' and 'structuralist' to describe 'them' versus 'us' type differences of opinion about the nature and development of cognition. In my opinion, they have become empty slogans or buzz words. . . . They actually interfere with communication because they give one only the illusion of understanding exactly what claims about the formal aspects of development are being made. . . . If someone told me [that he was a structuralist] today, I would: (1) have only a rough idea what he meant; and (2) suspect that he might also have only a very rough idea what he meant (p. 5).

If we substitute *soft-core information processing* for *structuralism* in this quotation, Flavell's argument is equally valid. Consider the nearly universal acceptance of theoretical constructs such as short-term and long-term memory, controlled and automatic processes, encoding, storage and retrieval, schemas, frames, declarative and procedural knowledge, and so on. As Flavell summarizes his position on structuralism: "How many cognitive developmentalists can you think of who do *not* believe that the child's mental contents and processes are complexly organized?" (p. 4). Similarly, who would deny that children's cognition involves the processing of information?

If this position is accepted, then the writer of a chapter on information processing has two choices: either write a comprehensive review of the state of the art in a large number of areas of cognitive development, or focus on a more limited domain—that of hard-core information processing. The main reason not to follow the first of these two paths is that it has been done repeatedly and ably in recent years (cf. Siegler, 1983, 1985; Miller, 1983; Kail & Bisanz, 1982), and it is unlikely that I could improve upon those efforts. Therefore, I have chosen to follow the second path, and, for the remainder of this paper, I shall focus on hard-core information-processing approaches to cognitive development. I will begin by describing what I mean by this term.

1.2 Hard-core Information-processing Approaches to Cognitive Development

The three hard-core features, shown at the bottom of Table 1, are: use of computer simulation models, non-metaphorical interpretation of such models, and creation of self-modifying systems as theories of cognitive development. These features can be viewed as the extreme points of several of the soft-core features listed in the upper portion of Table 1 described earlier (p. 133). Soft-core features S1, S2, S4, and S7, have an extreme form in H1, the use of computer simulation, and H2, the interpretation of the simulation as a theoretical statement. Methodological features S5 and S6 support the evaluation of such models, and H3 is the hard-core version of S3.

1.3 H1: Use of Computer Simulation

Computer simulation is often viewed as *the* criterial attribute of hard-core information processing.[4] Klahr and Wallace (1976) characterize the approach as follows:

> Faced with a segment of behavior of a child performing a task, we posit the question: "What would an information-processing system require in order to exhibit the same behavior as the child?" The answer takes the form of a set of rules for processing information: a computer program. The program constitutes a model of the child performing the task. It contains explicit statements about the capacity of the system, the complexity of the processes, and the representation of information—the data structure—with which the child must deal (p. 5).[5]

Although the resultant computer program may be sufficient to generate same behavior as the child, there is, of course, no guarantee that every component of the program is necessary, nor that the program is unique. How then, can we gain some confidence that the program is a plausible theory?

Simon (1972) proposed four general metatheoretical constraints that can be used to evaluate computer simulation models: (a) consistency with what we know of the physiology of the nervous system; (b) consistency with what we know of behavior in tasks other than the one under consideration; (c) sufficiency to produce the behavior under consideration; and (d) definiteness and concreteness. The extent to which these constraints have been met by computer simulators varies inversely with the order in which they are listed above. Any running program satisfies the last constraint, and if it is highly task-specific, then an ingenious programmer can usually satisfy criterion c. A common criticism of this kind of simulation is the non-identifiability of the proposed model. That is, for a single task, a model is typically ad-hoc, and, in principle, an infinite number of alternative models could account for the same data.[6] However, as we expand the range of data for which the model can account, the force of the non-identifiability criticism is weakened. For example, in the area of adult cognition, there are programs that can model behavior in a wide variety of tasks within a general category (e.g., Newell & Simon's General Problem Solver, or Feigenbaum & Simon's EPAM) and that therefore begin to satisfy constraint (b). Developmental examples are much harder to find: I can think of only one running simulation that is both constrained by a large amount of data on children's performance and applicable to a fairly disparate set of tasks (addition, multiplication, spelling, memory rehearsal), and that is Siegler's (1986) strategy choice model.

But even Siegler's work is unconstrained by the first of Simon's four criteria: the underlying physiology of the brain. Here, his model is in company with virtually all other symbolically-oriented simulations of higher order cognition, be they developmental or not. For many years, computer simulators simply ignored the physiological constraint, while acknowledging that, ultimately, symbol systems were grounded in a neural substrate. This is not to say that their models were inconsistent with what was known about physiology, only that there was no consistency check at all.

However, recent analysis by Newell (1986, 1988) of temporal constraints in cognition illustrates how the physiological constraint can be brought to bear on the computer simulation models. The path is indirect: It occurs through consideration of the different hierarchical levels of the human cognitive system and time scale of operation of each level. Each level is comprised of organized assemblies of the level below it, and it runs more slowly. Newell uses very rough approximations for the operational time scale of each level: 1 ms for neurons, 10 ms for neural circuits comprised of neurons, 100 ms for a deliberate cognitive act, 1 sec for a cognitive operation Newell (1988) concludes:

> The *real-time constraint on cognition* is that the human must produce genuine cognitive behavior in ~ 1 s, out of components that have ~ 10 ms operation times (p. 10). The significance of such a mapping, however approximate, should not be underestimated. For years, cognitive psychology has enjoyed the luxury of considering its analysis to be one that floats entirely with respect to how it might be realized in the brain. . . . The floating kingdom has finally been grounded (p 12).

How might we apply these time constraints in evaluating computer simulation models? To illustrate, I propose a particularly far-fetched example, by considering whether or not a artificial-intelligence program, written to play high-quality chess, could be taken as a plausible theory of how humans play the game. The program, called Hitech (Berliner & Ebeling, 1988), is currently rated at a level equal to the high end of the Master level for human tournament play, so it clearly meets the criterion of being sufficient to generate the behavior of interest. Hitech gets its power by generating a massive search (about 100 million positions per move). Although there is abundant evidence that humans do not generate even one millionth as many positions, we will limit this evaluation of Hitech to temporal considerations alone, and consider only the *rate* at which Hitech generates alternative positions—about 175,000 positions per second. Given the fact that the representation for a chess position is a complex symbol structure, requiring several elementary steps in its generation, and that the order of magnitude of neural firing rates is only about 1 ms, then the 5 *micro*seconds per position rate for Hitech simply rules it out as a plausible theory of human cognition. Even if we posit a massively parallel computation (indeed, Hitech is comprised of a set of simultaneous processors), this does not make Hitech any more plausible as a human model, for, as Newell (1988) notes, even connectionist models require time for "bringing the results of computations in one part of the network into contact with developing results in other parts of the network" (p. 91). Both serial, symbolically-oriented computing and parallel distributed computing are constrained by the temporal requirements of aggregating results over lower levels, and the elementary processing rates—determined by the underlying physiology of the neural tissue—could not support a theory based on the Hitech organization.

Note that Simon's criteria for evaluating computer simulation models are similar to the set of criteria for evaluating *any* representation—computer simulation or otherwise—listed in Section 1.1.2. However, they differ in two respects. First, since they are directed toward computer simulation, Simon's criteria are stricter about actually generating behavior and about definiteness. Second, they do not include the developmental tractability criterion listed earlier. Recall that the purpose of this criterion is to evaluate the extent to which different models of the child at two different points in time can be integrated into a transitional theory: one that can actually transform the early state into the later one. Regardless of the predictive power or elegance of a theory for a given level of knowledge, if there is no plausible mechanism that might have produced that state from some previous one, then, from the viewpoint of the developmental psychologist, such a theory is seriously deficient. Here too, Siegler's model gets good marks, because learning and performance are intertwined such that what the model does affects what it learns, and what it has learned depends on what it has done in the past.

However, if we run the clock backwards on Siegler's model, we run up against the developmentalist's equivalent of St. Augustine's musings about the "Prime Mover." Siegler's model implies that the distribution of associations between problems and responses derives from their previous distribution and environmental history. Current answers depend on answers generated in response to previous problems. But this backward induction cannot go on indefinitely, for at each of the earlier knowledge levels, we face the same question of how *that* knowledge got there. Ultimately, we come to the initial situation in which all answers have flat distributions of associations, and subjects must use fall-back strategies. But from where do those strategies, and the strategy-choice mechanism itself, originate?

Here we are forced to make assertions about what I have called the *innate kernel*. To the best of my knowledge, there are no complete proposals for what the innate information-processing system might have to contain (although Wallace,

Klahr, & Bluff, 1987, did outline some of the requirements). I believe that this remains one of the greatest challenges facing developmental theorists. The answer will undoubtedly require a convergence of analytic tools, such as the formulation of cognitive architectures and detailed studies of neonatal functioning. These empirical studies will be necessarily limited to the assessment of perceptual and motor behavior and will thus press the very boundaries of current approaches to information-processing psychology.

The "definiteness and concreteness" criterion is elaborated in Gregg and Simon's (1967) four main claims for the advantages of computer simulation models. The first has to do with avoidance of inconsistency: the same set of operations are used for all cases of testing the theory. While it is true that programs have an unlimited potential for points of modification, once a theory has been formulated as a program, it cannot be *inadvertently* "tuned" to special cases. My own experience in formulating several different strategies for the TOH problems (cf. Klahr & Robinson, 1981) made me appreciate how important it was to be confident that each program followed its unique rules in a consistent fashion for the 40 problems that it had to solve. The second item on Gregg and Simon's list of advantages is the elimination of implicit assumptions. Everything in a program must be stated as an unambiguous operation. Continuing the example, the creation of the alternative strategies made it very clear exactly what the differences were in each strategy, and what their implications were for performance. The third feature is unambiguous predictions: the program generates behavior that can be compared with human performance. Finally, Gregg and Simon emphasize encoding explicitness. The need to create data structures for the program to process avoids finessing questions about encoding and representation. Although one may disagree with any specific encoding, computer models require explicitness about just what goes into that encoding, and in some cases suggest further experimentation.

Neches (1982) offers a thoughtful tempering of these arguments. Although he points out that the claim for superiority of computer simulation over verbal or mathematically stated theories has sometimes been overstated, his own work on HPM—to be described later in this paper—actually exemplifies many of these merits. Furthermore, while it is true that the benefits listed above begin to accrue from *any* move toward formalization (as suggested by the earlier quotation from Siegler on his use of semantic nets and flow charts), the discipline of computer simulation represents a qualitative increase in all of them. Indeed, in subsequent work, Siegler's models of children's strategy choice on arithmetic tasks became sufficiently complex that the only feasible way to develop the theory and derive predictions from it was to use computer simulation (Siegler, 1986, p. 109).

There are several other instances in the developmental literature in which models initially stated in some noncomputer formalism were deemed by their creators to be sufficiently imprecise, complex, or ambiguous to require further specification as computer simulations: Shultz's (1987, 1988) models of causality, Halford's work on structure-mapping (Bakker and Halford, 1988), and Gentner's research on analogy and metaphor (Gentner, 1988; Falkenhainer, Forbus, & Gentner, 1986) all exhibit this tendency to move to computer simulation as theory development matures.

1.3.1 The Computer's Role in Simulation Models

Given the centrality of computer simulation to hard-core information processing, it may be useful to clarify a few essential points that are often misunderstood. First of all, it is important to distinguish between the theoretical content of a program that runs on a computer and the psychological relevance of the computer itself. Hard-core information-processing theories are usually sufficiently complex that it is necessary to run them on a computer in order to explore their implications, but this does not imply that the theory bears any resemblance to the computer on which it runs. Computer simulations of hurricanes do not imply that meteorologists believe that the atmosphere works like a computer. Furthermore, the same theory could be implemented on computers having radically different underlying architectures and mechanisms.

Failure to make this distinction leads to the common misconception that information-processing approaches can be arranged along a dimension of "how seriously they take the computer as a model" (Miller, 1983). It would be counterproductive for a developmental psychologist to take the computer at all seriously as a model for cognition, because the underlying computer does *not* undergo the crucial self-modification necessary for cognitive development. A similar misunderstanding of the role of the computer in hard-core information-processing models may have led to Brown's (1982) widely quoted (but misdirected) criticism that "A system that cannot grow, or show adaptive modification to a changing environment, is a strange metaphor for human thought processes which are constantly changing over the life span of an individual." I agree: later in this chapter, I will describe some hard-core information-processing approaches that propose very explicit mechanisms for "adaptive modification to a changing environment." The hard-core information-processing approaches are serious, not about the similarity between humans and computers, but rather about the extent to which intelligent behavior—and its development—can be accounted for by a symbol-processing device that is manifested in the physical world. The strong postulate for hard-core information-processing is that both computers and humans are members of the class of "physical symbol systems" (Newell, 1980), and that some of the theoretical constructs and insights that have come out of computer science are relevant for cognitive developmental theory.

1.3.2 *Recursive Decomposition and Emergent Properties*

One such insight is what Palmer and Kimchi (1986) call the *recursive decomposition* assumption: any nonprimitive process can be specified more fully at a lower level by decomposing it into a set of subcomponents and specifying the temporal and informational flows among the subcomponents. This is a good example of how abstract ideas from computer science have contributed to hardcore information processing: "it is one of the foundation stones of computer science that a relatively small set of elementary processes suffices to produce the full generality of information processing" (Newell & Simon, 1972, p. 29). An important consequence of decomposition is that

> ... the resulting component operations are not only quantitatively simpler than the initial one, but *qualitatively different* from it. ... Thus we see that higher level information-processing descriptions sometimes contain *emergent properties* that lower level descriptions do not. It is the *organization* of the system specified by the flow relations among the lower level components that gives rise to these properties (Palmer & Kimchi, 1986, pp. 52–53).

Palmer and Kimchi illustrate this point with the memory-scanning process described earlier: it is accomplished by the appropriate organization of simpler processes: matching one symbol to another, moving through an ordered list, setting an indicator for whether the probe has been matched or not, etc. None of these sub-processes, in isolation, does a memory scan. Indeed, each of them could be used in quite a different super-process, such as sorting a list. It is their *organization* that gives them the emergent property of being a scanning process.

The importance of emergent properties cannot be overemphasized, for it provides the only route to explaining how intelligence—be it in humans or machines—can be exhibited by systems comprised of unintelligent underlying components—be they synapses or silicon. Even if one defines "basic processes" at a much higher level—be it production systems or networks of activated nodes, emergent properties continue to emerge, for that is the nature of complex systems.[7]

Siegler's model of children's strategy choice in arithmetic provides an interesting developmental example of the emergent property of a rational choice of an efficient and effective strategy. In that model, strategy choices about whether to retrieve the answer to a multiplication problem from memory or to calculate the result are made without any rational calculation of the advantages and disadvantages of each strategy. As Siegler (1988) puts it: "Rather than metacognition regulating cognition, cognitive representations and processes are assumed to be organized in such a way that they yield adaptive strategy choices without any direct governmental process." Although this may sound like Adam Smith's "invisible hand" applied to the mental marketplace, it exemplifies the idea of emergent properties in the context of an important developmental phenomenon.

The emergent property notion provides the key to my belief that hard-core information processing has the potential to formulate powerful theories of cognitive development. The fundamental challenge is to account for the emergence of intelligence. Intelligence must develop from the innate kernel. The intelligence in the kernel, and in its self-modification processes, will be an emergent property of the *organization* of elementary (unintelligent) mechanisms for performance, learning, and development. As I noted earlier, we do not yet have a detailed proposal for what the innate kernel is, and, with respect to the ambitious goal of creating a full account of the development of the information-processing system, Siegler's example may seem like a small step, but it is a step in the right direction. I will describe a few others below.

1.3.3 Data Constraints

Another aspect of simulation models that tends to be misunderstood is the extent to which they can be said to account for data. For example, Liben (1987) claims that using simulation models to account for empirical results is circular because:

> . . . the competence model is empirically derived directly from observed performance, as illustrated in [work by Siegler and Shipley (1987)]. That is, given that the particular computer program was written expressly to simulate children's observed behaviors, it is not remarkable that there is a good match between them (p. 114).

Beilin (1987), echoing Liben, asserts that:

> Inasmuch as computer simulations usually mimic the data and performances they are designed to predict, such predictions usually turn out to be successful.

It is hard to make sense of these simplistic criticisms as they stand. A minor paraphrase of Liben reveals why:

> Given that Newton's inverse-square law of gravitation was formulated expressly to account for empirical observations of planetary motion, it is not remarkable that there is a good match between his theory and the actual motion of the planets.

The problem is that unless one understands *how* a theory generates its predictions, it is impossible to assess its circularity or remarkability. This is true no matter what the form of the theory: be it a computer simulation, a mathematical model, or a verbal statement. In the case of a computer model, one could generate a perfect fit to subjects' behavior by simply reading in a data table, derived from subject performance, and then printing it out again—hardly an interesting exercise. On the other hand, if the model is based on a set of basic processes and a few parameters, and if, furthermore, the model makes testable

predictions about data patterns that were not detected before the model was formulated, then it serves the role that any theory should. That is, it summarizes existing data patterns and predicts new ones on the basis of fundamental principles.

The additional advantage of computer simulation models over conventional
forms of theorizing is that they permit a very clear allocation of "credit" for
such fits and predictions to the various sources: the general theoretical principles,
the particular parameter values in the model (one can explore the parameter
space in a model to discover just which variables are critical, and to which ones
the model is relatively insensitive), or the particular encoding of the task environment. In contrast, with verbal models or even flow charts, it is never clear
how much of the interpretive work is being done by the theory, and how much
by the reader of the theory.

1.4   H2: Commitment to Elements of the Simulation
as Theoretical Assertions, Rather than just Metaphor
or Computational Convenience

This is another aspect of Miller's (1983) question about how seriously one
should take the computer as a model of thought. The degrees of seriousness here
are not about the correspondence between the computer and the theory, but about
the *program* and the theory. In some cases, the program is used as a convenient
format for stating a set of processes that could be implemented in many
equivalent forms and in many computer languages. The program's role is to
compute the behavior of the system under a set of specified inputs. Klahr and
Robinson's (1981) simulation models of children's performance on the Tower of
Hanoi puzzle exemplify this soft end of the computer-simulation attribute.

At the other end of the attribute, the program and the computational architecture that interprets it (i.e., runs the program) jointly comprise a theoretical statement about the general organization of the cognitive system and the specific
knowledge that is required to do the task at hand. Perhaps the most commonly
proposed architecture of this kind of hard-core model is a production system.
Both the production-system interpreter and the specific productions are proposed
as theoretical constructs, not just programming conveniences. For example,
Klahr and Wallace (1976) utilized Newell's original production system architecture[8] to formulate a theory of the development of quantitative processes including elementary quantification, class-inclusion, transitive reasoning, and
conservation of quantity. Programs for all of these tasks were constrained by the
theoretical principles embodied in the production-system architecture, and the
entire package was intended to be "taken seriously."

In production-system models, the productions and the architecture bear the
same relation to cognitive behavior as a particular molecular structure and
general laws of chemistry are taken to jointly explain the behavior of a sub-

stance. For the hard-core simulator using productions, it is no more appropriate to argue that productions are only functionally equivalent to some "real" mental item, than it is to say that molecules are only functionally equivalent to some real chemical entity. The production-system architecture is sufficiently important to hard-core information processing that I will describe it at length in Section 2.

1.5 H3: Goal of Creating a Complete Self-modifying Simulation that Accounts for Both Task Performance and Development

The objective:

- Specify an innate kernel—cast as a self-modifying production system—that characterizes the neonate information-processing system.
- Represent the external environment in such a way that the system can utilize its perceptual and motor operators to interact with the environment, and to learn from that interaction.
- Run the system and let it develop its own intelligence.

That is the Holy Grail of the hard-core information-processing approach to cognitive development. The question is whether the enterprise is under the control of Tennyson or Monty Python. My own bets are with the Idylls of the King, as I believe that self-modifying production systems are able to represent and account for the fundamental inseparability of performance and change. Some important pieces of this puzzle are already in place, but much remains to be accomplished before we will have the kind of total system envisioned above. In the following section, I will lay out some of the major issues in the use of production systems that must be resolved in order to achieve the ultimate goal.

2. PRODUCTION SYSTEMS: AT THE CORE OF THE CORE[9]

Production systems are a class of computer-simulation models stated in terms of condition-action rules. A production system consists of two interacting data structures, connected through a simple processing cycle:

1. A *working memory* consisting of a collection of symbol structures called working memory *elements.*
2. A *production memory* consisting of condition-action rules called *productions,* whose conditions describe configurations of working memory elements and whose actions specify modifications to the contents of working memory.

Production memory and working memory are related through the *recognize-act* cycle, which is comprised of three distinct processes:

1. The *match* process finds productions whose conditions match against the current state of working memory. The same rule may match against working memory in different ways, and each such mapping is called an *instantiation*. When a particular production is instantiated, we say that its conditions have been *satisfied*. In addition to the possibility of a single production being satisfied by several distinct instantiations, several different productions may be satisfied at once. Both of these situations lead to *conflict*.
2. The *conflict resolution* process selects one or more of the instantiated productions for applications.
3. The *act* process applies the instantiated actions of the selected rules, thus modifying the contents of working memory.

The basic recognize-act process operates in cycles, with one or more rules being selected and applied, the new contents of memory leading another set of rules to be applied, and so forth. This cycling continues until no rules are matched or until an explicit halt command is encountered. The many variations that are possible within this basic framework will be described in Section 2.3.

2.1 Notation or Theory?

The distinction made earlier between two related interpretations of the theoretical status of computer simulation models applies to production-system models. Under the first interpretation (feature S5), production systems are simply a formal notation for expressing models, and the object of interest is *model content*, rather than expressive form or interpretation scheme. For example, one might characterize the rules a person uses to perform some task in terms of a production system without necessarily committing to the psychological assumptions inherent in the production system interpreter. Other formalisms for expressing the same content are possible (e.g., scripts, LISP programs, and flowcharts), and one can debate their relative merits (see Klahr & Siegler, 1978).

In contrast, the hard-core view (feature H3) treats both the task-specific productions and the production-system interpreter as theoretical assertion about domain-dependent and domain-independent components of behavior. That is, the production system interpreter serves as a particular theory about the architecture of the human information processing system. This view was originally put forward by Newell (1967, 1972) and substantially extended by Anderson (1983). Most recently, it has been reformulated as a major theoretical statement by

Newell (1988). He asserts that humans actually employ productions in language, reasoning, motor skill, and every other form of intelligent behavior, and he describes a novel form of production system architecture—called Soar—that is proposed as a unified theory of human cognition.

The developmental relevance of this hard-core view derives from the ability of production system models to modify themselves in ways that capture many of the central features of learning and development. This potential for self-modification provides the major justification for the use of production systems in modeling cognitive development. In the following sections, I summarize some issues surrounding the adoption of production systems as a candidate for the cognitive architecture of the developing human.

2.2 Properties of Production-system Models

Newell and Simon (1972) summarized the production system features that recommend them for modeling human behavior as follows:

1. *Homogeneity.* Production systems represent knowledge in a very homogeneous format, with each rule having the same basic structure and carrying approximately the same amount of information.
2. *Independence.* Productions are independent of one another in the sense that one production makes no direct reference to any other production. Their interaction occurs only through their effects on working memory. Therefore it is easy to insert new rules or remove old ones. This makes production systems a very congenial format for modeling successive stages in a developmental sequence and also makes them attractive for modeling the incremental nature of much human learning.
3. *Parallel/serial nature.* Production systems combine the notion of a parallel recognition process with a serial application process; both features seem to be characteristic of human cognition.
4. *Stimulus-response flavor.* Production systems inherit many of the benefits of stimulus-response theory but few of the limitations, since the notions of stimuli and responses have been extended to include internal symbol structures.
5. *Goal-driven behavior.* Production systems can also be used to model the goal-driven character of much human behavior. However, such behavior need not be rigidly enforced; new information from the environment can interrupt processing of the current goal.
6. *Modelling memory.* The production-system framework offers a viable model of long-term memory and its relation to short-term memory, since the matching and conflict resolution process embody principles of retrieval and focus of attention.

2.3   Production Systems as Cognitive Architectures

As noted earlier, the term "cognitive architecture" denotes the invariant features of the human information processing system. Since one of the major goals of any science is to uncover invariants, the search for the human cognitive architecture should be a central concern of developmental psychology. The decision to pursue production system models involves making significant assumptions about the nature of this architecture. However, even if one accepts a production-system framework for formulating developmental theories, many decisions remain to be made. Theory formulation takes on the properties of a constrained design process. There is a general framework, within which particular architectural design options must be further specified. Once made, the resultant production-system interpreter represents one point in a large design space. That is, it is a specific theory of the human cognitive architecture, within the general production-system framework. The evaluation of the theory then rests on the kinds of criteria listed earlier. At present, there are no proposals for a complete developmental architecture of this type, but there are some candidates for the adult system that could be extended to play this role. Later in this chapter, I will briefly describe one such architecture.

Before getting to that, I will lay out the major dimensions of the space of production-system architectures. Within the general framework, production system interpreters can differ along four major dimensions: working memory management, the structure of production memory, conflict resolution policies, and self-modification mechanisms. I will discuss the first three of these briefly, and then in Section 2.5 elaborate the self-modification issue.

2.3.1   Working Memory Issues

1. *The structure of memory.* Is there a single general working memory, or multiple specialized memories (e.g., data and goal memories, or memories for interface with the perceptual and motor environments)? In the latter case, how are conditions in productions specialized to match particular memories?
2. *The structure of elements.* What is the basic form of working memory elements (e.g., list structures, attribute-value pairs)? Do elements have associated numeric parameters, such as activation or recency?
3. *Decay and forgetting.* Are there limits on the number of items present in working memory? If so, are these time-based or space-based limitations?
4. *Retrieval processes.* Once they have been "forgotten," can elements be retrieved at some later date? If so, what processes lead to such retrieval? For example, must productions add them to memory, or does "spreading activation" occur?

2.3.2 Production Memory Issues

1. *The structure of memory.* Is there a single general production memory, or are there many specialized memories? In the latter case, are all memories at the same level, or are they organized hierarchically?
2. *The structure of productions.* Do productions have associated numeric parameters (e.g., strength and recency) or other information beyond conditions and actions?
3. *Expressive power of conditions.* What types of conditions can be used to determine whether a rule is applicable? For example, can arbitrary predicates be included? Can sets or sequences be matched against? Can many-to-one mappings occur?
4. *Expressive power of actions.* What kind of processing can be performed within the action side of an individual rule? For example, can arbitrary functions be evoked? Can conditional expressions occur?
5. *Nature of the match process.* Are exact matches required or is partial matching allowed? Does the matcher find all matched rules, or only some of them? Does the matcher find all instantiations of a given production?

2.3.3 Conflict Resolution Issues

1. *Ordering strategies.* How does the architecture order instantiations of productions? For example, does it use the recency of matched elements or the specificity of the matched rules?
2. *Selection strategies.* How does the architecture select instantiations based on this ordering? For example, does it select the best instantiation, or does it select all those above a certain threshold?
3. *Refraction strategies.* Does the architecture remove some instantiations permanently? For example, it may remove all instantiations that applied on the last cycle, or all instantiations currently in the conflict set.

To summarize, the basic production-system framework has many possible incarnations, each with different implications about the nature of human cognition.[10] Of particular importance to cognitive development are the self-modification issues, but before turning to a more extensive discussion of them, I will briefly describe some *non*-self-modifying production-system models of children's performance in a few domains of importance to developmental psychology.

2.4 Some Examples of Production-system Models of Children's Performance

Even when cast as models of different performance levels, rather than as models of transition processes, production-system simulations can serve useful functions. In this section I describe four different ways—taken from my own research—in which *non*-self-modifying production systems have been used to model children's performance. The first example illustrates how production systems can be matched to chronometric data to produce some estimates of the duration of elementary components of the recognize-act cycle. The second example illustrates one of the most valuable features of production systems for modeling cognitive development: the ease with which different performance levels can be represented by a family of models having different production sets. The third example focuses on how production systems can include encoding and performance productions in the same general format, and the final example illustrates a kind of "vertical integration" in a production-system model that represents several levels of knowledge from general principles down to specific encoding rules.

2.4.1   Quantification: Matching Production Firings to Chronometric Data

Production-system models of thinking were initially developed to account for the verbal protocols generated by subjects working on puzzles requiring several minutes to solve (Newell, 1966). However, a much finer temporal grain of analysis was used in the first production-system models that actually ran as computer simulations. Newell (1973) introduced his production-system language (PSG)[11] in the context of the Sternberg memory-scanning paradigm (described in Section 1.1.2). In the same volume (Chase, 1973), I described a model, written in PSG, of elementary processes for quantification: subitizing, counting, and adding (Klahr, 1973). Both of these models were atypical of most subsequent production-system models in that they attempted to account for chronometric data in terms of the dynamic properties of the production-system execution cycle. That is, they estimated the duration of specific micro-processes within the recognize-act cycle (such as the time to do a match, or the time to execute an action) by relating the number of such micro-process executions to the reaction-time data.

Although neither of these early models dealt with developmental data, the model of elementary quantification processes was subsequently elaborated into one that did deal with the differences in subitizing rates between children and adults (Klahr & Wallace, 1976; Chaps. 3 and 8). The elaboration included two distinct "working memories": one corresponding to the traditional STM, and the other corresponding to an iconic store. Accordingly, the condition elements in productions could refer to either of these information sources, and the time parameters associated with matches in the two stores differed.

By attempting to constrain the model-building process with the chronometric data from very different domains, both of these models converged on a gross estimate of the time duration for the basic production-system cycle time of between 10 and 100 ms. While this may seem to be a fairly loose parameter estimate, it is important to note that it is not 1 ms, nor is it 1000 ms. That is, if the production cycle is constrained, even within these broad limits, then one can evaluate the plausibility of particular production systems in terms of whether they exhibit—within an order of magnitude—the same *absolute* as well as relative temporal patterns as do the humans they are modelling.

2.4.2 Production Systems for a Different Levels of Performance

In contrast to relatively rare chronometrically-constrained production systems, the "family of models" approach is the most common use of production systems by developmentalists. The goal here is to produce a family of production-system models for a specific task that represent different levels of performance. Once it has been demonstrated that the models can indeed produce the appropriate behavior at each level of performance, then one can examine the differences between successive models in order to infer what a transition mechanism would have to accomplish. Baylor and Gascon (1974) did this kind of analysis for levels of weight seriation, and Klahr and Siegler (1978) did it for the balance scale task. Siegler previously had produced an elegant analysis of rule sequences characterizing how children make predictions in several domains (Siegler, 1976), and the sequences were formulated as a series of increasingly elaborated binary decision trees. By recasting the rules as production systems, Klahr and Siegler were able to make a more precise characterization of what develops than was afforded by just the decision tree representation. Even without describing the models, the following quotation from their paper conveys the level of detail that was facilitated by the production-system formulation.

> We can compare the four models to determine the task facing a transition model. At the level of productions, the requisite modifications are straightforward: a transition from Model I to Model II requires the addition of P3; from Models II to III, the addition of P4 and P5; and from Models II to IV, the addition of P6 and P7 and the modification of P4 to P4'. (This modification changes the action side from random muddling through to "get torques.")
>
> We can compare the four models at a finer level of analysis by looking at the implicit requirements for encoding and comparing the important qualities in the environment. Model I tests for sameness or difference in weight. Thus, it requires an encoding process that either directly encodes relative weight, or encodes an absolute amount of each and then inputs those representations into a comparison process. Whatever the form of the comparison process, it must be able to produce not only a same-or-different symbol, but if there is a difference, it must be able to keep track of which side is greater. Model II requires the additional capacity to make these decisions about distance as well as weight. This might constitute a completely separate encoding and comparison system for distance representations, or it might be the same system except for the interface with the environment.
>
> Model III needs no additional operators at this level. Thus, it differs from Model II only in the way it utilizes information that is already accessible to Model II. Model IV requires a much more powerful set of quantitative operators than any of the preceding models. In order

to determine relative torque, it must first determine the absolute torque on each side of the scale, and this in turn requires exact numerical representation of weight and distance. In addition, the torque computation would require access to the necessary arithmetic production systems to actually do the sum of products calculations (p. 80).

2.4.3   Representing the Immediate Task Context

One advantage of a production-system formulation is that it facilitates the extension of a basic model of the *logical* properties of a task to include the processing of verbal instructions, encoding of the stimulus, keeping track of where the child is in the overall task, and so on. For example, in their analysis of individual subject protocols on the balance scale, Klahr and Siegler proposed some models to account for some children's idiosyncratic—but consistent—response patterns. One of these models included not only the basic productions for a variant of one of Siegler's four models for balance scale predictions, but also a lot of other knowledge about the task context:

> The model represents, in addition to the child's knowledge about how the balance scale operates, her knowledge about the immediate experimental context in which she is functioning. The trial-by-trial cycle during the training phase comprises (1) observation of the static display, (2) prediction of the outcome, (3) observation of the outcome, (4) comparison of the outcome with the prediction, and (5) revision if necessary of the criterion. . . . This model utilizes, in one way or another, representation of knowledge about when and how to encode the environment, which side has *more* weight or distance, which side has a *big* weight or distance, what the current criterion value is, what the scale is expected to do, what the scale actually did, whether the prediction is yet to be made or has been made, and whether it is correct or incorrect (Klahr & Siegler, 1978, p. 89).

This kind of model raises two issues that might otherwise escape notice. First, what kinds of knowledge are necessary to generate these different encodings, and where do they come from? It has long been known that "surface" variations in tasks can cause wide variation in children's performance—even on the tasks purported to index developmental level, such as class inclusion (Klahr & Wallace, 1972). Production-system formulations avoid the arbitrary dichotomy between "performance" demands and the so-called "logical" properties of a task, and force an unambiguous specification of all the processing necessary to complete the task. Second, how much of the encoded knowledge (i.e., the contents of working memory) must be available at any one moment? That is, in order to do the task, how much working memory capacity is required? Case (1986) addresses this issue informally in his proposed procedures for quantifying tasks in terms of their demands on the Short Term Storage Space. However, without a clear and principled specification of the grain-size and computational power of the routines that *use* the contents of STSS, it is difficult to apply his demand-estimating procedure to a new domain.

2.4.4 Multiple-level Production System: From Principles to Encodings

Klahr and Wallace (1976) describe a model of children's performance on Piaget's conservation of quantity task. Their model contains productions dealing with several different levels of knowledge. At the highest level are productions that represent general conservation principles, such as "If you know about an initial quantitative relation, and a transformation, then you know something about the resultant quantitative relation." (See Klahr & Wallace, 1973, for an elucidation of these conservation principles.) At the next level are productions representing pragmatic rules, such as "If you want to compare two quantities, and you don't know about any prior comparisons, then quantify each of them." At an even lower level are rules that determine which of several quantification processes will actually be used to encode the external display (e.g., subitizing, counting, or estimation). Finally, at the lowest level, are productions for carrying out the quantification process. These are the same productions that comprised the systems described earlier in our discussion about matching production systems to chronometric data.

Although I have described this system as if there were a hierarchy of productions, there is only the flat structure of a collection of productions. Each production simply checks for its conditions. If it fires, then it deposits its results in working memory. The hierarchy emerges from the specific condition elements in each production, which ensure that productions only fire when the current context is relevant.

2.4.5 Non-transition Models: A Summary

Recall that in preparation for this recent enumeration of computer simulations of developmentally-relevant phenomena, I first limited the discussion to production systems, then to state models, rather than transition models, and finally, for convenience, to the work I know best. As a result, I have traversed a familiar, but narrow, path. However, these four instances by no means exhaust the set of computer simulations of children's thinking processes. Rabinowitz, Grant and Dingley (1987) summarize over a score of other computer simulation models relevant to cognitive development, including those that use non-production-system architectures, and including both state and transition models. The production-system models include work on seriation (Baylor, Gascon, Lemoyne, & Pother, 1973; Young, 1976) and subtraction (Young & O'Shea, 1981). Computer simulations based on schema architectures have been proposed in the area of arithmetic (Greeno, Riley, & Gelman, 1984; Riley, Greeno, & Heller, 1983; Kintsch & Greeno, 1985) and language acquisition (Hill, 1983). Task-specific architectures have been used to model children's performance on addition (Ashcraft, 1987), multiplication (Siegler, 1988), subtraction (Brown & VanLehn, 1982), and series completion (Klahr & Wallace, 1970b).

As Rabinowitz et al. note, only a handful of these models include any self-modifying mechanisms. Nevertheless, the underlying assumption in all of the computer simulations is that by clarifying the nature of children's thought at any particular level of development, the requirements of a transition theory become better defined. Thus, regardless of their intrinsic merits, the principle value of all of these state models is that they provide promissory notes for a model of self-modification. Furthermore, I believe that production system architectures are both highly plausible and very tractable architectures within which to formulate theories of self-modification. In the following section, I consider this issue in detail.

2.5 Self-Modification

Self-modification can lay claim to being the central issue for a cognitive developmentalist. One way to approach self-modification from a production-system perspective is to assume the stance of a designer of a self-modifying production system, and consider the issues that must be resolved in order to produce a theory of self-modification based on the production-system architecture.

First, a definition. Rather than get side-tracked by attempting to distinguish between learning and development, I will use the more neutral term *change*, and it will be understood that the change is imposed by the system's own information-processing mechanisms (hence "self-modification"). Note that while learning is usually defined—in one form or another—as "the improvement of performance over time," such directionality is not necessarily implied by change. Indeed, in many areas of development, the measured trajectory is U-shaped, rather than monotone (Strauss, 1982), and a theory of change must account for this. So for now, I will use change as the generic term for self-modification, and later I will return to the question of whether self-modifying production systems are models of learning or development.

2.5.1 Mechanisms

Many general *principles* for change have been proposed in the developmental literature. These include things like equilibration, encoding, efficiency, redundancy elimination, search reduction, self-regulation, consistency detection, and so on. However, they are not mechanisms. Once we have adopted a production system architecture, we can pose the following focused questions about how these principles might be implemented as specific mechanisms.

1. *Change mechanisms.* What are the basic change mechanisms that lead to new productions? Examples are generalization, discrimination, composition, proceduralization, and strengthening.

2. *Conditions for change.* What are the conditions under which these change mechanisms are evoked: when an error is noted, when a rule is applied, when a goal is achieved, or when a pattern is detected?
3. *Interactions among mechanisms.* Do the change mechanisms complement each other, or do they compete for control of behavior? For example, generalization and discrimination move in opposite directions through the space of conditions.

The recognize-act cycle offers three points at which change can have an effect: a production system's repertoire of behaviors can be changed by affecting the outcome of (1) production matching, (2) conflict resolution, and (3) production application.

2.5.2 Change During the Match

The most commonly used technique for altering the set of applicable productions found by the matching process is to add new productions to the set. As long as matching is exhaustive, the new productions are guaranteed to be considered during the next recognize-act cycle. One way to generate the new productions is to modify the conditions of existing rules. Anderson, Kline, and Beasley (1978) were the first to modify production system models of human learning via *generalization* and *discrimination.* The first mechanism creates a new rule (or modifies an existing one) so that it is *more* general than an existing rule, meanwhile retaining the same actions. The second mechanism—discrimination—creates a new rule (or modifies an existing one) so that it is *less* general than an existing rule, while still retaining the same actions. The two mechanisms lead to opposite results, though in most models they are not inverses in terms of the conditions under which they are evoked.

Within production-system models there are three basic ways to form more general or specific rules, each corresponding to a different view of generality. First, one can add or delete conditions from the left-hand side of a production. The former generates a more specific rule, since it will match in fewer situations, while the latter gives a more general rule. The second method involves replacing variables with constant terms, or vice versa. Changing variables to constants reduces generality, whereas changing constants to variables increases generality. The final method revolves around class hierarchies. For example, one may know that both dogs and cats are mammals and that both mammals and birds are vertebrates. Replacing a term from this hierarchy with one below it in the hierarchy decreases generality, while the inverse operation increases generality.

These techniques have been used in programs modeling behavior on concept acquisition (Anderson & Kline, 1979), language comprehension and production at various age levels (Langley, 1982; Anderson, 1981), geometry theorem proving (Anderson, Greeno, Kline, & Neves, 1981), and various puzzle-solving tasks (Langley, 1982). Note that both methods require instances that have been clustered into some class, and both attempt to generate some general description of those classes based on the observed instances. These mechanisms are described in considerable detail by Langley (1987).

2.5.3 Change During Conflict Resolution

Once a set of matching rule instantiations has been found, a production-system architecture still must make some determination about which instantiation(s) in that set will be executed. Thus, conflict resolution offers another decision point in the recognize-act cycle where the behavior of the system can be affected. This turns out to be particularly important because many models of human learning attempt to model its incremental nature, assuming that learning involves the construction of successively closer approximations to correct knowledge over a series of experiences.

The knowledge represented in a new production is essentially an hypothesis about the correctness of that production. A self-modifying system must maintain a balance between the need for feedback obtained by trying new productions and the need for stable performance obtained by relying on those productions that have proven themselves successful. This means that the system must distinguish between rule *applicability* and rule *desirability*, and be able to alter its selections as it discovers more about desirability. Production systems have embodied a number of schemes for performing conflict resolution, ranging from simple fixed orderings on the rules in PSG (Newell and McDermott, 1975) and PAS (Waterman, 1975), to various forms of weights or strengths (Anderson, 1976; Langley, 1987), to complex schemes that are not uniform across the entire set of productions as in HPM (Neches, 1987), to no resolution at all, as in Soar (Newell, 1988).

2.5.4 Changing Conditions and Actions

Various change mechanisms have been proposed that lead to rules with new conditions *and* actions. *Composition* was originally proposed by Lewis (1978) to account for speedup as the result of practice. This method combines two or more rules into a new rule with the conditions and actions of the component rules. However, conditions that are guaranteed to be met by one of the actions are not included. For instance, composition of rules (**AB → CD**) and (**DE → F**), would produce the rule (**ABE → CDF**). Of course, the process is not quite this simple; most composition methods are based on instantiations of productions rather than the rules themselves, and one must take variable bindings into account in generating the new rule. Lewis (1987) discusses the situations under which such compositions are likely to have the desired effects.

Another mechanism for creating new rules is *proceduralization* (Neves & Anderson, 1981). This involves constructing a very specific version of some general rule, based on some instantiation of the rule that has been applied. This method can be viewed as a form of discrimination learning because it generates more specific variants of an existing rule. However, the conditions for application tend to be quite different, and the use to which these methods have been put have quite different flavors. For instance, discrimination has been used almost entirely to account for reducing search or eliminating errors, whereas proceduralization has been used to account for speedup effects and automatization.

A basic mechanism for change via chunking was initially proposed by Rosenbloom and Newell (1982, 1987) and first used to explain the power law of practice (the time to perform a task decreases as a power-law function of the number of times the task has been performed). The learning curves produced by their model are quite similar to those observed in a broad range of learning tasks. The basic chunking mechanism and the production-system architecture to support it has evolved into a major theoretical statement about the nature of the human cognitive system. The system (called "Soar") represents the most fully-elaborated candidate for complete cognitive theory—a "unified theory of cognition" (Newell, 1988)—and to give even a brief overview of Soar would require a substantial extension of the present chapter. I will comment on only its approach to self-modification. Soar contains one assumption that is both parsimonious and radical. It is that all change is produced by a single mechanism: chunking. The chunking mechanism forms productions out of the elements that led to the most recent goal achievement. What was at first a search through a hierarchy of subgoals becomes, after chunking, a single production that eliminates any future search under the same conditions. Chunking is built into the Soar architecture as an integral part of the production cycle. It is in continual operation during performance—there is no place at which the performance productions are suspended so that a set of chunking productions can fire. Chunking occurs at all levels of sub-goaling, and in all problem-spaces. (Soar operates entirely through search in problem spaces: spaces for encoding the environment, for applying operators, for selecting operators, etc.) Chunking reduces processing by extending the knowledge base of the system.

2.5.5 Are Other Mechanisms Necessary?

Langley, Neches, Neves, and Anzai (1980) have argued that self-modifying systems must address two related problems: including *correct* rules for when to perform the various actions available to the system and developing *interesting* new actions to perform. However, most of the models that have been developed in recent years have focused on the first of these issues, and some researchers (e.g., Anderson, 1983) have asserted that mechanisms such as composition, generalization, and discrimination are sufficient to account for all change.

Nevertheless, it appears that although these processes may be necessary components of a computational change theory, they may not be sufficient. The evidence for this comes from a number of studies that have tried to characterize differences between the strategies employed by experts and novices (Hunter, 1968; Larkin, 1981; Lewis, 1981; Simon & Simon, 1978). The reorganization necessary to get from novice to expert level involves much more than refinements in the rules governing when suboperations are performed. Such refinements could presumably be produced by generalization and discrimination mechanisms. However, producing this new procedure requires the introduction of new operations (or at least new goal structures). Those new operations, and the control structure governing the sequence of their execution, require the introduction of novel elements of goals—something that generalization, discrimination, and composition are clearly not able to do.

There are only a few studies in which change sequences, and the intermediate procedures produced within them, have been directly observed. Fortunately, a similar picture emerges from both studies. Anzai and Simon (1979) examined a subject solving and re-solving a five-disk Tower of Hanoi puzzle. They found a number of changes in procedure that seemed inconsistent with strict composition/generalization/discrimination models. These included eliminating moves that produced returns to previously visited problem states, establishing subgoals to perform actions that eliminated barriers to desired actions, and transforming partially specified goals (e.g., moving a disk off a peg) into fully specified goals (e.g., moving the disk from the peg to a specific other peg).

In the second study, Neches (1981) traced procedure development in the command sequences issued by an expert user of a computer graphics editing system. In doing this, he found a number of changes that involved reordering operations and replanning procedure segments on the basis of efficiency considerations. Subjects were able to evaluate their own efficiency at accomplishing goals and to invert new procedures to reach the same goals more efficiently.

The important point in both of these examples is that the change appears to involve reasoning on the basis of knowledge about the structure of procedures in general, and the semantics of a given procedure in particular. In each example, procedures were modified through the construction of novel elements rather than through simple deletions, additions, or combinations of existing elements.

2.5.6 Heuristic Procedure Modification

This class of self-initiated qualitative improvements is exemplified by children's acquisition of the min strategy for simple addition problems discussed earlier. When children are first instructed in addition, they are taught the "count all" algorithm, but they eventually develop the min strategy on their own. Their answers are correct under execution of either strategy (but not equally—see Siegler, 1987 for a careful analysis of the relation between errors and strategy choice) and there is no explicit instruction that tells children to *create* a min strategy. What kind of self-modification mechanism could account for this and other examples of the ubiquitous tendency for children to develop novel approaches to problems? Neches (1981, 1987) proposed a production-system architecture called HPM (for Heuristic Procedure Modification) that addresses these issues. The model demonstrates how a system can learn entirely from its own performance without relying on external feedback. From an architectural perspective, HPM's most important features are a goal trace, which leaves a record of goal accomplishments, and a production trace, which preserves information about the temporal order of production firing, and the context in which they fired.

The general idea that change systems should be able to observe their own performance appears under several rubrics, and it remains to be seen just how much they differ. HPM is one clear instantiation of the notion, and it also appears as the "time line" notion in the developmental model sketched by Wallace, Klahr, and Bluff (1987). It is also captured to some extent in the way that Soar forms chunks out of the goal trace and local context for satisfied sub-goals.

2.6 Summary: Production Systems as Frameworks for Cognitive Developmental Theory

In this section I have provided both a brief overview of production-system architectures and a perspective on the issues that arise in applying them to the areas of learning and development. The framework rests on three fundamental premises of the hard-hard-core approach:

1. *The structure of production-system architectures provides insight into the nature of the human information-processing system architecture.* This premise derives from observations about similarities in terms of both structural organization and behavioral properties. Structurally, production systems provide a plausible characterization of the relationship between long-term memory and working memory, and about the interaction between procedural and declarative knowledge. Behaviorally, strong analogies can be seen between humans and production systems with respect to their abilities to mix goal-driven and event-driven processes, and with their tendency to process information in parallel at the recognition level and serially at higher cognitive levels.

2. *Change is the fundamental aspect of intelligence; we cannot say that we fully understand cognition until we have a model that accounts for its development.* The first 20 years of information-processing psychology devoted scant attention to the problems of how to represent change processes, other than to place it on an agenda for future work. Indeed, almost all of the information-processing approaches to developmental issues followed the two-step strategy outlined in the Simon quotation that opened this chapter: first construct the performance model, and then follow it with a change model that operates on the performance model. In recent years, as people have finally started to work seriously on the change process, they have begun to formulate models that inextricably link performance and change. Self-modifying production systems are one such example of this linking.

3. *All information-processing-system architectures, whether human or artificial, must obey certain constraints in order to facilitate the process of change.* It is these constraints that give rise to the seemingly complex particulars of individual production system architectures. Thus, following from our second premise, an understanding of production-system models of change is a step toward understanding the nature of human development and learning.

I have tried to demonstrate how computer-simulation models in general, and production-system models in particular, enable us to sharpen and focus the question of self-modification in a way that is simply unattainable in more traditional verbal formulations of theories of state or transition. The early critics of information-processing models in cognitive development (Beilin, 1983; Brown, 1982) faulted these models for their lack of attention to issues of transition and change. However, they failed to understand the principal virtue of the early simulation models of distinct states: that they explicated many of the complex requirements for a self-modifying system (an explication entirely absent from Genevan accounts of equilibration). However, both the Rabinowitz et al. review and the listing in this section clearly indicate, several examples of self-modifying systems have been created and described in the literature. Nevertheless, echos of the "non-modifiability" theme are still appearing (cf. Liben, 1987, p. 117, citing Beilin, 1983), even though the existence of self-modifying systems in specific domains provides concrete evidence that the criticism is uninformed and unfounded.

3. CONCLUSION AND SPECULATION

In this chapter I have attempted to define and illustrate the major attributes of information-processing approaches to cognitive development. For rhetorical purposes, I proposed a dichotomy between soft-core and hard-core attributes, when in reality, they form several continua having complex and subtle interactions. The main point to be made was that at the soft end of these attributes, information-processing approaches are so pervasive as to be redundant modifiers of "cognitive development." Distinctive features only begin to appear as we approach the hard-core instances, particularly those that use computer simulation as a form of theory building. I then went on to describe the relevance and potential of a particular, theory-laden type of computer simulation: production systems. Several examples of how production systems have been used to model performance on developmentally important tasks were presented, and then I introduced self-modifying production systems and their potential for modelling change. In this final section, I will make a few general comments on the state of theorizing about developmental mechanisms, point to one area of great potential importance that has not been treated in the chapter, and speculate about the future of information-processing approaches to cognitive development.

3.1 Is This Trip Necessary?

Are computational models worth the effort? Why should someone interested in theories of cognitive development be concerned about the detailed architectural variations of the sort discussed earlier? The primary justification for focusing on such systems is my earlier claim that self-modification is *the* central question for cognitive developmental theory. My personal belief is that if we want to make theoretical advances, then we have no other viable alternatives than to formulate computational models at least as complex as the systems described here.

Some people have criticized the area for being insufficiently attentive to the issue of self-modification.

> I have asked some of my developmental friends where the issue stands on transitional mechanisms. Mostly, they say that developmental psychologists don't have good answers. Moreover, they haven't had the answer for so long now that they don't very often ask the question anymore—not daily, in terms of their research (Newell, 1988a, p. 325).

Is this too harsh a judgment? Perhaps we can dismiss it as based on hearsay: for Newell himself is not a developmental psychologist. But it is harder to dismiss the following assessment from John Flavell (1984)

> ... serious theorizing about basic mechanisms of cognitive growth has actually never been a popular pastime, ... It is rare indeed to encounter a substantive treatment of the problem in the annual flood of articles, chapters, and books on cognitive development. The reason is not hard to find: Good theorizing about mechanisms is very, very hard to do (p 189).

Even more critical is the following observation on the state of theory in perceptual development from one of the area's major contributors in recent years (Banks, 1987):

Put simply, our models of developmental mechanisms are disappointingly vague. This observation is rather embarrassing because the aspect of perceptual developmental psychology that should set it apart from the rest of perceptual psychology is the explanation of how development occurs, and such an explanation is precisely what is lacking (p. 342).

It is difficult to deny either Newell's or Bank's assertions that we don't have good answers, or Flavell's assessment of the difficulty of the question, but I believe that it is no longer being avoided: many developmentalists have been at least asking the right questions recently. In the past few years we have seen Sternberg's (1984) edited volume *Mechanisms of Cognitive Development*, MacWhinney's (1987) edited volume *Mechanisms of Language Acquisition*, and Siegler's (1989) *Annual Review* chapter devoted to transition mechanisms. So the question is being asked. Furthermore, the trend is in the direction of hardening the core. Only a few of the chapters in the Sternberg volume specify mechanisms any more precisely than at the flow-chart level, and most of the proposed "mechanisms" are at the soft end of the information-processing spectrum. However, only five years later, Siegler, in characterizing several general categories for transition mechanisms (neural mechanisms, associative competition, encoding, analogy, and strategy choice) is able to point to computationally-based exemplars for all but the neural mechanisms (e.g., Bakker & Halford, 1988; Falkenhainer et al., 1986; Holland, 1986; MacWhinney, 1987; Rumelhart & McClelland, 1986; Siegler, 1988).

To reiterate, as Flavell and Wohlwill (1969) noted 20 years ago: "Simple models will just not do for developmental psychology." A serious theory of cognitive development is going to be enormously complex. The formulation, adaptation, or extension of a universal theory of cognition of the scope of something like Soar is a major intellectual commitment.

A clear advantage of computational models is that they force difficult questions into the foreground, where they cannot be sidetracked by the wealth of detailed but unconnected experimental results, nor obscured by vague generalizations and characterizations about the various "essences" of cognitive development. The relative lack of progress in theory development—noted by Banks, Flavell, and Newell—is a consequence of the fact that, until recently, most developmental psychologists have avoided moving to computationally-based theories, attempting instead to attack the profoundly difficult question of self-modification with inadequate tools.

3.2 Connectionism and Cognitive Development

Earlier in this chapter, I justified the exclusion of information-processing models of perceptual/motor development on conventional grounds. The implication was that it was simply a matter of space constraints. However, there is a more critical interpretation of the exclusion of motor and perceptual areas from the core of information-processing approaches. This view argues that information-processing approaches of the symbolic variety are inherently inadequate to account for the important phenomena in perception and motor behavior. The gist of the argument is that, given the highly parallel and "presymbolic" nature of these areas, and given the serial and symbolic nature of most information-processing accounts of higher cognition, it follows that we should never expect to see symbol-oriented information-processing models of any value to either area.

Indeed, this weakness of information-processing models is, according to recent attacks from the connectionists (Rumelhart & McClelland, 1986), the Achilles heel of the symbolic approach to information processing. Furthermore, from a developmental perspective, the situation is particularly troublesome, for if we are to model a system from its neonatal origins, then we will have to invent new ways to model the interface between perceptual-motor systems and central cognition, particularly at the outset, when they provide the basis for all subsequent cognition. At present, there are not enough connectionist—or "parallel-distributed-processing" (PDP)—models of developmental phenomena to decide the extent to which they will replace, augment, or be absorbed by the symbolic variety of information-processing models described in this chapter. Nevertheless, the connectionist criticisms of symbol-oriented approaches to cognition in general, and the more developmentally relevant points listed above, warrant careful consideration.

3.3 Self-modifying Systems: Development or Learning?

Recall that earlier, I side-stepped the distinction between learning and development by using the term "change" for self-modification. However, I need to return to the issue, because a common criticism of the kind of systems described above is that while they may account for learning, they certainly do not capture the "essence" of development (cf. Beilin, 1981; Neisser, 1976). I disagree. If we look at the many dichotomies that have been used to distinguish development from learning, the self-modifying systems appear to be more appropriately placed in the development category than in the learning category.

- *Spontaneous versus imposed.* Much of development appears to occur "on its own," without any external agent instructing, inducing, or urging the change. But this is precisely the phenomenon that Siegler's strategy-choice model and Neches' HPM were designed to account for. In Soar, chunking occurs continuously and results in changes whenever the system detects the appropriate circumstances. It has the flavor of the experience-contingent spontaneity that purportedly distinguishes development from learning.

- *Qualitative vs. quantitative change.* This distinction has occupied philosophers and developmentalists for many years, and I can only suggest one modest clarification. Look at a program that has undergone self-modification, and ask whether the change is quantitative or qualitative. For example, in the Anzai and Simon (1979) work, it seems to me that the change from depth-first search to a recursive strategy could only be characterized as qualitative, and hence more of a developmental change than a learning one. Similarly, the HPM system transforms an inefficient strategy for addition (counting out the augend, counting out the addend, and then counting out the total set) into an efficient one (starting with the maximum of the two arguments and then "counting on" the other argument). It is difficult to characterize this as simply a change in which more of some pre-existing feature is added to the system: "qualitative change" seems the appropriate designation.

- *Structural reorganization vs. local change.* Developmental theories, particularly those with a strong emphasis on stages (cf. Fischer, 1980), usually demand structural reorganization as a requirement for development, while viewing local changes as the province of learning. Clearly, some of the basic mechanisms in self-modifying production systems operate on a relatively local basis. Indeed, one of the great advantages of production systems is that they do not require vast systematic knowledge of the consequences of local changes. But when we begin to look carefully at changes in information-processing systems, the distinction between "local" and "structural" changes becomes blurred. Changing a few conditions in an existing production (a local change) may radically alter the firing sequence of it and all its previous successors, producing very different patterns of activation in working memory. This in turn would result in different patterns of goals and subgoals, and, ultimately, in a different set of generalizations and rules. Thus, from local changes come global effects, and from incremental modifications come structural reorganizations.

- *Reflective abstraction vs. practice with knowledge of results.* The systems described in this chapter constitute a very different class of models from earlier models of paired-associate learning (Feigenbaum, 1963) or concept learning (Gregg & Simon, 1967). Such models were clearly intended to account for learning in situations with externally supplied feedback about the correctness of the current state of the system. In systems like HPM, or proposed systems like BAIRN (Wallace, Klahr, & Bluff, 1987), change is not dependent on explicit feedback from the environment. Instead, many of the processes that seek patterns are self-contained, in the sense that they examine the trace of the system's own encodings in the absence of any clear indications of a "right" or "wrong" response. Such processes can be viewed as a mechanization of Piaget's "reflective abstraction."

- *Active or Passive?* Information-processing models have been criticized for painting "a strikingly passive picture of the child" (Liben, 1987, p. 119). While a passive model might account for learning—especially learning from instruction—it could not, so the argument goes, account for the active, seeking, self-initiated nature of cognitive development. But it should be clear by now that computer simulation models must, by their very nature, make explicit statements about how goals are set, how agenda's are constructed, or how self-direction is initiated or maintained.[12] Assertions about the particular ways in which this "active" engagement with the environment occurs may well be inadequate or incorrect, but not until the creation of information-processing models was it possible to make unambiguous statements about these centrally important issues.

These dichotomies are not independent, nor do they exhaust the possible contrasts between development and learning. This listing should suffice, however, to show that at the level at which such contrasts are stated, there is little basis for the claim that information-processing models in general, or self-modifying production systems in particular, are inherently inadequate to capture the essence of cognitive development.

3.4 The Future of the Hard-core Approach

In the early years of computer simulation, the necessary resources were limited to very few research centers. Even today, only a handful of developmental psychologists have had any extensive training with computer simulation models. However, with the widespread distribution of powerful workstations, the proliferation of computer networks for transmitting programs and systems, and the increasing number of published reports on various kinds of computationally based cognitive architectures, the appropriate technology and support structures are relatively accessible. This accessibility will make it possible to include simulation methodology as a standard part of the training of cognitive developmentalists.

The situation appears somewhat like the early days of other kinds of computational technology, such as standard statistical packages, or scaling procedures. The earliest papers using those techniques usually required many pages of description about the fundamental ideas, before the task at hand could be addressed. Today, the reader of a paper using analysis of variance or multidimensional scaling is expected to have had several courses in graduate school learning the fundamentals. Similarly, early papers on production systems all included a brief tutorial on the basic concepts, before presenting a production system model of the specific domain.

Over the next 10 years, I expect to see theories of cognitive development couched in terms of extensions to systems like Soar, or Act*, or some other well-known (by then) cognitive architecture. The writers of those papers will be able to assume that readers need no more of a tutorial in the underlying system than current writers assume that they have to explain the conceptual foundations or computational details of an ANOVA. My vision is that, with respect to the hard-core information-processing approach to cognitive development, we will be able to expect the same level of technical training in the developmental psychologist of the future. Once we are fully armed with such powerful tools, progress on our most difficult problems will be inevitable. We will no longer talk of "approaches" to our problems, but rather, of their solutions.

ACKNOWLEDGMENTS

I would like to thank my colleagues Janet Davidson, Sharon Carver, Allan Newell and Robert Siegler for their careful and constructive comments on an earlier version of this paper. Preparation of the chapter was supported in part by the Personnel and Training Research Programs, Psychological Sciences Division, Office of Naval Research, under Contract No. N00014-86K-0349.

NOTES

1. As well as a stimulating paper by three of my fellow graduate students (Quillian, Wortman & Baylor, 1964) entitled "The Programmable Piaget."

2. For other recent definitions of the field, see Kail & Bisanz, 1982 and Siegler, 1983, 1986. For a thoughtful comparison between information processing and other major approaches to cognitive development, such as Piagetian, Freudian, Gibsonian, see Miller, 1983.

3. In fact, Naus and Ornstein (1983) used the memory scanning paradigm to show that third-graders used a less efficient strategy than sixth-graders and adults when searching lists that could be taxonomically organized.

4. To the best of my knowledge, Greene & Ruggles (1963) were the first to attempt to construct a developmental simulation model. It was an abstract characterization of Piaget's sensory-motor stages. It combined the symbol-oriented and connectionist techniques then available.

5. Interestingly, this quotation comes from a section entitled "*The* Information-processing paradigm," which contradicts my opening comments about multiple perspectives, and reveals how hard it is to keep an open mind about one's preferred approach to a field.

6. Although such alternative models are rarely forthcoming!

7. There is, at present, a vigorous debate taking place within cognitive science as to the appropriate level at which to represent the primitive, non-decomposable components, and how to account for their organization. The "symbol-processors" tend to start with the symbol, and to construct intelligence out of symbolic structures, while the "connectionists" (Rumelhart & McClellend, 1986)

start with distributed patterns of activation over networks of nodes. I will not go into that debate in this paper, but note that in both cases there is fundamental agreement that intelligence is an emergent property based on the organization of components. The intelligence derives largely from the architecture.

8. Although the use of production systems to model human performance had been introduced several years earlier by Newell (1968), it wasn't until the early 1970s that Newell produced a running system for general use (Newell, 1973; Newell & McDermott, 1975). This turned out to have a profound impact in two related domains: within cognitive psychology, it was the first serious proposal for a "tool kit" for building simulation models based on a well-defined cognitive architecture. (The expansion of Newell's original production-system architecture into a large *space* of such architectures will be discussed in the next section.) Within artificial intelligence, production systems spawned an industry dedicated to the creation of computer-based expert systems. (See Neches, Langley, & Klahr, 1987, for a brief history of production systems in psychology, and Brownston, Farrell, Kant and Martin [1985] for a tutorial on building expert systems.)

9. Parts of this section have been adapted from Neches, Langley and Klahr, 1987.

10. PRISM is a flexible production-system language that enables the user to construct an architecture with specific settings on most of the dimensions listed above (Langley, Ohlsson, Thibadeau, & Walter, 1984).

11. An acronym for "Production System G." This implies that six precursor versions had already been deemed unsuitable for public consumption; I take this as an indirect testimony to Newell's standards of excellence.

12. Given the importance of children's "active construction of their own environment" to neo-Piagetians, it is surprising and frustrating to search in vain through Piaget's theoretical formulations for a clear statement of how any of these processes operate.

REFERENCES

Anderson, J. R. (1976). *Language, memory, and thought*. Hillsdale, NJ: Erlbaum.

Anderson, J. R. (Ed.). (1981). *Cognitive skills and their acquisition*. Hillsdale, NJ: Erlbaum.

Anderson, J. R. (1983). *The architecture of cognition*. Cambridge, MA: Harvard University Press.

Anderson, J. R. (1987). Skill acquisition: Compilation of weak-method problem solutions. *Psychological Review, 94*, 192–210.

Anderson, J. R. & Kline, P. J. (1979). A learning system and its psychological implications. In *Proceedings of the Sixth International Joint Conference on Artificial Intelligence*. Tokyo: IJCAI.

Anderson, J. R., Greeno, J. G., Kline, P. J., & Neves, D. M. (1981). Acquisition of problem solving skill. In J. R. Anderson (Ed.), *Cognitive skills and their acquisition*. Hillsdale, NJ: Erlbaum.

Anderson, J. R., Kline, P. J., & Beasley, C. M., Jr. (1978). *A general learning theory and its application to schema abstraction* (Tech. Rep. 78-2). Department of Psychology, Carnegie-Mellon University.

Anzai, Y., & Simon, H. A. (1979). The theory of learning by doing. *Psychological Review, 86*, 124–140.

Ashcraft, M. H. (1982). The development of mental arithmetic: A chronometric approach. *Developmental Review, 2*(3), 213–236.

Ashcraft, M. H. (1987). Children's knowledge of simple arithmetic: A developmental model and simulation. In J. Bisanz, C. J. Brainerd, & R. Kail (Eds.), *Formal methods in developmental psychology: Progress in cognitive development research*. New York: Springer-Verlag.

Atkinson, R. C., & Shiffrin, R. M. (1968). Human memory: A proposed system and its control processes. In K. W. Spence & J. T. Spence (Eds.), *The psychology of learning and motivation*. New York: Academic Press.

Bakker, P. E., & Halford, G. S. (January 1988). *A basic computational theory of structure-mapping in analogy and transitive inference* (Tech. Rep.). Centre for Human Information Processing and Problem Solving, University of Queensland, Australia.

Banks, M. S. (1987). Mechanisms of visual development: An example of computational models. In J. Bisanz, C. J. Brainerd, & R. Kail (Eds.), *Formal methods in developmental psychology: Progress in cognitive development research.* New York: Springer-Verlag.

Banks, M. S. (1988). Visual recalibration and the development of contrast and optical flow perception. In A. Yonas (Ed.), *Perceptual Development in Infancy.* Hillsdale, NJ: Erlbaum.

Baylor, G. W., & Gascon, J. (1974). An information processing theory of aspects of the development of weight seriation in children. *Cognitive Psychology, 6,* 1–40.

Baylor, G. W., Gascon, J., Lemoyne, G., & Pother, N. (1973). An information processing model of some seriation tasks. *Canadian Psychologist, 14,* 167–196.

Beilin, H. (May 1981). Piaget and the new functionalism. Address given at the Eleventh Symposium of the Piaget Society, Philadelphia.

Beilin, H. (1983). The new functionalism and Piaget's program. In E. K. Scholnick (Ed.), *New trends in conceptual representation: Challenges to Piaget's theory?* Hillsdale, NJ: Erlbaum.

Beilin, H. (1987). Selective perspectives on cognitive/intellectual development. *Contemporary Psychology, 32*(12), 1010–1012. Review of M. Perlmutter, "Perspectives on intellectual development: The Minnesota symposia on child psychology," Vol. 19.

Berliner, H., & Ebeling, C. (1988). Pattern knowledge and search: The SUPREM architecture. *Artificial Intelligence* (in press).

Bisanz, J., Brainerd, C. J., & Kail, R. (Eds.). (1987). *Formal methods in developmental psychology: Progress in cognitive development research.* New York: Springer-Verlag.

Brainerd, C. J. (1987). Structural measurement theory and cognitive development. In J. Bisanz, C. J. Brainerd, & R. Kail (Eds.), *Formal methods in developmental psychology: Progress in cognitive development research.* New York: Springer-Verlag.

Brown, A. L. (1982). Learning and development: The problem of compatibility, access and induction. *Human Development, 25,* 89–115.

Brown, J. S., & Burton, R. R. (1978). Diagnostic models for procedural bugs in basic mathematical skills. *Cognitive Science, 2,* 155–192.

Brown, J. S., & VanLehn, K. (1982). Towards a generative theory of "bugs." In T. Romberg, T. Carpenter, & J. Moser (Eds.), *Addition and subtraction: A developmental perspective.* Hillsdale, NJ: Erlbaum.

Brownston, L., Farrell, R., Kant, E., & Martin, N. (1985). *Programming expert systems in OPS5: An introduction to rule-based programming.* Reading, MA: Addison-Wesley.

Card, S.K., Moran, T., & Newell, A. (1983). *Applied information processing psychology: The human-computer interface.* Hillsdale, NJ: Erlbaum.

Case, R. (1985). *Intellectual development: Birth to adulthood.* New York: Academic Press.

Case, R. (1986). The new stage theories in intellectual development: Why we need them; What they assert. In M. Perlmutter (Ed.), *Perspectives for intellectual development.* Hillsdale, NJ: Erlbaum.

Celle'rier, G. (1972). Information processing tendencies in recent experiments in cognitive learning-theoretical implications. In S. Farnham-Diggory (Ed.), *Information processing in children.* New York: Academic Press.

Chase, W. G. (Ed.). (1973). *Visual information processing.* New York: Academic Press.

Chase, W. G. (1978). Elementary information processes. In W. K. Estes (Ed.), *Handbook of learning and cognitive processes,* Vol. 5. Hillsdale, NJ: Erlbaum.

Chi, M. T. H. (1976). Short-term memory limitations in children: Capacity or processing deficits? *Memory and Cognition, 4,* 559–572.

Chi, M. T. H. (1977). Age differences in memory span. *Journal of Experimental Child Psychology, 23,* 266–281.

Chi, M. T. H. (1978). Knowledge structures and memory development. In R. Siegler (Ed.), *Children's thinking: What develops?* Hillsdale, NJ: Erlbaum.

Chi, M. T. H. (1981). Knowledge development and memory performance. In M. Friedman, J. P. Das,

& N. O'Connor (Eds.), *Intelligence and learning*. New York: Plenum Press.

Chi, M. T. H. & Klahr, D. (1975). Span and rate of apprehension in children and adults. *Journal of Experimental Child Psychology, 19*, 434–439.

Craik, F. I. M., & Lockhart, R. S. (1972). Levels of processing: A framework for memory research. *Journal of Verbal Learning and Verbal Behavior, 11*, 671–684.

Davidson, J. E. (1986). The role of insight in giftedness. In R. J. Sternberg & J. E. Davidson (Eds.), *Conceptions of giftedness*. New York: Cambridge University Press.

DeLoache, J. S. (1987). Rapid change in the symbolic functioning of very young children. *Science, 238*, 1556–1557.

DeLoache, J. S. (1988). The development of representation in young children. In H. W. Reese (Ed.), *Advances in Child Development and Behavior*. New York: Academic Press. In press.

Dunbar, K., & Klahr, D. (1989). Developmental differences in scientific discovery strategies. In D. Klahr & K. Kotovsky (Eds.), *Complex information processing: The impact of Herbert A. Simon*. Hillsdale, NJ: Erlbaum.

Ericsson, A. & Simon, H. A. (1984). *Protocol Analysis: Verbal Reports as Data*. Cambridge, MA: MIT Press.

Falkenhainer, B., Forbus, K. D., & Gentner, D. (1986). The structure-mapping engine. In *Proceedings of the American Association for Artificial Intelligence*. Philadelphia: American Association for Artificial Intelligence.

Farnham-Diggory, S. (Ed.). (1972). *Information processing in children*. New York: Academic Press.

Fay, A. L., & Mayer, R. E. (1987). Children's naive conceptions and confusions about LOGO graphics commands. *Journal of Educational Psychology, 79*(3), 254–268.

Feigenbaum, E. A. (1963). The simulation of verbal learning behavior. In E. A. Feigenbaum & J. Feldman (Eds.), *Computers and thought*. New York: McGraw-Hill.

Feigenbaum, E. A., & Simon, H. A. (1984). EPAM-like models of recognition and learning. *Cognitive Science, 8*, 305–336.

Fischer, K. W. (1980). A theory of cognitive development: The control and construction of hierarchies of skills. *Psychological Review, 87*, 477–531.

Fischer, K. W., & Pipp, S. L. (1984). Processes of cognitive development: Optimal level and skill acquisition. In R. J. Sternberg (Ed.), *Mechanisms of cognitive development*. New York: Freeman.

Flavell, J. H. (1982). Structures, stages, and sequences in cognitive development. In W. A. Collins (Ed.), *The concept of development*. Hillsdale, NJ: Erlbaum.

Flavell, J. H., & Wohlwill, J. F. (1969). Formal and functional aspects of cognitive development. In D. Elkind & J. H. Flavell (Eds.), *Studies in cognitive development*. New York: Oxford University Press.

Geary, D. C., Widaman, K. F., Little, T. D., & Cormier, P. (July 1987). Cognitive addition: Comparison of learning disabled and academically normal elementary school children. *Cognitive Development, 2*(3), 249–270.

Gentner, D. (February 1988). Metaphor as structure mapping: The relational shift. *Child Development, 59*(1), 47–59.

Goodman, N. (1968). *Languages of art*. Indianapolis: Bobbs-Merrill.

Greene, P. H., & Ruggles, T. L. (April-July 1963). Child and Spock. *IEEE Transactions on Military Electronics, MIL-7*(2&3), 156–159.

Greeno, J. G., Riley, M. S., & Gelman, R. (1984). Conceptual competence and children's counting. *Cognitive Psychology, 16*(1), 94–143.

Gregg, L. W., & Simon, H. A. (1967). Process models and stochastic theories of simple concept formation. *Journal of Mathematical Psychology, 4*, 246–276.

Groen, G. J., & Parkman, J. M. (1972). A chronometric analysis of simple addition. *Psychological Review, 79*, 329–343.

Hagen, J. W. (1972). Strategies for remembering. In S. Farnham-Diggory (Ed.), *Information processing in children*. New York: Academic Press.

Halford, G. S. (1970). A theory of the acquisition of conservation. *Psychological Review, 77*, 302–316.

Halford, G. S. (1975). Children's ability to interpret transformations of a quantity, I: An operational system for judging combinations of transformations. *Canadian Journal of Psychology, 29*, 124–141.

Hill, J. C. (1983). A computational model of language acquisition in the two-year-old. *Cognition and Brain Theory, 6*, 287–317.

Holland, J. H. (1986). Escaping brittleness: The possibilities of general purpose machine learning algorithms applied to parallel rule-based systems. In R. S. Michalski, J. G. Carbonell, & T. M. Mitchell (Eds.), *Machine learning: An artificial intelligence approach*. Los Altos, CA: Kaufmann.

Hoyer, W. J., & Familant, M. E. (1987). Adult age differences in the rate of processing expectancy information. *Cognitive Development, 2*(1), 59–70.

Hunter, I. M. L. (1968). Mental calculation. In P. C. Wason & P. N. Johnson-Laird (Eds.), *Thinking and reasoning*. Baltimore, MD: Penguin Books.

Inhelder, B. (1972). Information processing tendencies in recent experiments in cognitive learning-empirical studies. In S. Farnham-Diggory (Ed.), *Information processing in children*. New York: Academic Press.

Just, M. A., & Carpenter, P. A. (1978). Inference processes during reading: Reflections from eye fixations. In J. W. Senders, D. F. Fisher & R. A. Monty (Eds.), *Eye movements and the higher psychological functions*. Hillsdale, NJ: Erlbaum.

Kail, R. (1984). *The development of memory in children: Second edition*. New York: Freeman.

Kail, R. (1988). Developmental functions for speeds of cognitive processes. *Journal of Experimental Child Psychology, 45*, 339–364.

Kail, R. & Bisanz, J. (1982). Information processing and cognitive development. In H. W. Reese (Ed.), *Advances in child development and behavior*. New York: Academic Press.

Kail, R., Pellegrino, J., & Carter, P. (1980). Developmental changes in mental rotation. *Journal of Experimental Child Psychology, 29*, 102–116.

Keating, D. P., & Bobbitt, B. L. (1978). Individual and developmental differences in cognitive processing components of mental ability. *Child Development, 49*, 155–167.

Kellman, P. H. (1988). Theories of perception and research in perceptual development. In A. Yonas (Ed.), *Perceptual development in infancy*. Hillsdale, NJ: Erlbaum.

Kintsch, W., & Greeno, J. G. (1985). Understanding and solving word arithmetic problems. *Psychological Review, 92*, 109–129.

Klahr, D. (1973). A production system for counting, subitizing, and adding. In W. G. Chase (Ed.), *Visual information processing*. New York: Academic Press.

Klahr, D., & Carver, S. M. (1988). Cognitive objectives in a LOGO debugging curriculum: Instruction, Learning, and Transfer. *Cognitive Psychology, 20*, 362–404.

Klahr, D., & Robinson, M. (1981). Formal assessment of problem solving and planning processes in preschool children. *Cognitive Psychology, 13*, 113–148.

Klahr, D., & Siegler, R. S. (1978). The representation of children's knowledge. In H. W. Reese & L. P. Lipsitt (Eds.), *Advances in child development and behavior, Vol. 12*. New York: Academic Press.

Klahr, D., & Wallace, J. G. (1970a). The development of serial completion strategies: An information processing analysis. *British Journal of Psychology, 61*, 243–257.

Klahr, D., & Wallace, J. G. (1970b). An information processing analysis of some Piagetian experimental tasks. *Cognitive Psychology, 1*, 358–387.

Klahr, D., & Wallace, J. G. (1972). Class inclusion processes. In S. Farnham-Diggory (Ed.), *Information processing in children*. New York: Academic Press.

Klahr, D., & Wallace, J. G. (1973). The role of quantification operators in the development of conservation of quantity. *Cognitive Psychology, 4*, 301–327.

Klahr, D., & Wallace, J. G. (1976). *Cognitive development: An information processing view*. Hillsdale, NJ: Erlbaum.

Klahr, D., Langley, P., & Neches, R. (Eds.). (1987). *Production system models of learning and development*. Cambridge, MA: MIT Press.

Kolers, P. A., & Smythe, W. E. (1984). Symbol manipulation: Alternatives to the computational view of mind. *Journal of Verbal Learning and Verbal Behavior, 23,* 289–314.

Kuhn, D., & Phelps, E. (1982). The development of problem solving strategies. In H. W. Reese (Ed.), *Advances in child development and behavior.* New York: Academic Press.

Lachman, R., Lachman, J., & Butterfield, E. C. (1979). *Cognitive psychology and information processing: An introduction.* Hillsdale, NJ: Erlbaum.

Langley, P. (1982). Language acquisition through error recovery. *Cognition and Brain Theory, 5,* 211–255.

Langley, P., Ohlsson, S., Thibadeau, R., & Walter, R. (1984). Cognitive architectures and principles of behavior. In *Proceedings of the Sixth Conference of the Cognitive Science Society.* Boulder, CO.

Langley, P. (1987). A general theory of discrimination learning. In D. Klahr, P. Langley, & R. Neches (Eds.), *Production system models of learning and development.* Cambridge, MA: MIT Press.

Langley, P., Neches, R., Neves, D. M., & Anzai, Y. (1980). A domain-independent framework for procedure learning. *Policy Analysis and Information Systems, 4*(2), 163–197.

Larkin, J. H. (1981). Enriching formal knowledge: A model for learning to solve textbook physics problems. In J. R. Anderson (Ed.), *Cognitive skills and their acquisition.* Hillsdale, NJ: Erlbaum.

Lewis, C. H. (1978). *Production system models of practice effects.* Doctoral dissertation, University of Michigan.

Lewis, C. (1981). Skill in algebra. In J. Anderson (Ed.), *Cognitive skills and their acquisition.* Hillsdale, NJ: Erlbaum.

Lewis, C. (1987). Composition of productions. In D. Klahr, P. Langley & R. Neches (Eds.), *Production system models of learning and development.* Cambridge, MA: MIT Press.

Liben, L. S. (Ed.). (1987). *Development and learning: Conflict or congruence?* Hillsdale, NJ: Erlbaum.

Mackworth, A. K. (1987). What is the schema for a schema? *Behavioral and Brain Sciences, 10*(3), 443–444.

MacWhinney, B. J. (Ed.). (1987). *Mechanisms of language acquisition.* Hillsdale, NJ: Erlbaum.

MacWhinney, B. (1987). *Competition and cooperation in language processing.* In R. Tomlin (Ed.), Proceedings of the Pacific Conference on Linguistics. Eugene, Oregon: University of Oregon.

Madden, D. J. (1987). Aging, attention, and the use of meaning during visual search. *Cognitive Development, 2*(3), 201–216.

Mandler, J. M. (1983). Representation. In P. H. Mussen (Ed.), *Cognitive Development.* Vol. III: *Handbook of Child Psychology.* New York: Wiley.

Mandler, J. M., & Johnson, N. S. (1977). Remembrance of things passed: Story structure and recall. *Cognitive Psychology, 9,* 111–151.

Marr, D. (1982). *Vision: A computational investigation into the human representation and processing of visual information.* San Francisco: Freeman.

Miller, P. H. (1983). *Theories of developmental psychology.* San Francisco: Freeman.

Naus, M. J., & Ornstein, P. A. (1983). Development of memory strategies: Analysis, questions, and issues. In M. T. Chi (Ed.), *Trends in memory development research.* New York: Karger.

Neches, R. (1981). *Models of heuristic procedure modification.* Doctoral dissertation, Department of Psychology, Carnegie-Mellon University.

Neches, R. (1982). Simulation systems for cognitive psychology. *Behavior Research Methods and Instrumentation, 14,* 77–91.

Neches, R. (1987). Learning through incremental refinement of procedures. In D. Klahr, P. Langley, & R. Neches (Eds.), *Production system models of learning and development.* Cambridge, MA: MIT Press.

Neches, R., Langley, P., & Klahr, D. (1987). Learning, development and production systems. In D. Klahr, P. Langley, & R. Neches (Eds.), *Production system models of learning and development.* Cambridge, MA: MIT Press.

Neisser, U. (1976). General, academic and artificial intelligence. In L. B. Resnick (Ed.), *The nature of intelligence.* Hillsdale, NJ: Erlbaum.

Nelson, K., & Gruendel, J. M. (1981). Generalized event representations: Basic building blocks of cognitive development. In M. E. Lamb & A. L. Brown (Eds.), *Advances in developmental psychology, Vol. 1.* Hillsdale, NJ: Erlbaum.

Neves, D. & Anderson, J. R. (1981). Knowledge compilation: Mechanisms for the automatization of cognitive skills. In J. R. Anderson (Ed.), *Cognitive skills and their acquisition.* Hillsdale, NJ: Erlbaum.

Newell, A. (1966). On the representation of problems. *Computer science research review,* 18–33.

Newell, A. (1968). On the analysis of human problem solving protocols. In J. C. Gardin & B. Javlin (Eds.), *Calcul et formalization dan les sciences de l'homme.* Center de la Recherche Scientifique.

Newell, A. (1972). A note on process-structure distinctions in developmental psychology. In S. Farnham-Diggory (Ed.), *Information processing in children.* New York: Academic Press.

Newell, A. (1973). Production systems: Models of control structures. In W. G. Chase (Ed.), *Visual information processing.* New York: Academic Press.

Newell, A. (1980). Physical symbol systems. *Cognitive Science, 4,* 135–183.

Newell, A. (1980). Reasoning problem solving and decision processes: The problem space as a fundamental category. In R. Nickerson (Ed.), *Attention and performance, Vol. 8.* Hillsdale, NJ: Erlbaum.

Newell, A. (1989). Putting it all together: Final comments. In D. Klahr & K. Kotovsky (Eds.), *Complex information processing: The impact of Herbert A. Simon.* Hillsdale, NJ: Erlbaum. (b).

Newell, A. (1988). The 1987 William James Lectures: Unified theories of cognition. Departments of Computer Science and Psychology, Carnegie-Mellon University.

Newell, A., & McDermott, J. (1975). *PSG Manual.* Pittsburgh: Carnegie-Mellon University, Department of Computer Science.

Newell, A., & Simon, H. A. (1972). *Human problem solving.* Englewood Cliffs, NJ: Prentice-Hall.

Nisbett, R. E., & Wilson, T. D. (1977). Telling more than we can know: Verbal reports on mental processes. *Psychological Review, 84,* 231–259.

Norman, D. A., Rumelhart, D. E., & the LNR Research Group. (1975). *Explorations in cognition.* San Francisco, CA: Freeman.

Palmer, S. E., & Kimchi, R. (1986). The information processing approach to cognition. In T. J. Knapp & L. C. Robertson (Eds.), *Approaches to cognition: Contrasts and controversies.* Hillsdale, NJ: Erlbaum.

Pollack, R. H. (1972). Perceptual development: A progress report. In S. Farnham-Diggory (Ed.), *Information Processing in Children.* New York: Academic Press.

Quillian, M. R., Wortman, P. M., & Baylor, G. W. (1964). *The programmable Piaget: Behavior from the standpoint of a radical computerist.* C.I.P. Working Paper 78. Pittsburgh: Carnegie-Mellon University.

Rabinowitz, F. M., Grant, M. J., & Dingley, H. L. (1987). Computer simulation, cognition, and development: An introduction. In J. Bisanz, C. J. Brainerd, & R. Kail (Eds.), *Formal methods in developmental psychology: Progress in cognitive development research.* New York: Springer-Verlag.

Resnick, L. B., & Glaser, R. (1976). Problem solving and intelligence. In L. B. Resnick (Ed.), *The nature of intelligence.* Hillsdale, NJ: Erlbaum.

Riley, M. S., Greeno, J. G., & Heller, J. I. (1983). Development of children's problem-solving ability in arithmetic. In H. P. Ginsburg (Ed.), *The development of mathematical thinking.* New York: Academic Press.

Rosenbloom, P. S., & Newell, A. (1982). Learning by chunking: Summary of a task and a model. In *Proceedings of the Second National Conference on Artificial Intelligence.* Los Altos, CA: Morgan-Kaufmann.

Rosenbloom, P. S. & Newell, A. (1987). Learning by chunking: A production system model of practice. In D. Klahr, P. Langley & R. Neches (Eds.), *Production system models of learning and development.* Cambridge, MA: MIT Press.

Rumelhart, D. E., & McClelland, J. L. (1986). *Parallel distributed processing: Explorations in the microstructure of cognition.* Cambridge, MA: MIT Press.

Rumelhart, D. E. & Norman, D. A. (1981). Analogical processes in learning. In J. R. Anderson (Ed.), *Cognitive skills and their acquisition.* Hillsdale, NJ: Erlbaum.

Shultz, T. R. (1987). A computational model of judgments of causation, responsibility, blame, and punishment. Based on a paper delivered to the Meetings of the Society for Research in Child Development, Baltimore, April 1987.

Shultz, T. R. (1988). *Making causal judgments.* Department of Psychology, McGill University.

Siegler, R. S. (1976). Three aspects of cognitive development. *Cognitive Psychology, 8*(4), 481–520.

Siegler, R. S. (1981). Developmental sequences within and between concepts. *Monographs of the Society for Research in Child Development, Vol. 46.* (Whole No. 189).

Siegler, R. S. (1983). Information processing approaches to development. In P. H. Mussen (Ed.), *Volume 1: History, Theory, and Methods. Handbook of Child Psychology.* New York: John Wiley & Sons.

Siegler, R. S. (1986). Unities in strategy choices across domains. In M. Perlmutter (Ed.), *Minnesota symposium on child psychology.* Hillsdale, NJ: Erlbaum.

Siegler, R. S. (1988). Strategy choice procedures and the development of multiplication skill. *Journal of Experimental Psychology: General 117,* 258–275.

Siegler, R. S. (1989). Mechanisms of cognitive development. *Annual Review of Psychology, 117,* 258–275.

Siegler, R. S., & Shipley, C. (1987). The role of learning in children's strategy choices. In L. S. Liben (Ed.), *Development and learning: Conflict or congruence?* Hillsdale, NJ: Erlbaum.

Simon, H. A. (1962). An information processing theory of intellectual development. *Monographs of the Society for Research in Child Development, 27*(2, Serial No. 82).

Simon, H. A. (1972). On the development of the processor. In S. Farnham-Diggory (Ed.), *Information processing in children.* New York: Academic Press.

Simon, D. P., & Simon, H. A. (1978). Individual differences in solving physics problems. In R. Siegler (Ed.), *Children's thinking: What develops?* Hillsdale, NJ: Erlbaum.

Sperling, G. (1960). The information available in brief visual presentations. *Psychological Monographs, 74* (11, Whole No. 498).

Spitz, H. H., & Borys, S. V. (1984). Depth of search: How far can the retarded search through an internally represented problem space? In P. H. Brooks, R. Sperber, & C. McCauley (Eds.), *Learning and cognition in the mentally retarded.* Hillsdale, NJ: Erlbaum.

Stein, N. L., & Glenn, C. G. (1979). An analysis of story comprehension in elementary school children. In R. O. Freedle (Ed.), *New directions in discourse processing, Vol. 2.* Norwood, NJ: Ablex.

Sternberg, S. (1966). High speed scanning in human memory. *Science, 153,* 652–654.

Sternberg, R. J. (Ed.). (1984). *Mechanisms of cognitive development.* New York: Freeman.

Sternberg, R. J., & Rifkin, B. (1979). The development of analogical reasoning processes. *Journal of Experimental Child Psychology, 27,* 195–232.

Strauss, S. (Ed.). (1982). *U-shaped behavioral growth.* New York: Academic Press.

Wallace, J. G., Klahr, D. & Bluff, K. (1987). A self-modifying production system of cognitive development. In D. Klahr, P. Langley & R. Neches (Eds.), *Production system models of learning and development.* Cambridge, MA: MIT Press.

Waterman, D. (1975). Adaptive production systems. In *Proceedings of the Fourth International Joint Conference on Artificial Intelligence.* Cambridge, MA: Artificial Intelligence Laboratory, MIT.

Wilkinson, A. C., & Haines, B. A. (1987). Learning a cognitive skill and its components. In J. Bisanz, C. J. Brainerd, & R. Kail (Eds.), *Formal methods in developmental psychology: Progress in cognitive development research.* New York: Springer-Verlag.

Yonas, A. (Ed.). (1988). *Perceptual development in infancy.* Hillsdale, NJ: Erlbaum.

Young, R. M. (1976). *Seriation by children: An artificial intelligence analysis of a Piagetian task.* Basel: Birkhauser.

Young, R. M., & O'Shea, T. (1981). Errors in children's subtraction. *Cognitive Science, 5,* 153–177.

ECOLOGICAL SYSTEMS THEORY

Urie Bronfenbrenner

In this chapter, I undertake a difficult task—to be at once the critic and creator of my own work. The inherent conflict of interest is obvious, but I have been so long and so deeply involved in it that I can no longer escape. Ever since the publication of the *Ecology of Human Development* (Bronfenbrenner, 1979), now almost a decade ago, I have been engaging in a smuggling operation. In a series of articles written ostensibly for other purposes,[1] I have been pursuing a hidden agenda: that of re-assessing, revising, extending—as well as regretting and even renouncing—some of the conceptions set forth in my 1979 monograph. The invitation to contribute a chapter to the present volume therefore presents me with an opportunity, indeed an obligation, to perform this task explicitly and systematically.

I begin with a warning, and a reaffirmation. Any readers who might have welcomed the words "regret" and "renounce," in the preceding paragraph should note the absence of "recant." Those who choose to disregard the warning and read on will discover that the basic elements and imperatives of the ecological paradigm not only still stand, but, are further strengthened and extended both by scientific evidence and scientific argument. In the pages that follow, additions,

Annals of Child Development, Volume 6, pages 187-249.
Copyright © 1989 by JAI Press Inc.
All rights of reproduction in any form reserved.
ISBN: 0-89232-979-3

subtractions, and revisions, albeit substantial, apply almost exclusively to corollaries, not to fundamental theorems of an ecological paradigm for research on human development.

In evidence of that fact, I begin with what I regard as the cornerstone of the theoretical structure—then, as now, appropriately introduced as "Definition 1." It reappears unaltered, except for the addition of a clarifying phrase, identified by underscoring.

Definition 1.

The ecology of human development is the scientific study of the progressive, mutual accommodation, *throughout the life course*, between an active, growing human being, and the changing properties of the immediate settings in which the developing person lives, as this process is affected by the relations between these settings, and by the larger contexts in which the settings are embedded.

I. CONTEXT WITHOUT DEVELOPMENT

Alas, no sooner have I reaffirmed a first principle than I find myself obliged to acknowledge a first infirmity of equal magnitude. It infirms not the principle but its implementation. The principle defines as the ultimate aim of the scientific endeavor the systematic understanding of the processes and outcomes of human development as a joint function of the *person* and the *environment* Yet, an examination of the now substantial body of research conducted within an ecological perspective over the past decade reveals a striking imbalance. As I have documented in the series of articles and reviews cited above, existing studies in the ecology of human development have provided more knowledge about the nature of developmentally relevant environments, near and far, than about the characteristics of developing individuals, then or now.[2] As I have written elsewhere:

> It is an instance of what might be called 'the failure of success.' For some years I harangued my colleagues for avoiding the study of development in real-life settings. No longer able to complain on that score, I have found a new bête-noir. In place of too much research on development 'out of context,' we now have a surfeit of studies on 'context without development' (Bronfenbrenner, 1986a, p. 288).

Ironically, having made the criticism, I must now also acknowledge that it applies to my own writings. Anyone who takes the trouble to examine my 1979 monograph from this perspective (and there are some who have) will discover that it has much more to say about the nature and developmental contribution of the environment than of the organism itself. Moreover, this was the result of a deliberate decision; in the preface to that volume, I expressed "the conviction that further advance in the scientific understanding of the basic intrapsychic and interpersonal processes of human development" (p. 12), must wait upon the formulation and implementation of a more differentiated and dynamic conception of the environment. I then undertook what I regarded as the necessary prior task, deferring—for the time being—my primary interest in the psychological development of the individual.

I believed then, and still believe now, that, at the time, I made the right decision both on scientific and practical grounds. Nevertheless, the decision resulted in a conceptual model that, although intended to be useful both for basic research and its translation into policy and practice, was—from a strictly theoretical perspective—admittedly incomplete, or at least heavily one-sided. Indeed, were my disclaimer to be disregarded, I could justly be accused of having proposed a theoretical orientation that by default, assumed an "empty organism."

It is this conscious and reluctant omission that explains why, in subsequent articles written mainly for other purposes, I have been smuggling in theoretical ideas and relevant research findings that accord to the human organism a more explicit and powerful role in its own development. These organism-oriented ideas first began to emerge by indirection, from the top down, as by-products of a more general effort to formalize the construct of development both in theoretical, and then in operational terms. These formulations, however, were highly abstract, and bereft of concrete structure and substance, particularly with respect to the person side of the developmental equation. It was the need to provide body and soul for the formless figure that finally forced some specification of the characteristics of the person that constituted both the product and partial producer of developmental processes.

That undertaking, in turn, had an unanticipated result. It led to a reformulation and elaboration of my earlier conceptions regarding the structure of the environment and its role in the developmental process. Finally, the necessity of integrating the two newly-reconstructed domains had the further serendipitous effect of generating some new, and I believe promising, perspectives for future research on the ecology of human development. In presenting the product of these efforts, it seems appropriate, especially for a researcher committed to a developmental perspective, to follow the evolutionary sequence in which they occurred. Therefore, I begin with a proposed general formulation of the concept of development.

II. AN ECOLOGICAL PARADIGM FOR DEVELOPMENT IN CONTEXT [3]

The paradigm is derived from, and hence most appropriately introduced as, a transformed and extended version of Kurt Lewin's classical formula (Lewin, 1935, p. 73):

$B = f(PE)$ [Behavior is a joint function of person and environment]

The first transformation involves a provocative substitution:

$D = f(PE)$ [Development is a joint function of person and environment]

The substitution is provocative because it focuses attention on the conceptual difference between "behavior" and "development." The key distinction lies in the fact that development involves a parameter not present in Lewin's original equation—the dimension of time.[4] Thus, at a purely descriptive level, human development may be defined as *the phenomenon of constancy and change in the characteristics of the person over the life course.*

In light of this definition, careful consideration of the reformulated formula reveals that the "D" term refers not to the phenomenon of development, but to its outcome at a particular point in time. What the revised Lewinian equation does accomplish, however, is to move the formulation from description to process (or, in Lewin's terms, from phenotype to genotype); it does so by stipulating the existence of two types of forces that interact to generate constancy and change in development. By incorporating the implied dimensions of time, and substituting words for symbols, we may translate the formula as follows: *The characteristics of the person at a given time in his or her life are a joint function of the characteristics of the person and of the environment over the course of that person's life up to that time*

The time factor can be represented in the formula itself by means of subscripts:

$$D_t = f_{(t-p)} (PE)_{(t-p)}$$

where "t" refers to the time at which a developmental outcome is observed and "t–p" to the period, or periods, during which the joint forces, emanating both from the person and the environment, were operating over time to produce the outcome existing at the time of observation. Note that, on the right-hand side of the equation, the subscript (t–p) appears not only for the substantive (PE) term but also for the operator "f." This means that the process producing developmental change is not instantaneous, but one that takes place over time, and, like the other terms in the equation, can change over time. For example, the processes that operate as a child grows older will not necessarily be the same as those that took place earlier.

Having completed our transformation of the Lewinian equation we need to consider its relation to a definition of development. Strictly speaking, what the equation defines is not development, but its outcome. The primary concern of science, however, is not with effects, but with the processes that produce them.

Hence, from a scientific perspective, it is the right-hand side of the equation that identifies the focus of our primary interest. Translating symbols into text, it defines development as *the set of processes through which properties of the person and the environment interact to produce constancy and change in the characteristics of the person over the life course.*

The primacy of our interest, however, should not limit the scope of our concern; for, clearly, an ill-considered conceptualization and choice of developmental *outcomes* can trivialize the most scientifically elegant demonstration of the *processes* producing the observed effects. Fortunately, in the present instance, two circumstances operate to keep our attention focused on product as well as process. The first is the fact that characteristics of the person appear on both sides of the developmental equation. Simply put, *the developmental outcomes of today shape the developmental outcomes of tomorrow.* A second consideration, working in the same direction, is the stated intent to give due attention within this chapter to the previously neglected domain of the psychological properties of the person, which are also, of course, themselves outcomes of development.

With respect to the latter, the reader will note the absence in the present definition of development of any necessary implication of movement toward more effective, constructive, or—from a purely structural viewpoint—more complex or differentiated modes of psychological functioning, as opposed to a regressive trend toward increasing dysfunction, disorganization, and psychopathology. The issue is deliberately left open at the outset, so that it can be addressed in the broader theoretical context to follow.

With the transformed Lewinian equation before us, we can now examine its implications as a general theoretical paradigm for the study of development in context. To begin with, the presence of the three principal terms now requires researchers to confront the question of what are the *specific* characteristics of the person and of the environment that are to be regarded as the products and producers of development. The main body of this chapter is devoted to some suggested answers to this query.

But there is one other element in the equation that demands consideration because of its profound significance both for theory and research. Its importance is easily overlooked, for its existence is indicated only by the inconspicuous lower case letter "f," which stands for "function." As used by Lewin, this concept carries two signal implications. First, while indicating that the left hand term of the equation is the joint result of some combination of forces arising from both the person and the environment, Lewin explicitly ruled out the possibility that the combination was one of simple addition. Consistent with the Gestalt tradition in which Lewin's theory was developed, the whole was presumed to be different from the sum of its parts. The issue takes on added importance because, despite occasional theoretical assertions to the contrary, most developmental investigations in fact employ analytic models that assume only *additive* effects; that is, the influences emanating from the person and the environment are treated as operating independently of each other, with the net effect estimated from an algebraic sum of the various factors included in the model. Yet, in those instances in which more complex models have been applied, they have typically revealed important *interactive* effects; that is, particular environmental conditions have been shown to produce different developmental consequences depending on the personal characteristics of individuals living in that environment. It was this kind of person-environment interaction that Lewin envisioned in his original formulation. Its investigation in the sphere of human development constitutes one of the most promising, but at the same time theoretically and methodologically most challenging, directions for future research.

Lewin's concept of function had yet another implication of even greater significance for theory and research design. In his writings, he drew what he regarded as a fundamental distinction between two kinds of research paradigms (Lewin, 1931, 1935, 1951). The first he referred to as Aristotelian or *class-theoretical*. In such formulations, phenomena are "explained" by the categories to which they are assigned, as with Aristotle's four elements (earth, air, fire, and water). In opposition to such static concepts, Lewin argued for "field-theoretical" or "Galilean" paradigms that specify the particular *processes* through which the observed phenomenon is brought about. Typically in the historical development of a given science, class-theoretical concepts precede field-theoretical ideas, and are gradually replaced by the latter. Lewin wished to accelerate the process. As we shall see, however, although half a century has gone by since the publication of Lewin's seminal essay, Aristotelian concepts and research models still abound in the scientific study of human development. Moreover, I shall argue below that, given the incomplete stage of our knowledge, such paradigms may often be the strategies of choice for exploring uncharted domains. Like the surveyor's grid, they provide a useful frame for describing the new terrain.

Nevertheless, purely class-theoretical models, while often suggestive, do not reveal the mechanisms that account for observed relationships. As is the rule in all science, what is required for this purpose is a conceptualization of a particular process (or set of processes) presumed to produce a given effect—in this instance, to activate or to sustain development.

Lewin's distinction between class-theoretical and field-theoretical models provides a basic point of departure for our next task. Having formulated a general theoretical paradigm, we are now faced with the problem of its operational definition. For possible solutions of this problem, we turn to an analysis of research designs currently employed for the study of development in context to determine the extent to which they can be used or adapted to fit the requirements of our revised theoretical paradigm. In accord with Lewin's dichotomy, these designs are usefully distinguished in terms of those that do, versus do not, include in the model a consideration of the *processes* through which characteristics of person, environment, or of both together, can influence human development. The principal variants of each type are discussed below in order of their increasing complexity and completeness with respect to approximating the elements comprising our general paradigm.[5]

III. RESEARCH MODELS IN THE STUDY OF DEVELOPMENT IN CONTEXT

Because class-theoretical designs are more simple in structure, we begin with a consideration of these. Models in which the "f" term is omitted can take a variety of forms. The most common is one in which only the E term is present; that is, development is viewed solely as a product of environmental factors, but through some process or processes that remain unspecified. I have referred to this type of research design as a *social address model*[6] (Bronfenbrenner & Crouter, 1983, pp. 361–362). Among the most common "social addresses" appearing in the research literature are the following: social class, family size and ordinal position, rural vs. urban residence, differences by nationality or ethnic group, and, more recently, what I have referred to as the "new demography" (Bronfenbrenner & Crouter, 1983, p. 373)—one vs. two parent families, home care vs. day care, children in private vs. public schools; mother's employment status, how many times remarried, or—perhaps soon, the number of hours the father spends in child care and household tasks, or homes with and without computers.

The principal limitation of the social address model is readily apparent. Like all class-theoretical concepts, it is little more than a name. As I have written elsewhere, "One looks only at the *social address*—that is, the environmental label—with no attention to what the environment is like, what people are living there, what they are doing, or how the activities taking place could affect the child" (Bronfenbrenner & Crouter, 1983, pp. 382–383).

Albeit less frequent, an analogous form of class-theoretical design exists on the side of the person. Here only P appears; that is, development is examined only as a function of the characteristics of the individual at an earlier age. I have referred to this type of design as a *personal attributes model*.[7] A common example is found in studies of the constancy of IQ.

Finally, there are designs that combine the two domains—what I have called the *person-context model* (Bronfenbrenner, in press-a). Here characteristics *both* of the person and of the environment are taken into account *jointly*. Although this model suffers from the same limitations as the two preceding, from an ecological perspective, it possesses a structural feature that makes it useful in the study of development in context. The particular strength of person-context designs lies in their capacity to identify what I call *ecological niches*. These are particular *regions in the environment that are especially favorable or unfavorable to the development of individuals with particular personal characteristics.* Operationally, occupational niches are defined by the intersection between one or more social addresses and one more personal attributes of individuals who live at these addresses. For example, an analysis (Bronfenbrenner, 1988c) of data published annually by the National Center for Health Statistics reveals that a pregnant mother is more likely to have a low-birth-weight baby (under 2,500 grams or 5¹/₂ pounds) if she comes from an environmental background distinguished by two or more of the following features: the mother has had less than a high school education, lives in the central section of a large metropolitan city, or is unmarried. This probability almost doubles, however, if she is 19 or under, and doubles again if she happens to have been born black. Another group at special risk, albeit to a somewhat lesser degree, are mothers in the same environmental contexts who do not have their first child until they are 35 or over.

Although such findings are typically interpreted in terms of increased risk, the very same facts can be viewed from the perspective of positive growth (in this instance judged on a criterion of physical health). To wit, pregnant mothers least likely to have a low- birth-weight baby are white, college educated women living in middle-class neighborhoods who are married and have their first child when they are in their middle or late 20s.

Informative as such findings are, they do not tell us what it is about mothers' education, place of residence, marital status, or age and race that affects the weight of the babies they bear. In other words, how does the particular combination of environmental and personal characteristics defining a particular ecological niche operate to influence human development? To answer that question, we must move from what Lewin called a class-theoretical model to one that is field-theoretical by postulating some *process*, associated with the above characteristics that could account for the observed variation.

Fortunately, the annual report on the vital statistics of the United States includes data relevant to one such process. Since 1969, the annual volume on natality data has carried several tables documenting the distribution of live births by birth weight and by the month of pregnancy that prenatal care began. Among the facts revealed by analysis of these data (Bronfenbrenner, 1988b) are the following:

- In general, the percentage of low-birth-weight babies decreases the earlier prenatal care is begun.
- By far the highest frequency of premature births occurs among mothers who received no prenatal care at all—20%, as against 6% among those who received some prenatal care, even if only in the last month of pregnancy.
- Nearly a quarter of all babies born in 1985 were born to mothers who received no medical care during the critical first three months of pregnancy.

- The percentage of newborns whose mothers received prenatal care during the first trimester rose from 65% in 1969 to almost 75% in 1979, at which point the trend leveled off until 1985, when, for the first time since annual statistics have been published, the figure showed a drop from the previous year.
- The preceding turnabout is mirrored in the 1985 figures on the frequency of low birth weight. For the first time in two decades the percentage of newborns weighing under 2,500 grams increased. The increase of 1% in one year is equal to a preceding 1% decrease that had taken more than three decades to achieve.
- A further analysis of the above data with the effects of education and maternal age held constant revealed that the availability of prenatal care was associated with a reduction in the occurrence of low birth weight. This relationship was stronger among black families than among white.

Although the above analysis suffers from the well-known limitation of aggregate data (i.e., relationships at the individual level remain unknown), it nicely illustrates the distinction between class-theoretical and field-theoretical models, and also serves as an introduction to more comprehensive process designs to be discussed in the next section. Before proceeding to that discussion, however, it is important to provide an example of a more complex person-context model in which the developmental outcomes go beyond physical characteristics into the domain of psychological functioning.

Most of the studies in this sphere are concerned with identifying groups at psychological risk, probably because of the greater concern, both on the part of professionals and of the general public, with problem behavior. Hence, the question arises: What ecological niches are favorable to psychological growth, and what is to be understood by such a concept? One of the few studies that explicitly sought to identify some of the elements that define a "good ecology," which, in turn, fosters "good" psychological development, is Werner and Smith's monograph (Werner & Smith, [1982], provocatively entitled *Vulnerable but Invincible*. The work involves a longitudinal study of a group of Hawaiian children who, despite having been "born and reared in chronic poverty, exposed to higher than average rates of prematurity and perinatal stress, and reared by mothers with little formal education ... managed to develop into competent and autonomous young adults who 'worked well, played well, loved well, and expected well' " (p. 153). With respect to the topic at hand, the authors identified a number of characteristics early in life that appeared to differentiate these children from their matched controls, who had grown up in the same deprived environment and did exhibit the types and degrees of developmental impairment often observed in such settings. On the environmental side, the distinguishing characteristics of those who "escaped" included smaller family size; greater spacing between the index child and the next-born sibling; the number and type of alternate caregivers available to the mother within the household (in the Hawaiian context, these were all family members); steady employment of the mother outside the household; and the presence of a multigenerational network of kin and friends in adolescence. But the structure of the children's environment did not tell the whole story. From their earliest years onward, the youngsters themselves also exhibited a number of distinctive characteristics:

> The resilient high-risk boys and girls had fewer serious illnesses in the first two decades of life and tended to recuperate more quickly. Their mothers perceived them to be 'very active' and 'socially responsible' when they were infants, and independent observers noted their pronounced autonomy and social orientation when they were toddlers. Developmental examinations in the second year of life showed advanced self-help skills and adequate sensorimotor and language development for most of these children (p. 154).

We may note in passing the kinds of characteristics that are viewed as indicative of what might be called "healthy" psychological development. In this study, as in others to be mentioned below, they are of several kinds—here poetically, if not altogether precisely, summed up in the authors' description of their "invulnerable" children now grown-up: "competent and autonomous young adults who 'worked well, played well, loved well, and expected well' " (p. 152). We shall have occasion to examine such characteristics more systematically below, particularly in Section IV. For the moment, I would only point out that the attributes mentioned are those that are valued in Western—and especially American—white, middle-class culture.

Not only did the characteristics of both the person and the environment play a significant role in the subsequent developmental progress achieved by the Hawaiian children, but, through the use of a person-context design, the investigators were able to show that youngsters growing up in similar environmental circumstances developed differently as a function of their particular personal characteristics. One of the most striking examples of this phenomenon was the contrasting pattern of development observed for boys vs. girls. A distinctive feature of the pattern was the fact that it reversed itself over the first two decades of life.

> At birth, and throughout the first decade of life, more boys than girls were exposed to serious physical defects or illness requiring medical care, and more boys than girls had learning and behavior problems in the classroom and at home . . .
>
> Trends were reversed in the second decade of life: The total number of boys with serious learning problems dropped, while the number of girls with serious disorders rose. Boys seemed now more prepared for the demands of school and work, although they were still more often involved in antisocial and delinquent behavior. Girls were now confronted with social pressures and role expectations that produced a higher rate of mental health problems in late adolescence and serious coping problems associated with teenage pregnancies and marriages.

> While control of aggression appeared to be one of the major problems for the boys in childhood, dependency became a major problem for the girls in adolescence . . .
>
> Related to this trend was the cumulative number of stressful life situations reported by each sex. Boys with serious coping problems experienced more adversities than girls in *childhood*; girls with serious coping problems reported more stressful life events in *adolescence*. In spite of the biological and social pressures, which in this culture appear to make each sex more vulnerable at different times, more high-risk girls than high-risk boys grew into resilient young adults (pp. 153–154).

Note that, despite the richness of information obtained in this study about the environmental and personal characteristics of a group of highly vulnerable children who ultimately exhibited contrasting developmental outcomes, the specific processes and pathways that enabled some of them to "escape" remain unclear. The principal reason for this unclarity is that the analysis of processes requires a more differentiated research design, to be described below.

A. The Process-Person-Context Model

As its name implies, this design permits analysis of variations in developmental processes and outcomes as a *joint* function of the characteristics of the environment and of the person. The nature and power of the model are perhaps best conveyed by a concrete example. For this purpose, I select a study that addresses a scientific question made more urgent by the recent increase in the already high rate of babies born under 5½ pounds in the United States:[8] What are the consequences of low birth weight for subsequent psychological development, and what are the processes involved?

Perhaps the best demonstration of the scope of possible effects and the processes that underlie them is still to be found in a classic study conducted in Scotland a quarter of a century ago. In the 1950s and 1960s, Cecil Mary Drillien (1957, 1964), a physician and Professor of Child Life and Health at the University of Edinburgh, carried out a seven-year longitudinal investigation of psychological development in two groups: 360 children of low birth weight (under 2,500 grams, or 5½ pounds), and a control group selected "by taking the next mature birth from the hospital admission list" (1957, p. 29). In her follow-up assessments, the investigator found that the children of low birth weight were more likely to exhibit problems in physical growth, susceptibility to illness, impaired intellectual development, and poorer classroom performance, with all of these tendencies being more pronounced in boys (1964).[9] With respect to school achievement, a special analysis revealed that those with low birth weight were especially likely to be working below their mental capacity.[10] In relation to this finding, the author comments as follows: "In most cases, failure to attain a standard commensurate with ability was associated with problems of behaviour, which were found to increase with decreasing birth weight [and] to be more common in males" (1964, p. 209).

Drillien's research is replete with far more explicit evidence of the interplay between biological and environmental forces, including some findings that, when fully examined, reveal implications for preventive strategies. Of particular significance in this regard are data on what she refers to as "maternal efficiency," a composite rating based on observations during successive home visits throughout the preschool years. Items considered included mother-child relationships, management of the home, and family health practices. In general, ratings of maternal efficiency (by observers who had no information about the children's classification by birth weight) were appreciably lower for mothers of low-weight newborns than for those of the normal controls. The same relationship held for physical growth. In addition, "those males who were smallest at birth appear to be affected rather more by poor maternal care than females" (p. 69).

Although research findings on low-birth-weight babies are typically interpreted in terms of increased developmental risk, the very same data can also be viewed from the perspective of positive growth. To wit, *the more effective the maternal care, the better the development of the young child, particularly for low-birth-weight children. In other words, where the mother is willing and able to make the effort, she can do much to reduce the developmental risk that this handicap entails.*

It would be a mistake to assume, however, that the environment does the job all by itself, independent of the organism. Living organisms have the capacity, and indeed the active disposition, to heal themselves over time. We are all familiar with this phenomenon in the sphere of physical injury and illness, but we may not be as conscious of its operation in the psychological realm as well. An example appears in another of Drillien's analyses. Having demonstrated that children with low birth weight tended to be somewhat retarded in intellectual development, Drillien went on to show that, in successive assessments from 6 months up to 7 years of age, this difference tended to decrease. The improvement was especially marked during the period up to age 2. After that time, it declined slightly for infants with the lowest birth weight ((under 3½ pounds) but continued to increase for less handicapped cases so that, by school age, these youngsters were well within the normal range of intellectual functioning. In sum, *significant resources for counteracting effects of prenatal handicaps exist both on the side of the environment and of the organism itself.*

Unfortunately, on the environmental side, these resources are not equally available to all. Drillien was one of the first to document the substantially higher proportion of low-birth-weight babies born to lower class families. But she also went a significant step farther by identifying and investigating processes that could account for this difference. Drillien began by showing that the quality of maternal behavior (as classified and then rated by the home visitor) also varied systematically by the family's socioeconomic status, with care in lower class homes being less consistent and responsive. Drillien then went on to analyze the relationship between quality of care and developmental outcomes, *separately* within each combination of three levels of social class and of weight at birth, during each of two age periods: birth to two years, and from two to five years. Thus, the effectiveness of the mother-infant process was being examined as a joint function of characteristics of the broader environment (social class), and of the individual child (birth weight and age).[11]

The principal developmental outcome examined was the frequency and severity of reported behavior disturbances, such as hyperactivity, over-dependence, timidity, and negativism. The results revealed a general effect of maternal responsiveness in reducing both the incidence and severity of problem behavior, particularly as the children got older. With respect to social class, however, the pattern of relationships was more complex. The effect of maternal care in reducing the *number of* children exhibiting one or more forms of disturbed behavior was strongest in the two highest social class groups. In other words, it would appear that these mothers got a bigger return on their investment. Whereas this is the finding emphasized by Drillien, further examination of the data reveals another, equally pronounced trend with respect to the *severity* of the reported problem behavior. Here it was the children from families at the bottom of the socioeconomic scale whose behavioral problems, while still present, were most relieved by maternal attention and care. Finally, while there was an increase in both incidence and severity of problems as birth weight decreased, this effect was not as great as that associated with social class and quality of maternal care.

In sum, responsive maternal care can substantially reduce the severity of psychological problems associated with low birth weight among socioeconomically deprived families, and can subsequently reduce the number of low-birth-weight children experiencing any serious difficulty.

At a broader level, Drillien's research findings illustrate an important characteristic of the process of human development that is revealed through the application of process-person-context models; namely, the frequent occurrence of vicious or benign circles. The term *synergism* is use to describe a phenomena of this kind, in which *the joint operation of two or more forces produces an effect that is greater than the sum of the individual effects.* In this instance, the combination of low birth weight and disadvantaged socioeconomic status had greater negative impact than would have been expected from the seperate effects of each.

With respect to research design, Drillien's analyses, taken as a whole, illustrate the two key defining properties of a process-person-context model:

1. The design permits assessment not only of developmental outcomes but also of the effectiveness of the processes producing these outcomes.

2.   The design reveals how both developmental outcomes and processes vary as a joint function of the characteristics of the person and of the environment, thus permitting the detection of synergistic effects.

Stated more succinctly, the model identifies any *differences in developmental processes and outcomes associated with different ecological niches.*

What is the special scientific utility and importance of a model of this kind? The results of Drillien's analysis provide an illustration of the answer to this question. Prior to that time, the generally-accepted explanation for the observed correlation between low birth weight and subsequent psychological impairment assumed minimal brain damage as the intervening mechanism; indeed, this was the heading under which Drillien presented her discussion (p. 275). Her finding, however, that this correlation varied systematically by social class clearly implied a more complex set of processes. Drillien's speculations on this score focused mainly on a variety of physiological deficits (including minimal brain damage) associated with low birth weight that, in turn, could lower the resistance level to socio-environmental stress in later life (pp. 275–277). In her view, there was little possibility of separating out these factors, given the limitations of the then-available data.

Today, as the result of the earlier work of Drillien and others, the range of possible processes have broadened both in variety and complexity, but the prospect of sorting them out is now considerably brighter, again through the use of process-person-context models. Two scientific advances, in particular, have contributed to this changed situation. First, the development of modern imaging techniques, such as ultrasound, now permit the detection of a variety of physiological brain malfunctions (Catto-Smith et al., 1985; Stewart, 1983). The availability of such a measure makes it possible to assess both the independent and joint effects of a number of possibly handicapping organic factors often present together at the time of birth, such as minimal brain damage, congenital malformations (minor anatomical abnormalities), complications in the birth process, low birth weight, and early gestation age (age at birth calculated from estimated date of conception). Second, the recognition that conventional indices of social class are but a weak reflection of the quality of the environment affecting family life has led to the development of more powerful measures of the family's ecology; for example, indices that incorporate characteristics not only of the child's own family but those of families living in the same neighborhood or involved in the same social network (see below, pp. 233–234). Such more differentiated process-person-context designs, however, are still to be applied specifically in the study of long term effects of perinatal influences.[12]

As the preceding examples illustrate, the principal scientific power of the process-person-context model lies not so much in its capacity to produce definitive answers as to generate new questions by revealing the inadequacies of existing formulations in accounting for observed complexities. As the history of science shows, herein lies one of the principal keys to scientific advance.

A similar purpose is served by process models that include only one of the two other domains. Some examine how mechanisms and outcomes vary solely with respect to context (*process-context models*); others only in relation to contrasting characteristics of the individual (*process-person models*). Both of these truncated designs can contribute new knowledge and understanding of development, provided the lacunae in the model are taken into account.

B. The Chronosystem Model

Having sought to persuade the reader of the superiority of the process-person-context model over its contemporaries, I shall now, perversely, point to a major lacuna in this powerful design. The missing element is the same one that was omitted in Lewin's original formula—the dimension of time. This dimension has been given short shrift in most empirical work as well. For many decades, it was taken into account only as it applied to constancy and change in the characteristics of the person; the environment was treated as a fixed entity, observed only at a single point in time, and presumed to remain constant (for example, family composition and social class were dealt with as if they were unchanging structures).

Especially in recent years, however, research on human development has projected the factor of time along a new axis. In the mid 1970s, an increasing number of investigators began to employ research designs that took into account constancy and change not only in the person, but also in the environment. I have referred to designs of this kind as *chronosystem models*[13] (Bronfenbrenner 1986a; 1986c; in press-a). Particular attention was focused on developmental changes triggered by life events or experiences. These experiences may have their origins either in the external environment (e.g., the birth of a sibling, entering school, divorce, winning the sweepstakes), or within the organism (e.g., puberty, severe illness). Whatever their origin, the critical feature of such events is that they alter the existing relation between person and environment, thus creating a dynamic that may instigate developmental change.

Chronosystem models may be either short-term or long-term. In the former case, data are obtained for the same group of subjects both before and after a particular life experience or *life transition*. An early example is Baldwin's study (1947) of changes in parent-child interaction induced by the impending arrival of a sibling. The results revealed marked changes in the mother's behavior toward the first child before, during, and after the mother's pregnancy with the second child.

A long-term chronosystem design permits examining the often cumulative effects of a sequence of transitions in what sociologists, from as far back as the

1930s, have referred to as the *life course* (Clausen, 1986; Elder, 1985). The degree of scientific sophistication and power that such models have achieved in recent years is well illustrated in the work of Glen Elder and his colleagues (Elder, 1974; Elder & Caspi, 1988; Elder, Caspi, & Downey, 1986). Their studies have revealed the systematically different developmental paths, now extending across three generations, that were set in motion by the Great Depression of the 1930s. Elder's work represents a prototype—indeed, because of its elegance and imaginativeness, almost a paragon—of this type of chronosystem design.[14]

The description of the chronosystem model completes our discussion of formal paradigms and research designs for the study of development in context. We now more from the abstract to the concrete with the consideration of the substantive content of the two major substantive domains in the general paradigm—the developmentally-relevant characteristics of *persons* and of *environments*. Although the paradigm emphasizes the necessity for analyzing the interaction between these two spheres, such analysis requires prior understanding of the structure and content of each of the interacting domains.

IV. PROPERTIES OF THE PERSON FROM AN ECOLOGICAL PERSPECTIVE

In examining scientific conceptions of the developing person from an ecological perspective, one is struck by a curious fact: the overwhelming majority of these conceptions are *context free*; that is, the characteristics of the person are defined, both conceptually and operationally, without any reference to the environment, and are presumed to have the same meaning irrespective of the culture, class, or setting in which they are observed, or in which the person lives.

There have been, however, some violations of this unstated assumption. Most of them are implicit; that is, they occur at the level of method rather than explicit theory. Any findings that might call the assumption into question are treated as error in the form of method variance, and in this way dismissed from further consideration. But in a few instances, the assumption has been explicitly and systematically challenged. Until recently, the challenges have been overlooked, mainly because most of the challengers have been scholars from abroad or from disciplines other than developmental psychology.

In this section, we shall examine these challenges in terms of their implications for the scientific study of human development. Because the most systematic alternative conceptualizations have been formulated in relation to the nature and origin of the *cognitive capacities* of human beings, we shall begin our considerations in that sphere. We shall then cross the illusory and deceptive "great divide" in contemporary developmental psychology to undertake a similar analysis in a second domain—that of *socioemotional and motivational characteristics*, traditionally classified under the rubrics of temperament and personality.

A third and final category introduces a different, as-yet-untried, frame of reference for conceptualizing properties of the developing person. Consistent with an ecological view of organism-environment interaction, the orientation takes as its point of departure a conception of the *person as an active agent* who contributes to her own development. Correspondingly, personal characteristics are distinguished in terms of their potential to evoke response from, alter, or create the external environment, thereby influencing the subsequent course of the person's psychological growth. Because such active potentials simultaneously involve cognitive, socioemotional, and motivational aspects, the traditional separation between cognitive capacities, on the one hand, and qualities of temperament and personality, on the other, is not appropriate for this interactive domain.

A. Cognition in Context

As previously noted, most scientific conceptions and measures of cognitive capacities are characterized by an underlying assumption that the abilities in question (for example, formal operations in Piaget's sense) are invariant across place and time; that is, they are presumed to have the same psychological significance irrespective of social structure, culture, or historical era. This assumption characterizes a wide range of measures, including objective tests of intelligence, academic achievement, or personality; assessments of Piagetian or neo-Piagetian stages of cognitive[15] or moral[16] development; analyses of cognitive (Kagan, Moss, & Sigel, 1963; Kogan 1973, 1983) and personal style (Block, J. H. & Block J., 1980); characterizations of persons based on their patterns of response in laboratory experiments (Witkin, Dyk, Faterson, Goodenough, & Karp, 1962); and modes of cognitive functioning based on information theory and theories of artificial intelligence (Brown, Bransford, Ferrara, & Campione, 1983).

In progressive degree, the conceptualizations and methods of cognitive functioning that follow call this tacit assumption of contextual irrelevance into question.

1. Competence as an Achieved Status

This first sub-category challenges the above assumption only by implication and default. It does so by defining a person's level of competence solely by that person's achieved status in the environment. Entirely lacking is any specification of psychological qualities that may have enabled the person to attain the given status, but the underlying assumption is that such qualities do in fact exist. The most common examples are the number of years of schooling obtained, or the highest occupational status reached. Corresponding indices on the debit side include dropping out of school, ending up on welfare, failing to meet requirements for professional status, and the like. Note that the criteria of "positive" vs. "negative" outcomes of development implicit in such operational definitions are socioeconomic and social success vs. failure as defined by the society at large.

2. Competence Evaluated Within the Setting

While still focused on achieved status in a real life setting, this category adds two new elements. First, status is judged by persons within the setting who occupy roles that involve responsibility for evaluation. Second, the evaluation is made not with regard to general levels of ability or competence but with respect to capacity to function effectively in specific kinds of activities and tasks conducted within a particular type of setting in everyday life. The most common examples include teachers' grades given in various school subjects, or supervisors' ratings of subordinates' job performance. Here again there is an implicit criterion of positive vs. negative development, but this time it is defined operationally in terms of specific competencies deemed essential for success in the context of particular social institutions accorded status in the larger society.

An additional aspect of assessments of this kind is that, to the extent that the judges of performance continue to be participants in the person's life or to influence decisions on future opportunities (e.g., promotion), their judgments represent not only an evaluation of the person's present level of functioning but may also play a role in shaping his or her future career, and thereby influence the course of later development.[17] Recognition of this possibility points to the advantage of including both noncontextual and contextual measures of competence within the same research design, a topic to receive further consideration below.

3. Competence as the Mastery of Culturally-defined, Familiar Activities in Everyday Life

In both of the preceding sub-categories, the assessment of competence in real-life settings is based mainly on pragmatic considerations rather than on more general theoretical grounds. By contrast, the environmentally-oriented attributes described below are derived from a broad, a priori conception requiring the inclusion of context as an element essential to the very definition of competence. Because of the special significance of such formulations for the ecology of human development, I shall describe them in some detail.

Similar formulations have emerged from the work of researchers from rather different disciplines and intellectual perspectives. Perhaps the earliest and most explicit theoretical conception of competence in context is found in the writings and research of the Soviet psychologists Vygotsky (1929, 1978), Luria (1928, 1931, 1976, 1979, 1982), and Leontiev (1932, 1959, 1975). Although the latter two have each made original contributions to a common scientific endeavor, both acknowledge Vygotsky as the primary source of their own ideas. The group's conception of cognitive competence is deeply grounded in Vygotsky's theory of development, which, in turn, is built on a Marxist base. The basic tenets of the theory may be summarized as follows. Central to the formulation is the thesis that development in human beings is fundamentally different from that in other animals. Specifically, the human species, by virtue of its unique capacity to use tools and symbols, continually creates and elaborates its own environment in the form of culture. The evolution of culture, in turn, is seen as a historical process that has taken different forms across both time and place. Moreover, human beings are not only a culture-producing species, they are also culture-produced; that is, the psychological characteristics of the species are a joint, interactive function of the biological characteristics and potentials of an active organism, on the one hand, and, on the other, of the forms of psychological functioning and possible courses of development existing in a given culture at a particular point in its history. It follows that the repertoire of mental processes and outcomes available as possibilities for individual development can vary from one culture or subculture to the next, both within and across time. Taken as a whole, this conceptualization constitutes what Luria referred to as Vygotsky's theory of "the sociohistorical evolution of the mind" (Luria, 1978, p. 5)[18]

So sweeping a theory may appear to elude any possibility of an empirical test. The protagonists of the theory, however, thought otherwise, and acted accordingly. Luria (1976) tells the story in his autobiography.[19] The time was the early 1930s.

> We conceived the idea of carrying out the first far-reaching study of intellectual functions. . . . By taking advantage of the rapid cultural changes that were then in progress in remote parts of our country, we hoped to trace the changes in thought processes that are brought about by technological change. . . . At that time, many of our rural areas were undergoing rapid change with the advent of collectivization and mechanization of agriculture (p. 60).

The basic research design took advantage of the fact that the process of modernization had not been introduced in all areas of the region at the same time. As a result, it became possible to carry out a comparison of cognitive functioning in communities differing in their degree of exposure to social change. Vygotsky died of tuberculosis before this extraordinary investigation was completed. The following is Luria's succinct summary of the findings:[20]

> Our data indicate that decisive changes can occur in going from graphic and functional—concrete and practical—methods of thinking to much more theoretical modes of thought brought about by changes in social conditions, in this instance by the socialist transformation of an entire culture (Luria, 1976, p. vi).

In the Vygotskian framework, this same principle applies to intracultural contexts as well. For example, in what appears to be his first paper published in the United States, Luria (1928) delineates analogous developmental differences in the contrasts between preschool and school, and village and town.

> We consider [that] the development of the child's conduct can be reduced to a series of transformations, that these transformations are due to the growing influence of cultural environment, the constant appearance of new cultural inventions and habits, and that each invention of a new "artificial" habit involves the change of the structure of the child's conduct. Compare the conduct of a pupil in the first year at school with that of a preschool pupil. Compare the mental processes of these two and you will note two structures essentially different in principle. Compare the village boy with another boy of the same age who lives in town and you will be struck by the huge difference in the mentality of both, the difference being not so much in the development of natural psychical functions (absolute memory, the quickness of reactions, etc.) *as in the subject-matter of their cultural experience and those methods which are used by those two children in realizing their natural abilities* (p. 494).

What is the relation of such formulations to the cognitive characteristics of the child? A clue to the answer appears in the opening paragraph of the first and only journal article by Vygotsky published in the United States. In 1929, he wrote:

> In the process of development the child not only masters the items of cultural experience, but the habits and forms of cultural behavior and cultural methods of reasoning. We must, therefore, distinguish the main lines in the development of the child's behavior. First, there is the line of natural development of behavior which is closely bound up with the processes of general organic growth and maturation of the child. Secondly, there is the line of cultural improvement of the psychological functions, the working out of new methods of reasoning, the mastering of the cultural methods of behavior (p. 415).

The same point is made by Luria:

> The "cultural" aspect of Vygotsky's theory involved the socially structured ways in which society organizes the kind of tasks that the growing child faces and the kinds of tools, both mental and physical, that the young child is provided with to master those tasks (1979, p. 44).

It is this *mastery of culturally-defined and experienced tasks* that defines the basis of cognitive competence in the Vygotskian framework.

For specific examples, we turn to another perspective that led to a similar conclusion, but in a more concrete form. In his autobiography, Luria identifies as one of the significant influences on Vygotsky's thought the ideas of the English anthropologist W. H. R. Rivers (1926). Rivers was the forerunner of a number of contemporary ethnologists (Lancy & Strathern, 1981; Lave, 1977; Lave, Murtaugh, & de la Roche, 1984; Murtaugh, 1985; Super, 1980) who, on the basis of their field observations, argued that different environmental demands lead to the development of different patterns of ability. For example, the anthropologist Charles Super (1980) has documented the highly complex cognitive processes employed by the !Kung San people, a hunting-gathering society of West Africa. Yet, !Kung San adult men perform only at the level of Western children on IQ tests, Piagetian tasks and information processing problems, even when such measures are adapted for the local culture.

Other cultural anthropologists have reported analogous "cognitive dissonances" within American society. For example, Jean Lave and her colleagues (Lave, Murtaugh, & de la Roche, 1984; Murtaugh, 1985) have shown that shoppers, upon being confronted with multiple brand items of unequal size and price, can make highly complex, rapid, and accurate estimates of actual per-unit cost. But again, when these same shoppers were administered standardized tests of mental arithmetic, allegedly requiring the same mental operations, no relation was found between test performance and the subject's shopping accuracy.

A similar contrast for children has been demonstrated in a study of "Mathematics in the Streets and in Schools," with a sample of street urchins in Recife, Brazil who were engaged in commercial transactions (Carraher, Carraher, & Schliemann, 1985). "Performance on mathematical problems embedded in real-life contexts was superior to that on school-type word problems and context-free computational problems involving the same numbers and operations" (p. 21).

The two contextual approaches to cognitive development—Vygotskian on the one hand, anthropological on the other—have been brought together and impressively applied in the work of Michael Cole and his colleagues (Cole, Gay, Glick, & Sharp, 1971; Cole & Scribner, 1974; Laboratory of Comparative Human Cognition, 1983; Scribner & Cole, 1981).

Finally, in the most recent concerted effort to assess cognition in context, the experimental psychologist Stephen Ceci (in press) has turned anthropologist, but then returned to his root discipline by putting the laboratory itself in context. In a series of experimental studies, Ceci and his colleagues demonstrated that the same cognitive processes, in both children and adults, varied appreciably both in complexity and efficiency as a function of the context in which they were embedded. For example, processes supporting prospective memory progressively increased in efficiency as the same experiment was conducted with samples of children in a physics laboratory, a laboratory in a home economics building, and in the children's own home (Ceci & Bronfenbrenner, 1985). In a second experiment (Ceci, in press), the ability to educe complex visual patterns showed a quantum gain when the same stimulus patterns were depicted as small pictures of familiar objects embedded in a video game instead of by abstract geometrical figures embedded within a laboratory task. In a third study, appropriately titled "A Day at the Races," (Ceci & Liker, 1986) highly successful racetrack bettors were asked to handicap a total of 60 actual and experimentally-contrived races. "The analysis revealed that expert handicapping was a cognitively sophisticated enterprise, with experts using a mental model that contained multiple interaction effects and nonlinearity . . . involving as many as seven variables" [pertaining to the characteristics of the horse, the jockey, the other horses in the field, the weather, etc.] (Ceci & Liker, 1986, p. 255). Measures of expertise, however, were not correlated with the subjects' IQs, and four of the top handicappers had IQ scores in the lower to mid 80s.

On the basis of their findings, Ceci and his colleagues (Ceci, Bronfenbrenner, & Baker, 1988) conclude that "the context in which cognition takes place is not simply an adjunct to the cognition, but a constituent of it" (p. 243).

Viewed in a Vygotskian perspective, Ceci's study of successful gamblers raises an issue of both theoretical and practical significance. In effect, what Ceci is arguing is that complex cognitive functioning can take a wide variety of forms, all of them equally valid, in terms of the particular culture or subculture in which they evolved. But what if the modes of complex cognitive functioning available and acquired in the particular subculture in which a person has developed do not correspond to the equally complex modes of cognitive functioning expected in the broader culture in which one lives, or in another culture into which one has moved? Does this kind of situation, which exists for so many human beings in modern times, require a new process of enculturation extending over time; or are there more rapid developmental trajectories for achieving new levels of psychological integration across both worlds? The question constitutes one of the principal challenges to the ecology of human development, both as a science and as a context for evolving humane and constructive social policies.[21]

B. Implications for Theory and Research Design

We have now completed a tentative taxonomy of measures of cognitive competence and are in a position to consider its implications for the study of development in context. Such implications are most obvious, indeed they are made quite explicit, in the last group of conceptions outlined above, those that define cognitive competence in terms of processes and outcomes inextricably rooted in a cultural or subcultural context. It is useful for our purposes to summarize these implications, and others to follow, in a series of principles basic to an ecology of human development.

Principle 1. Differences in cognitive performance between groups from different cultures or subcultures are a function of experience, in the course of growing up, with the types of cognitive processes existing in a given culture or subculture at a particular period in its history.

This principle leads to a further implication in the realm of research design and interpretation. We shall use the term "corollary" to denote design-relevant implications of this kind.

Corollary 1.1 Any assessment of the cognitive competence of an individual or group must be interpreted in the light of the culture or subculture in which the person was brought up.

The next important point to be noted is less an implication than a descriptive fact. If we use the taxonomy we have constructed as a map on which to locate the areas in which scientific explorations have been conducted, it becomes clear that the overwhelming majority of empirical investigations have employed *acontextual* assessments of cognitive capacity—that is, on types of cognitive functioning assumed to be invariant across place, social structure, culture, and historical time. Specifically, scientists studying mental ability and task performance have relied primarily (in order of decreasing frequency) on objective tests of intellectual capacity and achievement, assessments of Piagetian-type stages, and measures of cognitive style. By comparison, investigations of cognition as it takes place in the real-life contexts of culture, subculture, or immediate setting have been comparatively rare. Thus, what might be called *the ecology of cognition and competence* remains largely an uncharted domain.

From the perspective of research, this descriptive fact has an obvious implication.

Corollary 1.2 Scientific progress in the study of development in context requires the increased use of contextually-based measures of cognitive ability and performance of the types described above.

This corollary, however, must immediately be followed by a caveat. *By no means should this recommendation be interpreted as arguing for the abandonment of acontextual measures.* Quite the contrary. As Vygotsky, Luria and their colleagues demonstrated in their studies of the cognitive effects of social change in Soviet Asia, one of the most productive scientific strategies for revealing the role of culture or subculture in the genesis of cognitive processes and outcomes is to employ measures that are, in varying degree, alien to the culture or subculture in question. In accord with the above stated corollary, it then becomes not only possible but essential to interpret the obtained results in the light of the culture or subculture in which the person was raised.

This injunction applies not only to groups but also to individuals—especially, to persons who have been brought up in a subculture in which patterns of activity and modes of thought differ from those of the broader culture in which the subculture is embedded. Particularly instructive in this regard are research designs that permit the assessment of developmental outcomes at two points in time differentiated by duration of the developing person's exposure to the majority world; for example, before and after school entry.

The juxtaposition of principle and practice points to yet another implication for research design. An ecologically-valid definition of cognitive competence emphasizes the *cultural significance* of the processes and tasks in which mastery can be achieved; that is, how these processes and their outcomes are perceived by members of the culture. Recognition of this precept leads to the following corollary for scientific strategy.

> *Corollary 1.3* Evaluations of a person's cognitive competence by members of that person's culture or subculture, judging from their own perspective, becomes a key element for understanding the developmental status achieved by particular individuals or groups.

With respect to research practice, the corollary accords greater scientific legitimacy and importance than has traditionally been granted to descriptions and judgments provided by persons within the society occupying social roles that include responsibility for evaluation, such as teachers and supervisors, as well as by colleagues and peers. Once again, this does not imply the abandonment of more commonly used acontextual measures of cognitive status and style by means of standardized tests, or analyses of Piagetian processes and stages. Quite the contrary, the use of both types of measures can illuminate, by similarity and contrast, the nature and social significance of cognitive processes and outcomes existing for a particular cultural or subcultural group. Hence, the next corollary:

> *Corollary 1.4* The scientific understanding of development in context is enhanced through the use of research designs that incorporate both contextual and acontextual assessments of cognitive processes and outcomes. Specifically, an analysis of their interrelationships in particular cultural and subcultural groups sheds light in two directions. First, it illuminates the differing meanings and roles of particular types of cognitive ability or skill in different cultural contexts. Second, it indicates the extent to which persons in particular social roles and contexts give weight, in their evaluations of cognitive ability and performance, to intellectual functions that are now commonly assessed acontextually, both in science and in society.

The theoretical and practical importance of both types of information is illustrated in several of the studies cited in the discussion of designs for future research in Section VI below.

Before proceeding to consideration of the next, rather different domain of personal characteristics, it is important to acknowledge major lacunae in each of the foregoing principles and corollaries: namely, in all of them, the terms "culture" and "subculture" remain undefined, and the models and methods to be employed for "interpreting results in the light of the culture or subculture in which the person was raised" remain unspecified. There is a reason for the omission: for a complete formulation must draw on a parallel, complementary analysis of environmental contexts, a topic that is treated below in Section VI. In the interim, it may be helpful to indicate in advance that the two terms "culture" and "subculture" as here used encompass a variety of social structures, each possessing certain defining properties to be specified below. Such structures are typically identified in research operations by phenotypic proxy categories in the form of social addresses, such as nationality, ethnicity, class, religion, region, community, and neighborhood. As the reader will recognize, however, these categories are class-theoretical in nature, and hence, by themselves, have no explanatory power. The corresponding "field-theoretical" constructs are still to come (see below Section V, p. 223ff.).

C. Assessments of Temperament and Personality

As one turns from the scientific description of cognitive characteristics of the person to the classification of emotional and social attributes, one is struck by a contrast in perspective. The frame of reference for the former is primarily developmental; that is, researchers have typically used as the basis for their assessment of cognitive processes the changes occurring in this domain as a function of age, particularly at the two extremes of the life span. By contrast, the principal point of orientation for describing socioemotional characteristics is that of psychopathology and deviant behavior. As a result, most of the categories employed, and of the data collected, in the study of human temperament and personality have to do with maladaptive modes of response. Positive features, to the extent that they exist, arise mainly by default, as the opposite poles of negative attributes (for example, "anxious vs. calm"). But even there one is more likely to find an equally problematic opposite extreme (as in "passive vs. hyperactive"). In the latter circumstance, students of healthy development are left to search on their own for positive markers in an as-yet-uncharted middle ground.

The concentration on polarities has yet another consequence. Because extreme forms of behavior are most likely to be invariant across place and time, contextually-oriented definitions of personality, character, and—especially—temperament are few and far between. In sum, prevailing research definitions of *socioemotional* attributes of the person are neither developmentally nor contextually based. The few departures from this generalization, therefore, especially merit attention.

To begin with, a developmental perspective is clearly implied in the definition and usage of the concept of *temperament*. Both classic (Allport, 1937) and modern (Campos, Lamb, Goldsmith, & Stenberg, 1983) formulations of this construct emphasize individual differences in arousal, tempo, and intensity of response that are presumed to be biological in origin, remain stable over time, and serve as the substratum for the subsequent development of intrapersonal and interpersonal processes that, in turn, affect future personality structure. Consistent with this view, the term temperament is more often employed in research on young infants and children, whereas studies of "personality" are conducted primarily with older children, adolescents, and adults.

To this writer's knowledge, the only other developmentally-linked descriptors of socioemotional characteristics of the person that have informed empirical work are rooted in Piagetian theories of moral development and find their principal implementation in the work of Kohlberg and his followers.[22]

From an ecological perspective, what is most striking about all of the above formulations is the underlying assumption of the universality of qualities of temperament and personality across time and space; that is, a given socioemotional attribute is presumed to have the same psychological significance irrespective of the cultural and subcultural context in which the person lives or has been raised. That assumption applies as well to the immediate settings and methods employed for measuring individual differences in personality characteristics. For example, studies of temperament in young children rely primarily on three methods for gathering data: (1) parental reports (secured through interviews or questionnaires); (2) observations by trained observers in the laboratory, or under controlled experimental conditions; and (3) observations by trained observers in the home, or other familiar settings. Any discrepancies in results obtained by these three methods (and such discrepancies are substantial) are treated as errors of measurement in the form of method variance. The justification for this view follows directly from the definition of temperament as an expression "of the individual's emotional nature . . . regarded as dependent on constitutional make-up, and therefore largely hereditary in origin" (Allport, 1937, p. 54). Consistent with this formulation, "individual differences in temperamental characteristics are expected to be maintained across time as well as across situations" (Campos et al., 1983, p. 832). Therefore, "the temperament construct should not be method bound. . . . Cross-method convergence is to be desired highly" (p. 832).

Yet, the cross-method convergence is in fact not very high, ranging from .20 and to .40 (p. 841). How is one to account for this substantial lack of correspondence? One possible explanation calls into question the assumption that temperament, in its basic origin and nature, is in fact context free. Evidence bearing on this issue comes from the contrasting patterns of heritability coefficients, to be described below, that were obtained in twins studies of infant temperament conducted under different ecological conditions (Plomin, and Rowe, 1979; Matheny, Wilson, Dolan, & Krantz, 1981).

These ecological conditions also have differential status in psychological science. Reflecting the roots of their discipline in the physical as against the natural sciences, psychologists are prone to attribute greater validity to findings based on laboratory methods. Witness the following statement in the latest edition of the *"Handbook of Child Psychology,"* regarding the growing application of such laboratory-tested techniques in research on infant temperament: "This paradigmatic trend promises to bring temperament research closer to the mainstream of developmental psychology" (Campos et al., 1983, p. 841).

A noteworthy conclusion emerging from such mainstream research is reported in the first of these studies by Plomin and Rowe. These investigators imported the Strange Situation paradigm from the laboratory into the home in order to assess heritability of temperament in a sample of infant twins between two- and three-years of age. Trained observers noted the infants' responses in such categories as smiling, looking, touching, cuddling, vocalization, and separation distress. The principal finding: "Comparisons between intraclass correlations for identical and fraternal twins yielded significant differences for social behavior directed toward the stranger, but not toward the mother.... We conclude that in infancy, heredity affects individual differences in social responding more to unfamiliar persons than to familiar persons" (Plomin & Rowe, 1979, p. 62).

Given this conclusion, one would not expect to find in other studies high heritability levels for behaviors directed by infants toward their mothers. Yet, two years later, Adam Matheny and his colleagues (Matheny et al., 1981) employing a sample of similar age, reported results hardly consistent with the stated generalization. The strongest differences in concordance rates between identical and fraternal infant twins were found for a behavior cluster (labeled *sociability*) again involving such responses as smiling, cuddling, social responsiveness, and vocalization. The data, however, were based not on observations by a trained observer but on reports by the mother, obtained in an interview, regarding the presence of similarities and differences between the two twins on a wide range of behaviors.

How is one to explain these contrasting findings with respect to basic psychological characteristics that are presumed to be biologically-grounded and to remain constant across situations? Note that the phenomenon to be explained is not that genetic effects were found in one study but not in the other; rather, such effects emerged in both settings, but in relation to different parties.

Specifically, the question arises why, in the first situation, should the genetic component in the infant's attachment to its mother manifest itself only in the behavior of the infant toward a stranger and not to the mother herself? This paradoxical result can hardly be attributed to method variance, since, in the first study, the same measurement techniques were employed in relation to the two parties. And why, in the second situation, should the previously-absent genetic component in the infant's response to the mother now emerge as prepotent, the principal difference being that the mother herself, instead of a trained observer, served as the source of information?

There are several possible answers to these questions, none of them denying the existence of genetically-based differences in temperament, but all of them hinging on the meaning of the observed behaviors in the *settings* in which they occurred. To begin with, in the first, more scientifically-controlled setting, the context was limited to the experimental situation, whereas in the second investigation the scope covered the full range of the mother's everyday experience with her infant. Moreover, the first study was indeed carried out in a "strange situation." Not only were the observations conducted in the presence of a strange adult, but, as required by the experimental conditions, mothers were asked to limit their responsiveness and, upon instruction, to go out of the room, leaving the infant alone with the stranger. Under such circumstances, it seems quite possible that well-developed patterns of mother-infant interaction, based in part on genetically-influenced characteristics of both infant and mother, may be temporarily disrupted, and hence not there to be observed. Instead, what comes to the fore is the infant's established pattern of response, again genetically-based, to an unfamiliar stressful situation centered in the person of a strange adult.

Whether this particular explanation is in fact correct cannot of course be determined from the available data, nor is the validity central to a broader generalization toward which the findings point; namely, the markedly contrasting results described above are consistent with the interpretation that the observed differences in temperament develop in the context of the early mother-infant relationship and—not despite, but because of a high genetic loading—may in fact not be manifested across all situations. To paraphrase and extend Ceci's cognitive thesis (see this chapter, p. 40) to another domain: "The context in which temperament is manifested is not simply an adjunct to the characteristic in question, but a constituent of it."

Given the above considerations, the widely recommended and applied cross-situational and cross-method criterion as a necessary condition for establishing individual differences in temperament may be inappropriate from the standpoint both of theory and of research operations. Instead, a scientifically more rigorous and productive approach would be one of viewing *temperament in context*; that is, examining the systematic variation across context and method as a defining element of the individual's characteristic pattern of differential response to varying types of environments.

Applying this principle in the study of infant temperament requires prior theoretical consideration of which aspects of temperament are likely to be activated in which types of social contexts. The contrasting findings from the two studies summarized above suggest that a particularly important dimension of context in this regard is familiarity vs. unfamiliarity of the situation, especially in terms of the identity of the persons in the infant's immediate environment. Consistency across situations in the expression of a particular temperamental attribute would then be expected only to the extent that the dimension of familiarity were kept constant (or systematically and similarly varied) in each of the situations in which temperament was being assessed.

But, contrary to the prevailing view, it is not in consistency over time that the developmental effects of temperament are most likely to be manifested. From a dynamic ecological perspective, what one should more often expect are synergistic effects set in motion by characteristics of temperament exhibited early in life that then evoke differential patterns of response from the environment. For example, a physically attractive easily-soothed infant may invite affection and attention leading to reciprocal patterns of progressively more complex patterns of interaction that, in turn, facilitate psychological growth, whereas a fussy baby may discourage such interaction. In short, the distinctive characteristics of the person at a given point in time, such as temperament, may be more likely to instigate progressive developmental change in a particular direction, depending on the environmental response, than to insure unchanging psychological traits throughout life. More extended consideration and illustration of such possibilities are offered below in discussing what are referred to as "developmentally instigative personal characteristics" (see Section G).

Similar considerations apply to prevailing approaches in the scientific study of the broader concept of *personality*. Here too variations across situations and sources of information have typically been dismissed as "method variance" (Campbell & Fiske, 1959), and the recommended strategy of choice, known as the "multitrait-multimethod design," "is simply to appraise the consistency of measurement properties across different observers, conditions, and instruments" (Messick, 1983, p. 490). As before, such a strategy fails to make a distinction between sources of random error and systematic differences in the manifestation and meaning of personality attributes in different contexts. As in the case of temperament, a given socioemotional characteristic is presumed to have the same meaning, be it in science or in life, irrespective of the culture, subculture, or immediate setting in which the characteristic is observed.

This underlying assumption is even more pervasive in the study of temperament and personality than of cognitive capacity and competence. Although, as documented above, Vygotsky's culturally-oriented and contextually-based definition of the individual characteristics of the person has made some headway in Western studies of cognition, it has yet to make any appreciable impact on contemporary investigations of the social, emotional, or motivational attributes of the person, and their development.

There is one notable exception to the foregoing statement, but it lies mostly outside the present borders of psychological science. The approach has its origins, and principal application, in the same discipline from which Vygotsky found his inspiration: cultural anthropology. Beginning with the seminal work of W. H. R. Rivers (1926) more than a half-century ago, the study of "culture and personality'' has been an active and valued research domain within the science of anthropology. Indeed, during the late 1930s to the mid-1950s, when, primarily under the influence of the American anthropologists Edward Sapir and Clyde Kluckhohn, this orientation also captured the imagination, and informed the work, of some influential personality psychologists.[23] Almost all of this effort, however, was focused on the relation between culture and personality in adults in preindustrial societies, with little attention either to younger age levels or to intracultural variation. One outstanding departure from this focus was the study of children in six cultures (including the United States) conducted under the leadership of John and Beatrice Whiting (1973, 1975). The investigation is noteworthy for combining, in complementary fashion, the standardized observational methods of developmental psychology with the ethnographic techniques of the anthropologist. As a result, the investigators were able to interpret their systematic observations and quantitative findings in the context of the culture and community in which the children lived. Unfortunately, few developmentalists have adopted this dual orientation in research on development in context.

The preceding point brings us back to our primary concern with the design of ecological paradigms most appropriate for research on the ecology of human development. *It should now be apparent that Principle 1 and its four corollaries, originally developed and applied in relation to cognitive characteristics of the person, is equally applicable to the socioemotional sphere.* Indeed, given the foregoing evidence and argument, it would appear essential that individual differences in temperament and personality be interpreted from the perspective of the culture and subculture in which the individual was raised. In addition, the prevailing theoretical orientation and associated practice, especially in the socioemotional domain, of treating as error variance differences in descriptions of the developing person obtained in diverse settings by observers differing in their role and relationship to the subject is to be called into question. This is not to imply that the individual personality does not show continuity across place and time. Rather, the continuity is manifested in the consistent way in which the person *varies* his behavior as a function of the situation. The phenomenon is one of continuity in change. This seeming paradox is sufficiently important theoretically to warrant statement in what becomes a second general principle:

Principle 2. Continuity of temperament and character is expressed primarily not through constancy of behavior across time and place but through consistency over time in the ways in which the person characteristically *varies* his or her behavior as a function of the different contexts, both proximal and remote, in which that person lives.

The principle finds its precedent in the role theory developed by George Herbert Mead and the Chicago school of sociologists (Mead, 1934; Thomas, 1927;

Thomas & Thomas, 1928; Thomas & Znaniecki, 1927). For example, one of Mead's students, L. S. Cottrell (1942), proposed the thesis that in the process of socialization the developing person internalizes both sides of the role of significant others in his or her life. In a characteristically down-to-earth example, Cottrell described the "bicycle rider personality," who "bows down to those above, and beats down on those below" (Personal communication, 1943). This kind of phenomenon may explain the emergence later in life, seemingly out of the blue, of personality characteristics that appear to contradict long-existing prior patterns of behavior. From Cottrell's perspective, these would represent the activation, in a new and now appropriate context, of the complementary side of a previously-learned role.

Beyond such case study examples, I know of no research evidence bearing directly on Principle 2. The issue, however, would appear to be altogether susceptible to rigorous investigation through the use of research designs focusing on the behavior of the same persons functioning in different social roles, such as superior vs. subordinate, spouse vs. parent, vendor vs. purchaser, or teacher vs. student.

Like its predecessor, Principle 2 carries implications for research design in the form of the following corollary:

Corollary 2.1 From an ecological perspective, a scientific understanding of the psychological characteristics of the person and their development is furthered by research designs that permit the systematic comparison and interpretation of assessments made in different contexts by observers who differ in their role and relationship toward that person; for example, parents, peers, teachers, supervisors, trained researchers and,—last but not least—the self perceptions of the subject.

Although the comparative analysis of perceptions of the same person from the perspective of significant others in various parts of that person's life is a common practice in case studies and clinical work, to date I have not been able to find any instance in which this approach was applied systematically as a scientific strategy in research on human development. While data on children's socioemotional attributes are occasionally obtained in more than one setting from more than one source, the comparison of findings, if it is done at all, is typically limited to methodological issues. Substantive variations by context in the manifestations of temperament and personality of the same child or adult have only begun to be explored (e.g., Hinde & Tobin, 1988; Plomin & Nesselrode, in press), and thus constitute a *terra incognita* in contemporary developmental science.

Especially from an ecological perspective, there is good reason to believe that exploration in this terrain will bring significant scientific rewards. Consider, for

example, two rather different spheres of considerable research activity in contemporary developmental studies: the first focuses on the effect of day care; the
second on the influence of parents vs. peers on personality development, particularly in early adolescence. In the former case, data on psychological outcomes are obtained almost exclusively in settings outside the home, either in the
day care center, the school, or the psychological laboratory. Information from
parents, if collected at all, is treated simply as another, typically secondary
source, and is accorded no distinctive importance. Yet, parents are known to be
the most powerful influence on children's development and the persons most
sensitive and responsive to their children's behavior. Hence, any changes that
parents perceive in their child's characteristics are especially likely to provoke
corresponding changes in their own parental behavior toward the child; this altered behavior, in turn, may introduce new forces that affect the child's subsequent psychological growth. A comparative analysis, especially over time, of
qualities attributed to the child at home, school and other settings may therefore
provide effective vantage points for tracing the dynamics of ongoing developmental change.

An analogous situation occurs with respect to studies of parent-peer influences
on adolescent development. Once again, we encounter the phenomenon of
primary reliance on a single source of data on psychological outcomes, in this instance, the adolescents' self-reports, obtained through personality inventories.
Parents' perceptions of the children are usually not taken into account; nor are
those of peers. This comment should not be misinterpreted as implying that
descriptions of the young person by significant others from different settings
provide a more valid assessment of personality than do self reports. Rather, the
argument is that availability of information from different vantage points in the
adolescent's ecology provides a picture of the latter's characteristic modes of
adaptation to *differing* life situations. Moreover, because these situations are
likely to recur, often cross settings with the same participants, each mode of
reciprocal adaptation creates a continuing synergistic dynamic that can drive and
accelerate the course of future development.

This last consideration suggests a new and different dimension for distinguishing properties of the person; namely, the degree to which a given type of personal characteristic becomes a dynamic force, a vector that both fuels and directs
the course of future psychological development. It is this orientation that constitutes the focus of a final, somewhat unconventional point of reference for conceptualizing and analyzing the psychological characteristics of human beings.

D. A Developmental Conception of the Developing Person

Most developmental research treats the cognitive and socioemotional characteristics of the person solely as dependent variables; that is as measures of out-

come. Much less often are such characteristics examined as precursors of later development, and even more rarely as moderating factors affecting the power or direction of developmental processes. In the latter respects, not all personal attributes have equal potential for influencing subsequent development; some are more likely to be consequential than others. For the researcher, this differential power in affecting subsequent psychological growth provides a useful criterion and conceptual frame for selecting and classifying those human qualities that are especially significant for the person's future development.

Such personal attributes, which I shall refer to collectively as *developmentally-instigative characteristics*, are distinguished by either, or both, of two features. The first, and more commonly recognized, are personal qualities that invite or discourage reactions from the environment of a kind that can disrupt or foster processes of psychological growth. Examples include a fussy vs. a happy baby; attractive vs. unattractive physical appearance; or social responsiveness vs. withdrawal. Half a century ago, Allport (1937) spoke of such characteristics as constituting "personality" defined in terms of its "social stimulus value." Accordingly, I shall refer to such personal features as *personal stimulus qualities.*

Probably more potent, but as yet seldom studied, are characteristics that, rather than merely evoking a reaction from others, involve an active orientation toward and interaction with the environment. For example, early in life, such an orientation is seen in an infant's initiation and maintenance of patterns of reciprocal interaction with the mother and other caregivers. A bit later, the dynamic potential becomes manifest in the visual and motoric exploration of the immediate setting, both with respect to its physical and social content. At older ages, the analogous tendency is expressed in such forms as a readiness to seek out and sustain human relationships; intellectual curiosity; a disposition to manipulate, select, elaborate, reconstruct, and even to create environments for self and others; and a conception of the self as an active agent in a responsive world. I shall use the term *developmentally-structuring attributes* to designate active personal orientations of this kind.

Alternatively, to the extent that such an active and responsive personal orientation to the environment exists only in limited degree, the developmental progression may proceed at a slower rate, and along fewer developmental pathways. Or, where the impulse to activity is high but not tempered by complementary responsiveness to the surroundings, the resulting expression of diffuse hyperactivity can, in the absence of concerted environmental counterstrategies, set in motion developmental trajectories of progressive incompetence and social disruptiveness.

Both types of developmentally-instigative characteristics, when they are manifested over time in particular settings, tend to evoke complementary patterns of continuing environmental feedback, thus creating progressively more complex developmental trajectories that exhibit continuity through time. The result is a person-specific repertoire of evolving context-based and context-differentiated dispositions that continues to be distinguishable over the life course, and hence constitutes what we recognize over the years as the person's individual personality.

In recent years, this synergistic process of development has been documented in a number of longitudinal studies. Regrettably, however, all of them thus far are confined to personal characteristics of the first type, what I have called *stimulus attributes*, qualities that evoke developmentally fostering or disruptive reactions from others. For instance, a striking effect of a purely physical feature is documented in one of the follow-up studies of children of the Great Depression by Elder and his colleagues (Elder, Van Nguyen, & Caspi, 1985). The investigators found that economic hardship adversely influenced the psychosocial well-being of girls by increasing the rejecting behavior of fathers; the effects of rejection, however, varied inversely as a function of the daughter's physical attractiveness. Indeed, in the authors' words, ''Attractive daughters were not likely to be maltreated by their fathers, no matter how severe the economic pressure . . . [The results] underscore the importance of viewing economic decline in relation to both the child's characteristics and parenting behavior'' (p. 361). Here we have a classic instance of the power of a process-person-context model in revealing the complex interactions between organism and environment that drive the process of development.

The next two examples move from the purely physical into the psychological realm. Caspi and his colleagues (Caspi, Elder, & Bem, 1987, in press) have documented what might be called a ''snowballing effect'' across both time and space of two contrasting childhood personality characteristics—an explosive temperament on the one hand, and a tendency toward social withdrawal on the other. In the first domain, children who, when studied between eight and ten years of age, had been described as exhibiting frequent or severe temper tantrums were more likely as adults to experience reduced educational attainment, downward occupational mobility, erratic work careers, and disrupted family life. These patterns were further differentiated by characteristics of both person and context. Thus, for women, the effects were greater in the sphere of family life than of work; females with a history of temper tantrums in childhood were especially likely to become ill-tempered mothers and to experience divorce. By contrast, for men the sequelae of early explosiveness were more apt to be manifested in a delayed and disrupted work history.

The gender contrast across the domains of work and family life emerged as even more pronounced in the life course patterns of shy children. Men who in childhood had been described as socially and emotionally withdrawn married later than matched controls, were more likely to experience divorce, and were slower and less successful in establishing their careers. Women with similar childhood histories, however, showed no particular problems later on (Caspi, Elder, & Bem, 1988). In the authors' words:

> Not only did they appear to "float through" early adulthood with little difficulty, they were more likely than other women in their cohort to follow a conventional pattern of marriage, childbearing, and homemaking. Clearly sex differences in the continuity and consequences of early personality are moderated by cultural and historical prescriptions of gender-appropriate behavior. For this cohort, shy and reserved behavior seemed to be more compatible—if not desirable—for women than for men. It is not clear, however, that sex-role changes in our society have altered the patterns observed here. A recent study of shyness and interpersonal relationships found that correlations were stronger for male than for female respondents, suggesting that the inhibitory effects of shyness on the development of relationships may still be greater for men than women (Jones & Briggs, 1984) (p. 829).

Although "explosiveness" and "shyness" represent rather different styles of childhood behavior that lead to somewhat different outcomes, Caspi and his colleagues propose that "the general mechanisms producing their continuity and consequences appear to be the same: Long-term continuities of personality are to be found in interactional styles that are sustained by the progressive accumulation of their own consequence." (p. 00).

The principle is surely both valid and powerful, but, from a dynamic, ecological perspective, it needs to be accompanied by a complementary caveat. If left unqualified, repeated findings of this kind could leave the impression that continuity in psychological development over the life course is the rule. Such a conclusion is, at best, premature. To begin with, most of the longitudinal studies of personality conducted to date, including the work of Caspi and his colleagues, deal with behavioral extremes. And as Clarke and Clarke (1980) documented in a recent review, "Greater constancies across time are to be expected in seriously deviant conditions compared with less abnormal development." (p. 3). Moreover, even with respect to the extreme patterns of childhood explosiveness and shyness studied by Caspi et al., an examination of the results suggests that continuity, while clearly present, characterizes only a minority of the cases. For example, the structural model for the sequelae of childhood temper tantrums—including all analyzed pathways, both direct and indirect—is associated with a total R^2 of .34. This means that, even after allowing for error in measurement, the amount of variance accounted for by continuity is not more than a third. Or, to put the issue more provocatively, most youngsters who exhibited patterns of marked explosive behavior in childhood did not experience significantly reduced educational attainment, occupational success, or family stability.

What are the forces that counteract the disruptive thrust of early maladaptive behaviors? Given our theoretical framework, the answer must be sought in processes set in motion by other characteristics of both person and context usually not included in most research designs employed to date. On the context side, an indication of a possible counteractive mechanism comes from a study by Crockenberg (1981). The investigator found that the beneficial impact of maternal social supports on mother-infant interaction varied systematically as a function of the infant's temperament. The effect was strongest for the mothers with the most irritable babies, and minimal for those whose infants were emotionally calm.

On the person side, the most likely countervailing personal qualities fall into our second class of "developmentally instigative characteristics," those that involve an active, structuring orientation toward the environment. Although the methods and opportunities for investigating these kinds of personal qualities are readily at hand, they have yet to be exploited in research designs that take into account processes of interaction between person and context. A tantalizing example of such a missed opportunity is found in the important longitudinal investigations conducted over many years by Jack and Jeanne Block (1980). Two well-known measures of children's personality that these investigators have constructed nicely fit the criteria for what I have called *developmentally-structuring personal attributes*. "Ego resiliency" refers to the capacity of children actively to cope under environmental stress or uncertainty. "Ego control" involves the ability to regulate impulse expression. The classifications are derived from Q-sorts of personality items made by trained judges familiar with the child, typically by teachers. Both measures have been widely used both as criteria of developmental outcome and as personality predictors of subsequent behavior, but I have been able to find no investigation that examined whether family or peer group processes had differential effect on the development of children initially exhibiting contrasting levels of ego resilience or control. Particularly intriguing from this perspective is a study by the Blocks and a colleague (Block, Block, & Keyes, 1988) of "early childhood personality and environmental precursors" of drug usage in adolescence. The researchers neatly demonstrated that both children's personality characteristics during the preschool years and early parental patterns of child rearing were related to substance use in adolescence, but, regrettably, the investigators did not examine the interplay between the domains of person and context.

A similar situation exists with respect to another type of developmentally-instigative personal characteristic, one that is often subsumed under the general rubric of personality, but, because of its special significance, merits separate consideration here. I refer to the individual's conception of self as an active agent in a responsive environment. The best known measure of this kind is Rotter's index of "locus of control" (Rotter, 1966), a personality inventory assessing the extent to which the person feels that the sources of failure or success lie within or outside the self. Subsequently, a more sophisticated formulation of the concept, and of its operationalization, was introduced by Bandura under the rubric of "self-efficacy" (Bandura, 1977, 1982). Despite the widespread use of measures of this kind, I am aware of only one study of the impact of self-concept on subsequent development (as distinguished from behavior at the moment). Employing a longitudinal design with a sample of schoolchildren, Newman (1984) was able to show, by causal modeling, that between Grades 2 and 5 mathematics achievement influenced self-ratings of ability, but not the reverse; and even this effect diminished in the higher grades.

Although evidence appears to be lacking for any effect of children's own belief systems on their later development, a set of findings emerging from a doctoral dissertation by Tulkin (Tulkin, 1973, 1977; Tulkin & Cohler, 1973; Tulkin & Kagan, 1972) does point to the potency of parental belief systems in this regard. The investigator began by studying social class differences both in the behaviors and the beliefs of mothers of ten-month-old girls. The research was conducted in the home, employing both interviews and observations. Middle-class mothers were distinguished from their working-class counterparts not only by higher levels of reciprocal interaction with their infants, but also in their views about what a ten-month-old could do and about their own abilities to influence their baby's development; specifically, the more advantaged mothers attributed greater potentials both to their infants and themselves. In addition, the correlations between maternal behavior and attitudes were substantially greater in middle-class than in lower-class families. Several years later, Tulkin and a colleague (Tulkin & Covitz, 1975) reassessed the same youngsters after they had entered school. The children's performance on tests of mental ability and language skill showed significant relationships to the prior measures of reciprocal mother-infant interaction.

Taken as a whole, the foregoing research findings suggest an additional principle bearing on the role of personal attributes in shaping human development in real life contexts.

Principle 3. The attributes of the person most likely to shape the course of human development are modes of behavior or belief that reflect an active, selective, structuring orientation toward the environment and/or tend to provoke reactions from the environment. The term *developmentally-instigative characteristic* is used to designate personal attributes of this kind. The effect of such characteristics on the person's development depends in significant degree on the corresponding patterns of response that they evoke from the person's environment.

The preceding principle, and especially the impressive research findings marshalled in its support, might lead the reader to conclude that human beings themselves are the primary shapers of their own development, with environment playing only a secondary, essentially reactive role. Such an interpretation would be mistaken. It is true that individuals often can and do modify, select, reconstruct, and even create their environments. But this capacity emerges only to the extent that the person has been <u>enabled</u> to engage in self directed action as a joint function not only of his biological endowment but also of the environment in which he or she developed. There is no one without the other.

To return to the consideration of developmentally-instigative characteristics, their potential range goes far beyond the particular attributes of temperament, personality, and beliefs involved in the investigations cited. For instance, they could include customary strength and speed of response, patterns of exploratory behavior, cognitive styles in interpreting and organizing the environment, or expectations and future plans. As this sequence of examples suggests, such characteristics, while exhibiting some continuity over time, evolve progressively in form and complexity as a function of biological and psychological maturation.

A final set of developmentally-instigative characteristics that deserve explicit mention involves a variety of purely physical factors that have no psychological substance in themselves, but often do lead to psychological sequelae. Three types of such characteristics are usefully distinguished:

1.   Forms of organic injury or maldevelopment that threaten subsequent psychological growth. Common examples include low birth weight and other complications of pregnancy, congenital anomalies, physical handicaps, severe illness, and damage to brain function through accident or degenerative processes.

2.   Bodily characteristics or changes associated with differing developmental outcomes; for example, body size and type, physical appearance and attractiveness, physical and physiological changes associated with puberty, menopause, or old age.

3.   The third set possesses a special distinction; it includes a set of three physical characteristics deemed so potent in influencing the course of future development that they need to be distinguished in every study, irrespective of the particular hypothesis under investigation. These are the familiar demographic factors of age, sex, and race.

Note that all three are class-theoretical concepts, and hence have no explanatory power in themselves. Under these circumstances, the sweeping scientific injunction clearly demands justification. Explanation is also called for on additional grounds: both the reason for and the design implications of the requirement are more complex than the injunction itself conveys. What is involved is not the familiar methodological admonition to control for the possibly confounding effect of these three factors on measures of outcome. The rationale for the requirement is substantive rather than methodological, and focuses primarily on possible differences not in outcome but in process. As evidenced by the results of a number of studies described in the preceding pages—and others still to come—processes often operate in different ways, with different effects, in the two sexes; for subjects at different ages; and for persons from different racial groups. The reasons for such differences are themselves highly complex. For example, while obviously rooted in physical characteristics, their dynamics are also driven by the social response to these characteristics in a particular culture or subculture. But whatever their origin, the differences in process associated with these three factors occur so frequently that failure to provide for this possibility in study design entails significant scientific cost.

The cost is of two kinds. First, there is the risk of over-generalization, arising from the possibility that the reported phenomenon may in fact differ substantially as a function of the gender, age, and race of the subjects. Equally if not more important, however, is the missed scientific opportunity of discovering variations in human development that can stimulate the revision and further explication of existing theory and knowledge. It is the very nature and power of science that it moves forward through the systematic discovery and acknowledgement of its own errors.

The point under discussion is sufficiently important to warrant status as a design corollary to Principle 3.

Corollary 3.1   Every research design for the study of human development should provide for the possibility of differences in process and outcome associated with the factors of gender, age, and race, to the extent that they differ within the research sample.

With this paradoxically-specific universal injunction, we conclude our analysis of the properties of the person as viewed from an ecological perspective. As the analysis has revealed, that perspective incorporates a universal injunction of its own that is far more general. Stated in the form of a fourth and final principle, that universal tenet reads as follows:

Principle 4.   No characteristic of the person exists or exerts influence on development in isolation. Every human quality is inextricably embedded, and finds both its meaning and fullest expression, in particular environmental settings, of which the family is a prime example. As a result, there is always an interplay between the psychological characteristics of the person and of a specific environment; the one cannot be defined without reference to the other.

This phenomenon of interaction is of course fundamental to an understanding of how human beings develop. An adequate conceptualization of it must simultaneously take into account diverse properties of the person, and of the environment in which the person is embedded. Having completed an analysis of the former, I turn next to an elaboration and, in some instances reformulation, of the environmental paradigms set forth in the 1979 monograph on the "Ecology of Human Development" (Bronfenbrenner, 1979).

V. PARAMETERS OF CONTEXT FROM A DEVELOPMENTAL PERSPECTIVE

As previously noted, because of the one-sided emphasis given to the environment in the aforementioned work, there already exists a working taxonomy of contexts that can serve as a basis for further work. As originally formulated, the taxonomy consisted of a hierarchy of systems at four levels moving from the most proximal to the most remote. The systems were identified by the successive prefixes; micro-, meso-, exo-, and macro. While these environmental constructs appear to have stood the test of trial and time, my subsequent efforts to right the imbalance on the organism side of the ecological equation have unexpectedly led to an expansion and reformulation on the context side as well. The most conspicuous of these changes involves the introduction of significant new elements in the definition of the micro- and the macrosystem. These changes, and their rationale, are presented below.

A. The Microsystem Revisited and Revised

In its original form, the definition of this system read as follows:

> A *microsystem* is a pattern of activities, roles, and interpersonal relations experienced by the developing person in a given face-to-face setting with particular physical and material features.

Examples of settings included home, school, peer group, or the workplace.

With the sobering wisdom of hindsight, I find myself struck by what now appears as a glaring omission in this formulation. To the extent that the definition recognizes other human beings as existing in the setting, it is solely in terms of their social roles and relationships; that is, they have no existence as persons possessing distinctive characteristics of temperament, personality, or systems of belief. Thus, the short shrift that had been given to the person side of the equation in the initial formulation of the ecological paradigm is reflected as well in the initial specification of the environment.

Unfortunately, the same one-sidedness is also found in contemporary empirical work. Relatively few studies of development in context examine the influence on psychological growth of the personality characteristics of significant others in the developing person's life. A signal exception appears in the recent work of Elder and his colleagues (Elder et al., 1986). Exploiting cross-generational data from the Berkeley Guidance Study, the investigators showed that the disruptive developmental effects of the Great Depression were particularly severe for children with irritable, explosive parents. As adults, these children were themselves likely to be more ill-tempered. This general characteristic, in turn, affected both their marital relationship, and, their behavior as parents. Finally, upon looking at these parents' children and grandchildren, the researchers found evidence that "the legacy of undercontrolled behavior persists into the fourth generation" (p. 329). Note that this legacy was not simply a manifestation of the constancy of temperament over time, but a product and projection (using these terms almost in their mathematical sense) of the initial combination of a particular kind of person in a particular kind of situation-specifically, a somewhat irascible adult male under economic duress.

Findings of this sort point to the importance of including within the formal definition of the developing person's immediate environment the developmentally-relevant characteristics of the *other persons* present and participating in that environment. Potentially, such characteristics cover the same range of attributes as that set forth in the preceding section. Thus, depending on the research question being posed, they might include demographic features such as age and sex, cognitive abilities and skills, or, as in the study cited above, aspects of temperament or personality. As the foregoing study illustrates, the aspects of the person most likely to produce powerful interactive effects are what we have called *developmentally-instigative* characteristics.

To highlight the potential importance for development of the personal characteristics of significant others in the immediate environment, I have added to the original definition of microsystem the final phase *italicized* below:

A *microsystem* is a pattern of activities, roles, and interpersonal relations experienced by developing person in a given face-to-face setting with particular physical and material features, *and containing other persons with distinctive characteristics of temperament, personality, and systems of belief.*[24]

The definitions of the next two systems levels remain unchanged, and are repeated here solely for the reader's convenience.

The *mesosystem*, comprises the linkages and processes taking place between two or more settings containing the developing person (e.g., the relations between home and school, school and work place, etc.). In other words, a mesosystem is a system of microsystems.

The *exosystem*, encompasses the linkage and processes taking place between two or more settings, at least one of which does not ordinarily contain the developing person, but in which events occur that influence processes within the immediate setting that does contain that person (e.g., for a child, the relation between the home and the parent's work place; for a parent, the relation between the school and the neighborhood group).

B. The Macrosystem Concretized

Ironically, the beginning effort to spell out developmentally-relevant properties of the person had its greatest impact on the environmental side in enriching the theoretical conception and importance of the most distal and expansive region of the environment—the *macrosystem*. The impact has its origin mainly in two context-oriented definitions of person characteristics. The first source is Vygotsky's theory of the "sociohistorical evolution of the mind" (Luria, 1976, p. 5); in particular, his thesis that from earliest childhood onward the development of one's characteristics as a person depends in significant degree on the options that are available in a given culture at a given point in its history. The second source is the concept of *developmentally-instigative personal characteristics*, in particular, systems of belief. As highlighted in the revised definition of the microsystem, such dynamic attributes are critical features not only of the developing person but also of significant others in the person's environment. Furthermore, with respect to macrosystems, consistent with Vygotsky's formulation, the repertoire of available belief systems, as well as their intensity, is defined by the culture or subculture in which one lives, and hence may vary appreciably over both space and time. It is from this repertoire that parents, teachers, and other agents of socialization draw when they, consciously or unconsciously, define the goals, risks, and ways of raising the next generation. *It follows that scientific recognition of the belief systems prevailing in the world of the developing person is essential for an understanding of the interaction of organismic and environmental forces in the process of development.* Such belief systems therefore constitute a developmentally-critical feature of every macrosystem.[25]

In addition, the concept of a cultural repertoire of belief systems raises the possibility of other kinds of repertoires that can create or constrain developmental opportunity. Thus, there may be other features of the macrosystem that are not merely structural, but also developmentally-instigative. The application of this already familiar construct at the level of the macrosystem signals yet another instance of how efforts to expand the person side of the ecological equation have led to key expansions on the environmental side.

Specifically, consideration of these issues has resulted in the addition of a key dynamic complement to the formal definition of the macrosystem. The revised definition, with the addition underscored, reads as follows:

The *macrosystem* consists of the overarching pattern of micro-, meso-, and exosystems characteristic of a given culture, subculture, or other broader social context, *with particular reference to the developmentally-instigative belief systems, resources, hazards, life styles, opportunity structures, life course options, and patterns of social interchange that are embedded in each of these systems*. The macrosystem may be thought of as a societal blueprint for a particular culture, subculture, or other broader social context.

Several aspects of this expanded definition merit further consideration. Thus we must ask: What are the "other broader social contexts" that also constitute macrosystems, and how do they differ from, and what do they share in common with cultures and subcultures as macrosystems? To address the easiest part of this question first, what all macrosystems share in common are the elements specified in the above definition. Over and above these commonalities, cultures and subcultures have two distinguishing features. First, they constitute the highest order, overarching macrostructures that encompass all other, intracultural forms. Second, they differ from these other constituent forms in possessing an additional, critical quality: namely, the patterns of belief and behavior characterizing the macrosystem are passed on from one generation to the next through processes of socialization carried out by various institutions of the culture, such as family, school, church, workplace, and structures of government.

Finally, to return to the initial part of the question: What are the principal types of macrosystems existing within a culture or subculture? Like these latter, superordinate systems, they are typically identified by proxy variables in the form of social address labels, such as social class, ethnicity, or region (e.g, rural vs. urban). Other possibilities include different professions (e.g., doctors vs. lawyers), or cohorts experiencing different historical events, epochs or life styles (e.g., "Children of the Great Depression," "Vietnam veterans," "the Sixties generation," the "women's movement," "yuppies"). But, as previously noted, these are all class-theoretical concepts, mere labels that have no explanatory power in themselves. *In the last analysis, what defines the macrosystem is sharing in common the kinds of characteristics specified in the above formal definition (i.e., similar belief systems, social and economic resources, hazards, life styles, etc.). From this perspective, social classes, ethnic or religious groups, or persons living in particular regions, communities, neighborhoods, or other types of broader social structures constitute a macrosystem whenever the above conditions are met.* This also means that, over the course of history, newly evolving social structures have the potential of turning into subcultures by developing a characteristic set of values, life style, and other defining features of a macrosystem. A case in point is the evolution, within the American middle class, of a new—and now predominating family pattern—that of the two-wage-earner family. Another, contrasting example, is the low-income, single-parent household. The test of whether the label of macrosystem is legitimately applied to each of these phenomena is the demonstration that they do in fact exhibit characteristic life styles, values, expectations, resources, and opportunity structures that distinguish them both from each other, and from the more traditional family form in which the male is the sole breadwinner and "family head." There is a growing body of research evidence indicating that, in both instances, the criteria for the existence of a distinctive macrosystem are indeed well met.[26]

The critical, or merely curious, reader may ask why it is necessary to introduce the neologism of "macrosystem" when the already existing terms "culture" and "subculture" would seem to capture much the same concept. There is indeed some overlap, but it is far from complete. All cultures and subcultures qualify as macrosystems, but the reverse proposition does not hold. For instance, the former terms do not typically connote such social structures or institutions as neighborhoods, cohorts, family types, or systems of day care or education; yet, as some the foregoing examples reveal, such systems can, under certain circumstances, acquire the properties specified in the above definition of a macrosystem.

And, once evidence for the existence of a macrosystem is found, it becomes possible to investigate the nature of various aspects of that system as they affect developmental processes at more proximal levels.

It becomes possible, but it is rarely done. To put it more precisely, in developmental research the analysis of macrosystem elements seldom goes beyond an operational definition based solely on a proxy variable (i.e., a social address), its use for purposes of statistical control, and a report of the effect on developmental outcomes associated with the label in question (for example, class or ethnic differences in IQ or self-esteem[27]).

What else can and should be done? Stating the issue more broadly, what are the implications of the more differentiated conceptualizations of both person and environment set forth in the preceding pages for further advance in the scientific study of human development?

VI. FORM AND SUBSTANCE FOR FUTURE RESEARCH

Possible answers to the preceding question emerge from an integration of the formal ecological paradigms and models presented in the first part of this chapter (Sections I–III) with the structural and substantive aspects of person and context elaborated in the second part (Sections IV–V). I refer to "possible" answers because all of them are implications derived mainly from theoretical considerations. Relevant empirical evidence is lacking, or fragmentary at best. The justification for exploiting this lop-sided state of affairs lies in the research potential of the possible answers. From its very beginning, the ecology of human development was defined as a scientific undertaking "in the discovery mode" (Bronfenbrenner, 1979, pp. 37–38). The aim was not to test hypotheses, but to generate them. Even more broadly, the goal was to develop a theoretical framework that could provide both structure and direction for the systematic study of organism-environment interaction in processes of human development.

Given this objective, the "possible answers" take the form of a series of *priority propositions*, each defining a particular element of the broader framework that, when operationalized in empirical work, could serve to illuminate developmental processes and permit the formulation of more fruitful and precise concepts and hypotheses. Hence, each proposition consists of a theoretical statement, along with a specification of an operational research model suitable for investigating the proposition in question. Thus, in this concluding section, issues of theory and research design are no longer treated separately (as principles vs. corollaries) but presented together in a way that reveals the necessary close relation between the two.

For reasons that will become apparent, the propositions begin with the outermost region of the environment—the macrosystem.

Proposition 1.

To the extent that is practically possible, every study of development in context should include a contrast between at least two macrosystems. In terms of research design, this means that, whatever questions or hypotheses are under investigation, the analysis is conducted separately for each macro-domain, thus making it possible to determine the extent to which the hypothesized processes operate in the same way in different macrosystems.

The preceding recommendation is not quite as demanding as might appear, for rarely would an investigator choose a sample so narrowly defined that it would not include within it substantial representation from two or more macrosystem domains. Moreover, the domains that occur most frequently are also those especially likely to offer contrasts in belief systems, resources, life styles, patterns of social exchange, and life course options that are especially significant for developmental processes and outcomes. For example, the contrasting macrosystems most salient in modern societies are those associated with differences in social class, family structure, gender, ethnicity, parental employment patterns, and linkages between home, school, and community. These are precisely the domains in which processes are apt to function differentially. Nevertheless, even if such contrasting groups are present in sufficient size, stratification of the sample inevitably reduces the statistical power of the design, while at the same time substantially increasing the scope and the cost of analysis.

What, then, would be the scientific yield of such expansion that could justify the increased expense? Fortunately, in this instance there is a concrete example that demonstrates the added gain. The example comes from a four-year longitudinal study conducted by Helen Bee and her associates (Bee, Barnard, Eyres, Gray, Hammond, Spietz, Snyder, & Clark, 1982). Relevant data were collected at five successive age periods during early childhood, beginning at birth. As we shall see shortly, the overall research findings testify to the developmental importance of aspects of both person and context delineated in the preceding pages. But first, we must take note of a distinctive feature of the investigation especially relevant for the topic at hand: the authors carried out a separate analysis of their data for mothers at each of two levels of schooling (those with some education beyond high school, in comparison with those with high school or less). The justification for conducting such a dual analysis was not based on the kinds of theoretical issues being raised here, but on the more conventional ground of the need to control for what are viewed as possible confounding factors in order to establish the generality of the findings. In the authors' words, "if we are to move closer to statements of causal connections between environmental measures and measures of the child's intellectual development, we must be able to show that the significant environmental variables are predictive within as well as across social class groups" (p. 1136).

The results of the analysis, however, revealed a rather different picture. In general, the predictive relationships were considerably stronger in the low education group. Specifically, in predicting final outcome measures both of intelligence and receptive language, almost all of the correlations (ten in each case) were significant, ranging in magnitude from .20 to .63, with a median above .40. By contrast, in the high education group, only three environmental predictors were significant, none above an r of .31.

The authors offer two explanations for this striking result.

> First, it is possible that we are dealing here largely with differences in variance between the two groups. For example, most of the fathers in the high-education group were present during the pregnancy and were strongly supportive of the mother. Among the low-education group, there were a number of single mothers and others whose partners were less supportive. The fact that social support is predictive of IQ and language for the low-education group may, thus, be a simple reflection of the fact that only in that subgroup did the score vary widely.
>
> An alternative explanation, however, is that there may be a different interactional dynamic operating in the high- and low-education families. For example, perhaps mothers with less education respond differently for high levels of life change or low levels of social support. These mothers may be less able to "buffer" the child against the vicissitudes in their own personal relationships (p. 1152).

The authors' second explanation represents a classic example of process-context interaction. It would clearly be instructive were it possible to differentiate between the two alternative hypotheses through further analysis of the available data.

Fortunately, thanks to the care the authors had taken in reporting basic descriptive statistics, such a possibility exists. To begin with, an examination of the published standard deviations of the independent variables reveals that, in every case, the sigma is significantly greater for the low education group. Hence, the authors' first alternative hypothesis finds empirical support.

But that is not the whole story. Although no regression coefficients are reported, the availability of the standard deviations along with the r's made it possible to calculate the regression of IQ and language scores on each independent variable, again separately for the two education groups.[28] The results of this reanalysis were indeed instructive. Certain variables did have greater impact per unit input in the low education group; specifically, social supports, maternal expectations, and life changes. Certain other variables, however, had greater impact per unit input in the high education group. These were measures of mother-infant interaction, and of cultural resources present in the home [as assessed by Bradley & Caldwell's HOME scale (1977)].

While such essentially serendipitous findings obviously require cross validation, they do exhibit a consistent pattern in terms of the theoretical framework presented in the preceding pages. Thus, one might hypothesize that the developmental impact of *microsystem* processes within the family is enhanced by the kinds of resources that are associated with parents' education beyond the high school years. By contrast, the parent's linkages and orientations to the world outside the family (in this instance, in the form of social support, and belief systems about one's own and one's child's capacity to cope) have greater developmental power in families deprived of the resources that higher socioeconomic status might otherwise provide.[29]

My purpose here is not to claim validity for any particular hypothesis derived from this reanalysis of Bee's data, but rather to illustrate the scientific importance of providing for the analysis of macrosystem contrasts in research development in context. Such provision is highly desirable for several reasons. First, [there is] the danger, in the absence of one or more macrosystem contrasts, of overgeneralizing findings and conclusions. The reality of this risk is illustrated by the results of a recent study by Dornbusch and his colleagues of the relation of parenting style to adolescent school performance (Dornbusch, Ritter, Leiderman, Roberts, & Fraleigh, 1987). One of the most widely cited findings in the socialization literature is Diana Baumrind's demonstration, in a series of studies (Baumrind, 1971, 1973; Baumrind and Black, 1967), of the superiority of what she has called the "authoritative" pattern of child rearing, distinguished by a combination of firmness and support, as contrasted to more one-sided authoritarian or permissive styles. Dornbusch and his coworkers, employing a much larger and more representative sample of almost 8,000 subjects, obtained general support for Baumrind's thesis. "We found that both authoritarian and permissive parenting styles were negatively associated with grades, and authoritative parenting was positively associated with grades" (Dornbusch et al., 1987, p. 1244). The size and diversity of the sample, however, also permitted carrying out separate analyses for four ethnic groups: Black, Asian, Hispanic, and non-Hispanic White. The results revealed that the expected relationships clearly held for whites and blacks, but not for Asians or Hispanics. Asians, in particular, showed a widely discrepant pattern; the correlations of grades with both the authoritative and the permissive styles were near zero. Moreover, "compared to whites, the Asian high school students of both sexes reported that their families were higher on the index of authoritarian parenting and lower on the index of authoritative parenting. Yet, counter to the general negative relation of such parenting patterns to academic achievement, the Asians as a group received high grades in school'' (p. 1256). The authors acknowledge that "the success of Asian children in our public schools cannot be adequately explained in terms of the parenting styles we have studied,'' and suggest that "careful studies of the meaning of specific behaviors as interpreted by members of various social groups, particularly ethnic groups, could produce a major advance in our knowledge'' (p. 1256).

The foregoing statement nicely captures Lewin's distinction between a class-theoretical model, in which ethnicity is treated simply as a social address, and a field-theoretical macrosystem model, which permits the analysis of the particular contextual elements, and personal attributes and belief systems characterizing a particular ethnic group. Herein lies the second and more compelling reason for urging the introduction of macro-domains as a common denominator in studies of development in context. *The reason lies in the generative power of macrosystem designs in illuminating the sources and operation of forces affecting the pace and content of psychological growth.* This potential cannot be realized, however, if the macrosystem is indexed only by its social address; *the research design must also include provision for assessing at least some of the substantive elements set forth in the formal definition of a macrosystem.* Unfortunately, most research models currently employed in studies of development in context do not incorporate these substantive features. From this viewpoint, the Bee study is a rare exception. The special strength of the work derives precisely from its com-prehensiveness in obtaining and analyzing data at no less than three systems levels: micro- (e.g., mother-child interaction), exo- (e.g., mother's support networks), and macro- (e.g., contrasting levels of mother's education).

But even this exceptional study fails to take advantage of some rewarding prospects that would have been provided by a more differentiated ecological paradigm. The first of these missed opportunities arises from the fact that, in the present research, the investigators moved too quickly to more complex analyses, thus by-passing productive possibilities existing in the available data. For example, they were in a position to discover and describe the distinctive patterns of risk, belief systems, modes of mother-child interaction, and life changes that characterize families in the two macrosystems operationally defined by the proxy variable of maternal education. This could have been accomplished simply by examining differences in means for the two education groups on each of the environmental measures included in the study.

There was an even greater, and theoretically richer, missed opportunity as well. It was created by the availability of data not only in the realm of context, but also in the person domain. Beginning with the assessment of perinatal complications at birth, the investigators obtained successive measures of the young child's developmental status based on mental tests, mother's reports, and observations of language behavior. These data were used, however, exclusively for the purpose of analyzing the relative predictive power, at successive ages, of the characteristics of the child as against those of the environment. The main finding in this regard was that "assessments of child performance were poor predictors prior to 24 months, but were excellent predictors from 24 months on" (Bee et al., 1982, p. 1134).

This finding may well underestimate the importance for future development of the infant's early characteristics, because of the restricted research paradigm guiding the analysis. What the paradigm neglects is the possibility, indeed the likelihood, of an interaction, observable from the youngest ages onward, between the organism and the environment. For example, was the effect of mother-infant reciprocal activity the same for infants who had experienced perinatal complications versus those who had not? Analogous questions can be raised with respect to children who differed in developmental status at successive ages as assessed by tests, or perhaps more relevantly, as perceived by their mothers. Finally, returning to the level of the macrosystem, did these diverse developmental trajectories differ for children of mother's in the two educational groups? In sum, the investigators missed an opportunity to apply a full process-person-context model in their chronosystem design.

The preceding examples illustrate both the scientific need and the scientific gain of analyzing macrosystem contrasts in developmental research. All of the preceding investigation, however, were field studies concerned primarily with *social* processes. Is the injunction to employ macrosystem models equally applicable to research on basic *cognitive* processes in the laboratory? The results of previously-cited studies bearing on this question (see above, pp. 28–30) suggest that the case for employing macrosystem contrasts in the latter domain is equally if not more compelling. In terms of research design, two types of models merit consideration. The first, though more demanding, promises a richer scientific yield. It involves replicating each laboratory study in a natural setting with tasks that require analogous processes, but draw on the subjects' experience in everyday life. The second, more economical strategy extends to the laboratory the principle of exploiting macrosystem contrasts already present within the sample, perhaps strengthened through the selection of subjects in a stratified design. There is good reason to believe that the systematic application of one or both of these models in studies of such basic cognitive processes as memory, concept formation, logical operations, and reasoning will not only challenge existing conceptions and conclusions, but—more importantly—lead to more sophisticated formulations that, when implemented in appropriate research designs, will significantly enhance our understanding and knowledge of cognitive development in context.

The next proposition takes as its point of departure a feature previously incorporated as a new element in the revised definition of the microsystem; namely, the recognition of the developmental importance of the characteristics of significant others in one's life. This same element also has key relevance for the nature of the proxy variables employed to identify macrosystems. At the present time, these variables are typically limited to background characteristics of the research subjects themselves; i.e., *their* social class, ethnicity, place of residence, etc. An ecological perspective suggests, however, that equally pertinent would be the background characteristics of the *other persons* living in the same environment; for example, neighbors, friends, associates at work. I have been able to find few investigations that have taken such factors into account; but when this was done, the effects were substantial. An early example is a study by Kawi and Pasamanick (1959) on the role of prenatal factors in the development of childhood reading orders. The sample was drawn from the greater Baltimore area and consisted only of white males. Instead of using a conventional measure of social class based on parents' education and occupation, the investigators classified families on the basis of census tracts ranked by decile in terms of the median rental cost. In other words, the index took into account not only the socioeconomic status of the subjects' families, but also of their neighbors. Within each decile, children with and without reading problems (retardation of two years or more) were matched on an impressive array of background variables. For example, the control group was selected on the basis of the next birth in the same hospital (i.e., a child of the same age), of the same sex, and mother's age as the index child.

The effect of class background in this study was much greater than is usually obtained in developmental research. Moreover, the influence of what, from a macrosystem perspective, one might call different socioeconomic macrosystems was reflected not only in a marked contrast in levels both of prenatal complications and reading disorders, but also in the relation between these two factors. For example, the ratio of birth complications among nonreaders vs. matched controls was 12 to 1 in the two lowest census tract deciles, but 1 to 1 in the top two. In other words, in the latter case, there was no difference at all; as in Drillien's work cited earlier (pp. 21–26), families living in good ecologies are in a position to avoid any serious problems for their children's later development arising from complications of pregnancy.

A second instructive example appears in a comparative study by Blau (1981) of competence, socialization, and social structure in a sample of black and white children and their families. As one measure of socioeconomic status, Blau calculated "the proportion of close neighbors in white-collar occupations, of college educated neighbors, and of neighbors with a child who has gone to college" (Blau, 1981, p. 18). She appropriately called the measure "social milieu," and, perhaps more precisely, "middle class exposure." In a multiple regression of the five "best" predictors for IQ and achievement test scores in the sample as a whole, this index had an independent effect second only to race, and slightly ahead of both education and occupational status. The impact of middle class exposure was especially strong in the black sub-sample.

The preceding theoretical and empirical considerations lead to the following proposition:

Proposition 2.

The concept of macrosystem includes not only the subculture in which the person has been raised, but also the subculture in which the person lives. The latter is defined by the personal and background characteristics of those with whom the person associates in the settings of everyday life. Any research design that includes a macrosystem contrast should therefore, to the extent possible, provide for securing identifying criteria from both of these domains. This provision is especially important when the person has been raised, or lives in, two different subcultures (as in the case of minority or immigrant groups).

The recommendation to include a macrosystem contrast in every study of development in context accords special importance to the structure and substance of the particular macrosystems in question. The next proposition addresses this issue by taking cognizance of the fact that the macrosystem, as the outermost region of the environment, encompasses all the other systems.

Proposition 3.

The macrosystem is defined by the structure and content of constituent systems, with particular reference to the developmentally-instigative belief systems, resources, hazards, life styles, patterns of social exchange opportunity structures, and life course options that are embedded in each of these systems. The power of a macrosystem model is therefore enhanced to the extent that provision is made for assessing the foregoing characteristics in the research design for constituent micro-, meso-, or exo-systems.

Accordingly, the next set of propositions deals with these constituent systems, proceeding in descending order.

Exo- and mesosystems have a key feature in common: both deal with the *relations between two or more settings*. In my 1979 monograph, I pointed out that such intersetting linkages could take a number of forms, among them the participation of the same persons in more than one setting, communications between settings, and the availability of information in one setting about the other. The preceding propositions dealing with the macrosystem call attention to yet another key dimension of relations between settings. The domain constitutes the focus of the next proposition.

Proposition 4.

The nature and power of developmental processes at the level of the meso-
or the exosystem are influenced to a substantial degree by the belief systems and expectations existing in each setting about the other. Provision
for assessing such bidirectional orientations should therefore be incorporated as a key element in research designs involving the relation between two settings.

Existing empirical evidence for the above proposition is as yet only indirect,
being based solely on research findings, such as those previously cited, indicating the developmental importance of belief systems, first at the personal and then
at the cultural level. Despite the extensive research literature in such areas as the
relation between family and day care, home and school, school and peer group,
and family and workplace, I have been unable to find any study that systematically addressed the issue of intersetting beliefs and expectations.

I turn next to a set of three propositions pertaining to the microsystem. As the
reader will observe, all of them reflect, and indeed follow from, the four principles (and their associated design corollaries) that emerged from the effort
above to construct a tentative topology of the developmentally-relevant characteristics of the person.

Proposition 5.

In a microsystem paradigm, the developing person is viewed as an active
agent who inevitably plays some part in any developmental process taking
place in the microsystem. Any research design for a microsystem must
therefore take this active role into account. In addition, the scientific power
of a microsystem model is enhanced to the extent that it provides for each
of the following:

- the assessment of cognitive competence, socioemotional attributes, and con-
  text-relevant belief systems of the developing person, with particular emphasis on those qualities that meet criteria for being characterized as
  developmentally-instigative.
- the assessment and interpretation of personal characteristics from the differing viewpoints of the person herself, familiar significant others in the setting, and a trained observer, as well as from the perspective of the culture(s)
  and subculture(s) in which the developing person has been raised and has
  lived.

Proposition 6.

The developmental processes taking place within a setting can vary substantially as a function of the personal attributes of significant others present in the setting. Of particular significance are qualities of others that are developmentally-instigative for the subject. The scientific power of a microsystem model is therefore further increased to the extent that such characteristics are assessed.

Proposition 7.

Each member of a microsystem influences every other member. In terms of research design, it is therefore important to take into consideration the influence of each relationship on other relationships; for example, within the family the effect of the husband-wife relationship on the parent-child relationship, the effect of the mother-child relationship on the father-child relationship, and vice versa.[30] The appropriate design for this purpose is a process-person-context model in which each relationship is treated as a context for processes taking place in the other.[31]

The eighth and final proposition is all-pervasive, for it invokes a parameter that is critical to the functioning of every ecological system in all of its parts. I refer to *the stability and predictability of the system's operation.* In short, does the system operate consistently over time? The most extensive evidence bearing on this issue comes from a longitudinal study conducted by the Finnish psychologist, Lea Pulkkinen. Beginning when the children were eight years of age, she investigated the effect of environmental stability and change on the development of children through adolescence and young adulthood. The "steadiness" versus "unsteadiness" of family living conditions was measured by the frequency of such events as the following: the number of family moves, changes in day care or school arrangements, extent of family absence, incidence of divorce and remarriage, and altered conditions of maternal employment. Greater instability in the family environment was associated with greater submissiveness, aggressiveness, anxiety, and social problems among children in later childhood and adolescence, leading to higher risks of violence and criminal behavior in early adulthood (Polkkinen, 1983; Pulkkinen & Saastamoinen, 1986). Moreover, the factor of stability of family living conditions appeared to be a stronger determinant of subsequent development than was the family's socioeconomic status.

Other findings pointing to the disruptive effect of environmental instability on developmental processes come from a variety of sources. For example, in her classic study of the developmental seqelae of low birth weight (see above pp. 195–198), Drillien investigated the role of what she called "family stress" in increasing the risk that the child would experience subsequent problems in development. Her index of stress was quite similar to that developed by Pulkkinen a decade later in Finland, including such items as divorce or separation, employment of the mother, and placement of the child in a residential nursery. (Pulkkinen does not seem to have been familiar with Drillien's earlier investigation). When related to behavioral outcomes, Drillien's measure of family stress proved to be an even stronger predictor of developmental problems than socioeconomic status. In particular, the tendency of children of low birth weight to exhibit problem behavior in school was especially strong for those youngsters who had grown up in unstable family environments.

Analogous findings for the contemporary American scene were obtained by Moorehouse (1986) in a study of how stability vs. change over time in the mother's work status during the child's preschool years affected patterns of mother-child communication, and how these patterns in turn influenced the child's achievement and social behavior in the first year of school. A key analysis involved a comparison between mothers who had maintained the same employment status over the period of the study, and those who had changed in either direction: that is, to working more hours, fewer hours, or none at all. The results revealed that significant effects of work status were pronounced only in the group that had changed their working status. Although the disruptive impact was greatest among those mothers who had moved into full time employment, it was still present even for those who had reduced their working hours or had left the labor force. Moorehouse concluded that "instability, on the whole, is associated with less favorable school outcomes than stability" (p. 103).

Further support for this conclusion emerged from a reanalysis of data reported in the previously-cited study by Dornbusch and his colleagues (1987). The results indicated that by far the lowest school grades were obtained by adolescents whose parents had exhibited mixed or inconsistent child rearing styles. At the same time, there is evidence from this same investigation that too much rigidity in a given system may also lead to developmental dysfunction. The reader will recall that, in the reported results, the poorest performance was shown by adolescents whose parents consistently exhibited an authoritarian pattern of child rearing, a result in accord with the earlier findings of Baumrind (see above p. 231). At a broader level, an investigation conducted in rural and urban areas of Switzerland (Meili & Steiner, 1965; Vatter, 1981) indicated that the superior cognitive functioning observed in city children was a function of the richer and more diversified environment typifying the urban scene. Not only were these results independent of social class, but the community factors exerted a stronger influence than intrafamilial variables.

Such findings point to some optimal middle ground between extreme fluidity of systems, on the one hand, and extreme rigidity, on the other. This point is incorporated in the following proposition.

Proposition 8.

The degree of stability, consistency, and predictability over time in any element of level of the systems constituting an ecology of human development is critical for the effective operation of the system in question. Extremes either of disorganization or rigidity in structure of function represent danger signs for potential psychological growth, with some intermediate degree of system flexibility constituting the optimal condition for human development. In terms of research design, this proposition points to the importance of assessing the degree of stability vs. instability, both with respect to characteristics of the person and of context, at each level of the ecological system.

Some readers may regard the preceding proposition as too indeterminate to warrant scientific status, particularly as the final statement in a series of precepts defining directions for future research. In response, I can do no better then quote the succinct and elegant answer given to this same question by the philosopher of language, John Searle: "It is a condition of the adequacy of a precise theory of an indeterminate phenomenon that it should precisely characterize that phenomenon as indeterminate" (Searle, 1983).

Retrospect and prospect. The preceding series of proposition marks the completion of the task undertaken in this chapter. How close has the effort come to achieving its aim? One way to answer this question is to look again at out disembodied Lewinian equation, and ask to what extent it is now possible to substitute concrete substance for the empty symbols. Here, once again, is the reformulated formula:

$$D_t = f_{(t-p)} (PE)_{(t-p)}$$

At first glance, it would appear that all is well. In every domain, including the previously neglected sphere of properties of the person, there is now much material. Indeed, the supply may even exceed the demand; there may not be enough researchers to go round. All any one of them need do is to choose a research question that fits the magic paradigm, apply the mighty process-person-context model—perhaps even with a timely chronosystem component—and a rich research reward is sure to come.

But that is only on the first glance. Alas, a second look reveals a new lacuna. The all-essential key to scientific discovery is missing. In all the preceding pages, what is there to substitute for the fateful "f" in the formula? What is the *process* that person and context are to generate? The original monograph of a decade ago contained no less than 50 hypotheses—all neat and numbered. The hopeful reader who looks back through the preceding pages will find nary a one. The task, however, is not being neglected; it is the subject of a book manuscript to which this chapter is but a prologue. I offer the prologue now, in advance, in the hope that others too may be moved to get into the act. "The play's the thing."

ACKNOWLEDGMENTS

The author is indebted to a number of his colleagues at Cornell and elsewhere for their constructive criticisms and suggestions on earlier drafts of this chapter. Particular appreciation is expressed to Stephen Ceci, who, in the course of our collaboration in research and many conversations in between, has contributed more than I can any longer distinguish to the ideas developed here, especially in Section IV.

NOTES

1. Bronfenbrenner, U. (1982, 1985a, 1985b, 1986a, 1986b, 1986c, 1987, 1988a, 1988b, 1988c); Bronfenbrenner & Crouter (1983); Bronfenbrenner, U., Kessel, F., Kessen, W., & White, S. (1986); Bronfenbrenner, Moen, & Garbarino, 1985; Silbereisen (1986).

2. What is being criticized here is the failure to give adequate consideration to the developmental impact of the person *in contemporary ecological research*. Personal characteristics have of course received an enormous amount of attention in traditional studies of personality development, but relatively few such investigations have been conducted in an ecological perspective. A number of researches that do examine the *joint* contribution of person and context to development are cited below.

3. The exposition that follows draws on and extends a formulation first introduced in Bronfenbrenner (1988a).

4. The issue here raised is one that Lewin himself never fully addressed, or—perhaps putting it more precisely—it is an issue that he finessed by defining psychology as an ahistorical science. Lewin's failure to include this factor in his formula was not accidental, but deliberate. In his view, science was by its very nature ahistorical. In psychology as in physics, he argued, present events can be influenced only by forces existing in the present situation. In psychology, however, the latter consisted of what Lewin called the "psychological field"; that is, the situation defined not objectively but as perceived by the person. Hence, historical events could become "field forces" only to the extent that they existed in the person's present awareness. It was perhaps Lewin's predilection for the paradigms of physics, and their ahistorical orientation, that led him, and many other psychologists as well, to be far more interested in the study of behavior than of development. (For further discussion of these issues see Bronfenbrenner (1951); Lewin (1931, 1951).

5. Henceforth, the term "paradigm" will be used to refer to the *conceptual* definition of the general paradigm or any of its components, whereas the term "model" will be applied to denote *operational* definitions of these concepts.

6. Although the social address model has limited scientific utility, it is useful as a marker for identifying what I have called *macrosystems*, overarching environmental structures at the level of the culture and subculture that define the nature of more proximal systems (see section V. below).

7. For more detailed discussion of the nature, uses, and limitations of social address and personal attribute models see Bronfenbrenner and Crouter (1983) and Bronfenbrenner (in press).

8. See above, pp. 192–193.

9. It is an interesting question whether the effects are as severe today, given the subsequent progress in scientific knowledge and treatment strategies. Unfortunately, the absence of comparable data does not permit an answer.

10. The analysis involved comparing the children's school performance to what would have been expected on the basis of their scores on an intelligence test.

11. Regrettably, the analyses did not include any breakdown by sex of child.

12. For additional discussion of these issues see Rutter (in press).

13. The term "chronosystem," which characterizes a particular type of research design, is not to

be confused, through "clang association" with a series of concepts employed in the 1979 monograph, as well as later in this chapter, to differentiate various types of environmental systems (micro-, meso-, exo-, and macro-) that serve as contexts of development (see Section V. below). The chronosystem is a methodological construct; the remaining four are theoretical, but can also become substantive when put to empirical use.

14. For a summary of Elder's original studies, see Bronfenbrenner, 1979, pp. 273–284.

15. For reviews see Bullinger and Chatillon (1983), Case (1985), Gelman and Baillargeon (1983).

16. For a comprehensive review of this literature see Rest, J. R. (1983).

17. The same consideration also applies to more objective measures of ability and achievement to the extent that the individual's scores become known to teachers or superiors, or are used as the basis for selection or recommendation. Such possibilities are often not taken into account by researchers, especially in the interpretation of measures of mental ability.

18. The theory was first introduced to American psychologists in the late 1920s in a series of two articles, both under the same title, in the *Journal of Genetic Psychology*. The first article was authored by Luria (1928), the second by Vygotsky himself (Vygotsky, 1929).

19. In a preface to the English edition of the full report of the research, Luria indicates that the original idea for the study was suggested by Vygotsky (see Luria, 1979, p. v.).

20. The publication of the study in the Soviet Union was held up for more than three decades. The reasons for the delay are described by Michael Cole in his preface to the American edition: "The status of national minorities has long been a sensitive issue in the USSR (not unlike the issue of ethnic minorities in the United States). It was all well and good to show that uneducated, traditional peasants quickly learned the modes of thought characteristics of industrialized socialist peoples, but it was definitely not acceptable to say anything that could be interpreted as negative about these people at a time when their participation in national life was still so tenuous (for source, see Luria, 1978, p. xiv).

21. A promising strategy for future work in both of these is the application of what I have called meso- and exosystem models that link the family to other principal contexts of development such as school, peer group, and the parents' workplace (see below, pp. 225, 235; also Bronfenbrenner 1986c, 1986d).

22. For a comprehensive review of this literature see Rest, J. R. (1983).

23. For documentation see Plant, J. S. (1937) and Kluckhohn, C. Murray, H. A. (1948, 1952).

24. This revised definition, along with that for the macrosystem to follow, has important implications for research design. Because these implications involve research models that relate systems-properties of the environment to characteristics of the person, specification of these designs is deferred to the final section of this chapter, which deals with paradigms and models for future research.

25. In a sense, a place for this feature was accorded in the original definition of macrosystem through reference to "belief systems or ideology" [See reference #1, p. 26]. But the reference was little more than that, since no implications were spelled out.

26. For reviews of the research literature on both of these new family forms, see Bronfenbrenner & Crouter (1982), and Hetherington, Cox, & Cox (1982).

27. Often this last seemingly basic feature is left unspecified; the text will merely state that a given hypothesis was (or was not) supported after control for a set of background variables, without indicating whether the latter had any effects and what they were.

28. The raw (unstandardized) regression coefficient measures the change in the dependent variable for each unit change in the independent variable, irrespective of the degree of variation in the latter. In short, it may be thought of as measuring "the bang for the buck." Ordinarily, this statistic is not useful for purposes of comparison, since regression coefficients are specific to the particular pair of independent and dependent variables involved. In the present instance, however, the same vari-

ables appear at each education level. Hence, it becomes possible to compare the relative impact of each environmental factor in the two education groups.

29.   Support for this tentative hypothesis also emerged in an analysis of the effects of mother-infant interaction on the child's subsequent adjustment upon entering school. The mother's joint activity with her baby at age three significantly facilitated early school performance and behavior, but only in families in which the mother had had some education beyond high school. [See Bronfenbrenner (in press).]

30.   The proposition addresses what I referred to in my 1979 monograph as the *second-order* or *third party* effect, defined as "the indirect effect of third parties on the interaction between members of a dyad." (See Bronfenbrenner 1979, pp. 68, 77–81.)

31.   For discussion of statistical models appropriate to this design, see Bronfenbrenner (in press).

REFERENCES

Allport, G. W. (1937). *Personality: A psychosocial interpretation*. New York: Holt.

Allport, G. W. (1937). *Personality: A psychosocial interpretation* (p. 54). New York: Holt.

Baldwin, A. L. (1947). Changes in parent behavior during pregnancy. *Child Development, 18*, 29–39.

Bandura, A. (1977). Self-efficacy: Toward a unifying theory of behavior change. *Psychological Review, 84*, 191–215.

Bandura, A. (1982). Self-efficacy mechanism in human agency. *American Psychologist, 37*, 122–147.

Baumrind, D. (1971). Current patterns of parental authority. *Developmental Psychology Monograph 4*, 1–103.

Baumrind, D. (1973). The development of instrumental competence through socialization. In A. D. Pick (Ed.), *Minnesota symposium on child psychology* (Vol. 7, pp. 3–46). Minneapolis: University of Minnesota Press.

Baumrind, D. & Black, A. E. (1967). Socialization practice associated with dimensions of competence in preschool boys and girls. *Child Development, 38*, 291–327.

Bee, H. L., Barnard, K. E., Eyres, S. J., Gray, C. A., Hammond, M. A., Spietz, A. L., Snyder, C., & Clark, B. C. (1982). Prediction of IQ and language skill from perinatal status, child performance, family characteristics, and mother-infant interaction. *Child Development, 53*, 1134–1156.

Blau, Z. B. (1981). *Black children/white children: Competence, socialization, and social structure* (p. 94). New York: Free Press.

Block, J. H. & Block J. (1980). The role of ego-control and ego-resiliency in the organization of behavior. In W. A. Collins (Ed.), *Minnesota Symposia on Child Psychology, 13*, 39–101. Hillsdale, N.J.: Erlbaum.

Block, J., Block, J. H., & Keyes, S. (1988). Longitudinally foretelling drug usage in adolescence: Early childhood personality and environmental precursors. *Child Development, 59*, 336–355.

Bradley, R. H. & Caldwell, B. M. (1977). Home observation for measurement of the environment: a validation study of screening efficiency. *American Journal of Mental Deficiency, 81*, 417–420.

Bronfenbrenner, U. (1951). Toward an integrated theory of personality. In R. R. Blake & G. V. Ramsey (Eds.), *Perception: An approach to personality* (pp. 206–257). New York: Ronald Press (see especially pp. 210–216).

Bronfenbrenner, U. (1979). *The ecology of human development*. Cambridge: Mass.: Harvard University Press.

Bronfenbrenner, U. (1982). Child development: The hidden revolution. In *National Research Council: Issues and studies*. (pp. 41–45). Washington, D. C.: National Academy Press.

Bronfenbrenner U. (1985a). Midtveis i den menneskelige utviklings okologi (The ecology of human development in mid-passage). In I. Bö (Ed.), *Barn i miljo (Children in the environment)* (pp. 36–69). Oslo: J. W. Cappelens Forlag.

Bronfenbrenner, U. (1985b). Contextos de crianza del nino. Problemas y prospectiva. *Infancia y Aprendizaje, 29*, 41–55.

Bronfenbrenner, U. (1986a). Recent advances in research on human development. In R. K. Silbereisen, K. Eyferth, & G. Rudinger (Eds.), *Development as action in context: Problem behavior and normal youth development* (pp. 287–309). Heidelberg and New York: Springer-Verlag.

Bronfenbrenner, U. (1986b) Dix années de recherche sur l'écologie du développment humain. In M. Crahay & D. Lafontaine (Eds.), *L'art et la science de l'enseignement* (pp. 283–301). Bruxelles: Editions Labor.

Bronfenbrenner, U. (1986c). Ecology of the family as a context for human development. *Developmental Psychology, 22,* 723–742.

Bronfenbrenner, U. (1986d). Alienation and the four worlds of children. *Phi Delta Kappan, 67,* 430–436.

Bronfenbrenner, U. (1987). La cambiante ecologia de la infancia. Implicaciones en el terreno del la ciencia y de la accion. In A. Alvarez (Ed.). *Psicologia y education. Realizaciones y tendencias actuales en la investigacion y en la practica* (pp. 44–56). Madrid: Mec y Visor Libros.

Bronfenbrenner, U. (1988a). Interacting systems in human development: Research paradigms: Present and future. In N. Bolger, A. Caspi, G. Downey, & M. Moorehouse (Eds.), *Persons in context: Developmental processes* (pp. 25–49). New York: Cambridge University Press.

Bronfenbrenner, U. (1988b). Foreword. In A. R. Pence (Ed.), *Ecological research with children and families* (pp. ix–xix). New York: Columbia University Teachers' College Press.

Bronfenbrenner, U. (1988c). Paradoxes of prenatal care: A case for vitality from our vital statistics. *Early Childhood Update 4,* 2–7.

Bronfenbrenner, U. & Crouter, A. C. (1982). Work and family through time and space. In Kamerman, S. B. & Hayes, C. D. (Eds.), *Families that work: Children in a changing world* (pp. 39–83). Washington, D.C.: National Academy Press.

Bronfenbrenner, U. & Crouter, A. C. (1983). The evolution of environmental models in developmental research. In P. H. Mussen (Ed.), *Handbook of child psychology: Vol. I. History, theory, and methods* (W. Kessen, Volume editor) (pp. 357–414). New York: Wiley.

Bronfenbrenner, U. Kessel, F., Kessen, W., & White, S. (1986). Toward a critical history of developmental psychology. *American Psychologist, 41,* 1218–1230.

Bronfenbrenner, U., Moen, P., & Garbarino, J. (1982). Child, family, and community. In R. D. Parke (Ed.). *Review of child development research. Vol. 7: The family* (pp. 283–328). Chicago: University of Chicago Press.

Brown, A. L., Bransford, J. D., Ferrara, R. A., & Campione, J. C. (1983). Learning, remembering, and understanding. In P. H. Mussen (Ed.), *Handbook of child psychology: Vol. III. Cognitive Development* (J. H. Flavell and E. M. Markman, Volume editors) (pp. 77–166). New York: Wiley.

Bullinger, A. & Chatillon, J. F. Recent theory and research of the Genevan school. (1983). In P. H. Mussen (Ed.), *Handbook of child psychology: Vol. III. Cognitive Development* (J. H. Flavell and E. M. Markman, Volume editors) (pp. 231–262). New York: Wiley.

Campbell, D. T., & Fiske, D. W. (1959). Convergent and discriminant validation by the multitrait-multimethod matrix. *Psychological Bulletin, 56,* 81–105.

Campos, J. J., Caplovitz, C., Lamb, M. E., Goldsmith, H. H., & Stenberg, C. (1983). Socioemotional development. In P. H. Mussen (Ed.), *Handbook of child psychology: Fourth Edition: Vol II.* (p. 832). N.Y. Wiley.

Carraher, T. N., Carraher, D. W., & Schliemann, A. D. (1985). Mathematics in the streets and in schools. *British Journal of Developmental Psychology, 3,* 21–29.

Case, R. (1985). *Intellectual development birth to adulthood.* Orlando, Fla.: Academic Press.

Caspi, A., Elder, G. H., Jr., & Bem, D. J. (1987). Moving against the world: Life-course patterns of explosive children. *Developmental Psychology, 22,* 303–308.

Caspi, A., Elder, G. H., Jr., & Bem, D. J. (in press). Moving away from the world: Life-course patterns of shy children. *Developmental Psychology 24,* 824–831.

Catto-Smith, A. G., Yu, V. Y., Bajusk, B. Orgill, A. A. & Astbuty, J. (1985). Effect of neonatial periventricular haemorrhage on neurodevelopmental outcomes. *Archive of Disease in Childhood, 60*, 8–11.

Ceci, S. H. (in press). *On intelligence: A bioecological view of intellectual development.* Cambridge, Mass.: Harvard University Press.

Ceci, S. J. & Bronfenbrenner, U. (1985). "Don't forget to take the cupcakes out of the oven": Prospective memory, strategic time-monitoring, and context. *Child Development, 56*, 150–165.

Ceci, S. J., Bronfenbrenner, U. & Baker, J. G. (1988). Memory in context: The case of prospective memory. In F. Weinert & M. Perlmutter (Eds.), *Universals and changes in memory development* (pp. 243–256). Hillsdale, N.J.: Erlbaum.

Ceci, S. J. & Liker, J. (1986). A day at the races: IQ, expertise, and cognitive complexity. *Journal of Experimental Psychology: General, 115*, 255–266.

Clarke, A. M. & Alan, D. B. (1988). The adult outcome of early behavioral abnormalities. *International Journal of Behavioral Development, 11*, 3–19.

Clausen, J. A. (1986). *The life course: A sociological perspective.* Englewood Cliffs, NJ: Prentice-Hall.

Cole, M. J., Gay, J., Glick, J., & Sharp, D. W. (1971). *The cultural context of learning and thinking.* New York: Basic Books.

Cole, M. & Scribner, S. (1974). *Culture and thought.* New York: Wiley.

Cottrell, L. S. (1942). The analysis of situational fields in social psychology. *American Sociological Review, 7*, 370–382.

Crockenberg, S. B. (1981). Infant irritability, other responsiveness, and social support influences on the security of infant-mother attachment. *Child Development, 52*, 857–865.

Dornbusch, S. M., Ritter, P. L., Leiderman, P. H., Roberts, D. F., and Fraleigh, M. J. (1987). The relation of parenting style to adolescent school performance. *Child Development, 58*, 1244–1257.

Drillien, C. M. (1957). The social and economic factors affecting the incidence of premature birth. *Journal of Obstetrical Gynaecology, British Empire, 64*, 161–184.

Drillien, C. M. (1964). *The growth and development of the prematurely born infant.* Edinburgh and London: E. & S. Livingston Ltd.

Elder, G. H., Jr. (1974). *Children of the Great Depression.* Chicago: University of Chicago Press.

Elder, G. H., Jr. (1985). Perspectives on the life course. In G. H. Elder, Jr. (Ed.), *Life course dynamics* (pp. 23–49). Ithaca, N.Y.: Cornell University Press.

Elder, G. H., Jr. & Caspi, A. (1988). Stressful times in children's loves. In N. Bolger, A. Caspi, G. Downey, & M. Moorehouse (Eds.), *Persons in context: Developmental processes* (pp. 77–113). New York: Cambridge University Press.

Elder, G. H., Jr., Caspi, A., & Downey, G. (1986). Problem behavior and family relationships: Life course and intergenerational themes. In A. Sørensen, F. Weinert, & L. Sherrod (Eds.), *Human development and the life course: Multidisciplinary prespectives* (pp. 293–340). Hillsdale, N.J.: Erlbaum.

Elder, G. H., Jr., Van Nguyen, T. V., & Caspi, A. (1985). Linking family hardship to children's lives. *Child Development, 56*, pp. 361–375.

Gelman, R., & Baillargeon, R. (1983). A review of some Piagetian concepts. (1983). In P. H. Mussen (Ed.), *Handbook of child psychology: Vol. III. Cognitive Development* (J. H. Flavell and E. M. Markman, Volume editors) (pp. 167–230). New York: Wiley.

Hetherington, E. M., Cox, M., & Cox. (1982). Effects of divorce on parents and children. In M. Lamb (Ed.), *Nontraditional families* (pp. 233–288). Hillsdale, N.J.: Erlbaum Associates.

Hinde, R. A. & Tobin, C. (1986). Temperament at home and behavior at preschool. In G. A. Kohnstamm (Ed.), *Temperament discussed* (pp. 123–132). Holland: Swets & Zeitlinger.

Jones, W. H., & Briggs, S. R. (1984). The self-other discrepancy in social shyness. In R. Schwarzer (Ed.), *The self in anxiety, stress, and depression* (pp. 93–108). Amsterdam: North Holland.

Kagan, J., Moss, H. A., & Sigel, I. E. (1963). Psychological significance of styles of conceptualization. (pp. 73–124). In J. C. Wright, & J. Kagan (Eds.) *Basic cognitive processes in children. Monographs of the Society for Research in Child Development, 28* (2, Serial No. 86).

Kawi, A. A. & Pasamanick, B. (1959). Prenatal and paranatal factors in the development of childhood reading disorders. *Monographs of the Society for Research in Child Development, 24* (4, Serial No. 74).

Kogan, N. A. (1973). *Creativity and cognitive style: A life-span perspective.* In P. B. Baltes & K. W. Schaie (Eds.), *Life span developmental psychology: Personality and socialization* (pp. 146–180). New York: Academic Press.

Kogan, N. A. (1983). Stylistic variation in childhood and adolescence. P. H. Mussen (Ed.), *Handbook of child psychology: Vol. III. Cognitive Development* (pp. 695–706). New York: John Wiley.

Laboratory of Comparative Human Cognition (1983). *Handbook of child psychology: Vol. I. History, theory, and methods* (W. Kessen, Volume editor) (pp. 295–356). New York: Wiley.

Lancy, D. F. & Strathern, A. J. (1981). Making two's: Pairing as an alternative to the taxonomic mode of representation. *American Anthropologist, 83,* 773–795.

Lave, J. (1977). Tailor-made experiments and evaluating the intellectual consequences of apprenticeship training. *The Quarterly Newsletter of the Institute for Comparative Human Development, 1,* 1–3.

Lave, J. Murtaugh, M., & de la Roche, D. (1984). The dialectic of arithmetic in grocery shopping. In B. Rogoff & J. Lave (Eds.), *Everyday cognition: Its development in social context.* Cambridge, Mass: Harvard University Press.

Leontiev, A. N. (1932). The development of voluntary attention in the child. *Journal of Genetic Psychology, 40,* 52–83.

Leontiev, A. N. (1959). *Problemy razvitiya psikhiki [Problems of mental development].* Moscow: Izdatel'stvo Moskovskogo Gosudarstvennogo Universiteta. Published in English as *Problems in the development of mind.* Moscow: Progress Publishers, 1982.

Leontiev, A. N. (1975). *Deytel'nost', soznanie, lichnost' [Activity, consciousness, personality].* Leningrad: Izdatel'stvo Polilticheskoi Literaturi. Published in English as *Activity, consciousness, personality.* Englewood Cliffs, N.J.: Prentice-Hall, 1978.

Lewin, K. (1931). The conflict between Aristotelian and Galilean modes of thought in contemporary psychology. *Journal of Genetic Psychology, 5,* 141–177.

Lewin, K. (1935). *A dynamic theory of personality.* New York: McGraw-Hill.

Lewin, K. (1951). *Field theory in social science.* New York: Harper & Brothers.

Luria, A. R. (1928). The problem of the cultural behavior of the child. *Journal of Genetic Psychology, 35,* 493–506.

Luria, A. R. (1931). Psychological expedition to Central Asia. *Science, 74,* 383–384.

Luria, A. R. (1976). *Cognitive development.* Cambridge, Mass: Harvard University Press.

Luria, A. R. (1978). *Cognitive development: Its cultural and social foundations.* Cambridge, Mass: Harvard University Press.

Luria, A. R. (1979). *The making of mind.* Cambridge, Mass: Harvard University Press.

Luria, A. R. (1982). *Language and cognition.* New York: Wiley Intersciences.

Matheny, A. P., Jr., Wilson, R. S., Dolan, A. B., & Krantz, J. Z. (1981). *Child Development, 52,* 579–588.

Mead, G. H. (1934). *Mind, self, and society.* Chicago: University of Chicago Press.

Meili, R. & Steiner, H. (1965). Eine Untersuchung zum Intelligenzniveau elfjähriger der deutschen Schweitz. *Schweizerische Zeitschrift für Psychologie und ihre Anwendungen, 24*(1), 23–32.

Messick, S. (1983). Assessment of children. In P. H. Mussen (Ed.), *Handbook of child psychology: Vol. I. History, theory, and methods* (W. Kessen, Volume editor) (pp. 477–526). New York: Wiley.

Moorehouse, M. (1986). *The relationships among continuity in maternal employment, parent-child communicative activities, and the child's school competence.* Unpublished doctoral dissertation. Cornell University, Ithaca, N.Y.

Murtaugh, M. (1985). The practice of arithmetic by American grocery shoppers. *Anthropology and Education Quarterly,* Fall.

Newman. R. S. (1984). Children's achievement and self-evaluations in mathematics: A longitudinal study. *Journal of Educational Psychology, 76,* 857–873.

Plant, J. S. (1937). *Personality and the cultural pattern.* New York: Commonwealth Fund.
Plomin, R. & Nesselrode, J. R. (in press). Behavior genetics and personality change. *Journal of Personality.*
Plomin, R. & Rowe, D. C. (1979). Genetic and environmental etiology of social behavior in infancy. *Developmental Psychology, 15,* 62.
Pulkkinen, L. (1983). Finland: The search for alternatives to aggression. In A. P. Goldstein & M. Segall (Eds.), *Aggression in global perspective* (pp. 104–144). New York: Pergamon Press.
Pulkkinen, L. & Saastamoinen, M. (1986). Cross-cultural perspectives on youth violence. In S. J. Apter & A. P. Goldstein (Eds.), *Youth violence: Programs and prospects* (pp. 262–281). New York: Pergamon Press.
Rest, J. R. (1983). Morality. In P. H. Mussen (Ed.), *Handbook of child psychology: Fourth Edition: Vol III.* (pp. 556–629). N.Y. Wiley.
Rivers, W. H. R. (1926). *Psychology and ethnology.* New York: Harcourt, Brace.
Rotter, J. (1966). Generalized expectancies for internal versus external locus of control of reinforcement. *Psychological Monographs: General and Applied, 80,* 1–28.
Scribner, S. and Cole (1981). *The psychology of literacy.* Cambridge, Mass.: Harvard University Press.
Searle, J. (1983, Oct. 27). The world turned upside down (p. 79). *New York Review of Books* (pp. 74–79).
Silbereisen, R. K. (1986). Entwicklung und ökologischer Kontext: Wissenschaftsgeschichte im Spiegel persönlicher Erfahrung—Ein Interview mit Urie Bronfenbrenner (Development in ecological context: History of psychological science through the mirror of personal experience—an interview with Urie Bronfenbrenner). *Psychologische Erziehung und Unterricht, 33,* 241–249.
Stewart, A. (1983). Severe perinatal hazards. In M. L. Rutter (Ed.), *Developmental neuropsychiatry.* New York: Guilford Press.
Super, C. M. (1980). Cognitive development: Looking across at growing up. In C. Super & M. Harkness (Eds.), *New directions for child development: Anthropological perspectives on child development, 8,* 59–69.
Thomas, W. I. (1927). *The unadjusted girl.* Boston: Little, Brown.
Thomas, W. I. & Thomas, D. S. (1928). *The child in America.* New York: Knopf.
Thomas, W. I. & Znaniecki, F. (1927). *The Polish peasant in Europe and America.* Chicago: University of Chicago Press.
Tulkin, S. R. (1973). Social class differences in infants' reactions to mother's and stranger's voices. *Developmental Psychology, 8*(1), 137.
Tulkin, S. R. (1977). Social class differences in maternal and infant behavior. In P. H. Leiderman, A. Rosenfeld, & S. R. Tulkin (Eds.). *Culture and infancy.* New York: Academic Press, 495–537.
Tulkin, S. R. & Cohler, B. J. (1973). Child-rearing attitudes and mother-child interaction in the first year of life. *Merrill-Palmer Quarterly, 19,* 95–106.
Tulkin, S. R. & Covitz, F. E. (1975). *Mother-infant interaction and intellectual functioning at age six.* Paper presented at the meeting of the Society for Research in Child Development, Denver.
Tulkin, S. R. & Kagan, J. (1972). Mother-child interaction in the first year of life. *Child Development, 43,* 31–41.
Vatter, M. (1981). Intelligenz und regionale Herkunft. Eine Langsschnittstudie im Kanton Bern. In A. H. Walter (Ed.), *Region und Sozialisation* (Volume I. pp. 56–91). Stuttgart: Frommann-Holzboog.
Vygotsky, L. S. (1929). II. The problem of the cultural development of the child. *Journal of Genetic Psychology, 36,* 415–434.
Vygotsky, L. S. (1978). *Mind in society.* Cambridge, Mass.: Harvard University Press.
Werner, E. E. & Smith, R. S. (1982). *Vulnerable but invincible.* New York: McGraw-Hill.
Whiting, B. B. & Whiting J. W. M. (1975). *Children of six cultures: A psychocultural analysis.* Cambridge, Mass.: Harvard University Press.
Whiting, J. W. M. & Whiting, B. B. (1973). Altruistic and egoistic behavior in six cultures. In L.

Nader & T. W. Maretzki (Eds.), *Cultural illness and health: Essays in human adaptation.* Washington, D.C.: American Anthropological Association, 1973.

Witkin, H., Dyk, R. B., Faterson, H. F., Goodenough, D. R., & Karp, S. A. (1962). *Psychological differentiation.* New York: Wiley.

ETHOLOGICAL AND RELATIONSHIPS APPROACHES

Robert A. Hinde

INTRODUCTION

The futility of a dichotomy between the biological and social aspects of human nature is now generally recognized. Nevertheless many research workers still place their main emphasis either on biological or on social factors as the primary determinants of human development, and the means for a synthesis have been hard to find. However a route offering considerable promise is now beginning to appear. This results from a combination of "ethological" and "relationships" approaches to child development.

Ethology had its roots in the study of animal behavior. Although direct parallels between human and animal behavior are usually misleading, the orienting attitudes of ethology and many of its concepts are of considerable importance to child developmentalists. A relationships approach involves the recognition that

Annals of Child Development, Volume 6, pages 251-285.
ISBN: 0-89232-979-3

children must be seen not as isolated entities, but as forming part of a network of social relationships, and requires a delicate balance between conceptions of the child as an individual and as a social being. It has arisen partly from psychology (Duck & Gilmour, 1981; Kelley et al., 1983) and partly from ethological primatology (Hinde, 1976, 1979, 1983; Kummer, 1982).

Many of the contributions of ethology to the study of child development, and the nature of a relationships approach, have been reviewed recently (Hinde, 1983; Hinde & Stevenson-Hinde, 1987a), so no attempt to provide a detailed survey of either has been made here. Rather the pages allocated have been used to highlight some issues that emerge from combining ethological and relationship perspectives, and to consider their implications for future research. First, however, some characteristics of ethology on the one hand, and of the relationships approach on the other, must be sketched briefly.

THE ORIENTING ATTITUDES OF ETHOLOGY

Although ethology started with the observational study of animal behavior in natural or near-natural conditions, it is limited neither to the study of animals nor (as is too often supposed) to the use of observational methods. However ethologists do put emphasis on the observation and description of behavior as a *preliminary* to its analysis, and on proper consideration of the nature of the units of behavior studied. For example, both ethologists and psychologists—and the distinction is used with reference to an era when it was meaningful, not with any implication that it should now be maintained—have been concerned with the definition of aggressive behavior, and reached similar conclusions about the necessity to subdivide children's aggression (Feshbach, 1970; Manning, Heron, & Marshall, 1978). Now ethologists are suggesting an additional step, arguing that further light can be thrown on the sub-categories by the recognition that they are motivationally complex. Thus while "specific" or "instrumental" aggression is due to both acquisitive and aggressive motivations, "teasing" or "hostile" aggression results primarily from aggressive motivation, possibly coupled with a desire to enhance the actor's status (in the eyes of the actor him or herself, if not in the eyes of peers) (Attili & Hinde, 1986). No doubt further analysis will be necessary as research progresses.

While emphasizing that behavior must be first described and then analyzed through successive levels of behavioral and physiological complexity, ethologists insist that it is also necessary constantly to be aware of the relations between those levels, and to resynthesize the products of analysis to compare them with the starting point. We shall see how this principle applies to the study of social behavior in a later section.

In discussing development, ethologists have placed much emphasis on the *mutual* influences between organism and environment at every stage. For instance, female canaries build nests under the influence of changing daylengths and temperature. These external factors induce hormonal changes that lead to changes in responsiveness to external stimuli (e.g., male courtship) and in behavior (nest-building). The latter results in new external stimuli (from the nest), and there are concomitant hormone-induced changes in sensitivity to those stimuli (breast tactile sensitivity) that induce further changes in behavior (e.g., in selection of further nest material) and in hormonal state, which in turn have further consequences (Hinde, 1965). The relations between the child and the various influences that impinge upon him/her are certainly no less complicated.

The founders of ethology, who were biologists, emphasized the study of fixed action patterns (i.e., more or less stereotyped movement patterns that were characteristic of the species), because of their value for taxonomy. This has led to the erroneous view that ethologists were primarily interested in "fixed" aspects of behavior. In practice, from the earliest days ethologists have been interested in learning processes, but they do not regard these as impinging on an undifferentiated background. Rather, as discussed in a later section, the importance of constraints on and predispositions for learning is emphasized. A recent discussion of ethological views on development is given by Bateson (in prep.).

Ethologists are concerned not merely with questions about the immediate causation and development of behavior, but also with its function and evolution. Thus, they might ask not only what makes a child smile, and what is the developmental course of smiling in the individual, but also how did smiling evolve (e.g., what expressive movements in ancestral species did it evolve from), and what were the advantageous consequences of smiling through which natural selection acted in the course of its evolution (e.g., van Hooff, 1972)? We shall later see that questions of evolution and function can provide important new perspectives on human behavior, but are not ubiquitously applicable.

It might be argued that an ethological approach to the study of causation and development, with its roots in the study of animal behavior, was unlikely to be applicable to the study of human behavior. Our possession of a verbal language, the cognitive abilities that that requires and permits, our propensities to teach and to learn, (Premack, personal communication), and the diversification of cultures with their institutions and roles, values and beliefs, these and many other issues surely imply that our behavior is a different kind from that of other species? To some extent that is true, but our behavior depends on psychological mechanisms elaborated during the course of human evolution, and no theory of human behavior could be complete if it did not take that into account. It will indeed be argued that the orienting attitudes of ethology pose new questions and can provide important guidelines to answering old ones in the study of child development.

THE RELATIONSHIPS APPROACH

Data on children's social behavior mostly concern interactions of relatively limited duration between individuals. Most interactions are embedded in longer-term relationships in which each interaction is affected by preceding ones and by expectations about future ones. Such relationships are likely to form part of a network of relationships with more or less clearly defined boundaries such as the family, or the school class (Hinde, 1979).

Each of these levels of social complexity has properties not relevant to lower levels. Thus the behavior of two children in an interaction may mesh or be discordant with each other, but these are properties not relevant to an isolated individual; a relationship may be uniplex, containing interactions of only one type (e.g., some teacher-pupil relationships), or multiplex, containing diverse interactions—a distinction not relevant to interactions; and a group may be structured linearly or centrifocally, properties of patterning not relevant to dyadic relationships. Such properties must be considered as parts of the social setting in which a child lives: the meaning of interactions with peers may depend crucially on whether or not those interactions form part of relationships, and "sociability," in the sense of a propensity to engage in social interaction, is not necessarily associated with the formation of relationships.

Furthermore each of these levels affects and is affected by other levels (Figure 1). Thus the behavior shown in an interaction depends on the characteristics of both individuals involved and, because the participants are affected by past interactions and by expectations of future ones, on the nature of the relationship in which it is embedded. But the nature of a relationship depends on that of its con-

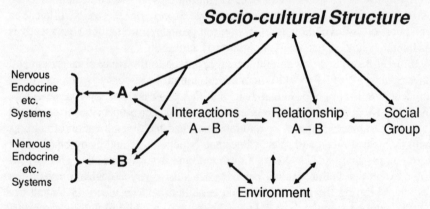

Figure 1. Dialectical relations between successive levels of social complexity. (From Hinde, 1987).

stituent interactions, and in the long run the behavior that individuals can show depends on the interactions and relationships they have experienced in the past. The properties of the family or group affect, and are affected by, those of the constituent relationships on the one hand and of other groups on the other. Thus the successive levels of social complexity are connected by a series of dialectical relations: indeed interactions, relationships and groups are to be seen not as entities but as processes in continuous creation through the agency of these dialectics.

All that has been said so far concerns behavior. But behavior is accompanied by and, one may presume, is determined by, subjective wishes, feelings, needs, and so on. These are related not only to the individual's egocentricity: indeed of special importance in the present context are wishes and feelings related to the relationships and groups of which the individual is a member. In practice we can regard relationships and groups as having two aspects—an objective one, as seen by an outside observer, and a subjective one, existing in the minds of the participants. Important also are the beliefs and values that individuals share (to a greater or lesser extent) with other individuals, and the rights and duties proper to the roles they see themselves as playing in the institutions of their society. We may refer to these institutions with their constituent roles, and to the beliefs, values, myths, legends and so on held in common, as the sociocultural structure of the society. This also has two aspects—objective and subjective, the latter existing in the minds of the individuals of the society, and perhaps taking a slightly different form in each individual. The sociocultural structure must also be seen as a process in continuous creation through dialectical relations with the successive levels of social complexity.

Relationships, groups and certain aspects of the sociocultural structure form the most important part of the environment of individuals, but the physical environment also is important, itself affecting and affected by the behavior of individuals. And all these levels of social complexity, the sociocultural structure and the environment, exist in time, and cannot be fully understood independently of their history.

A relationship approach does not of course demand that one takes all these levels of complexity into account all the time, but it does mean that one must be constantly ready to cross and re-cross the levels as the problem demands. It also means that an understanding of child development requires an appreciation not only of both the biological and the social forces determining its course, but also of the relations between them. It is perhaps natural for the developmental psychologist to take many of the societal influences on child development as givens, but it must be remembered that they have been created by human minds that have themselves been influenced by the forces of natural selection and shaped in a social environment, and a full understanding of the development of individual personality requires also an understanding of the genesis of the social forces that influence its course.

Emphasis on the importance of coming to terms with the properties of dyadic and higher order relationships has come both from ethology and psychology. Ethologists studying nonhuman primates were early forced to recognize that the influences between mother and infant were mutual (Hinde, Rowell, & Spencer-Booth, 1964), that the relationships within a social group affect each other, that social groups may develop their own special properties, that these may be affected by environmental factors, that the development of individuality is affected by early relationships, and so on (e.g., Hinde, 1972, 1983). At the same time psychologists studying the bases of inter-individual attraction came to realize that different principles operated on initial attraction and subsequently (Duck & Miell, 1983), and exchange, interdependence and equity theorists came to focus on the processes involved in dyadic relationships (Homans, 1961; Kelley, 1979; Kelley et al., 1983).

SOME CONSEQUENCES OF ADOPTING A RELATIONSHIPS APPROACH

In this section some special aspects of a relationships approach to child development will be emphasized.

The Initial Data

The initial data on children's social behavior concern interactions. It is crucial to remember that the nature of every interaction (and relationship) depends on both or all of the individuals involved. It is easy to regard how often a child cries as a characteristic of the child, but it depends in part on how quickly the mother goes to it when it does cry. And the latter is not simply a characteristic of the mother, but depends also on how often the child cries. This consideration is relevant also to interview or questionnaire data. Thus temperament dimensions, obtained from a maternal interview or questionnaire, reflect aspects of the mother's behavior as well as that of the child. Stevenson-Hinde (1985) has suggested that it is convenient to think of measures as arranged along a continuum from those concerned solely with individual characteristics to interaction or relationship measures. Height and weight, but few psychological measures, lie at the individual end, though temperament measures would lie nearer to it than to the relationship end, while the reverse would be true for measures of security of attachment.

Given that measures of an interaction or relationship depend on both partners, it is sometimes desirable to separate their roles. This can be done only if the questions being asked are phrased very precisely. Thus the issue of whether changes in a mother or changes in a child are responsible for changes in a given relationship is a different question from whether differences between mothers or differences between children are responsible for differences between mother-child relationships. Some methods are discussed elsewhere (Hinde, 1979).

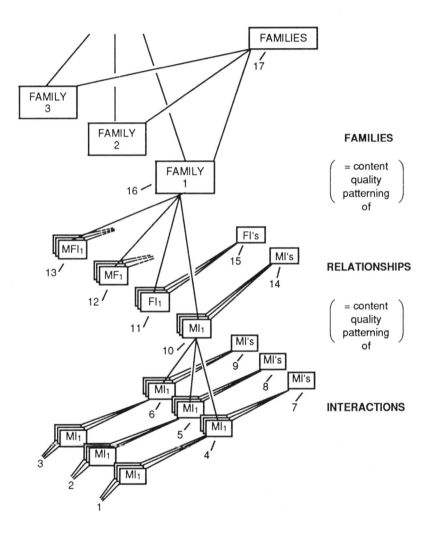

Figure 2. The relations between interactions, relationships and families, illustrating the two routes for generalizations from data on interactions. (In Hinde & Stevenson-Hinde, 1987).

Two Routes to Generalizations from Interactions

In most research in developmental psychology, data are obtained on a particular type of interaction (e.g., mother-infant play) from a number of dyads, and generalizations obtained by pooling data across dyads. Thus studies of the relations between particular independent variables (e.g., sex or age of child) and particular dependent variables may be presented as a relation between independent or dependent variables with each representing the mean of a number of individuals.

A relationships approach, by contrast, takes cognizance of the fact that different types of interaction may affect each other within the same relationship. Thus a mother who has to go to a crying child often at night may be less inclined to play with her in the daytime. It is thus necessary to examine the relations between different types of interaction in the same relationship. Indeed some of the most important properties of relationships depend not on the incidence of particular types of interaction, but on the relative frequency of different types (e.g., Baumrind, 1967, 1971; Maccoby & Martin, 1983). A given number of inhibitory commands from a mother who also often expresses affection is unlikely to have the same meaning for the child as the same number of commands from a mother who never expresses affection.

This implies that we must search for a route to generalizations different from that usually used in developmental studies. The issue is illustrated in Figure 2, which illustrates the principles involved in abstracting generalizations from behavioral data on interactions in two parent, one child families.

Rectangles 1, 2 and 3 represent specific instances of three types of interaction between a particular mother and her infant—say mother inhibits and child complies, mother inhibits and child ignores, and mother speaks affectionately. We can then make generalizations about the incidence of these three types of interaction in that mother-infant dyad (4, 5 and 6). The rectangles behind 4 represent similar data on maternal inhibitions with child compliance for other mother-infant dyads, those behind 5 for maternal inhibition without compliance and those behind 6 for maternal affection. The usual route to generalizations involves remaining at the same level of complexity, seeking for generalizations about *each type* of interaction *across dyads*, as at 7, 8 and 9. This is the procedure used in most studies of the relations between particular independent variables (e.g., age of child) and particular dependent variables (e.g., maternal inhibition). Similar procedures could be followed for interactions between father and infant, between mother and father, and for triadic interactions.

A second route involves proceeding to the relationship level of social complexity, examining the incidence of and the relations between *different types* of interaction in the *same dyad*. Thus in the figure, 10 represents aspects of this particular mother-infant relationship (and the rectangles behind it comparable aspects of other mother-infant relationships). These will include the frequencies of different types of interactions, their relative frequencies (e.g., were affectionate interactions more or less common than hostile ones?), the sequential relations between different types of interaction (e.g., were maternal inhibitions accompanied by expressions of affection, or were these two maternal modes always separated in time?), and other properties (see below).

Comparable procedures allow generalizations about other relationships in that family, i.e., father-infant (11), mother-father (12), and their triadic relationship (13), and in other families.

From here we can again remain at the same level, seeking generalizations about mother-infant relationships for a number of dyads (14), father-infant relationships (15), etc.; or we can proceed to the group level, in this case examining the nature and structure of that particular family (16). The latter would include the relations between the intrafamilial relationships. This could lead in turn either to generalizations about families (17) or to descriptions of higher order groups within which the families were located (not shown).

It will be noted that attempts to obtain generalizations about relationships (14, 15) from generalizations about specific interactions (7, 8 and 9) would lose information about those properties of relationships that depend on the relative frequency and patterning of different types of interactions. The numbers and the proportions of maternal inhibitions complied with provide information about very different aspects of the mother-child relationship, and a given number of commands from a mother who also often expresses affection is unlikely to have the same meaning for the child as the same number of commands from a mother who never expresses affection would have.

Similarly, attempts to obtain generalizations about families (17) from generalizations about relationships (14, 15) would lose information about how relationships are patterned and affect each other within families. A mother-child relationship involving frequent inhibitions might have quite different impacts on the child, depending on whether or not the father-child relationship was also inhibitory. Furthermore the properties of the mother-child relationship may affect the father-child relationship, and the manner in which it does so may depend on the nature of the marital relationship. Such issues would be lost if we merely examined the properties of the several relationships.

All this implies that relationships can never be fully assessed along a single scale. Of course the same is true of interactions: aggression must be assessed not only in terms of frequency, but also in terms of quality, context dependence, and so on. But the problem is much more severe in the case of relationships, where at best we can categorize them according to where they stand along a limited number of dimensions. Although any method involves a loss of information that may be important, there are a number of possible partial solutions to this difficulty (e.g., Hinde & Stevenson-Hinde, 1988). Sometimes it is possible to use the frequency of one particularly salient type of interaction as an index of the properties of the relationship (e.g., Dunn, 1988). At others the affective properties of the relationship can be used (Radke-Yarrow et al., 1988), or the degree of conflict shown (Christensen & Margolin, 1988). In other cases a profitable approach may be to categorize relationships according to the properties (frequency, quality, etc.) of a number of key types of interactions (see below).

For simplicity of presentation, the discussion in this section has, so far, referred primarily to behavioral aspects of relationships. That, of course is not all: the next section is concerned with a wider framework for the description of relationships.

The Description of Relationships

Ethologists emphasize the importance of the initial descriptive phase in the analysis of behavior, and this is especially important in the analysis of relationships. The generalizations we make, and the validity of the explanatory concepts we use, will depend upon the sorts of relationships with which we are concerned. As a first step towards ordering the almost infinite variety of data about relationships, it has been suggested (Hinde, 1979) that the most important dimensions fall into eight categories. These proceed from those concerned primarily with the nature of the interactions to those concerned with more global properties of the relationship, and from its more behavioral to its more subjective aspects:

a. The content of the interactions. (What do the participants do together?). Content dimensions provide an initial basis for differentiating among relationships. The content of the mother-child relationship may differ from that of the father-child relationship (Lamb, 1976; Lytton, 1980), and preschool children do different things with friends and non-friends (Hinde, Titmus, Easton, & Tamplin, 1985). Whether it matters how interactions of different types are "parcelled up" into relationships is an open issue raised by a relationships approach. For instance, in two-parent families fathers are involved in more physical play with the baby than are mothers. If, in a one-parent family, the mother attempted to provide the same amount of physical play, would the fact that the rambunctious play now came from the same individual who provided tender loving care make any difference to the personality development of the child?

b. The diversity of the interactions. (How many different sorts of things do they do together?). This depends in part on the level of analysis involved: thus a mother-child relationship could be described as uniplex, involving only maternal—filial responses, or multiplex, involving nursing, playing, protecting and so on. A greater diversity of interactions provides more opportunities for interactions of one type to be influenced by those of another type. The diversity of interactions involved may contribute to the special nature of the mother-child relationship.

c. The qualities of the several types of interaction. (e.g., Does the mother hold the baby gently, sensitively, firmly, etc.?). Though difficult to evaluate, this is one of a relationship's most crucial properties. What matters in the mother-child relationship is not just what they do together, but how they do it. If the mother responds sensitively to the child's needs (Ainsworth, Bell, & Stayton, 1974), or shows herself to enjoy physical contact (Main & Stadtman, 1981), the relationship may take a course quite different from that which it would take if the mother were insensitive or resistant to physical contact. The affect displayed by the two partners may be a valuable criterion for the overall quality of a relationship (e.g., Radke-Yarrow et al., 1988).

d. Qualities that emerge from the relative frequency and patterning of different types of interaction. (e.g., *Not* how often the child does what it is told, *but* on what proportion of the occasions on which it receives an instruction does it comply?). Several different issues may be involved here. First, the global labels that the participants (and outsiders) apply to a relationship may depend on the extent to which a number of different properties co-vary: we describe a relationship as "warm" or "competitive" on the basis of behavior in many different contexts. Second, the relative frequencies of interactions may be more important than their absolute frequencies: what matters is not only how often A comforts B, but how often A comforts B relative to how often B needs to be comforted. A third issue concerns properties of relationships consequent upon interactions of different sorts. For instance, a child who is always ready to play with another when invited might be seen as compliant, but one who sometimes refuses and at other times insists on playing might be seen as contrary or controlling.

e. The complementarity vs. reciprocity of the interactions. (e.g., Is one participant nurturant and the other succorant? One dominant and the other submissive? Or do they each behave similarly?). Whereas mother-child or teacher-pupil relationships involve mainly complementary interactions, peer relationships involve more reciprocity. Most close personal relationships involve an interweaving of reciprocal and complementary interactions. Complementary and reciprocal relationships may play quite different roles in personality development (Youniss, 1980).

f. Intimacy. (Do they reveal themselves to each other?). As yet, we know little about the development of intimacy, though the sharing of secrets is of obvious importance in peer relationships.

g. Interpersonal perception. (Do they see each other as they really are? Do they understand each other? Do they feel understood?). For A to see B as B "really" is or as "B sees B" it is necessary for A to comprehend B even when B's thoughts and feelings are different from A's own (cf. Chandler & Greenspan,

1972). Anecdotal data indicate that children understand how to needle or comfort each other in the context of long-term relationships long before such abilities are revealed by laboratory assessments in less intimate situations (e.g., Dunn & Kendrick, 1982; Lewis, Young, Brooks, & Michalson, 1975; Mueller & Brenner, 1977; Radke-Yarrow, 1975). Furthermore, we know that adults who can understand another's point of view do not always do so, so we must specify not just whether children are capable of mutual understanding, but the extent to which it actually influences the course of their friendships.

    h.   Commitment. (Do they strive to continue the relationship or to improve its properties?). In the parent-child relationship, commitment arises more or less inevitably. It may become an important issue in children's friendships quite early on. Thus remarks such as "June said she was my friend but she went and played with Mary" suggest that fidelity may be important even to preschoolers.

    These categories are concerned with dimensions seen as important in everyday life. Clearly some are more relevant to the relationships of young children than others. And it must not be forgotten that a relationship is not a static entity but a dynamic process in continuous creation through time. Thus any description can apply to only a limited span of time.

Crossing the Levels of Social Complexity

    Awareness of the dialectics between successive levels of social complexity brings recognition of the need to cross levels in order to understand the dynamics of changes in or differences between relationships. An elegant example is provided by the study by Sroufe et al. (1985) of mothers showing a "seductive" pattern with their two-year-old sons. Such mothers tended to be not seductive but hostile and deriding towards their daughters. Thus the seductive pattern depends critically on the relationship, and cannot be seen as a maternal trait expressed in all relationships. However the differences between the mother/son and mother/daughter relationships were understandable in terms of psychological processes in the mothers related to a history of emotional exploitation by their own fathers, and the resulting dissolution of generational boundaries. These processes appeared to involve the reconstruction by the mothers of relationship patterns that they had known in their own families of origin. The mothers had a reported history of emotional exploitation by their own fathers: Sroufe et al. regard their behavior with their sons as a means to satisfy their own emotional needs, used by these women because they had learned that parents may attempt to meet their emotional needs through their children. In showing hostility to and depreciation of their daughters, it is suggested that they were reconstructing the relationship pattern they had known with their own mothers. Understanding thus requires at the least an appreciation of the dialectical relations between the mothers' relationships with their parents, aspects of the mothers' personalities, and the mothers' interactions and relationships with their daughters and sons.

Consistency/Inconsistency: Continuity/Discontinuity

The need to cross between the levels of social complexity raises a matter of central importance to child developmentalists, namely the extent to which children behave similarly or differently in different situations, and the extent to which they retain their behavioral characteristics across time. Since the nature of interactions depends on both participants, a relationships approach would predict that children's behavior might change with changes in the social situation. Conversely, continuities in children's behavior over time may be explicable in terms of continuities in their relationships as well as in terms of continuities in their basic characteristics.

It is of course well established that children behave differently according to whom they are with. A one-year-old's relationship with father and mother, as assessed in the Ainsworth Strange Situation, may differ dramatically (Main & Weston, 1981), and Dunn and Kendrick (1982) found that first-born girls who had difficult relationships with their mothers tended to have positive relationships with their younger siblings. Again, 4-year-olds behave differently to teachers and to peers, and even show different behavior to peers who are best friends from that displayed to more casual acquaintanceships (Hinde et al., 1985). Young children even adjust the language that they use according to whom they are with (Gelman & Shatz, 1977; Shatz & Gelman, 1973; Snow, 1972).

This issue is familiar enough in studies of adults. It is implicit in the symbolic interactionists' description of individuals as having a number of "role identities" which, though emerging as a consequence of interaction with a particular other, also provide both plans for action and the criteria by which action is evaluated (e.g., Goffman, 1959; McCall, 1970, 1974). Or, to take a different theoretical perspective, the interdependence theorist's view that the course of a relationship depends on rewards and costs, and the expectation of rewards and costs, accruing in the course of each interaction (e.g., Kelley, 1979) implies that every relationship is, in part, a product of its own history and anticipated future and is thereby differentiated from other relationships.

Such a view is also entirely in harmony with current trends in the study of personality. Earlier criticisms of trait theories, based on the relatively low cross-situational consistency of the traits (Mischel, 1968), at first led to an emphasis on situational determinants and an excessive neglect of person variables (Block, 1977). However, studies evaluating the contributions of Person, Situations, and Person x Situation interaction to the variance in behavior indicate the importance of the latter (e.g., Endler & Magnusson, 1976a, 1976b). One approach has been to search for "moderator variables" which allow for the way in which supposed

basic dispositions might be affected by age, sex, or by other individual characteristics and by aspects of the situation (Alker, 1972), although this approach has
encountered methodological, statistical, and conceptual difficulties (e.g., Wallach & Leggett, 1972; Zedeck, 1971). But if all people are not consistent some of
the time about some things, at least some of the people are consistent some of the
time about some things (Bem & Allen, 1974; Bem & Funder, 1978, Kenrick &
Stringfield, 1980), and a variety of new approaches are now re-vitalizing the
study of personality (e.g., Buss & Craik, 1984). However the long-term success
of these approaches is likely to depend on their ability to come to terms with the
coherence underlying apparent cross-situational inconsistency in behavior.

This is not an easy task, and in the child development field it would seem that
research workers are not well equipped to tackle it. A specific example may illustrate some of the issues that arise. In a study of the behavior of preschoolers at
school and at home, correlations between similar measures in the two situations
were seldom significant (Hinde & Tamplin, 1983). For example children who interacted much with their mothers did not necessarily interact much with teachers
or peers, and children whose interactions with their mothers were often positive
did not necessarily tend to have positive interactions in school. Cross-situational
consistency was thus low. Furthermore, in a later study assessments of children's
temperamental characteristics at home and at school showed very low inter-cor-
relations (Hinde & Tobin, 1987). However there were meaningful *patterns* of
correlations between the two situations: for instance infrequent warm intercourse
with the mother was correlated with greater overall sociability in school, but the
interactions tended to be negative in character, involving hostile and controlling
behavior to adults and peers (Hinde & Tamplin, 1983). In seeking to understand
the bases of the observed differences between home and school behavior a number of issues must be borne in mind:

a.   It is essential first that measures of behavior, and to a lesser extent
measures of temperament, be seen as in part measures of relationships, and not
directly of individual characteristics.

b.   In some cases, linear correlational techniques give a misleading picture,
and other methods must be found. For example, the boys who were most aggressive in school had mothers who exercised little control at home, moderately aggressive ones tended to have controlling mothers, and unaggressive boys were
again subject to little control at home. Partly for this reason the application of
different statistical techniques (correlation, multiple regression, continuous discriminate analysis, discrete discriminant analysis) to the same data set can indicate different relations between home and school measures (Hinde & Dennis,
1986).

c.   Temperamental characteristics, insofar as they reside in the individual, may be expressed differently at home and at school. Interpretation of such differences is sometimes aided by considering boys and girls separately. For example, in the above study girls assessed as assertive on the basis of maternal descriptions of their behavior at home tended to have tensionful relationships with teachers, while assertive boys tended to interact seldom with teachers but often with peers (Hinde, Stevenson-Hinde & Tamplin, 1985).

d.   The relations between home and school behavior can often be understood better by considering patterns of home variables, rather than individual ones. Thus maternal warmth coupled with moderate control at home is associated with least aggression in school (Baumrind, 1967, 1971; Hinde & Tamplin, 1983). And the above findings on the correlates of warm intercourse with the mother can be partially understood in terms of combinations of child characteristics. Children high on the temperamental characteristics Active and Moody tended to have few positive interactions with their mothers at home, but Moody children tended to interact frequently with peers in school, and Active children to have a high proportion of interactions involving hostility. It is a reasonable supposition that the lack of positive interactions at home was a consequence of a tensionful mother-child relationship induced in part by the child's characteristics, and that those characteristics were expressed in a different way in school (Baumrind, 1967, 1971; Hinde and Tamplin, 1983, Hinde, 1985, 1987).

All this suggests that new ways of analyzing such data must be found. An application of a relationships approach that offers considerable promise for understanding the above data on home and school behavior is as follows. The observational material concerned interactions with mother and siblings at home, and with teachers and peers in school: questionnaire and interview data concerning such issues as temperamental characteristics, self concept, etc. were also obtained. Using a small number of key interactions (e.g., aggressive behavior, prosocial behavior), separate cluster analyses for behavior with each type of interactant permitted categorization of the children according to similarities in their relationships. In the case of the mother and sibling, these could fairly be said to be similarities in their child/mother and child/sibling relationships; in the case of the school teachers and peers, they concerned similarities in behavior with classes of interactants. Comparison of the clusters with each type of interactant permitted the identification of subclusters of individuals who behaved similarly *to each other* with two or more types of interactant, even though their *actual behavior* to each was different. The variances in the (independently assessed) temperamental characteristics of the individuals in each cluster and subcluster were significantly less than that of the sample as a whole, providing some validation of the procedure. Further examination of the behavioral characteristics and temperamental characteristics of each cluster and subcluster permits generalizations about the nature of cross-situational (or cross-relationship) coherence, and can open the way for a deeper understanding of process than is possible from the study of individual interactions.

The discussion so far concerns consistency or coherence across situations or relationships at the same age. The issue of continuity vs. discontinuity over time involves an additional problem, because constancy or change in behavior may be due to constancy or change in the subject, in the situation, or both. Furthermore, there are many difficulties in the interpretation of the evidence for continuity/discontinuity arising from the varied definitions of continuity, the possibly misleading nature of correlational evidence, other statistical issues, and possible changes in the mechanisms underlying specific aspects of behavior (Hinde & Bateson, 1985; Hinde in press (a); Rutter, 1987). In any case the fact of continuity/discontinuity is of minor interest unless it leads to understanding of the psychological mechanisms involved. As the data on seductive mothering (Sroufe et al., discussed above) show, apparent discontinuities may yet involve psychological coherence which can be understood by the investigator willing to cross and recross the levels of social complexity. As another example, a much discussed issue amongst developmental psychologists concerns continuity in the "difficultness" of children. Assessed in terms of temperamental characteristics of the child, continuity may be relatively low, and correlations of particular symptoms (e.g., perceived "lack of sootheability, restlessness") are also often low. However if attention is focussed on what matters to the mother, a different picture emerges. Engfer (1986) found that at 4 months "lack of sootheability," at 18 months frequent crying and restlessness, and at 43 months aggressive noncompliance were the most important constituents of child difficultness. Furthermore restlessness at 18 months was related to perceived lack of sootheability at 4 months ($r = .49$) rather better than to restlessness at 4 months ($r = .34$, difference not significant), and restlessness at 18 months was related to perceived difficultness at 43 months rather more strongly ($r = .49$) than to restlessness at 43 months ($r = .28$, difference $p < .10$).

Furthermore child difficultness at 4 and 18 months as perceived by the mother was associated more with lack of maternal sensitivity at 0 and 8 months respectively than with any of the measured characteristics of the baby. Perceived difficultness at 18 months was significantly associated with aspects of the baby's behavior at that age—namely with crying and restlessness, the behavior problems that the mothers then found most difficult. In turn, perceived difficultness at 18 months was related to lack of cooperativeness in the developmental testing situation at 33 months, and this in turn to perceived child difficultness at 43 months. Since at this age maternal characteristics predicted child difficultness only weakly, Engfer deduced that some sort of chaining had taken place. "Initially maternal lack of sensitivity made the babies look more difficult to the mothers at 4 and 18 months. But later on these children displayed observable characteristics substantiating these maternal perceptions and thereby stabilizing the maternal view that their children in fact *are* difficult'' (see also Maccoby 1984; Belsky, 1984).

Relations to Other Approaches

One thing is certain: no one approach will provide us with all the answers to the problems of child development. While not wishing to claim validity for an ethological/relationships approach to the exclusion of others, its properties can be emphasized by comparisons with three other approaches to which it is closely related.

The emphasis of social forces on the individual is even more strongly emphasized in Bronfenbrenner's (1979) "ecological" approach to child development. His concepts of micro-, meso-, exo- and macrosystems involve a more detailed analysis of the influences of group and of sociocultural structure than that discussed here, but are in no way incompatible with it. The difference is primarily one of emphasis: whilst Bronfenbrenner attempts to correct the previous over-emphasis on person as opposed to setting variables by focussing on the latter, here the aim is to come to terms with the dialectical relations between the two. And whilst Bronfenbrenner acknowledges the importance of the biological side of the biological/social interaction, he puts the issue on one side pending further analysis of the social side. By contrast the present approach holds that the influence of both biological and social factors are interdependent and must be examined together.

Second, in an important series of studies of the dynamics of children's groups, Strayer (1980) has adopted an ethological approach. This involved first examining the dominance/submissive relations between the children: this showed that the individuals could be arranged in more or less linear dominance hierarchies. He then studied interactions involving prosocial behavior, and was able to draw a network of prosocial relations in each class studied. Such an approach tells us a great deal about the dynamics of children's groups, but it is less useful for telling us about the relations between hostile and prosocial behavior within relationships.

The third comparison is with family systems approaches (e.g., Minuchin, 1985). Here again there are many points of overlap with the present approach. Thus both emphasize the importance of social context, the complex relations between part and whole, the importance of relations between relationships, and so on. However in their anxiety to correct the previous bias in favor of the parts at the cost of the whole, many systems theorists seem to swing too far the other way. It is necessary to see the individual both as a part of the whole and as a person in his or her own right, carrying the influences of the family environment to other social contexts. And some of the concepts used by systems theorists, such as family tasks and family goals, often have a reality only inside the minds of individuals, owing their commonality to common properties of those minds. Similarly, the property of homeostasis that many families show, and that plays an important part in the formulations of system theorists, often resides in properties of individuals or of dyadic relationships, rather than in the family as a whole (see Hinde, in press (b); Keller et al., 1987 for further discussion).

In this context it must be emphasized that the term "relationships" approach is used only because relationships are central between individual and family, because individuals cannot be considered independently from their relationships, and because influences between individuals and between families are mediated by relationships. But the important issue is to cross and recross the dialectical relations between levels.

BASIC PROPENSITIES: CONSTRAINTS ON AND PREDISPOSITIONS FOR LEARNING

All humans share certain behavioral properties. We all tend to avoid pain, to repeat responses that bring us food, to try to make sense of the world, to imitate others, to speak and so on. Each of these propensities itself has a developmental history, and as a result they vary in strength between individuals, but they are invariably present.

Such propensities affect the course of learning (Seligman & Hager, 1972; Hinde & Stevenson-Hinde, 1973). The human infant is not a tabula rasa, but tends to attend to some patterns rather than others, to learn some responses more easily than others, to find some events rewarding and others aversive. In animals, such constraints on and predispositions for learning are well established. Thus the seeds a finch selects to eat are determined in part by the nature of its bill: it learns to select those seeds that it can dehusk most efficiently (Kear, 1962). Again, song development in many birds depends on imitative learning, but the song repertoire that each individual acquires is often more or less limited to that characteristic of the species. This limitation is achieved in different ways in different species: the chaffinch seems to imitate selectively songs with a particular kind of note structure, whereas the bullfinch tends to imitate the male that helped to rear it (Thorpe, 1961; Marler, 1984).

Similar predispositions occur in humans, but they are closely interwoven with influences from the social environment and the sociocultural structure. For instance, at about 2–3 years of age children who have never seen a snake start to show fear of a snake moving on the ground. The extent to which the fear of snakes develops varies markedly between individuals: some develop snake phobias (Prechtl, 1950; Delprato, 1980). One important influence is the behavior of the caregiver: children, like monkeys (Emde, 1984; Seyfarth & Cheney, 1986) learn rapidly what is and is not to be feared from the behavior of their caregivers. The importance of snakes in our mythology may also be an important issue: in the Garden of Eden and many other contexts snakes symbolize evil. Indeed it is reasonable to suggest that these issues are not unrelated: the initial propensity to fear snakes, the snake mythology and snake phobias may influence each other. This exemplifies a principle that is emphasized repeatedly in this chapter: an understanding of the mutual influences between initial propensities, interpersonal relationships and aspects of the sociocultural structure are crucial for the study of child development.

FUNCTIONAL ISSUES

Ethologists address the issue of the functional significance of behavior in terms of its success in achieving the biological goals of survival and reproduction—or more precisely, perhaps, in terms of the survival of the genes they carry or of identical genes in other individuals (Dawkins, 1976). A relationships approach, however, suggests that we should assess also the functions of behavior in terms of culturally prescribed goals. As we shall see, sometimes the two coincide, but sometimes they differ: recognition of the extent to which the two coincide or differ is crucial for integrating ethological and relationships approaches (see later).

Ethologists tend to presume that ubiquitous behavioral propensities must have been established through the agency of natural selection—that is, that they must have or have had consequences that favor, or favored at some point in our evolutionary past, the survival and reproduction of the individual (and/or those of his close relatives). In point of fact, proof of the biological function of a behavioral characteristic depends on showing that individuals possessing it are at an advantage over individuals who do not, and this is in principle impossible to obtain when the characteristic is ubiquitous. However, often the character in question seems to be so well suited to ensuring survival or reproduction, that a biological function is hard to deny. For example, the distress of a child confronted by a stranger or left alone in a room of toys seems functionless in a secure civilized society, but would certainly have promoted survival in our "environment of evolutionary adaptedness" when an infant was dependent on maternal proximity for protection as well as food. Of course this "argument by design" is dangerous (Gould & Lewontin, 1979), but sometimes it can be supported by comparative evidence: for instance the Moro reflex can be related to a behavior pattern assisting monkeys to cling to their mothers (Prechtl & Beintema, 1964), and the origins of the human smile and laughter can be seen in our nonhuman primate relatives (van Hooff, 1972).

Furthermore, even ubiquitous behavioral propensities vary in some aspects (e.g., strength, intensity) between individuals, and it is sometimes possible to ask whether individual variation in the display of a given behavioral propensity is correlated with greater reproductive success. Over many issues (e.g., the acquisition of wealth as defined by culture specific standards) evidence from non-Western societies is in keeping with the biological hypothesis. Thus among the Turkmen of Persia, those more successful in accumulating money (Irons, 1979, 1980), among the Kipsigis of Africa those who accumulate most cows (Borgerhoff Mulder, 1987a, b), among the Ifaluk those who accumulate most wealth (Turke & Betzig, 1985), and among the Ache of Paraguay those most successful at hunting (Kaplan & Hill, 1985), leave the most offspring. There are, of course, two issues here. It is reasonable to suppose that, in our environment of evolutionary adaptedness, assertiveness and/or acquisitiveness led to biological success in leaving more offspring. The goal towards which these propensities are directed, however, is culturally defined. Presumably it has become defined in each group through the agency of brains which have themselves been shaped by natural selection for this sort of function (Irons, 1979). Interestingly, in Western societies, social success or prestige is not necessarily correlated with reproductive success (Vining, 1986): the culturally defined goals have become emancipated from biological considerations.

A functional approach can also be applied not only to differences between individuals, but also to variations in the behavior of individuals. For example, evolutionary theory predicts that individuals would be more likely to show prosocial behavior to related individuals (who carry largely the same genes) than to nonrelated individuals, and to those who were likely to reciprocate in preference to those who were not. The data indicate that to be the case (Essock-Vitale & McGuire, 1985).

It is important to emphasize that the application of a functional approach does not imply biological determinism. Indeed ethologists insist that, even among animals, natural selection has operated to produce alternative strategies to meet the diverse situations that an individual may encounter. Thus it pays to be at the top of a status hierarchy if you can, but individuals who cannot are equipped with alternative strategies (e.g., stealth, cunning) to achieve their goals. Another example comes from studies of maternal behavior in baboons. Altmann (1980) found she could divide baboon mothers into those who were "restrictive" and those who were "laissez-faire." The former had infants who might be more likely to survive in the early months because they were less exposed to kidnapping, predation, and so on. However, such mishaps were less likely to happen to infants of high status females than to those of low status. Furthermore, "restrictive" mothering tends to lead to independence being achieved more slowly, and a laissez-faire style could lead to infants better able to survive if orphaned. It may therefore be better for high status mothers to be laissez-faire and low status ones to be restrictive. On this view there would be no best mothering style, and natural selection would act to favor individuals who showed a mothering style appropriate to the situation in which they found themselves. This is even more true of man, whose brain is adapted both to set his proximate goals (see discussion of wealth, above) and to find means to achieve them.

This functional approach prompts questions seldom asked by the developmental psychologist. For instance, while attachment theorists argue that sensitively responsive mothering produces a securely attached child, who in turn will be socially competent, they do not often ask why that should be so. It could be the other way round, that sensitive mothering ''spoils'' the child, and/or makes the child overly dependent on one person and unlikely to form new relationships. It is usually implied that humans are ''just built that way.'' The answer to why they are ''built that way'' must be in functional/evolutionary terms. We can presume that natural selection would have affected the response to childhood experiences in such a way that the sequelae would augment the survival and reproductive potential of the individual in the environments likely to be experienced. The only predictor of the later environments available to the young individual is the current environment, so that one would expect natural selection to have shaped young individuals to use the quality of their early environment as an index of what life would be like when they grew up, and to develop personalities suitable to their anticipated environment. In general, the data seem to be in agreement with this view: sensitive, warm, loving care produces children who are sensitive and loving to their own children and to others (Grossmann, Fremmer-Bombik, Rudolph, & Grossmann, 1988; Main, Kaplan & Cassidy, 1985), while authoritarian parenting is associated with aggressive and assertive children (e.g., Baumrind & Black, 1967; review by Maccoby & Martin, 1983). Furthermore, one would expect individuals to show some flexibility, with some readjustment of personality possible if conditions change. This also is in harmony with the studies of both attachment theorists and psychiatric epidemiologists, which show that the consequences of adverse early experiences can be ameliorated by subsequent supportive relationships (Grossmann et al., 1988; Main, Kaplan, & Cassidy, 1985; Rutter, in press).

Draper and Harpending (1982) have used a similar approach in discussing the influence of father-involvement on the child's personality development. They suggest that children are constituted in such a way that, if they have a family-involved father, they tend to develop attributes conducive to maximizing reproductive success in a situation where males form long-lasting relationships and contribute substantially to their offspring, while if they have a noninvolved father they develop attributes more suitable for a situation in which males compete for access to females but contribute less to their offspring. Such suggestions are impossible to prove, but have an important merit: they open up the possibility that the diverse developmental pathways that actually occur need not be seen as aberrations from an ideal, but rather as adjustments to probable adult environments predicted on the basis of early experience.

A functional approach can also be applied to aspects of human relationships. While clear proof of the functional significance to each participant of pan-cultural characteristics of human relationships is hard to obtain, a functional approach can be of value in the conceptual integration of properties otherwise apparently unrelated. The argument here depends on the biological generality that the anatomy, physiology and behavioral characteristics of a species form a co-adapted whole. Thus birds have wings; they have muscles, a nervous system and a circulatory system suitable for flying; and they use flight in their life. In the same way, many aspects of the mother-child relationship can be seen as parts of a coadapted complex contributing to the reproductive success of the mother and the survival and eventual reproduction of the infant. Thus the composition of the milk is suited to the near-continuous nursing found in most cultures, the attachment behavior of the infant fits the maternal propensities for sensitive care and protection, and the potential for conflict at weaning can be seen as a consequence of the mother's attempts to promote the infant's independence in order to husband her resources for future babies at a time when it is in the infant's interests to exploit her care (Trivers, 1972; Hinde, 1984). Similar principles apply to other types of human relationships (see below and Hinde, 1987).

Of course there are limitations to the use of the biological approach here. For instance, we do not know whether modern environments are or are not within the range of our species environments of evolutionary adaptedness in matters relevant to aspects of personality development: what was biologically good then may not be so now. Indeed we do not know whether the relations between early relationships and adult personality are the same now as they were then: the forces impinging on the individual in the intervening years may be very different. In any case natural selection acted only within a range of environments: quite different principles of development may apply outside that range. And perhaps most important of all, in Western cultures maximization of reproductive success is not what we are primarily interested in.

That brings us to questions of function from a cultural viewpoint. Cultural norms prescribe the behavior appropriate for individuals and are as or more potent than biological propensities. But the relations between the two must not be seen as a simple dichotomy. Culture is part of being human, not something imposed from outside. Culture is based on human propensities—to teach, to use adults as models, to be guided by tradition, and so on—that have themselves presumably been selected for in our environment of evolutionary adaptedness (Boyd & Richerson, 1986).

However, although the sociocultural structure of a society depends upon propensities that have been established by natural selection, they may direct behavior into channels that are incompatible with biological success. The cultural imperative that decrees "Dulce et decorum est, pro patria mori" can rarely augment the inclusive fitness of the individual concerned. We shall consider some possible reasons for this later.

In practice, in attempting to achieve either biological or cultural desiderata, individuals must choose between alternative strategies according to the constraints of their situation. Thus Main & Weston (1982) have argued that babies who have an "avoidantly secure" attachment relationship with their mothers are adopting the best strategy open to them, given that they have a mother who is somewhat inexpressive and does not promote physical contact.

INTEGRATING ETHOLOGICAL AND RELATIONSHIP APPROACHES

Full understanding of development requires an integration of many approaches and many types of knowledge. In this section, new insights obtainable from bringing together ethological and relationships approaches are exemplified. The examples in fact concern a principle introduced in an earlier section, where it was suggested that understanding of the development of a fear of snakes required consideration of a ubiquitous propensity to fear snakes, presumably adaptive in our environment of evolutionary adaptedness, the relationship with the caregiver, and aspects of the sociocultural structure. Two further examples follow.

Crossing the Levels—Gender Differentiation

The genesis of gender differences is a problem too often muddied by an overemphasis on *either* biological *or* social factors, and a synthesis is especially desirable. The issues can be set out as follows.

1. In rhesus monkeys, young males and females show some behavioral differences from a few weeks after birth. These differences are partly due to the influences of prenatal hormones. Genetically female foetuses treated with testosterone during the early months of gestation develop into individuals showing male behavioral characteristics (Goy, 1978).

2. That the gender role behavior of young humans is similarly influenced by prenatal hormones is indicated by the consequences of treating pregnant women with steroids (Money & Ehrhardt, 1972).

3. The sex-typical behavior of rhesus monkeys can however be influenced by the social conditions of rearing (Goldfoot & Wallen, 1978).

4. Social experience is undoubtedly even more important in humans. A num-

ber of mechanisms are involved. These include differential treatment by the
parents, differential imitation of the parents, internalization of gender-specific
norms, and so on.

5. Basic to all these mechanisms are the sexual stereotypes of the sociocultural structure which affect the parental norms concerning behavior appropriately
shown to and displayed by little boys and little girls. In general these stereotypes
present gender differences much greater than those actually existing in the
society in question, and have a major influence on the behavior of parents. For
example, in a study near Cambridge, shy girls tended to have warmer relationships with their mothers than non-shy girls, whereas shy boys tended to have
worse ones. The probable explanation lies in the mother's values concerning behavior appropriate for boys and for girls: it is a good thing for a little girl to be
shy, but a bad thing for a boy (Hinde & Stevenson-Hinde, 1987b; see also
Radke-Yarrow et al., 1988).

6. Two problems thus arise. First, why do the gender differences implied by
the stereotypes take the direction they do? Second, why are the differences implied by the stereotypes so much greater than those that actually occur?

7. With regard to the direction of the differences, these show surprising
cross-cultural generality. In spite of the enormous cultural differences in socio-
sexual arrangements, men are nearly always perceived as more assertive, aggressive and sexually promiscuous than women, women are more nurturant and care
more about dyadic relationships than men. Furthermore male sexual jealousy is
institutionalized in nearly all societies, whereas this is much rarer for female
sexual jealousy. These are exactly the sorts of differences that would be expected
had natural selection acted to ensure that men and women were equipped to
maximize their individual inclusive fitness in our environment of evolutionary
adaptedness, given the assumption that some male parental help was required for
rearing the young. While it is not possible to pursue the argument in detail here,
the principle points are:

a. In mammals in general, the degree of size difference between males
and females is related to the degree of polygyny. This is because male
reproductive success is determined by the number of females fertilized:
males therefore compete for females, and male success in competition has
been selected for. The human size differential suggests a mild degree of
polygyny in our environment of evolutionary adaptedness: this is in keeping with most modern societies.

b. While male reproductive success depends on the number of females
fertilized, female reproductive success depends on the time needed to rear
the young. For that reason, if an infant is lost, a female must expend more
of her biological resources (i.e., lower her life-time reproductive success)

to replace it than must a male. If male help were needed to rear the young, male-female bonds would be more important to females than to males.

c. Males can be cuckolded, females cannot: hence male sexual jealousy. From a biological point of view, paternal care devoted to another male's infant would be wasted (unless perhaps the other male were a close relative).

d. Comparative studies of the genital anatomy and sexual physiology of the great apes suggest that sex was important for bonding as well as fertilization (Short, 1979). The argument here again depends on the biological generalization that the characters of anatomy, physiology and behavior in each species form a co-adapted whole. Thus chimpanzee females mate with several males in succession: male reproductive success depends in part on sperm competition, and correlated with that, the males have very large testes and accessory organs. By contrast the gorilla male, who usually has undisputed access to several females, has very small testes. The human characteristics of an exceptionally large penis and sexually attractive breasts, small testes, and other issues suggest that sex was important in bonding as well as for reproduction, and are in harmony with the view that each male had undisputed access to one or more females. The concealment of ovulation would have required a male to stay near a female to avoid being cuckolded, and to copulate frequently (Short, 1979; Alexander & Noonan, 1979; Symons, 1979).

Of course this argument concerns only the direction of gender differences, and has nothing to say about their extent, their immutability or their desirability. And it is based on an argument concerned with the biological desideratum of maximizing reproductive success, not with culturally differentiated goals. But the ethologist holds that the basic propensities that humans acquired in their environment of evolutionary adaptedness must be taken into account in understanding their behavior today, even though those propensities are *not determinants* of behavior. And this evolutionary argument does integrate a surprising wealth of facts about the *direction* of gender differences. Their *extent* is another issue.

8. The reasons why sexual stereotypes so grossly exaggerate reality are not known. However these reasons must lie not in some mysterious social given, but in the properties of the human minds that shaped the sociocultural structure. It can reasonably be suggested that they are related to the processes of self concept formation. Individuals categorize themselves as members of groups, including the male or female sex, and in doing so tend to exaggerate the difference between their own and other groups, and the desirability of their own (cf. Tajfel, 1978). In addition, individuals may give themselves an advantage in mate selection by ex-

aggerating those characteristics conventionally associated with their own sex. For instance, 10-year-olds may gain in status among their same sex peers by deriding girls as "sissy" or boys as "dirty"; while a few years later a member of either sex may be better able to acquire the partner of the opposite sex that they prefer if they exaggerate in themselves the characteristics deemed attractive in their own.

Thus the combination of ethological and relationship approaches, involving causal, developmental, functional and evolutionary arguments, provides a rather cohesive picture of the genesis of gender differences (see also Hinde, 1987).

Crossing the Levels—Attachment Theory

Attachment theory originated with the work of John Bowlby, a London psychoanalyst. Although it combines strands from a number of theoretical perspectives, ethological theory and a relationships perspective have played a crucial role.

Two issues were important in Bowlby's early thinking. First, he found that a high proportion of youths treated for behavior problems in adolescence had had disruptions in their early relationships with their mothers (Bowlby, 1944). Second, he recognized that the so-called "irrational fears of childhood"—fear of being left alone, of falling, of darkness—would have made very good sense in our environment of evolutionary adaptedness, where the infant's survival would have depended on the maintenance of proximity between mother and infant.

This, aided no doubt by Bowlby's psychoanalytic background, led to a focus on the crucial importance of the integrity of the mother-child relationship. The security provided by proximity was seen as more crucial than milk or other conventional reinforcers to the healthy development of the infant. Bowlby used the ethological concept of a "behavior system"—a "software" description of the relations between different functionally related behavior patterns (Baerends, 1976). His "attachment behavior system," incorporating such patterns as crying, smiling, clinging, etc., with the set-goal of maintaining proximity to the mother, integrates a surprising wealth of facts about infant behavior in a functional framework.

An important step forward was provided when Ainsworth (Ainsworth et al., 1978) devised the "strange situation" to access the patterns of attachment of one-year-olds to their mothers. This involves a series of episodes with child, mother and/or a stranger in a laboratory room, on the basis of which the child could be categorized as securely attached, avoidantly attached or ambivalently attached to mother or father. The findings that the categorization of attachment to the mother remained consistent from 12 to 18 months in relatively stable middle-class families and that the same child could be classified differently when tested with father and with mother (Main & Weston, 1981), clearly established that the attachment category was a relationship and not an individual measure. But the work of Ainsworth and her colleagues showed that the pattern of attachment appeared to depend upon the nature of the mother's behavior within the mother-child relationship, secure relationships being associated with maternal behavior sensitive to the child's needs.

The pattern of attachment to the mother at 12 months has considerable capacity for predicting later child characteristics—for instance aspects of cognitive development and social functioning in preschool (review Bretherton, 1985). Recently two independent studies have demonstrated relations between a child's strange situation categorization and that of his/her mother in her own childhood. The latter is determined retrospectively from an adult attachment interview developed by Main. On the whole, mothers who remember their own childhood relationships as secure are likely to have secure relationships with their own children. So also are mothers who have less positive recollections, but who described them in a coherent way, and have in some way come to terms with their early attachment experiences. But mothers who are still enmeshed with their past, or who can remember little about it, tend not to have securely attached children (Main & Goldwyn, in press; Grossmann et al., 1988).

It is important to note that the attachment classification does not depend on the assessment of specific behavioral items. Indeed the manifestations of a secure attachment naturally change with the age of the child. The attachment category in which a particular child is placed can be regarded as the result of the infant's use of a particular alternative strategy in the face of the behavior of the mother.

Differences in the proportions of the different categories have been found in different samples. How far these are due to differences in the suitability of the categorization procedure in different samples, how far they represent differences in the proportions of children that will grow up into "psychologically healthy" adults, and how far they are related to cultural differences in the desiderata for adult personality, are at present all still controversial issues. Be that as it may, the attachment classification of the mother-child relationship is surprisingly predictive of behavior some years later (Bretherton & Waters, 1985; Sroufe & Fleeson, 1988).

Principles for Future Research

No one approach to understanding child development is going to sweep the board, rendering earlier ones obsolete. Rather the success of any new approach—and this includes both ethological and relationships approaches and, as emphasized below, the attachment theory derived from them—is to be judged by the extent to which they can be integrated with previous ones. However it is legitimate to ask where the future special contributions of an ethological/relation-

ships approach are likely to lie. Here we are concerned not with the extent to
which the findings or principles derived from this approach have already made
their impact (see Hinde, 1983), but rather with current growing points. Although
the choice is somewhat arbitrary, six principles may be selected for special mention.

1. Constraints on and predispositions for learning. At each stage, there are
limitations on what an individual learns that are not merely limitations of
capacity. In other words, a given experience may "mean" different things to different individuals, and have different consequences for their subsequent development. Some of these constraints and predispositions are part of human nature; in
some cases they may differ between the sexes; in yet others they are consequences of the previous experience of the individual concerned.

2. Functional/evolutionary approaches. Understanding of children's behavior
can be enhanced through consideration not only of the questions of causation and
development, but also of function and evolution. Three issues have been mentioned:

   a. Individuals have alternative strategies for use in different situations.
   Departures from behavior construed as "normal" for a given society may
   represent the result of developmental processes that, at some stage in our
   past, have been adaptive for particular life-situations.

   b. The consequences of experience in development may be seen as
   resulting from developmental processes adapted to produce an adult organism fitted to the later circumstances predicted by its circumstances of
   development.

   c. A functional approach can integrate diverse aspects of human behavior and human relationships into a conceptually coherent whole—as
   summarized, for instance, in the above discussions of mother-child and
   male-female relationships.

3. Relationships. Individuals may behave differently in different contexts,
and the most important aspect of the context is usually the social or relationship
one. The importance of this for interpreting measures of behavior has been
stressed in this article. However the relationships context is equally important in
assessments of cognitive development (McGarrigle & Donaldson, 1974; Samuel
& Bryant, 1984); in contributing to cognitive and emotional development (Doise
& Mugny, 1984; Perret-Clermont & Brossard, 1985; Wertsch & Sammarco,
1985; Youniss, 1980; Radke-Yarrow et al., 1988); in determining the nature of
cognitive functioning in specific situations (Carraher, Carraher, & Schliemann,
1985) and in many other ways.

4. *Individuals and Groups.* A relationships approach, with its emphasis on the dialectical relations between levels of social complexity and the need to cross between those levels, has the capacity to integrate exclusively individual-oriented and systems approaches. It points the way to a more dynamic approach to personality that focusses on coherence rather than consistency across situations, and on the processes involved in consistency/inconsistency. It can aid understanding of the effects of relationships on relationships within families and groups (e.g., Hinde & Stevenson-Hinde, 1988) and while sharing many principles with a systems approach, avoids ascribing to groups properties (e.g., homeostasis) when they can be understood by processes at a lower level.

5. *The Sociocultural Structure.* Although it may seem a long journey, an approach with its roots in ethology that insists on the importance of dyadic relationships as part of the social environment must inevitably also embrace the values, beliefs and other aspects of the sociocultural structure that are brought to the individual through the agency of relationships. Its dialectical approach also provides a route for coming to terms with the ways in which that sociocultural structure is fashioned through the agency of individuals, so that its properties reflect or distort the properties of human minds as well as its own history, environment and so on. It also indicates the importance of coming to terms with the consequences on the sociocultural structure and on individual minds of attempts by individuals to impose coherence on that structure.

6. Finally, perhaps the most exciting advances are likely to come from a marriage between an ethological/relationships approach and others already in the field. Attachment theory provides a clear example. Bowlby integrated his psycho-analytic background with ethology and with systems theory, and incorporated elements from a number of other sources. Ainsworth added the insights of a developmental psychologist as well as the strange situation technique. There is hope for further integration in the future. For instance, attachment theorists use the concept of "internal" working models of the self, attachment figures and/or relationships (Bretherton, 1985, 1987; Main, Kaplan, & Cassidy, 1985). This concept has had great heuristic value but, as used at present, is loosely defined and can too easily explain anything. However aspects of the "internal working model" have much in common with concepts which have already been put to good use in developmental psychology, such as the self concept, object constancy and perspective taking. Further progress can be expected when attachment theorists integrate the concept of an "internal working model" with such concepts from other approaches to the study of child development and of cognitive processes. Such a course would also serve to provide a developmental perspective which, though advocated by some attachment theorists (e.g., Marvin, 1977; Greenberg & Marvin, 1982), is largely lacking in discussions of the internal working model.

CONCLUSION

The aim of this chapter is essentially integrative. It is suggested that the combination of an ethological approach, originally concerned with studies of animals but applied to child development by a number of authors in recent years (e.g., Blurton Jones, 1972), with a relationships approach, originating independently in social psychology and ethological primatology, can provide new insights for the study of child development. Many aspects of child development can be more fully understood if an appreciation of the child's initial propensities, including its learning predispositions, is brought together with a functional approach, with its capability for integrating diverse facts about human development into a cohesive framework. It is necessary also for the analysis to cross and recross the successive levels of social complexity, and to take cognizance both of the influence of cultural forces on the developing child and the genesis of those cultural forces themselves.

REFERENCES

Ainsworth, M. D. S., Bell, S. M., & Stayton, D. J. (1974). Infant-mother attachment and social development: "socialization" as a product of reciprocal responsiveness to signals. In M. P. M. Richards (Ed.), *The integration of a child into a social world.* London: Cambridge University Press.

Ainsworth, M. D. S., Blehar, M. C., Waters, E., & Wall, S. (1978). *Patterns of attachment.* Hillsdale, N.J.: Erlbaum.

Alexander, R. & Noonan, K. M. (1979). Concealment of ovulation, parental care and human social evolution. In N.A. Chagnon & W. Irons (Eds.), *Evolutionary biology and human social behavior.* N. Scituate, Mass.: Duxbury.

Alker, H. A. (1972). Is personality situationally specific or intrapsychically consistent? *Journal of Personality, 40,* 1–16.

Altmann, J. (1980). *Baboon mothers and infants.* Cambridge, Mass.: Harvard University Press.

Attili, G. & Hinde, R. A. (1986). Categories of aggression and their motivational heterogeneity. *Ethology and Sociology, 7,* 17–27.

Baerends, G. P. (1976). The functional organization of behavior. *Animal Behavior, 24,* 726–738.

Bateson, P. (in prep.). *The origins of behavior: the biology of behavioral development.* Cambridge: Cambridge University Press.

Baumrind, D. (1967). Child care practices anteceding 3 patterns of preschool behavior. *Genetic Psychology Monographs, 75,* 43–88.

Baumrind, D. (1971). Current patterns of parental authority. *Developmental Psychology Monograph, 4* (1, Part 1).

Baumrind, D. & Black, A. E. (1967). Socialization practices associated with the dimensions of competence in preschool boys and girls. *Child Development, 38,* 291–327.

Belsky, J. (1984). The determinants of parenting: a process model. *Child Development, 55,* 83–96.

Bem, D. J. & Allen, A. (1974). On predicting some of the people some of the time: the search for cross-situational consistencies in behavior. *Psychological Review, 81,* 506–520.

Bem D. J. & Funder, D. C. (1978). Predicting more of the people more of the time. *Psychological Review, 85,* 485–501.

Block, J. (1977). Advancing the science of personality: paradigmatic shift or improving the quality of research? In D. Magnusson & N. S. Endler (Eds.), *Psychology at the crossroads: current issues in interactional psychology.* Hillsdale, N.J.: Lawrence Erlbaum Associates.

Blurton Jones, N. G. (1972). *Ethological studies of child behavior.* Cambridge: Cambridge University Press.

Borgerhoff Mulder, M. (1987a). Kipsigis bridewealth payments. In L. L. Betzig, M. Borgerhoff Mulder & P. W. Turke (Eds.), *Human reproductive behavior: a darwinian prospective.* Cambridge: Cambridge University Press.

Borgerhoff Mulder, M. (1987b). Reproductive success in three Kipsigis cohorts. In T. H. Clutton-Brock (Eds.), *Reproductive Success.* Chicago: University of Chicago Press.

Bowlby, J. (1944). Forty-four juvenile thieves: their characters and home life. *Int. J. Psycho-Anal., 25,* 19–52 and 107–127.

Bowlby, J. (1969). *Attachment and loss, 1. Attachment.* London: Hogarth.

Boyd, R. & Richerson, P. J. (1985). *Culture and the evolutionary process.* Chicago: University of Chicago Press.

Bretherton, I. (1985). Attachment theory: retrospect and prospect. In I. Bretherton & E. Waters (Eds.), *Growing points of attachment theory and research* (pp. 3–38). Monog. Soc. for Research in Child Development, Vol. 50, Nos. 1–2.

Bretherton, I. (1987). New perspectives on attachment relations: security, communication and internal working models. In J. D. Osofsky (Ed.), *Handbook of infant development* (pp. 1061–1100). New York: Wiley.

Bretherton, I. & Waters, W. (1985). *Growing points of attachment theory and research.* Monog. Soc. for Research in Child Development, Vol. 50, Nos. 1–2.

Bronfenbrenner, U. (1979). *The ecology of human development.* Cambridge, Mass.: Harvard University Press.

Buss, D. M. & Craik, K. H. (1984). Acts, dispositions and personality. In B. A. Maher & W. B. Maher (Eds.), *Progress in experimental personality research.* New York: Academic Press.

Carraher, T. N., Carraher, D. W., & Schliemann, A. D. (1985). Mathematics in the streets and in the schools. *Brit. J. Develop. Psychol. 3,* 21–29.

Chandler, M. J. & Greenspan, S. (1972). Ersatz egocentrism: a reply to H. Borke. *Developmental Psychology, 7,* 104–106.

Christensen, A. & Margolin, G. (1988). Conflict and alliance in distressed and nondistressed families. In R. A. Hinde & J. Stevenson-Hinde (Eds.), *Relationships within families.* Oxford: Oxford University Press.

Dawkins, R. (1976). *The selfish gene.* Oxford: Oxford University Press.

Delprato, D. (1980). Hereditary determinants of fears and phobias: A critical review. *Behavior Therapy, 11,* 79–103.

Doise, W. & Mugny, G. (1984). *The social development of the intellect.* Oxford: Oxford University Press.

Draper, P. & Harpending, H. (1982). Father absence and reproductive strategy: an evolutionary perspective. *J. Anthropological Research, 38,* 255–273.

Duck, S. & Gilmour, R. (1981). *Personal relationships, 1, 2 and 3.* London: Academic Press.

Duck, S. W. & Miell, D. E. (1983). Mate choice in humans as an interpersonal process. In P. Bateson (Ed.), *Mate choice.* Cambridge: Cambridge University Press.

Dunn, J. (1988). Connections between relationships: implications of research on mothers and siblings. In R. A. Hinde & J. Stevenson-Hinde (Eds.), *Relationships within families.* Oxford: Oxford University Press.

Dunn, J. & Kendrick, C. (1982). *Siblings: love, envy and understanding.* Cambridge, Mass: Harvard University Press.

Emde, R. (1984). The affective self. In J. D. Call, E. Galenson & R. L. Tyson (Eds.), *Frontiers of infant psychiatry.* New York: Basic Books.

Endler, N. S. & Magnusson, D. (1976a). Toward an interactional psychology of personality. *Psychological Bulletin, 83,* 956–974.

Endler, N. S. & Magnusson, D. (1976b). *Interactional psychology and personality.* New York: Wiley.

Engfer, A. (1986). Antecedents of perceived behavior problems in children 4 and 18 months of age—a longitudinal study. In D. Kohnstamm (Ed.), *Temperament discussed*. Amsterdam: Swets & Zeitlinger.

Essock-Vitale, S. M. & McGuire, M. T. (1985). Women's lives viewed from an evolutionary perspective. 2. Patterns of helping. *Ethology and Sociobiology, 6*, 155–173.

Feshbach, S. (1970). Aggression. In P. H. Mussen (Ed.), *Carmichael's manual of child psychology, Vol. II*. New York: Wiley.

Gelman, R. & Shatz, M. (1977). Speech adjustments in talk to 2-year-olds. In M. Lewis & L. A. Rosenblum (Eds.), *Interaction, conversation and the development of language*. New York: Academic Press.

Goffman, E. (1959). *The presentation of self in everyday life*. New York: Doubleday Anchor.

Goldfoot, D. A. & Wallen, K. (1978). Development of gender role behaviors in heterosexual and isosexual groups if infant rhesus monkeys. In D. J. Chivers & J. Herbert (Ed.), *Recent advances in primatology, I*. London: Academic Press.

Gould, S. J. & Lewontin, R. C. (1979). The Spandrels of San Marco and the Panglossian paradigm: a critique of the adaptionist programme. *Proc. Roy. Soc. B., 205*, 581–598.

Goy, R. W. (1978). Development of play and mounting behavior in female rhesus virilized prenatally. In D. J. Chivers & J. Herbert (Eds.), *Recent advances in primatology, 1*, London: Academic Press.

Greenberg, M. T. & Marvin, R. S. (1982). Reactions of preschool children to an adult stranger: a behavioral systems approach. *Child Development, 53*, 481–490.

Grossmann, K., Fremmer-Bombik, E., Rudolph, J., & Grossmann, K. E. (1988) Maternal attachment representations as related to patterns of infant/mother attachment and maternal care during the first year. In R. A. Hinde & J. Stevenson-Hinde (Eds.), *Relationships within families*. Oxford: Oxford University Press.

Hinde, R. A. (1965). Interaction of internal and external factors in integration of canary reproduction. In F. Beach (Ed.), *Sex and behavior*. New York: Wiley.

Hinde, R. A. (1972). *Social behavior and its development in subhuman primates*. Condon Lectures, Eugene, Oregon.

Hinde, R. A. (1976). Interactions, relationships and social structure. *Man, 11*, 1–17.

Hinde, R. A. (1979). *Towards understanding relationships*. London: Academic Press.

Hinde, R. A. (Ed.), (1983). *Primate social relationships. An integrated approach*. Oxford: Blackwell Scientific Publications.

Hinde, R. A. (1983). Some principles of ethology relevant to child psychology. In P. H. Mussen (Ed.), *Handbook of child psychology*, (Vol. II. pp. 27–93). New York: Wiley & Sons.

Hinde, R. A. (1984). Biological bases of the mother-child relationship. In J. D. Call, E. Galenson & R. L. Tyson (Eds.), *Frontiers of infant psychiatry*. Vol. II. pp. 284–294). New York: Basic Books Ltd.

Hinde, R. A. (1985). Home correlates of aggressive behavior in preschool. In J. M. Ramirez & P. F. Brain (Eds.), *Aggression. Functions and causes*. Seville: Publicaciones de la Universidad de Sevilla.

Hinde, R. A. (1987). Individuals, Relationships and Culture. Cambridge: Cambridge University Press.

Hinde, R. A. (in press, a). Continuities and discontinuities: conceptual issue and methodological considerations. In M. Rutter (Ed.), Minister Lovell workshop on Risk and Protective Factors in Psychosocial Development.

Hinde, R. A. (in press, b). Reconciling the family systems and the relationships approaches to child development. In K. Kreppner & R. M. Lerner (Eds.), *Family systems and life-span development*. Hillsdale, N.J.: Erlbaum.

Hinde, R. A. & Bateson, P. (1984). Discontinuities versus continuities in behavioral development and the neglect of process. *Int. J. Behavioral Development, 7*, 129–143.

Hinde, R. A. & Dennis, A. (1986). Categorizing individuals: an alternative to linear analysis. *International Journal of Behavioral Development, 9*, 105–119.

Hinde, R. A. & Stevenson-Hinde, (Eds.), (1973). *Constraints on learning: limitations and predispositions*. London: Academic Press.

Hinde, R. A. & Stevenson-Hinde, J. (1987a). Interpersonal relationships and child development. *Developmental Review, 7*, 1–21.

Hinde, R. A. & Stevenson-Hinde, J. (1987b). Implications of a relationships approach for the study of gender differences. *Infant Mental Health Journal*.

Hinde, R. A. & Stevenson-Hinde, J. (Eds.), (1988). *Relationships within families*. Oxford: Oxford University Press.

Hinde, R. A. & Tamplin, A. (1983). Relations between mother-child interaction and behavior in preschool. *British Journal of Developmental Psychology, 1*, 231–257.

Hinde, R. A. & Tobin, C. (1987). Temperament at home and behavior at preschool. In G. A. Kohnstamm (Ed.), *Temperament discussed*. Lisse: Swets & Zeitlinger B. V.

Hinde, R. A., Rowell, T. E., & Spencer-Booth, Y. (1964). Behavior of socially living rhesus monkeys in their first six months. *Proc. Zool. Soc. Lond. 243*, 609–649.

Hinde, R. A., Stevenson-Hinde, J., & Tamplin, A. (1985). Characteristics of 3- to 4-year-olds assessed at home and their interactions in preschool. *Developmental Psychology, 21*, 1. 130–140.

Hinde, R. A., Titmus, G., Easton, D., & Tamplin, A. (1985). Incidence of "friendship" and behavior toward strong associates versus nonassociates in preschoolers. *Child Development, 56*, 234–245.

van Hooff, J. A. R. A. M. (1972). A comparative approach to the phylogeny of laughter and smiling. In R. A. Hinde (Ed.), *Non-verbal communication*. Cambridge: Cambridge University Press.

Homans, G. C. (1961). *Social behavior: its elementary forms*. London: Routledge & Kegan Paul.

Irons, W. (1979). Cultural and biological success. In N. Chagnon & W. Irons (Eds.), *Evolutionary biology and human social behavior*. N. Scituate, Mass.: Duxbury.

Irons, W. (1980). Is Yomut social behavior adaptive? In G. W. Barlow & J. Silverberg (Eds.), *Sociobiology: beyond nature/nuture?* Boulder, Colorado: Westview.

Kaplan, H. & Hill, K. (1985). Hunting ability and reproductive success among male Ache foragers. *Current Anthropology, 26*, 131–133.

Kear, J. (1962). Food selection in finches with special reference to interspecific differences. *Proc. Zool. Soc. Lond., 138*, 163–204.

Keller, H., Wolk, G., Gauda, G., & Scholmerich, A. (1987). System und Person: Einige entwicklungspsychologische Uberlegungen. In J. Kriz, & A. v. Schlippe (Eds.), *Gemeinsames— Kontroverses*. Bericht des ersten Weiheimer Symposiums in Osnabruck 1986. Verlag Mona Bogner-Kaufmann.

Kelley, H. H. (1979). *Personal relationships*. Hillsdale, N.J.: Erlbaum.

Kelley, H. H., Berscheid, M. E., & Christensen, A., et al., (1983). *Close relationships*. New York: Freeman.

Kenrick, D. T. & Stringfield, D. O. (1980). Personality traits and the eye of the beholder. *Psychological Review, 87*, 88–104.

Kummer, H. (1982). Social knowledge in free-ranging primates. In D. R. Griffin (Ed.), *Animal mind, human mind*. Berlin: Springer-Verlag.

Lamb, M. E. (Ed.). (1976). *The role of the father in child development*. New York: Wiley.

Lewis, M., Young, G., Brooks, J., & Michalson, L. (1975). The beginning of friendship. In M. Lewis & L. A. Rosenblum (Eds.), *Friendship and peer relations*, pp. 27–66. New York: Wiley.

Lytton, H. (1980). *Parent-child interaction: the socialization process observed in twin and singleton families*. New York: Plenum.

McCall, J. G. (1970). The social organization of relationships. In G. J. McCall et al., *Social relationships*. Chicago: Aldine.

McCall, J. G. (1974). A symbolic interactionist approach to attraction. In T. L. Huston (Ed.), *Foundations of interpersonal attraction*. New York: Academic Press.

McGarrigle, J. & Donaldson, M. (1974). Conservation accidents. *Cognition, 3*, 341–350.

Maccoby, E. E. & Martin, J. A. (1983). Socialization in the context of the family: parent-child interaction. In M. Hetherington (Ed.), Mussen: *Handbook of child psychology, IV*. 1–103. New York: Wiley.

Maccoby, E. E. (1984). Socialization and developmental change. *Child Development, 55*, 317–328.

Main, M. & Goldwyn, R. (in press). Interview-based adult attachment classifications related to infant-mother and infant-father attachment.

Main, M. & Stadtman, J. (1981). Infant response to rejection of physical contact by the mother. *J. Amer. Acad. Child Psychiatry, 20*, 292–307.

Main, M. & Weston, D. R. (1981). The quality of the toddler's relationship to mother and father: related to conflict behavior and the readiness to establish new relationships. *Child Development, 52*, 932–940.

Main, M. & Weston, D. R. (1982). Avoidance of the attachment figure in infancy. In C. M. Parkes & J. Stevenson-Hinde (Eds.), *The place of attachment in human behavior*, London: Tavistock.

Main, M., Kaplan, N. & Cassidy, J. (1985). Security in infancy, childhood, and adulthood: a move to the level of representation. In I. Bretherton & E. Waters (Eds.), *Growing points of attachment theory and research*. Monog. Soc. for Research in Child Development. Vol. 50, Nos. 1–2.

Manning, M., Heron, J. & Marshall, T. (1978). Styles of hostility and social interactions at nursery, at school and at home. An extended study of children. In L. A. Hersov & D. Shaffer (Eds.), *Aggression and anti-social behavior in childhood and adolescence*. Oxford: Pergamon Press.

Marler, P. (1984). Song learning: innate species differences in the learning process. In P. Marler & H. S. Terrace (Eds.), *The biology of learning*. Berling: Springer-Verlag.

Marvin, R. S. (1977). An ethological-cognitive model for the attenuation of mother-child attachment behavior. In T. Alloway, P. Pliner & L. Krames (Eds.), *Attachment behavior. Advances in the study of communication and affect* (vol. 3. pp. 25–29). New York: Plenum Press.

Minuchin, P. (1985). Families and individual development provocations from the field of family therapy. *Child Development, 56*, 281–288.

Mischel, W. (1968). Toward a cognitive social learning reconceptualization of personality. *Psychological Review, 80*, 252–283.

Money, J. W. & Ehrhardt, A. A. (1972). *Man & woman, boy & girl*. Baltimore: John Hopkins University Press.

Mueller, E. & Brenner, J. (1977). The origins of social skills and interaction among playgroup toddlers. *Child Development, 48*, 854–861.

Perret-Clermont, A-N. & Brossard, A. (1985). On the interdigitation of social and cognitive processes. In R. A. Hinde, A-N. Perret-Clermont & J. Stevenson-Hinde (Eds.), *Social relationships and cognitive development* (pp. 309–327). Oxford: Oxford University Press.

Prechtl, H. F. R. (1950). Das Verhalten von Kleinkindern gegenuber Schlangen. *Weiner Zeitz. f. Philosophie, Psychologie und Paedagogie, 2*, 68–70.

Prechtl, H. R. F. & Beintema, D. J. (1964). *The neurological examination of the full term newborn infant*. London: Heinemann.

Radke Yarrow, M. R. (1975). Some perspectives on research on peer relations. In M. Lewis & L. A. Rosenblum (Eds.), *The origins of behavior: friendship and peer relations*. New York: Wiley.

Radke-Yarrow, M., Richters, J., & Wilson, W. E. (1988). Child development in a network of relationships. In R. A. Hinde & J. Stevenson-Hinde (Eds.), *Relationships within families*. Oxford: Oxford University Press.

Rutter, M. (1987). Continuities and discontinuities from infancy. In J. Osofsky (Ed.), *Handbook of Infant Development (2nd Edition)*. New York: Wiley.

Samuel, J. & Bryant, P. E. (1984). Asking only one question in the conservation experiment. *J. Child Psychol. Psychiatry, 25*, 315–318.

Seligman, M. E. P. & Hager, J. L. (Eds.), *Biological boundaries of learning*. New York: Appleton Century Crofts.

Seyfarth, R. M. & Cheney, D. L. (1986). Vocal development in vervet monkeys. *Animal Behavior, 34*, 1640–1658.

Shatz, M. & Gelman, R. (1973). The development of communication skills: modifications in the speech of young children as a function of the listener. *Monog. Soc. Res. Child Devel. 38*. No. 5.

Short, R. (1979). Sexual selection and its component parts, somatic & genital selection, as illustrated by man and the great apes. *Adv. Study Behavior, 9*, 131–158.

Snow, C. (1972). Mother's speech to children learning language. *Child Development, 43*, 549–564.

Sroufe, A., Jacobvitz, D., Mangelsdorf, S., De Angelo, E., & Ward, M. J. (1985). Generational boundary dissolution between mothers and their pre-school children: a relationship systems approach. *Child Development, 56*, 317–325.

Sroufe, A. & Fleeson, J. (1988). The coherence of family relationships. In R. A. Hinde & J. Stevenson-Hinde (Eds.), *Relationships within families*. Oxford: Oxford University Press.

Stevenson-Hinde, J. (1985). Towards a more open construct. In G. A. Kohnstamm (Ed.), *Temperament discussed* (pp. 97–106). Lisse: Swets & Zeitlinger B. V.

Strayer, F. F. (1980). Child ethology and the study of preschool social relations. In H. C. Foot, A. J. Chapman & J. R. Smith (Eds.), *Friendship and social relations in children*. Chichester: Wiley.

Symons, D. (1979). *The evolution of human sexuality*. Oxford: Oxford University Press.

Tajfel, H. (1978). Contributions to Tajfel, H. (Ed.), *Differentiation between social groups*. London: Academic Press.

Thorpe, W. H. (1961). *Bird song*. Cambridge: Cambridge University Press.

Tivers, R. L. (1972). Parental investment and sexual selection. In B. Campbell (Ed.), *Sexual selection and the descent of man, 1871–1971*. Chicago: Aldine.

Turke, P. W. & Betzig, L. L. (1985). Those who can do: wealth, status and reproductive success on Ifaluk. *Ethology and Sociobiology, 6*, 79–87.

Vining, D. R. (1986). Social vs. reproductive success. *Behavioral and Brain Sciences, 9*, 167–216.

Wallach, M. A. & Leggett, M. I. (1972). Testing the hypothesis that a person will be consistent: stylistic consistency versus situational specificity in size of children's drawings. *Journal of Personality, 40*, 309–330.

Wertsch, J. V. & Sammarco, J. G. (1985). Social precursors to individual cognitive functioning: the problem of units of analysis. In R. A. Hinde, A-N. Perret-Clermont & J. Stevenson-Hinde (Eds.), *Social relationships and cognitive development* (pp. 276–293). Oxford: Oxford University Press.

Youniss, J. (1980). *Parents and peers in social development*. Chicago: University of Chicago Press.

Zedeck, S. (1971). Problems with the use of "moderator" variables. *Psychological Bulletin, 76*, 295–310.

Jessica Kingsley Publishers
116 Pentonville Road, London. N1 9JB Tel: 071-833 2307

Grief in Children
A Handbook for Adults
Atle Dyregrov
ISBN 1 85302 113 X pb

'A whole range of emotions, reactions and issues are dealt with in the book
and the practical advice relating to the specifics of helping children undergoing such trauma is especially well presented...this is a useful book for all
adults who may be faced with comforting and supporting children in times
of grief. Teachers, social workers, nurses and parents will all be able to utilize
the information provided.'

- Nursing Times

Many children experience the death of a relation or friend, or of other known adults
or children. At such times it is important for parents, teachers, social workers and
other responsible adults to know how to respond appropriately to the child's needs.
This practical book explains children's understanding of death at different ages and
gives a detailed outline of exactly how the adults around them can best help them
cope with the death, whether it is of a parent or sibling, other relation or friend, or
of class mate or teacher. It deals with the whole range of responses, from those on
the physical and pragmatic level to psychological reactions which may be less
obvious to the caring adult, and describes the methods that have been shown to work
best. The book addresses in depth the consequences of sudden death - sudden and
dramatic deaths create more anxiety and give rise to more reactions than anticipated
deaths. One chapter discusses how the matter should be handled at the child's school
and also provides guidelines for dealing with a larger-scale tragedy where several
people known to the children die at once.

Atle Dyregrov is a clinical psychologist and is Director of the Centre for Crisis Psychology
in Bergen, Norway. For more than 10 years he has worked with families who are the victims
of crisis surrounding sudden death.

CONTENTS: Introduction. 1. Children's Grief and Crisis Reaction. 2. Different Types of
Death. 3. Death and Crisis at Different Developmental Levels. 4. What Makes the Grief
Worse? 5. Sex Differences in Children's Grief. 6. Care for Children in Grief and Crisis. 7.
Guidelines for Taking Care of Children's Needs. 8. Handling Death in the Kindergarten and
at School. 9. Crisis - Or Grief-Therapy for Children. 10. Bereavement Groups for Children.
11. Caring for Oneself. Appendix A: Grief in Children - Guidelines for Care. References.

Jessica Kingsley Publishers
116 Pentonville Road, London. N1 9JB Tel: 071-833 2307

How and Why Children Hate
A Study of Conscious and Unconscious Sources
Edited by Ved Varma
ISBN 1 85302 116 4 hb
ISBN 1 85302 185 7 pb

Hate is a most potent factor in undermining feelings of love and all that it implies. It is very disturbing and destructive. We all hate from time to time, but children hate more than adults. Paradoxically, they are also more amenable to improvement and treatment. Yet, surprisingly that these matters are still not sufficiently openly discussed.

This book describes how to recognise and handle hatred in a practical way. The contributors include psychiatrists, social psychologists, psychotherapists, educationalists and sociologists. Their differing perspectives enable the reader to obtain a comprehensive picture of available models and management approaches to children's primitive hatred and shows that individual symptoms and types of hatred need to be assessed by relating them to the social and family contexts within which they occur.

CONTENTS: Introduction, Ved Varma. 1. Hatred in Nursery Rhymes. Captive Audience: Essential Message, Dr Robin Higgins, *MB BCh DPM BMus, Consultant Psychiatrist* 2. Unconscious Communication of Hatred Between Parents and Children, Francis M.J. Dale, *Principal Child Psychotherapist, Torquay.* 3. The Family Scapegoat: An Origin for Hating, Christopher Dare, PhD, *Senior Lecturer, Institute of Psychiatry, University of London; Honorary Consultant, Psychotherapy Unit, The Maudsley Hospital.* 4. Child Abuse and Hatred, Dr K N Dwivedi, *Consultant Psychiatrist, Northants.* 5. Hatred Between Children, Neil Frude, PhD, *Senior Lecturer in Psychology, Cardiff University.* 6. The Therapeutic Importance of Racial Identity in Working with Black Children who Hate, Joycelyn Maxime, PhD, *Principal Clinical Psychologist, London Borough of Hackney .* 7. Children and Hate: Hostility Caused by Racial Prejudice, Nandini Mane, *Educationalist, London.* 8. Religion, Hatred and Children, Robert Bocock, *Senior Lecturer in Sociology, The Open University.* 9. Authority and Hatred, Kevin Epps *Senior Clinical Psychologist, Glenthorne Youth Treatment Centre, Birmingham* and Clive Hollin, PhD, *School of Psychology, University of Birmingham.* 10. Gender and Hatred, *Helen Barrett, Research Fellow, Birkbeck College, University of London* and David Jones, *PhD, Department of Psychology, Birkbeck College, University of London.* 11. Class and Hatred, *David Jones and Helen Barrett.* 12. Hate and Mental Handicap: Issues in Psychoanalytical Psychotherapy with Children with Mental Handicap, Valerie Sinason, Principal Child Psychotherapist, The Tavistock Clinic, London.

Jessica Kingsley Publishers
116 Pentonville Road, London. N1 9JB Tel: 071-833 2307

How and Why Children Fail
Edited by Ved Varma
ISBN 1 85302 108 3 hb
ISBN 1 85302 186 5 pb

All of us under function at one time or another, in our health, at home, in school, in our work or in all these and other areas as well. But it can be argued that underfunctioning is likely to be most evident during periods of rapid change and difficulty; since childhood is the period during which we develop most rapidly, underfunctioning is especially prevalent in children. Afraid, bored, confused and underfunctioning mentally, socially and physically, they fall short, and their failures are sometimes not noticed by busy professionals. As the future generation of parents and adult citizens, it is essential to try to understand children, and help them understand and help themselves as they develop towards maturity.

This book, whose contributors are all experts in their field, is a rare search for answers to the question why and how children underfunction. It will provide essential reading for students and practitioners in psychology, psychiatry, education and social work.

CONTENTS: Introduction, Ved P Varma. 1. Creativity and Underfunctioning: Some Consequences for Society, Robin Higgins *MB BCh DPM BMus, Consultant Psychiatrist* 2. Fear and Underachievement, Herb Etkin *Consultant Psychiatrist, Clinical Director, Ticehurst Young People's Unit*. 3. Boredom, High Ability and Achievement, Joan Freeman *President, European Council for High Ability*. 4. Limited Intelligence and School Failure, Michael J Howe *Professor of Psychology, University of Exeter*. 5. Confusion and Underfunctioning in Children, Kedar Nath Dwivedi, PhD *Consultant Child, Adolescent and Family Psychiatrist, Northampton*. 6. The Effects of Physical Illness, Philip Barker *Professor, Dept of Psychiatry and Paediatrics, University of Calgary; Director, Dept of Psychiatry, Alberta Children's Hospital*. 7. The Effects of Child Abuse, Philip Barker. 8. The Child From the Chaotic Family, Philip Barker. 9. Racial Prejudice and Underfunctioning, Gerry German *Principal Education Officer, Commission for Racial Equality*. 10. The Lack of Proper Social Relationships in Childhood Failure, Clive Hollin PhD *University of Birmingham, Glenthorne Youth Treatment Centre*. 11. Gender and Failure: A Motivational Perspective, Colin Rogers *Lecturer in Education, Lancaster University*. 12. Inappropriate Curricula, Teaching Methods and Underfunctioning, Carl Parsons *Christ Church College, Canterbury*. 13. The Dyslexic Child, Robert Povey *Educational Psychologist, Christ Church College, Canterbury* and Janet Tod *Educational Psychologist, Christ Church College, Canterbury*.

Jessica Kingsley Publishers
116 Pentonville Road, London. N1 9JB Tel: 071-833 2307

Vulnerability and Resilience in Human Development
Edited by Barbara Tizard and Ved Varma
ISBN 1 85302 105 9 hb

This collection of original essays presents a unique contribution to the discussion of vulnerability and resilience in human development – a topic which is perceived as of increasing importance. The authors are, without exception, writers of distinction, well-known for the empirical research and scholarship in fields as diverse as the origins of behaviour disorders, recovery from brain injury, curricular development for the learning disabled, and creative ability in elderly people.

CONTENTS: Introduction, Barbara Tizard. Vulnerability and Resilience of Adults who were Classified as Mildly Mentally Retarded in Childhood, Stephen A Richardson and Helene Koller, *Albert Einstein College of Medicine of Yeshiva University*. Preventing mental handicap: a biomedical perspective, Joe Berg. A new look at nature and nurture, Michael Rutter. Resilience and Vulnerability in Child Survivors of Disaster, Bill Yule, *Institute of Psychiatry*. Rehabilitation of patients after strokes, R Fawcus and Fawcus. Troubled and Troublesome – perspectives on adolescent hurt, Masud Hoghugi, *Honorary Professor of Psychology at the University of Hull, Director of the Aycliffe Centre for Children*. The 1981 Act and the National Curriculum, Peter Mittler, *Director, School of Education, University of Manchester*. Escaping from a bad start, Doria Pilling. Early experience and the parent-child relationship, Rudolf Schaffer, *Professor of Psychology, University of Strathclyde*. Personality and Behaviour in People with Down's Syndrome: assests and deficits, Janet Carr, *PhD, C Psychol, FBPsS, Regional Tutor in the Psychology of Mental and Multiple Handicap, St George's Hospital Medical School*. Interactions between offspring and parents in development, Alexander Thomas and Stella Chess. Implications of the Warsaw Study for social and educational planning, Ignacy Wald, *Institute of Psychiatry and Neurology, Warsaw*, and Anna Firkowska-Mankiewicz, *Polish Academy of Sciences, Warsaw*. Recovering from cerebral injury, Edgar Miller.

Jessica Kingsley Publishers
116 Pentonville Road, London. N1 9JB Tel: 071-833 2307

Good Grief

Exploring Feelings, Loss and Death with Under 11's
Barbara Ward and Associates
ISBN 1 85302 161 X pb

'Good Grief has been put together with love and deep understanding of children's needs in facing loss and death.'

Barbara Kahan, National Children's Bureau

Loss comes in many forms – a favorite toy lost or misplaced, change of school/teacher/culture, a divorce, the death of a close relative. *Good Grief* helps explore and demystify this most sensitive area within the framework of the National Curriculum with over twenty educators contributing ideas piloted with children of different abilities and backgrounds in their care. Suitable for all professionals, carer's and parents involved with the under 11's, it is activity based, facilitating the use of children's own experiences and encouraging improvisation and extension. *Good Grief* should be included in the resources of every establishment involved with this age group.

CONTENTS: Aims and Objectives. Statistics for Britain. Foreword. Contents. Contributors. 1. INTRODUCTION AND BACKGROUND. 1.1 Why teach about loss and death? 1.2 Educator's notes. 1.3 Understanding Loss. 1.4 Divorce and Separation. 1.5 How to help someone who is suffering from loss. 1.6 Tracing Western attitudes to death. 1.7 Stages of grief. 1.8 Difficulties in grieving. 1.9 Grief in children. 1.10 Dying children and their families. 1.11 Preparation for a child's funeral. 1.12 Children's reaction to death. 1.13 Death of a child – a school's response. 1.14 Loss of a child – helping the parents. 1.15 When a child in your school is bereaved. 1.16 Bereavement in the junior school – a teacher's experience. 1.17 Glossary of words associated with death. 2. ACTIVITIES. 2.1 Creative activities. 2.2 Feelings. 2.3 Living with loss. 2.4 What is death? 2.5 How can we help? 2.6 Self esteem and self image. 3. APPENDICES. 3.1 Unhappy ever after. 3.2 Caught in the middle. 3.3 Helen House. 3.4 What to do when someone dies. 3.5 Why do we have funerals? 3.6 Rituals and customs. 3.7 How will Mummy breath and who will feed her? 3.8 I can't write to Daddy. 3.9 Heavenly bodies. 3.10 Value of hospitalized children's artwork. 3.11 Additional resources 3.12 Books for bereaved children. 3.13 Children's booklist. 3.14. Educator's and adult's booklist. Useful addresses. Attributions.

Jessica Kingsley Publishers
116 Pentonville Road, London. N1 9JB Tel: 071-833 2307

Good Grief

Exploring Feelings, Loss and Death with Over 11's and Adults
Barbara Ward and Associates
ISBN 1 85302 162 8 pb

CONTENTS: SECTION 1: INTRODUCTION AND BACKGROUND. 1.1 Educators notes. 1.2 Why teach about loss and death. 1.3 Understanding loss. 1.4 Teamwork. 1.5 How to help someone who is suffering from loss. 1.6 Divorce and separation. 1.7 Tracing western attitudes to death. 1.8 Helping young people grieve. 1.9 Working with young people facing death. 1.10 Explaining death. 1.11 Suicide. 1.12 My father died. 1.13 Teenagers. 1.14 Preparation for a childs' funeral. 1.15 The effects of disasters on children. 1.16 The management of trauma and bereavement. 1.17 The sixth of March 1987. 1.18 Helping schools to deal with death and dying. 1.19 When a child in your school is bereaved. 1.20 Loss of a child - helping the parents. SECTION 2: ACTIVITIES. 2.1 Setting the scene. 2.2 Making your own glossary. 2.3 Creative activities. 2.4 Living with loss. 2.5 What is death? 2.6 How can we help? 2.7 Listening skills. 2.8 Self esteem and self image. 2.9 A matter of life and death. 2.10 Last Rites. SECTION 3: APPENDICES. 3.1 Articles. 3.2 Additional Resources. 3.3 Student's booklist. 3.4 Educators booklist. 3.5 Useful addresses. 3.6 Attributions.

Family Response to Chronic Childhood Disease

Christine Eiser
ISBN 1 85302 168 7 pb

The presence of a chronically sick or handicapped child in the family creates considerable physical and emotional strain on parents, healthy siblings and even extended relations. Yet there are also more positive aspects. This book, drawing on both theoretical and practical sources, acknowledges the potential for distress involved in caring for a sick child but also emphasises the coping resources and skills that can be, and frequently are, adopted by families. The author demonstrates that the consequences of chronic childhood disease vary systematically with the development of the child and suggests ways in which coping resources can be developed and promoted.

CONTENTS PART I Chronic childhood disease. 1. Introduction: Impact of chronic diseases as a developmental phenomenum. 2. Infancy and pre-school. 3. Middle childhood. 4. Adolescence. PART II Implications for the family 1. Introduction. 2. Sibling responses. 3. Maternal responses. 4. Relationships between parent behaviour and child adjustment. 5. Interventions. 6. Implications.